# Dynamic Economic Decision Making

Founded in 1807, John Wiley & Sons is the oldest independent publishing company in the United States. With offices in North America, Europe, Australia, and Asia, Wiley is globally committed to developing and marketing print and electronic products and services for our customers' professional and personal knowledge and understanding.

The Wiley Finance series contains books written specifically for finance and investment professionals as well as sophisticated individual investors and their financial advisors. Book topics range from portfolio management to e-commerce, risk management, financial engineering, valuation, and financial instrument analysis, as well as much more.

For a list of available titles, visit our web site at www.WileyFinance.com.

# Dynamic Economic Decision Making

*Strategies for Financial Risk,*
*Capital Markets,*
*and Monetary Policy*

JOHN E. SILVIA

Lloyd,
Thank for your interest
in my research
+ your time with
the team. John

John & Silvia
8/27/13
VA
Arlington, VA
Isa 40:30-31

WILEY

John Wiley & Sons, Inc.

Published by John Wiley & Sons, Inc., Hoboken, New Jersey.
Published simultaneously in Canada.

For general information on our other products and services or for technical support, please contact our Customer Care Department within the United States at (800) 762-2974, outside the United States at (317) 572-3993 or fax (317) 572-4002.

Wiley also publishes its books in a variety of electronic formats. Some content that appears in print may not be available in electronic books. For more information about Wiley products, visit our web site at www.wiley.com.

*Library of Congress Cataloging-in-Publication Data:*

Silvia, John E.
   Dynamic economic decision making : strategies for financial risk, capital markets, and monetary policy / John E. Silvia.
       p. cm.—(Wiley finance series)
   Includes index.
    ISBN 978-0-470-92051-0 (cloth); ISBN 978-1-118-10093-6 (ebk);
    ISBN 978-1-118-10094-3 (ebk); ISBN 978-1-118-10095-0 (ebk)
  1. Decision making.   2. Strategic planning.   I. Title.
   HD30.23.S553 2011
   339.5–dc22                                                    2011011041

Printed in the United States of America

10  9  8  7  6  5  4  3  2  1

*Dedicated to the generations before and after:*

*To Deolinda and Luperce Silvia,*
*Joe, Kat, and Andrew*

# Contents

**Preface**     xiii

**Acknowledgments**     xvii

**CHAPTER 1**
**Dynamic Decision Making**     1
   Problems Change—Why Not Solutions?     3
   Developing a Dynamic Decision-Making Process     7
   Discussion Questions     19
   Notes     21

**CHAPTER 2**
**Measuring Economic Benchmarks**     23
   Benchmarking Growth     24
   Components of the GDP     27
   Benchmarking Inflation: Pricing Power and the Cost of
     Goods Sold     36
   Interest Rates: Real Nominal, the Short and Long End of
     It All     41
   Exchange Rates: A Relative Price with Many Relatives     45
   Profits     48
   Unbiased Information: Biased Users     50
   Discussion Questions     51
   Notes     52
   Recommended Reading for Serious Players     53

**CHAPTER 3**
**Cyclical and Structural Change**     55
   Forces of Economic Success     55
   Cyclical Patterns, Linear Projections     57
   Leading, Coincident, and Lagging Economic Indicators     59
   Identifying Trends and Cycles     64
   Bias in Decision Making     66
   Cycles, Structural Change, and the Evolution of
     a Framework     73

Discussion Questions                                                            78
Notes                                                                           79
Recommended Reading for Serious Players                                          80

**CHAPTER 4**
**Economic Dynamism: Growth and Overcoming the Limits of Geography    81**
A Framework for Growth                                                          83
Population Growth and the Westward Expansion of the
  United States                                                       88
Institutions and the Savings/Investment Decision                               90
Why Does Capital Not Flow to Poor Countries?                                    92
Overcoming Geography: Stretching the Production
  Possibilities Curve                                                 92
The Competitive Implications of Altering the Exchange Rate                      95
Growth, Opportunity, and Preservation                                          96
Discussion Questions                                                            97
Notes                                                                           99
Recommended Reading for Serious Players                                          99

**CHAPTER 5**
**Information: Competitive Edge in the Twenty-First Century            101**
Information in an Existing Business                                             102
Information as an Input to Today's Competitive Advantage                        103
Information in a New Growth Business                                            104
Information as Input to the Decision Process for Firms
  and Households                                                      106
Three Steps of Information Processing for Decision Makers                       107
Information in the Decision Maker's Framework                                   116
Information as Part of the Business Model                                       117
Choices and Information Choke Points                                            119
Discussion Questions                                                            119
Notes                                                                           121
Recommended Reading for Serious Players                                          122

**CHAPTER 6**
**Risk Modeling and Assessment                                        123**
Economics and the Risk Modeling Process                                        124
Housing Prices: Deflation and the Shock to the
  American Psyche                                                     129
Managing Economic Risk within the
  Decision-Making Process                                             132
Assessing Risks Using Econometric Models                                       138
Identifying Change                                                             141

Principles for a New Model 153
Discussion Questions 155
Notes 157
Recommended Reading for Serious Players 158

**CHAPTER 7**
**Money, Interest Rates, and Financial Markets** **159**
Markets before Institutions 162
Markets: Interdependence and the Driving Force of
    Unexpected Events 162
Change and Putting Our Framework through Its Paces 166
Short-Run to Long-Run Adjustment 170
Quality Spreads, the Economic Cycle, and Accounting
    for Risk 172
Evolution of the Money, Inflation, and Interest
    Rate Framework 173
Lessons for Decision Makers 175
Discussion Questions 176
Notes 177
Recommended Reading for Serious Players 178

**CHAPTER 8**
**Strategy, Risk, Uncertainty, and the Role of Information** **179**
Four Levels of Strategic Thinking 180
Discussion Questions 197
Notes 198
Recommended Reading for Serious Players 198

**CHAPTER 9**
**Capital Markets: Financing Operations and Growth** **199**
Engine of Analysis: The Market for Real Capital and the
    Market for Funds 200
Perspective of Change over Time 201
Economic Change as Driver of an Evolving Capital
    Market Framework 203
Complex Interactions: Economics, Expectations,
    and Information 205
The 1980s: Another Decade, Another New Normal for
    the Financial Markets, and the Critical Role of the
    Recency Bias 208
Internal Cyclical Changes in Capital Markets and the
    Overconfidence Bias 210

Two Underappreciated Forces in Financial Markets
   Are Irony and Paradox                                           211
The Great Recession of 2007 to 2010: Under the Heading
   That Facts Don't Matter until They Do                           212
Economic Evolution and the Changing Risk/
   Reward Calculation                                              213
Price Dichotomy: Traded and Non-Traded Goods                       215
Introducing the Wake-Up Call                                       216
Precise Mathematics Gives Way to Imprecise Reality: What
   Happens to Markets When the Average Expected Return
   and the Variability of Returns Become Uncertain?                217
Choices: Reacting to Feedback—The Most Dangerous Phase
   of the Credit Cycle                                             221
Credit Crunches: When Markets Don't Clear                          224
Capital Markets and the Life Cycle of an Institution               226
Capital Markets and the Allocation of Capital                      230
Discussion Questions                                               232
Notes                                                              233
Recommended Reading for Serious Players                             235

**CHAPTER 10**
**Financial Ratios: The Intersection of Economics and Finance      237**
Financial Ratios                                                   237
Developing a Framework within a Broader Economic Setting           240
Financial Ratios as Information                                    248
Discussion Questions                                               267
Notes                                                              268
Recommended Reading for Serious Players                             270

**CHAPTER 11**
**Fiscal Policy as Agent of Change                                 271**
Fiscal Policy over Time: Altering Incentives and Rewards of
   Risk Taking                                                     272
Public Policy and Private Expectations—the Lucas Critique          284
Interdependence between Fiscal and Monetary Policy                 285
Policy in the Context of Expectations and Information              289
Long-Run Equilibrium versus Short-Run Equilibrium                  292
When the Long-Run Outlook Impacts Today's Behavior                 294
Political Business Cycle: Political Realities for Private
   Decision Makers                                                 296
Fiscal Policy in an Open Economy: The United States in the
   Twenty-First Century                                            298

Discussion Questions 298
Notes 300
Recommended Reading for Serious Players 301

**CHAPTER 12**
**Global Capital Flows: Financing Growth, Creating Risk and Opportunity** **303**
Building a Framework for Understanding 304
A Model of Capital Flows to Frame Our Decisions 306
The American Framework in Global Capital Markets: The
  Evolution of Imbalances 313
Global Interest Rates 320
Risks and Opportunities: Not All Countries Fit One Mold 323
Implications for Decision Makers: Introducing Risk into the
  Global Capital Markets 328
Feedback, Altered Expectations, and Building the
  New Framework 330
A New Framework and the Overconfidence Bias 332
Discussion Questions 332
Notes 333
Recommended Reading for Serious Players 334

**CHAPTER 13**
**Innovation and Its Role in Economics and Decision Making** **335**
Innovation and the Economy 336
Innovation and the Patterns of Progress 349
Risk, Innovation, and Prospect Theory 352
Innovation, Economic Thought, and the Big Challenges of
  the Day 354
Discussion Questions 357
Notes 358
Recommended Reading for Serious Players 359

**APPENDIX**
**The Hodrick-Prescott Filter** **361**
Autoregressive Conditional Heteroscedasticity (ARCH) 365

**About the Author** **369**

**What's on the Companion Web Site** **370**

**Index** **371**

# Preface

The Great Recession of 2008 to 2010 demonstrated the power that macroeconomic and financial forces have to alter the risks and rewards that frame choices for both private and public sector decision makers. Moreover, these forces completely overwhelmed the complex, micro mathematical strategies that were the rage at many institutions. Many books about decision making, finance, and economics, especially textbooks, are more like cookbooks—they tell you how to prepare a specific meal, step by step, but not teach the fine art of being the gracious host who leads the guests through a wonderful evening. Most technique-oriented business strategy books are not reader-friendly for those who must make real world decisions. The focus of many of those writings is almost exclusively on fine techniques of micromanagement, while ignoring the reality of the broader set of macro scenarios faced by actual decision makers involving the many changes in economic growth, finance, and globalization that are ongoing in our world. Is it any wonder that failure and surprise accompany the economic shocks of the day? Our finest financial engineers fail in the face of real world change.

This book is drawn from both my professional and teaching experience. In college undergraduate and graduate business courses, many students are given laundry lists of techniques for solving specific problems, with each problem treated as an isolated case. The breadth of factors that impact an economy and how to place these factors in the context of a model of the economic world is often ignored. The spreadsheet has become a crutch for many, and also, unfortunately, a barrier to leadership. Professionally, having lived through numerous business cycles, I have seen complex, precise, microeconomic decision making based on "management economics" come to grief because of the frequent shocks from the macroeconomy that are simply unaccounted for, or worse, assumed away in so many models and professional papers. We have techniques without context, precision without purpose, solutions without realistic settling of the problem.

In contrast, effective strategy, in my opinion, involves connecting the dots across disciplines. In this book, I intertwine three intellectual disciplines—economics, business, and decision making. Each has a role in the economy, but traditionally each has been taught separately in classrooms and treated as a separate activity in most organizations. I believe effective decision making needs to be open-ended in order to solve problems as they evolve over time.

For economics, I focus on the driving forces of change in economic fundamentals and the challenges that each change represents. These forces include five major economic factors—growth, inflation, interest rates, the dollar exchange rate, and profits—and the influences they exert on successful business strategy both over a business cycle and over longer-term secular trends. Spectacular success or failure in business is often the result of misreading the economic tea leaves, rather than the day-to-day micro techniques of conducting a business. The framework of this book follows the major elements of business strategy in the macroeconomic sense of focusing on the fine art of presenting the feast, not on the detailed menus for each course. Those details are left to the reader. For senior managers who have to make strategic decisions the discussion is focused on the macroeconomic trends of growth and business cycles—the roles of information and innovation in decision making, for example, among other fields. The lessons of the Great Recession are not the necessity of gathering and processing more detail, but the wisdom and foresight to put the decisions we make into a broader context of a continually evolving economy. Economics favors analysis in a framework that makes a decision maker focus on key factors while also recognizing that all facts are not equally relevant. Fact gathering must also not fall into decision-making traps such as depending on what data is immediately available or what data confirms our prior reasoning.

In business, I draw on many examples where economic changes require an alteration of business plans. I will also focus on the context of strategic decisions in the fields of risk, policy innovations, and the globalization of capital markets. Economic and business tools unaccompanied by a sense of future situations are merely a collection of tools without a project to build; unfortunately, this is the way many business and public policy leaders are taught today. The recent subprime lending financial crisis reflects micromanagement decisions that failed in the face of macroeconomic surprises. Forcing decision making into conceptual boxes defined by much business education is counterproductive, since real-world decision making is open-ended, a continuous process of discovery.

Finally, in the discipline of strategic decision making, I discuss a process of recognizing change and to responding to it in an ongoing way. I will also emphasize the need to recognize that leaders' decision-making prejudices frequently limit their ability to make effective decisions.

In my capstone course for MBA students at Wake Forest University, I weave the contributions of each area together by recognizing the role of each as independent contributors but not as stand-alone disciplines. Decision making without economic or business context is sterile. Decision making outside the context of economics has produced a long history of failure. This is similar to war—techniques chosen without the context of the battlefield are a prescription for defeat—witness, for example, Gettysburg or Gallipoli. Great victories involve using proper techniques while also choosing the proper battlefield—Waterloo and Marathon being classic examples.

Books on economics traditionally address an already articulated body of problems, data, and theory, most often in the framework to which the business community is committed at the time. This approach expounds the body of accepted theory, not the process of continued learning going forward. This tactic gives the appearance that current practice is a static result of past learning—that once current practice is known, the toolbox is complete. However, the process of leadership, along with properly processing information, is dynamic, not static. It requires constant learning. Current, accepted, business practice can proceed only so long as the business community accepts without question the particular problem solutions already achieved. That, however, is not acceptable for the real world we confront every day.

JOHN E. SILVIA

# Acknowledgments

Special thanks are due to the faculty at the MBA program at Wake Forest in Charlotte for giving me the opportunity to teach the course on which this book is based. Special thanks also to the students in those classes who asked the good questions and were willing to extend their education beyond the mundane, and who twice awarded me the outstanding educator in last three years at the MBA program.

Thanks for the intellectual debts I owe to writers such as Stephen Ambrose, Doris Kearns Goodwin, Jim Grant, Niall Ferguson, Jim Collins, John Steele Gordon, Michael Roberto, Steven Roach, Thomas Sowell, Robert Barro, Richard Neustadt and Ernest May, and the late Peter Bernstein. I enjoyed their writing and their ability to combine business and economics in exciting narrative. I also owe thanks to the authors of the many business school cases I have used over the years and that I have referenced here.

Thanks to my Economics team at Wells Fargo, who have worked with me on many of these issues over the years, including Sam Bullard, Tim Quinlan, Michael Brown, Azhar Iqbal, Sarah Watt, Tyler Kruse, and Peg Gavin.

Finally thanks to Adrianna Johnson at John Wiley & Sons for shepherding this effort and to editing efforts by Larry Rothstein, Kyle H. Lee, and Jeannette Brichaux.

J.E.S.

# CHAPTER 1

# Dynamic Decision Making

*We are what we repeatedly do. Excellence, then, is not an act but a habit.*

—Aristotle

**C**ompletion of the first transcontinental railroad across the United States, ably told by Steven Ambrose, is a story of a very imperfect success, with numerous changes in how, where, and by whom the railroad was built. While imperfect, the railroad's completion is also a study in the flexibility of decision making where the paradigm of how, where, and by whom was always modified to fit the realities of building the road. Choices were constantly made and then modified on issues of where the track would go, how it would be financed, the construction, and, not to be overlooked, what political strings were to be pulled to get the railroad finished at a profit. Other than completing the railroad, there was not a set of proscribed rules; instead, a framework for decision making was set up, modified with new information, then choices were made and a new model put in place.

Successful decision making is a process, not an event, with constant modifications and interactions among the moving parts that evolve over time. In sports, many franchises win a championship once in a while. Yet repeat championships are driven by a model of decision making that generates winners.[1] The focus remains on the correct process that can be replicated over time and across circumstances rather than on a one-off correct decision that is more a matter of luck than skill. Good decision making must be replicable.

How do we go about seeking the correct process rather than the one-time correct decision? First, in economics, a framework must be developed that accurately characterizes the driving forces about the market we are concerned with for our decision. This framework is both a filter and a structure around which we develop our decision making. The framework is a filter because it identifies the relevant information needed to address the problem. Not all facts are equally relevant. In decision making, for example, two biases can throw off the building of any framework. First, the recency bias is the temptation to take the most recent data and treat that as the critical input to any framework. Recent data is often the most readily available and often the impetus, especially if unanticipated, for an examination of operations. But recent data may also be the most distorted by other factors, such as weather, and, while easily available, may be just too convenient to the lazy researcher in search of easy answers.

Confirmation bias is a second source of problems for any model/framework builder. In this case, when decision makers are in the early stage of model development there is a tendency to grasp at models or data that confirm the initial prejudices of the researcher. Yet we know from watching mystery thrillers that the initial suspect is often not the real criminal. The same initial problem/phenomenon can be framed or interpreted differently in several ways and the great detective—as opposed to the hapless detective—chooses a framework that stands up to the evidence as it develops over time rather than as it is initially presented.

Successful framework development does not attempt to force problems into conceptual boxes supplied by post-secondary education. Too often, newly minted managers are too anxious to put well-learned tools to work even if the problem itself is not carefully defined. In laymen's terms, the rookie wishes to use a hammer to solve every problem, because he knows how to use a hammer, even when the solution calls for a screwdriver.

Assumptions are another problem for framework development. There is a delicate balance between assumptions that simplify a problem too much and assumptions that introduce false premises that constrain or even prevent a solution. We can simplify a problem too much in those cases where we essentially assume away a problem that comes back later to destroy us. Over the last three years, the assumption of liquidity and marketability was taken as gospel in a marketplace where neither was present to support the underlying asset prices when the system was shocked. Alternatively, certain assumptions can complicate or misrepresent the problem. In their classic book, Neustadt and May[2] make the case for a careful use of analogies in developing proper frameworks/models of the problem at hand rather than misrepresenting the problem as something similar to what we are comfortably familiar with. Finally, there is often an assumption of symmetry in our frameworks that simply is not there in real life—especially in finance. There are often few limits on the upside for profitable companies or investment strategies, but there are limits on the downside—bankruptcy. For state and local governments there are budget and liquidity constraints that limit the ability of decision makers to adopt certain financial strategies and risky options.

Education propels us forward on a body of accepted wisdom within a particular view of the world. This wisdom includes a traditional set of axioms or rules along with accepted problem-solving techniques that are consistent with the received wisdom. Our education provides the accepted theory and the accepted problem-solving techniques. However, once outside the bounds of traditional models, how do we discover a way to approach the new problems of the Great Recession, for example? The model solutions we have learned are seldom open-ended; they do not allow the practitioner room to solve new problems that are significantly different from the received wisdom. Often, unfortunately, the models and problems we are educated about reflect a tradition born of a very specific learning style that limits progress in learning. This was famously demonstrated in the case of Isaac Newton, who had to overcome the orthodox Cartesian limits of the English universities of his time to develop his insight into the workings of gravity. In our traditional educational systems, the study of problem-solving models prepares us for membership in the business/government leadership community in which we will later practice, but not necessarily stretch, the boundaries of that knowledge throughout our professional careers.

A problem-solving framework reflects the accepted model or pattern for pursuing a particular solution based on our education, but is not necessarily appropriate for the new set of problems we will face later in our careers. Traditional approaches to learning match existing facts with established theory. The focus here is to develop an approach that recognizes the constant evolution of the model itself as the facts of the economic environment change, and highlights the need for leaders to recognize change and make choices in a very dynamic world. The established models can proceed without change only so long as leaders accept without question the particular problem-solving methods and solutions already achieved—but this approach is not acceptable for effective decision making over time.

## PROBLEMS CHANGE—WHY NOT SOLUTIONS?

Our models of how the world works are often cast in concrete more often in our minds than in the real world. We give lip service to the argument that change is constant, but then build business models that are resistant to change. In his book, *Leading Change*, James O'Toole identifies a culture at General Motors that was unable to recognize the implications of change in the competitive environment and the breakdown of their business model.[3]

Our world poses problems of endless variety. There are two aspects of problem variation. First, each problem we confront is not representative of all problems we face. In our education, we are often given a method for addressing a type of problem which is, of course, very useful. Unfortunately, we tend to use the methods taught to us more broadly than is appropriate. We fit problems to the methods of solution with which we are intellectually comfortable. Further, we tend to look for the set of problems where our model solutions are useful and fail to recognize the possible class of problems that are too difficult to solve given our familiar models. Problems that are highly unlikely cannot be ignored. Many states of nature are possible, so that, to our chagrin, zero probability events show up more often than we expect. This is the fat tail problem or the 100-year flood that shows up more often than once every 100 years.

Another dynamic characteristic of problems is that they are not solved for all time—they morph and generate new problems. In fact, we often find that decisions to address one problem generate a response from society and/or our business competitors that lead to further change along the way. We see this in the pricing wars that often accompany gas station or retail competition in America.

In recent years we have witnessed a decline in information costs and accelerated adaptability to innovation by both businesses and consumers. This has shortened the life span of our solutions to problems and prompted new solutions more rapidly than many decision leaders had anticipated. Moreover, growth is not simply a function of labor, capital, and the growth of the stock of knowledge and technology. Growth and change are driven by the interaction of these factors as well as the disasters along the way. The technology of the Internet and the laptop computer had existed for some time, but in the mid-1990s the scale of these activities and their interaction generated a leap in personal productivity and innovation in software, pushing the growth in economic activity further than anyone had anticipated.

## Barriers to Change

Often the sources of poor performance in both private and public sectors reflect the ability of decision makers to overcome the barriers to change. Unfortunately, the ability of organizations to alter operating models is hampered by our cultural/social heritage as exemplified by the concept of path dependence. The degree to which our decision-making culture can change is not well understood. Too often change is superficially incorporated in business. For example, economic models are often adapted by changing a numerical entry on a spreadsheet. This change leads to a new solution without any change in the underlying equations and does not address any relationship within that spread sheet. Such an approach may simplify learning, but it seriously misrepresents the process of decision making in the real world.

There are many sources of resistance to any of the choices we make in response to any change in the exogenous environment. The institutional structure, assumed or made explicit in our models, is inherited from the past and reflects a set of beliefs that may be significantly impervious to change—either because the proposed changes run counter to the belief system or because the proposed alteration in institutions threatens the leaders and entrepreneurs of existing organizations.

Change, especially if the implications of that change offer a different vision of the underlying socioeconomic structure, is very difficult to implement when trying to reach a solution within the current viable institutional arrangements that would support significant change. It seems that change is constant, but sometimes not implemented when met by entrenched interests. Enlightened management, for example, Grove at Intel, encourages open debate on the business model as standard operating procedure, much like the writers were encouraged to work on the TV program *Your Show of Shows*.[4]

Our inherited institutional structure reflects a set of beliefs about how the world works that is impervious to change because many in leadership roles have a vested interest in keeping the process working in a way they understand. When change runs counter to belief system or the alteration of the model threatens political/economic interests, decisions made in response to change may not reflect the economically optimal solution. Another complication to effective decisions that can occur in implementing a response to change is the recognition of interdependencies—change in just one area of business practice is incomplete and sometimes counterproductive if not complemented by changes elsewhere in the organization or the marketplace. An additional complication to responding to change is the time inconsistency among players. Not all parties have the same sense of urgency.

Moreover, two further complications make any change to the inherited structure uneven in its impact. First, altering the performance of an organization in response to an economic shock takes time—often longer than the time horizon of the business leader/political decision maker who must approve of these changes. The costs of economic adjustment often show up before the benefits; selling change therefore becomes a challenge to decision makers. The costs of adjustment to higher energy costs in the 1970s led to immediate problems for the automobile industry and electrical utilities, yet over time the energy efficiency improvements led to gains in auto quality, reliability, and a better environment. Second, consideration must also be given to people and businesses that are hurt by any change. For example,

British Prime Minister Peel's attempt to repeal the Corn Laws would have meant a loss of trade protectionism for English landowners who benefitted from high agricultural profits, since the Corn Laws limited grain imports. When the Corn Laws were eventually repealed, the balance of economic power in England shifted permanently away from the landed gentry to the industrialists and trading economic interests. In the United States the deregulation of airlines in 1978 lowered prices for consumers and opened up more travel options to regional markets in selected areas. Yet, for airlines such as Eastern and Braniff, the drop in fares led to eventual bankruptcy, as neither firm could compete in a lower fare marketplace.[5]

Incentives provide a focal point for thinking through our decision-making approach. A poor performance institutional matrix does not provide incentives for productivity-improving activities. Some groups within organizations have a vested interest in existing structure, and so incentives (carrots and sticks) must be found to overcome entrenched interests. In organizations there are complex relationships between formal rules and informal constraints. Organizational decision-making structures are man-made, and to function properly they must be continually altered to reflect the continued evolution of human desires and ways of living. As the cultural/economic heritage of a society changes, so must the models we use to characterize that change. Over time, there is no set formula for economic development, so there is unlikely to be one framework that will provide a magic formula for all time. Model developers must understand the process of economic growth before a framework for analysis is created. Developers must then understand that changes in society will dictate changes in our model.

### Sources of Change: Economics

For public and private decision makers five economic factors—growth, inflation, interest rates, the dollar exchange rate, and profits—provide the context for success of any enterprise over time. The source of change in our models and our actions is often precipitated by the gap between what we expect and what we get for each of these five factors.

1. For **growth,** recessions are the surprises that throw us off but in 2008 to 2010, there was also the gap between how we modeled the world and what we thought was our future.
2. For **inflation,** the experience pre/post Paul Volcker's era at the Federal Reserve defines two very different models of the economy.
3. **Interest rates** take on a different character over the business cycle, along the yield curve and between instruments of different credit quality.

4. **Exchange rate** fluctuations have been the source of disaster for some financial institutions, including Barings and Franklin National, as well as the bane of countries over time.
5. Volatility in **corporate profits** influences the pace of investment in the economy and the wealth of investors.

## DEVELOPING A DYNAMIC DECISION-MAKING PROCESS

Decision making is a dynamic process—not a solution—having two dimensions. First, decisions in the current period can be either our own as we anticipate change or as we respond to actual changes made elsewhere by others in the current economic environment. Second, this process is also dynamic because decisions made do not stand alone, but these decisions are part of a long sequence of decisions and responses. Once we make a decision, or face the challenge of decisions made by others, then we need to anticipate the implications of those decisions over time as well as how we respond to that change and subsequent changes down the road. In this sense decision making is like a perpetual chess match, in which moves and countermoves continue to offer short-term advantages, but never long-term dominance unless a company's winning position is guaranteed by a state or federal government. Moreover, each move is made after due consideration of the possible responses competitors may make to adapt to the initial move. Too often, decisions are portrayed in education or business literature as one-off responses to specific changes without the understanding that, like chess, we must anticipate and study not only our first move but the possible changes and responses in the environment in response to any decision we make.

### Creating a Framework

Any starting point for a picture of the economic framework facing any decision maker is by necessity very arbitrary and misrepresents the continuity of history. Long-term changes accompany any current snapshot, and yet we must start somewhere. In our initial framework we must start with some view of how our markets clear and the liquidity of the marketplace. In some cases, markets clear smoothly, as in the years 2003 to 2007 for housing and asset-backed securities, and yet, with the hindsight of history, liquidity and asset values were really not what they appeared to be.

When liquidity was not as expected, and actual did not equal anticipated, this information drove investors and households to react—sharply.

Financial disruption from mid-2007 to mid-2008 led to further market re-actions and feedback that forced a new vision of the available financial opportunities for all. Choices were then made in the context of a new vision of the risks and opportunities. A new framework or model had to be patched together where continuous market clearing did not hold and the value of collateral and the creditworthiness of both borrower and lender were in question. Moreover, the speed of the correction to market models was swift—yet the adjustment over time to a new, stable, market is still going on. The market adjustments in the short run may not lead quickly to the ultimate long-run model, which may be a very different equilibrium over time. For example, the current low yields on Treasury bonds is unlikely to remain as the long-run yields, given the size of current and expected future deficits.

Our process recognizes the constant evolution of framework develop-ment, change, and the modification of the framework in response to the implications of change and the response to that change. Our first step is to define the framework, or economic context of our business model. Then we introduce a shock or change. For the decision maker, the next step is to estimate the impacts of the changes and then choose a response. Finally, we need to decide whether and how to alter our original model based on the change we have witnessed.

For the economic framework, we develop an understanding of the supply/demand fundamentals underlying our marketplace and how these fundamentals may be evolving over time. Our challenge here is twofold. We need to carefully balance our choices of fundamentals to capture the essence of the marketplace without overly detailing the model as to pro-duce analysis/paralysis. We face a number of challenges in putting together a framework. First, there is a tendency to develop a framework around what we are familiar with, which means something current and often very comfortable. Hidden in this approach is the temptation to make implicit as-sumptions about how the world works when such assumptions may reflect the model/framework builder's prior bias, not the path in the future. We build around what is rather than what will be.[6]

Two sources of bias are particularly prevalent here that may distort the reliability of the framework. First, the structure and variables chosen for the model may reflect a confirmation bias. This bias reflects the ten-dency to gather information that confirms our prior beliefs about how the world works or our professional expertise. In the history of science we are familiar with the constant reworking of the Ptolemaic system so that new observations were fitted to an increasingly complex model of the universe. Another temptation for model building is framing where our assumptions in the model reflect the relative value we attach to risks/rewards for any given challenge. Often this framing will define why some leaders decide to pursue a certain course while others do not.

## Introducing Change

Two distinct paths are available to decision makers—we can anticipate change or react to change imposed on us. In the optimum approach, we seek out our possible problems and then go about seeking a solution before there is big trouble. While that may be the best path, it is most often the path least followed.

Leaders, anticipating change, will first ask the right questions. Then these leaders design decision-making processes to engage everyone in seeking the right solutions. In this case, leaders recognize that the economic system is constantly evolving and what is expected is often what we don't get. Testing assumptions—and recognizing hidden assumptions—are the keys to success. Do home prices always go up? Are credit ratings really foolproof? Are these financial instruments really as liquid and marketable as we assume?

Change can sometimes appear invisible, like rot beneath a staircase, but breakdowns in the economic models of our institutions often evolve over time. Business standards are compromised. Guidelines are fudged. Sometimes our belief structure filters the information derived from experience and we see what we believe; we do not take a disinterested view of economic developments, but instead emphasize our past commitments and investments, thereby falling prey to the sunk costs bias of decision making.

Introducing change into our framework can be both enlightening and misleading. If the model framework is specified carefully and thoughtfully and change is properly introduced, the results can be enlightening. Stress testing a portfolio or business model can reveal the sensitive points in our framework. The essential element of successful building construction is proper testing. Expectations do not equal actual results and thereby we are moved to react. The sources of many shocks and surprises that we must deal with are often a surprise, since our expectations are priced into the actions we have taken in the past in either our professional or financial choices.

However, stress testing a model is often not carried out in order to reveal problems, but rather to reassure management that everything is all right. There are two aspects of ineffective change simulations. First, we change the impacts on the model by modest amounts or we only alter those factors that we feel comfortable that the model can handle. Unfortunately, once the model faces the real world such ineffective testing is quickly revealed—often with catastrophic results. While our knowledge about sources and the magnitude of change are always imperfect, we are wise not to compound our ignorance by using incomplete models of change.

Second, within the real world experience, analysts often downplay information that contradicts or disproves their prior beliefs about the world, and there is therefore a recognition lag in many areas of human knowledge where change precedes the recognition of that change. From the view of cyclical change we have a history of changes in economic growth, inflation, and interest rates that alter course, sometimes rapidly, so that change leads to many business and political decision makers being behind the curve. With a longer view, there is a theme of creative destruction suggesting that over time, the common wisdom of our view of the world will be turned over by significant change.[7] Creative destruction represents a transformation that accompanies radical innovation. It is often driven by entrepreneurs, and effectively alters the path of economic growth as it destroys the value of established companies and laborers that enjoyed some degree of monopoly power derived from previous technological, organizational, regulatory, and economic paradigms.

## Choice: Innovation or Staying with the Old Model

Since change is constant, then so are our choices. Continuous novel change requires constant innovation and therefore a revaluation of our framework. We upgrade our education, our standard practices, and our information-gathering networks. Once we introduce a shock or surprise into our framework, then we must recognize that any change, however dramatic or subtle, will be either an incentive that will reveal weaknesses in our existing framework—as was the lack of true liquidity in the subprime mortgage secondary market—or an incentive to move our economic activity in a certain direction—as was true of the rapid rise of both inflation and interest rates in the late 1970s.

Economic shocks on the supply side can come from many sources, such as drought or floods, changes in laws and property rights, and the emergence or collapse of an international commodity cartel. For decision makers the approach has to recognize that such economic shocks or changes mean that the economy will not return to the original equilibrium model or state of nature. To paraphrase Euripides, you can never step into the same river twice. Yet public policy sometimes attempts to go back into the old river. For example, in economics, the British government attempted to reestablish the Gold Standard after World War I with disastrous results.

Change, and its associated risk, is not symmetrical in its impact. For example, equal changes in opposite directions for growth and interest rates have significant different implications when faced by liquidity, budget, or financial constraints. Over the last five years the implications of a 10 percent appreciation in home prices is significantly different from a 10 percent depreciation of home prices that wipes out the borrower's home equity and therefore significantly alters the risk of default.

Finally, we recognize that changes can be easily simulated in a spreadsheet based on fixed mathematical relationships. Each change alters the model itself as actors in the economic world will react to change in defensive or innovative ways that cannot be captured or anticipated in a model based on fixed relationships. Moreover, relationships such as elasticity (a relationship based on percentage changes) along the supply and demand curves, change along the curve even if the absolute period to period changes are equal.

## Feedback: What We Get Is Often What We Least Anticipate

What are the implications of a given change to the business directly and then, more interestingly, what are the possible implications for the framework itself? In most cases, we recognize that there is a range of possibilities for the implications of change and that this range of possible outcomes (and risks) depends on the time horizon of the decision makers.[8]

Moreover, even in a seemingly stable, short-run situation, there are undercurrents of dynamic change, such as demographics, that can be significantly impacted so that the future path of society/economy can be significantly different, depending not so much on the actual change, but rather on the state of the long-run changes in the economy. Tax policy, for example, has significantly different impacts between sectors of the economy. Demographics can be a harsh master with the evolution of Social Security and health care burdens over time.

From an opposite view, sometimes the same change implemented in an economy may have far more limited feedback given the cultural/historical context for the economy. For the analyst, estimating the feedback on the organization's prospects from any given change also faces, beyond the economic context, a number of decision-making impediments that will influence the path of any feedback response to change. Three bias factors are very common hindrances to getting the feedback estimate right: anchoring bias, recency bias, and illusory correlation. Anchoring bias allows an initial reference point to distort our expectations of the feedback. Organizations often start with the belief that the organization's basic model is correct and only small modifications are needed.[9] Anchoring bias is common in negotiating situations such as real estate and auto dealerships, where posted prices set a benchmark around which negotiations focus, even though in some cases the listed prices can be very far from market prices.[10] Meanwhile, the recency bias refers to the practice of referring to the last transaction or piece of information as the basis for the foundation point for future transactions.

Finally, there is the illusory correlation where two activities appear to move together, therefore creating an assumption of cause and effect. Unfortunately, the illusory correlation is too often the lazy path to analysis, resulting mainly in the creation of a significant number of sound bites.

The existence of the illusory correlation bias helps explain the tendency of many analysts to rely on truisms to characterize events rather than spending a bit more time thinking about the real underlying relationship.[11] In addition, there is also a tendency to pick the last straw on the camel's back to explain a collapse while ignoring the pile of prior straws. Unfortunately, the problem often is not the proximate cause of the collapse but the real problem was the weakened economic/financial state of the economy/company before the final straw.

In the history of economics we recognize one illusory correlation that was quite popular for a while: sunspot theory. While such a theory may have had some merit in an agrarian society, any correlation in the industrial age has certainly disappeared.

Today, the feedback effect on our model and any business framework has been altered by the emergence of globalization of markets for goods, capital, and, increasingly in recent years, labor markets. For many twenty-first century decision makers, the reality of an open, global economy is increasingly becoming part of the basic framework for the way forward.

### Choices: Taking Advantage of Change

Choices are part of the dynamic process of change and response—trial and error—that defines constant adjustment to an ever-changing economic landscape. Choices are constantly tweaked based on feedback we anticipate. That is, we choose a certain path anticipating what the market or our competition will do. We are familiar with this in such activities as chess or professional football. We also choose certain actions in anticipation of the news we will receive over time. Once again, we invest, for example, anticipating that the future earnings of a company will improve over time. Sometimes, the choices we make lead to dead ends or failure. But such mistakes also provide new information that can result in better solutions and, ultimately, success.

Often leaders see their decisions as confirming the continuation of the present framework. At other times decisions are made to be consistent with what leaders believe the new framework will be. There is a temptation to interpret history backward, that is, we interpret our historical experience in light of what we now know to be true so that we can say "everything worked out in the end." Yet, in fact, we had very little clear vision of what was happening at the time. We also have a tendency to make history linear or cumulative; we connect all the dots we see as relevant to fitting our view of history. That is, we connect the dots we remember in our past whereas often history is random and many bits of our history are essential and others are purely accidental. Yet we tend to make the present situation appear to be the perfectly logical outcome from the past.

With every change in the the business environment, the opportunity arrives to build a better mousetrap. However, the other two legs of the tripod—economics and decision making—need to be considered. Leaders also need to recognize that economics is a science of choice, of tradeoffs, of risks. But biases in their decision making are prevalent. Whether leaders are conscious of it or not, choices are made from frameworks of their minds and these frameworks and their biases can mislead the best of policymakers.[12] In this section, the focus is on these tricks, what we call *biases*, and this focus is applied throughout the rest of the book.

Behind the range of choices open to decision makers is the concept of path dependence. This concept highlights how the set of decisions a person faces for any given circumstance is limited by the decisions that person has made in the past, even though past circumstances may no longer be relevant. Essentially, history matters but is not deterministic. Path dependence also recognizes the impact of a nation's or a company's culture when making decisions. Because of its experience after World War I, German culture is staunchly anti-inflation. Japan has a culture of caution and respect for personal relationships within business while companies in the United States have had a mixed culture toward workers and innovation.

Culture extends to the application of prospect theory when leaders make choices. Prospect theory suggests that the way we see the prospects of any choice—in favor of risk or leaning toward reward—will bias our decision one way or another. When we see an opportunity for reward we will interpret information in a way to bias our decision to seek the reward. Where we anticipate risk, we see the risks and avoid the activity. In addition, some people are risk-averse and others are risk takers. Therefore, decision makers and their organizations can look at the same problem and yet assess risk differently. For some investors a given price is an opportunity to buy or an opportunity to sell.

In addition, decision makers will make different risk/reward choices based on the size of the bets they make. This helps explain why lotteries still attract a lot of buyers even though the probability of winning is very low. The size of the potential gains or losses will influence the willingness to bet one way or another, even when the actual probabilities of winning or losing are the same. When the lottery value is very high, there is a tendency for some people to bet, while when the lottery value is much less they would not bet. The mental model that a decision maker and an organization have of risk and reward influences the choices they make in situations where there is risk. Despite these mental models, in reality, there are few choices that do not involve risk.

Framing, which simply means that someone frames a choice based on his or her view of the world, is another aspect of the choices that face decision makers. Commonly expressed, do you see the glass half-empty or half-full? In economics, we assume that all consumers make choices in the same way. In finance, we assume that all investors see risk/reward the same way. However, not all consumers or investors will make the same decision, even if the underlying circumstances are the same. Investors can view any change as either a threat or an opportunity. Often, leaders become rigid in their thinking when facing a threat—they hunker down, pull in their horns, and get defensive. In contrast, when they frame a challenge or threat as an opportunity, they become more flexible and adapt in ways that will enable them to succeed in that situation. They innovate. They make lemons out of lemonade. They focus on the gains and not on the losses.

Another reality of making choices is that any institution or rule adopted for a particular time, even if optimal then, may no longer be effective because the business environment has changed. How decision makers deal with new developments is a key to success. Rationing during wartime gives way after a war to open markets and often rapid inflation. How would a decision maker adjust to free markets, competition, and, in some cases, the loss of government subsidies? In recent years in America, airlines, trucking, and long-distance phone service were deregulated. Many firms adapted successfully. Many firms did not.

In some cases, systematic relationships—the relationships that are the core of the spreadsheets so many business decisions are based on—change over time in unpredictable ways and create fundamental uncertainties. During the 1970s, the rapid rise in inflation wrecked the long-held business model of savings and loans associations. The globalization of capital markets upset the links between the economy, interest rates, and the money supply, causing the Federal Reserve to drop the use of monetary targets. The emergence of Asian economic powers, first Japan and then China, has led American firms to question their competitiveness as well as how and where they do business.

The choices for action are frequently conditioned by leaders' personal experiences and, most importantly, their education. They apply what they have learned, and often they apply, metaphorically, a hammer to different situations even when they should be using a screwdriver. In this chapter, the focus is on three mental biases that shape the choices of leaders. In later chapters, other biases are discussed.

The first mental bias is that of sunk costs. These costs represent the time, effort, and financial investment a person has put into a project that cannot be recouped if he or she stops working today. People then have a tendency to escalate commitment to the same course of action while ignoring the marginal costs and benefits of a project. A person grits his teeth and commits to finishing a job no matter what. He reasons: Look at how much I've put into the project already. Good money is now thrown after bad. For example, investors double down on their bets, convinced that an investment they own, even if losing money, will turn around if only given enough time. The commitment by the French under Ferdinand De Lesseps, chief engineer, to build the Panama Canal failed. The French continued to pour money into the project far beyond the initial budget estimates while many workers died of malaria. The French never completed the project and the Panama Canal Company declared bankruptcy in 1888. The continued commitment to complete the Panama Canal, even after years of losses, represents sunk cost bias.

A second mental bias is the overconfidence bias, or hubris. This bias is particularly evident in successful entrepreneurs and can, in a favorable situation, lead to success and innovation, and yet can be associated with failure when the entrepreneur pushes her luck and attempts a project outside her capabilities or the project itself is just too big or difficult for the economic environment. Day traders, chefs as restaurant owners, and home builders are susceptible to this bias, which helps explain the high failure rates for these groups.

Overconfidence often comes to grief when entrepreneurs or organizations believe that their efforts can overcome the devastating winds of a recession or financial shock. Individuals vow to succeed but the history of railroads, commodity corners such as Jay Gould's attempt to corner the gold market shortly after the Civil War and the Hunt brothers' attempt to corner the silver market during 1978 and 1979, and interest rate volatility suggest otherwise. As the great economist John Maynard Keynes said, "The market can stay irrational longer than you can stay solvent."[13]

A third mental bias is that of anchoring. This bias occurs when a person allows an initial reference point to distort his estimates of the true value of a financial asset or good he wants to purchase. In recent years, this bias was seen in the real market price of many financial assets. For example, dot-com stocks were selling at prices far higher than the advertised prices of these assets at their initial public offering, and houses were listed at prices far above market value. This bias limits a person's choices because he negotiates from the position the seller would like to start from, not from a careful assessment of the true value of the asset.

In the early post–World War II period, policy makers feared the economy might fall into another Great Depression. In the early 1980s, policy makers feared the economy might again experience the rapid inflation of the previous decade. Overcoming these kinds of anchoring biases usually takes one of two paths:

1. Outside experts or a newcomer to a company often can evaluate the framework of an enterprise and the overall economy with a fresh eye to the opportunities and risks that are ahead.
2. An intellectual leader inside the company, such as Andy Grove at Intel or Steve Jobs at Apple, can cut through conventional business assumptions and identify the way forward. Many business leaders, central banks, presidents, and generals build their strategy and framework around "fighting the last war."

Beyond the biases, there are also three patterns of our decision making that can result in poor decisions. First, leaders may pursue a linear path to their goal and use familiar rules to recreate the future in line with the familiar past. For example, this is particularly true for investors who follow specific stock screening strategies so closely that many opportunities are passed over when the company does not fit criteria or rules. Many investors have little incentive to change the framework because it is mentally comfortable for them even though they recognize that they are missing some investment opportunities. In a way, this is an example of the bounded rationality we will discuss later. Sometimes decision makers know how the current decision-making system works, at least under the old rules, even if anomalies appear from time to time. For example, today we recognize that the model assumes that asset returns are normally distributed random variables and yet the investment returns in equity and other markets are not normally distributed. This is the fat tail problem where unusually large returns, positive or negative, appear more often than predicted in a normally distributed model.[14]

Second, decisions made by one firm often give rise to a response from competitors. The process of achieving the firm's goal proceeds more like a chess game than a preplanned, linear decision process where specific steps follow prior steps in lockstep.

Third, decision makers, particularly political leaders, may not consider the long-run implications of current decisions because their costs fall to a future generation. This is the time inconsistency problem that bedevils so many issues today, for example, entitlements (Social Security, federal and state pensions, and post-retirement health care) and the federal deficit. In each case, political officeholders make promises to current voters, but these promises will have to be paid for by future voters. Third, there is a distinction between risk and uncertainty that often becomes confused and leads to poor decisions—especially in finance.[15] Risk refers to the probability of different outcomes based on experience with similar outcomes in the past. Uncertainty is associated with the problem of not seeing this pattern in the past and having very little to go on to make a call on its probability. Lloyds of London, a British insurance market, is famous for betting on cases of uncertainty. Las Vegas sports betting reflects risk.

## Decision Making as a Method of Making Choices

Economics is a discipline that focuses on choices. Choices never stop. Even when the environment appears quiet, inaction is also a choice. Challenges, shocks, and problems appear constantly, causing decision makers to reinvent the economy and their business models. Moreover, since the Enlightenment, when reason began to replace theology as a source of explanation and authority for science in the real world, each generation has pursued the study of its own unique problems and opportunities independent of ecclesiastical doctrines such as the writings of Descartes and Isaac Newton.[16] With the emphasis on science, the way forward led eventually to men landing on the moon.

Moreover, the view here is not that just the problems have changed but the network of fact, theory, and the economic/business models has shifted. Leaders solve the problems of the old paradigm only to find that the paradigm has changed and, therefore, new, more complicated problems appear. In this sense, we never solve the problems of disease, poverty, or financial crisis simply because the model and the problems constantly evolve. Life spans get longer and the diseases of old age become a new source of research. People are richer today in modern industrial societies, yet the sources of poverty evolve. We are told that the latest financial regulatory reform will end financial crisis—yet history teaches us that financial crises are repeated, each with a slightly different set of causes and patterns.

In fact, it is the newness of the problems that make what economists do so exciting. They are not solving the same textbook problems over and over again. Instead they are stretching their model and themselves to examine a new model in new ways to achieve progress. Their choices also force them to reexamine first principles and stretch the boundaries of the old model, which is narrow and rigid and does not solve their problems. These choices extend their mental and emotional comfort zone and lead to a new paradigm, a new way of defining our world. This new framework can be labeled globalization.

## Evolution of Our Frameworks

Globalization has meant that business decisions and processes that were successful in a closed economy are no longer effective in an open global economy. This can be seen in the auto and furniture industries in the United States where customer desires evolved faster than domestic producers could alter their production capabilities. In the field of international finance, the debt crisis in Greece in 2010 altered what was once thought to be a very stable euro framework.

To be truly successful, a new decision-making framework must explain and incorporate old behavior while designing a working model of how the world now functions. In reality, strategic decisions often evolve over time and proceed through an iterative process of choice, model building, and action. Each action is evaluated, the framework is tested, and then decisions are made on how to move forward. This is done with the expectation that the future differs from the past and that what was once successful in one area or time may not be successful in another area or time.

Three attributes of a new framework are important:

1. The framework must account for past mistakes and failures. If the same shocks and changes were to occur again, the new framework must be able to withstand the test.
2. The framework must allow decision makers to be flexible when responding to future shocks and changes.
3. The new framework must allow for the reality that it will change over time.

Decision making is a continuous process. Economies evolve, competition responds, and so must decision making. Over the last 50 years, there have been significant changes and shocks in the five central economic drivers— growth, inflation, interest rates, exchange rates, profits, and our expectations of each in the past. Institutional frameworks that did not allow for rapid changes in growth (recession) failed, including those of retailers such as W.T. Grant and Circuit City. Other examples include the rapid rise in inflation during the 1970s, doomed wage-price controls, and the model of lending practiced by the traditional savings and loan associations. Interest volatility altered the basic framework of the bond investor and the long-term debt bond issuance. Exchange rate volatility destroyed institutions such as Franklin National and forced the European community to reduce its exchange rate to one currency—a very innovative solution. Finally, profit volatility caused businesses to diversify, sign long-term supply contracts, and use hedging for critical supplies and output prices. Agricultural futures markets in Chicago began as an attempt not to speculate but as a way of hedging crop delivery prices so as to stabilize revenues in a volatile farming environment.

The reality is that the framework in the financial markets, as in all other markets, is constantly changing. Therefore, new rules and frameworks must be designed to deal with new problems that were unforeseen (unintended consequences in some cases) in the past.

Change is constant and needs to be accommodated in your thinking. At each step along the way, you need to be aware of decision-making biases that hinder your thinking and can lead to a suboptimal decision. Finally, five economic drivers are essential to all strategic business thinking. In fact, the biggest mistakes in most business decisions have little to do with the lessons learned in the traditional business curriculum. Instead, the greatest business failures revolve around not accounting for the unexpected movements of the five economic factors. This is covered in the next chapter.

## DISCUSSION QUESTIONS

1. In professional sports, opening day begins with all teams tied for first place, yet the history of league championships reveals that a select few franchises appear in the finals far more often than by chance.

    In examining this record of success (or in some cases you might want to identify why some franchises continue to fail), begin with your assessment of the correct process for winning in professional sports. What is your framework? When teams appear in championships across several decades (Yankees and Cardinals, Cowboys and Steelers, Celtics and Lakers, Canadiens and Redwings) what does that signify about their ability to react to change and develop a new framework for winning? Some franchises find a one-time solution, an outstanding player, such as Michael Jordan or Wayne Gretzky, but cannot sustain success after that player leaves. Why?

2. In business, Jim Collins, in his book, *Good to Great*, identifies companies that have sustained success over time despite the constant changes in the economic scene. For example, Collins examines the different approaches to labor and technology that Nucor and Bethlehem Steel adopted and the implications for each company over time.

    You have been recently appointed the CEO of a very large industrial equipment company that is not performing well.

    a. Define the economic framework for your company. One immediate challenge you have is that you are tempted to force the company's underperformance problems into conceptual boxes supplied by your post-secondary education.

    b. How might your framework be influenced, and therefore how can you avoid, the recency and confirmation bias problems that might cause you to define your framework by the recent experience of the company?

    c. Does your framework enlighten the perspective on the company or are you oversimplifying the company's framework?

    d. How does your framework reflect the path dependence of prior CEO decisions? How did you get to where you are today, and does that limit your options for the future?

    e. What are the entrenched institutional arrangements that you recognize in your framework? What are the vested interests of the current division leaders who directly report to you?

3. You have been appointed regional manager of a casual-dining restaurant chain in a moderate sized (1.5 million population) metropolitan area in the United States.

    a. Explain the underlying economic structure of the demand and supply relationships for your business that define your economic framework.

    b. What are the sunk costs associated with your current framework? Before you make a single decision, what types of anchoring bias should you be aware of going forward? How well do you know yourself as a risk taker or risk avoider, i.e., how would you see yourself in the spectrum of prospect theory?

    c. Lehman Brothers has failed and the outlook for the economy has darkened quickly. What feedback does this change signal for your business? List three options for your action and suggest a choice for the business. What is your new framework for the business and how does that differ from the initial framework?

    d. In an effort to make up for lost revenue, the county where your chain of five restaurants is located introduces a special tourism tax of 15 percent on all restaurant meals to pay for a new baseball stadium. Repeat the process of recognizing change, estimating feedback, making choices, and developing a new framework, and discuss how the influence of an anchoring bias impacts your judgment of closing one restaurant and moving to a new county.

    Explain your expected feedback from such a change and then your choices to deal with this change.

4. Leadership sometimes has its own interests at heart, with often tragic consequences. Consider the following circumstances and offer your

assessment on the impact of leadership, or lack thereof, in the following actions. Consider for a moment, too, what framework the leader had adopted and how that might be different from what others had expected.

a. General McClellan's preference for parading troops rather than fighting and Lincoln's response.

b. The Central Intelligence Agency's view of the Bay of Pigs operation and President Kennedy's assumption about their input to his decision making.

c. Polaroid's failure to pursue digital photography and their shareholder expectations.

d. The role of some of Enron's senior management and the expectations of the workers and shareholders.

e. Trade protectionism and earmarks within the framework of a congressman doing the best for his constituents or for the general welfare.

These are not easy problems and often represent a conflict of the framework or vision and that conflict is part of real world decision making, not the product of a textbook exercise with a neat, precise solution.

## NOTES

1. For baseball, Michael Lewis's book, *Moneyball* (New York: W.W. Norton, 2003) represents a shift in the model of how baseball championships are won.
2. Richard E. Neustadt and Ernest R. May, *Thinking in Time: The Uses of History for Decision-Makers* (New York: The Free Press, 1986).
3. James O'Toole, *Leading Change* (San Francisco: Jossey-Bass, 1995).
4. Richard Tedlow, *Andy Grove: The Life and Times of an American* (New York: Penguin Publishers, 2006). *Your Show of Shows* appeared from 1950 to 1954 on NBC and featured a team of famous writers who spent considerable time debating every show.
5. See A. E. Kahn, "Surprises of Airline Deregulation," *American Economic Review*, Papers and Proceedings 78, no. 2 (May 1988): 316–322.
6. See Jim Collins's discussion of Kroger and A&P in *Good to Great* (New York: HarperCollins, 2001).
7. Joseph A. Schumpeter, *Capitalism, Socialism and Democracy* (New York: Harper & Brothers, 1942).
8. Hugh Courtney, Jane Kirkland, and Patrick Viguerie, "Strategy Under Uncertainty," *Harvard Business Review* (November–December, 1997).
9. This reluctance to alter a winning formula was characteristic of Montgomery Ward and Ford Motor as written up in John Steele Gordon's essay on "The

Perils of Success" in his book *The Business of America* (New York: Walker & Co., 2001).

10. Price and wage expectations can be slow to adjust to the realities of the market-place as we have seen in both housing and labor markets over the period 2007 to 2010.

11. For a good example in the historical context, see Neustadt and May, *Thinking in Time*.

12. Douglas North, *Structure and Change in Economic History* (New York: W.W. Norton, 1981), 11.

13. John Maynard Keynes, *Essays in Persuasion* (New York: Harcourt, Brace & Co., 1931).

14. Popularization of this concept appears in Nassim Taleb, *The Black Swan* (New York: Penguin, 2007). The original insights come from Benoit Mandelbrot, a French-American mathematician who observed that financial prices, as well as cotton prices, did not follow the expected normal distribution. Thus fat tails in the distribution were very common in many statistical and economic series and hence outliers, termed *black swans*, were much more common than previously expected.

15. Frank Knight, *Risk, Uncertainty, and Profit* (Boston: Houghton Mifflin, 1921).

16. Descartes' *Discourse on the Method* and Newton's *Principia Mathematica* are considered founding tracts for the Enlightenment.

# CHAPTER 2

# Measuring Economic Benchmarks

Theory and statistics compose most of the graduate curriculum in economics for many master's degree programs in business as well as economics. This is a shortcoming that has immediate costs, since most students will soon enter the private sector and not stay in academia. The popular approach fails to provide a rudimentary exposure to the actual data these professionals have to examine and compare to the benchmarks of performance for the economy against their companies' own performance. In this section we focus not on the standards of abstract theory or statistics but rather on the basics for understanding and analyzing economic time series that students most often will encounter after graduation.

In the early post–World War II period, many policy makers and economists, as well as businesspeople such as Montgomery Ward, were concerned that the country would again enter another Great Depression. Montgomery Ward built his company's strategy around the weak, recession-prone forecast for the post–World War II period. He was wrong, and his company's performance suffered. Fear of another depression was based on the then popular framework of the consumption function as described by the famed British economist John Maynard Keynes. Keynes argued that as incomes grew, a household's average consumption rate fell (the Absolute Income Hypothesis). Keynes also reasoned that as incomes grew so would the propensity to save, and therefore the economy would slow down over time as savings rates rose as income grew. Simon Kuznets, then at the University of Pennsylvania, argued that Keynes' predictions did not work in the long run.[1] Kuznets would later win a Nobel Prize in Economics for this work. Kuznets gathered data dating back to 1869 that indicated that the ratio of consumption to income was, in fact, quite stable, despite the increased income over that period. The savings rate remained fairly constant, despite increases in income, and therefore the economy did not naturally slow down because of excess savings.

Another Great Depression did not appear. Households didn't assume a defensive position. Instead, they adopted an attitude of growth and spending that generated a consumer boom in the 1950s. Montgomery Ward was on the wrong side of that economic bet.

Notice the dynamic decision framework in action in the previous example. Keynes assumed a short-run orientation; from this perspective, he predicted a certain set of results. Kuznets brought a new data set to challenge that framework and provided a different framework of consumer behavior over the long run. Businesses such as Sears and Kroger, which adopted Kuznets' longer-run perspective, made different decisions than Montgomery Ward and A&P, which followed the short-run view of Keynes. Sears bet on the growth of the American consumer economy and the wishes of new families after World War II to have the homes and appliances that would satisfy their dreams. Kroger met the need for a broader selection of foods in a suburban environment. Montgomery Ward and A&P bet on a return to the past. The performance of these four consumer companies over the next 30 years reflected the adoption of a new framework that allowed for change over time. Since then, the inability to see the long-run evolution of household trends has led to the decline of many consumer franchises.

## BENCHMARKING GROWTH

In isolation, the statement that a company's sales are up 5 percent is meaningless. Five percent compared to what? Up over what time period? Are those real or nominal sales? The importance of aggregate economic concepts such as the gross domestic product (popularly termed GDP) real final sales, consumer spending, and business investment is that they provide a benchmark for analyzing an institution's performance over time. A company whose sales are growing 5 percent while the economy's nominal growth is 8 percent is likely losing ground. In contrast, a company growing 5 percent while the economy is growing 3 percent is gaining share. Over the last 60 years, the private and public institutions in America have developed a wealth of data for analyzing the economy.

### Three Applications for Benchmarking

Three measures are critical in determining the success of an economic framework and the choices leaders make when faced with changes to that framework:

1. National income.
2. Prices.
3. Factor returns, such as interest rates and corporate profits.

National income, one measure of which is the GDP, is often the primary way to judge whether an economy is growing and whether public policy is working. Prices, and its cousin inflation, provide a hint on the incentives to produce and sell at the micro level and on the success of public policy, particularly monetary policy, at the macro level. Finally, factor returns indicate the attraction of saving and investing, and provide the incentive to grow over time. Measures of income and prices provide the sources of data, the inputs needed to define the patterns of demand, supply, and incentives that drive the framework for decision making.

## Measuring Growth: Benchmark for Cyclical Change and Secular Growth

The GDP is the most simple and standard benchmark for gauging the performance of an overall economy, public policy, and the relative success of any enterprise. This measure allows decision makers to answer several key questions: How is the economy growing relative to the past or the promises of the future? How is the economy performing relative to the promises of the current political leadership? How is my company or institution growing or shrinking relative to the overall economy? Table 2.1 highlights the major

**TABLE 2.1**   Real Gross Domestic Product and Related Measures

| | Percent Change from Preceding Period | | | | |
|---|---|---|---|---|---|
| | 2007 | 2008 | 2009 | Q1 2010 | Q2 2010 |
| Total GDP | 1.9 | 0 | −2.6 | 3.7 | 2.4 |
| Personal Consumption Expenditure | 2.4 | −0.3 | −1.2 | 1.9 | 1.6 |
|   Durable Goods | 4.2 | −5.2 | −3.7 | 8.8 | 7.5 |
|   Nondurable Goods | 2 | −1.1 | −1.2 | 4.2 | 1.6 |
|   Services | 2.2 | 0.9 | −0.8 | 0.1 | 0.8 |
| Gross Private Domestic Investment | −3.1 | −9.5 | −22.6 | 29.1 | 28.8 |
|   Structures | 14.1 | 5.9 | −20.4 | −17.8 | 5.2 |
|   Equipment and Software | 3.7 | −2.4 | −15.3 | 20.4 | 21.9 |
|   Residential | −18.7 | −24 | −22.9 | −12.3 | 27.9 |
| Net Exports of Goods and Services | | | | | |
|   Exports | 9.3 | 6 | −9.5 | 11.4 | 10.3 |
|   Imports | 2.7 | −2.6 | −13.8 | 11.2 | 28.8 |
| Government Consumption Expenditure and Gross Investment | 1.3 | 2.8 | 1.6 | −1.6 | 4.4 |
|   Federal | 1.2 | 7.3 | 5.7 | 1.8 | 9.2 |
|   State and Local | 1.4 | 0.3 | −0.9 | −3.8 | 1.3 |
|   Final Sales of Domestic Product | 5.2 | 2.7 | −1.1 | 2.1 | 3.2 |

*Source:* U.S. Department of Commerce.

breakdown of the GDP for the first half of 2010 and serves as the reference point for benchmarking economic performance in the first year of this economic recovery.

Gross domestic product, as prepared by the Bureau of Economic Analysis (BEA) of the United States Department of Commerce, measures the total market value of final goods and services produced in the United States during a certain time period and is therefore a summary measure of the economic process. One tremendous advantage of the GDP is that it is widely recognized as the most reliable and best available economic data in an imperfect world. It can be easily accessed through the Department of Commerce web site. The concept of final goods is significant because it eliminates the purchases of one intermediate institution from another in the calculation of the GDP. In Figure 2.1 there is a clear pattern to the real GDP that should set off alarm bells for those analysts familiar with the tendency for many public policy and private managers to rely solely on a single straight line projection of future growth.

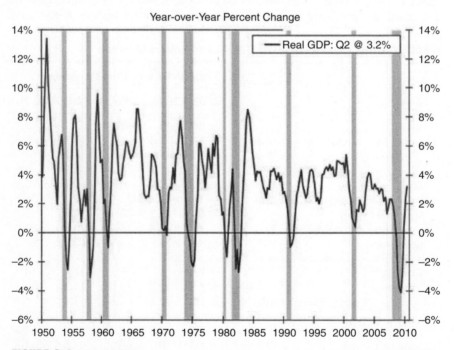

**FIGURE 2.1**   Real GDP

*Source:* U.S. Department of Commerce and Wells Fargo Securities, LLC.

## COMPONENTS OF THE GDP

For undergraduate students one of their first memories of economics is the equation of C + I + G + NX as the sum of the components that enter into the calculation of the GDP. For private and public decision makers the patterns of each of these components will set the tone for top line revenue sales and thereby the success of their enterprise. For this reason we review each of these components here.

### Personal Consumption

Personal consumption represents the largest component of the GDP in the United States. Personal consumption includes goods and services purchased by households, along with the operating expenses of nonprofit institutions, as well as the value of in-kind goods and services received by individuals. For an analyst, the breakdown of personal consumption into consumer durables, non-durables, and services provides a useful benchmark for viewing how these three components of consumer spending behave over time. Figure 2.2

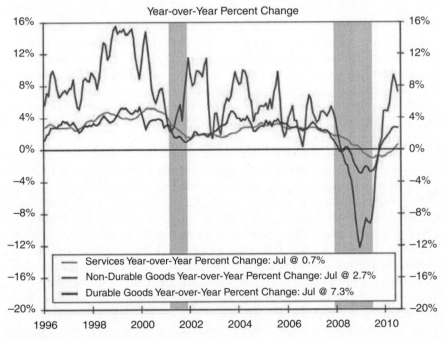

**FIGURE 2.2** Consumer Spending Components
*Source:* U.S. Department of Commerce and Wells Fargo Securities, LLC.

highlights the behavior of each major subcomponent. In-kind values must be imputed, which is a source of considerable controversy. Families that live in their own home enjoy the same type of housing services that someone renting receives. The market value of the rent for the house is estimated and considered part of the GDP.

Consumer durable spending (automobiles, furniture, appliances) tends to be more cyclical than the other components. Decision makers in this sector face greater cyclical risk and therefore need to carefully control inventories as gauge changes in the economy's rate of growth over time. Non-durable goods (food and clothing) last only a short period of time. This gives an impetus to consumer spending no matter how difficult the economy. Buying a new car or microwave can be postponed, but the dog must be fed. In a similar way, services (telephone or cable, haircuts or hair styling, doctors and the kids' orthodontist) must continue, and this gives a certain momentum to the economy over time.

## Gross Private Domestic Investment

Gross private domestic investment includes two components, business investment and residential investment. Business investment consists of the fixed capital goods purchased by private business and nonprofit institutions, as well as the value of the change in physical volume of inventories held by private businesses. Residential investment includes all private purchases of residential structures, either bought for owner occupancy or for a tenant.

Investment is broken down into several subcomponents that provide detail needed to benchmark performance. Nonresidential construction includes nonfarm office buildings, mining, and utilities as well as a separate farm construction estimate.

Producers' durable equipment is estimated by the BEA primarily from shipments data and includes the many types of electrical, non-electrical, high tech, and trucks, buses, and planes that represent the wide variety of investment spending. Figure 2.3 highlights the behavior of durable equipment over recent business cycles. The cyclical nature of spending is apparent. Business investment reflects the forces of expected business sales, financing costs, and business profitability—each of which has its own cyclical character. Businesses invest because they expect to make a profit. Expectations are a driving force and a potential source of opportunity or error depending on the quality of foresight at a firm. Financing costs bring in the influence of interest rates and the availability of credit. In a delicate balancing act, business leaders must judge whether the relative cost of credit is exceeded by the expected rate of return on the investment. The framework for decision

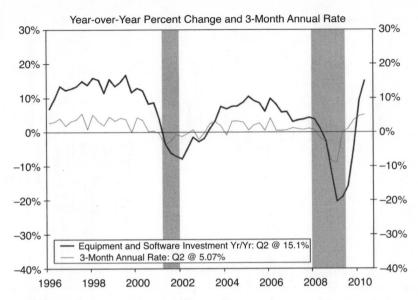

**FIGURE 2.3** Equipment and Software Spending
*Source:* U.S. Department of Commerce and Wells Fargo Securities, LLC.

making must include the expected rate of return of the investment, which, in turn, is derived from a business leader's model of the marketplace.

Residential investment, Figure 2.4, is more than just new housing. The data includes additions and renovations, for example. Once again, the developer and builder, as well as the buyer, have a framework for how the housing market works, and the balancing point revolves around the real cost of financing the house over time. For the buyer, the real interest rate and the monthly payment is compared to monthly income, but the importance of home price appreciation (or in recent years, depreciation) is also a driving force on whether the home purchase makes sense. Recent history highlights the dynamic changes that can arise for the business frameworks and particularly the unrecognized assumptions (home prices always go up) that business leaders take for granted in their models and that often leads to ruin.

Inventories are interesting and a caution note is warranted. In the GDP accounts, the change in inventories is actually incorporated in the GDP, not inventories per se. We are looking at the change in the physical volume of inventories valued at average prices over the period under study. Whenever a firm adds to its inventory of goods to be sold later, that increase in

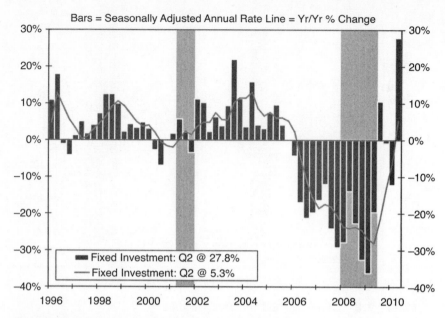

**FIGURE 2.4**   Real Residential Fixed Investments
*Source:* U.S. Department of Commerce and Wells Fargo Securities, LLC.

goods is an increase in current production and therefore adds to the GDP. We measure it as an addition to the GDP because the increase of goods inventory does represent current production. Inventory changes are also a signal to a company to increase or decrease production and thereby alter the pace of economic growth. Decision makers therefore must be aware of why inventories are changing over time. If demand in the economy is slowing down, inventories may rise as a result of reduced consumer spending. See Figures 2.5a and 2.5b. This is a signal to firms to reduce production today and gradually work off the excess inventory on their books.

In fact, the delicate balance between desired inventories and expected sales provides the internal dynamics of the national business cycle and the performance of selected industries. When such a balance crumbles, the impact on the economy and individual businesses is dramatic. In the years 2004 to 2007, there was a dramatic shortage of housing in certain markets (California, Florida, Nevada, and Arizona) relative to expected demand. This led to a rapid growth in housing construction in these regions. However, the boom was quickly followed by an equally dramatic falloff in housing demand and therefore an excess of housing stock relative to demand. Housing inventories rose quickly. Since World War II, dramatic imbalances

(a)

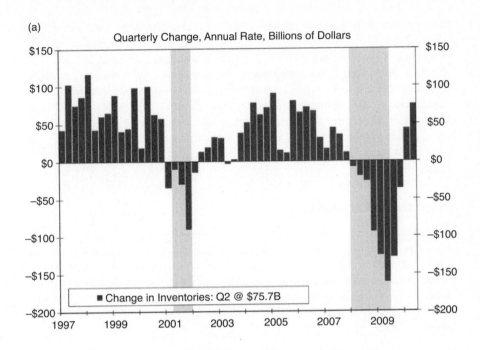

(b)

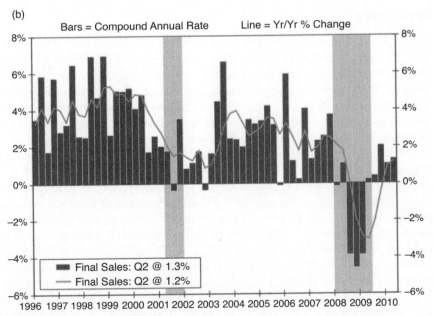

**FIGURE 2.5** (a) Inventory Change in GDP (b) Real Domestic Final Sales
*Source:* U.S. Department of Commerce and Wells Fargo Securities, LLC.

have occurred in housing as well as in automobiles, appliances, and computer chips. These imbalances are often the product of changes in business frameworks that cause leaders to alter their business models. Change is constant and it is often represented in the imbalance of inventories and expected final sales. For a new analyst, this imbalance of sales and inventories is a useful tool to use in beginning to explore the inner dynamics of any product market. Inventory and sales (shipments) data are published monthly by the Census Department and contain a wealth of information on the balance (or imbalance) of inventories and shipments in a number of sectors in the economy.[2]

## Government Purchases

The government purchases of goods and services component of the GDP is composed of the compensation of government employees and purchases from businesses. This includes federal military spending, state spending on highways, and local education expenditures. Government spending does not, however, include transfer payments to individuals, such as Social Security and welfare. Transfer payments are not made for current production of goods and services; they only reallocate income.

## Net Exports

Net exports of goods and services are exports less imports of goods and services. Services include factor incomes, measured as compensation of employees, interest, and corporate profits. However, the net aspect of this category hides the rising globalization of the American economy, which is of paramount importance to strategic thinking in any enterprise today. Figure 2.6 highlights the sum of exports and imports as a percentage of the GDP. As is evident, the globalization of the United States economy is relentless.

GDP also has its income side, as evidenced in Table 2.2. The concept of gross national product (GNP) differs from the GDP because the GNP accounts for net payments to factors of production between payments abroad less payments made to those abroad. The GDP measures the total income produced in the United States, while the GNP measures the total income earned by residents of the United States. Wages earned by a foreign national working in the United States is part of our GDP, but is not part of the older concept of GNP. GDP is a newer concept adopted by the BEA to conform to international standards. The movement from GNP to GDP occurred in 1991. The relationship between GDP and GNP is reviewed in Table 1.7.5 of the National Income and Product Accounts from the United States Bureau of Economic Analysis in the Department of Commerce.

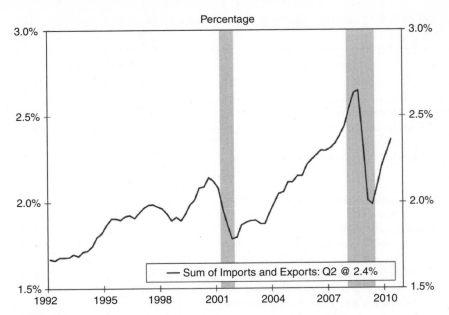

**FIGURE 2.6** Sum of Imports and Exports as Percentage of GDP
*Source:* U.S. Department of Commerce and Wells Fargo Securities, LLC.

Compensation of employees, which comprises more than 70 percent of income, is the income accruing to employees as payment for their work. Compensation is the sum of wages and salaries and of supplementary benefits, including employer contributions for social insurance that comes from Social Security. Proprietor's income is the income and income in kind received by small business and partnerships as well as tax-exempt cooperatives. Rental income is simply the rental income of persons from the rental of real property. Corporate profits, of which more is to be said later, are the income of corporations. Profits are adjusted for changes of inventory valuations and capital consumption adjustments (depreciation).

Benchmarking growth using GDP data provides a decision maker several insights. First, there is a sense of the historical pattern of the benchmark or target variable over the economic cycle and over the long run. How fast has consumer spending grown over the last 20 years? How does this component of consumer spending behave over the cycle? What is the responsiveness (beta) of consumption to changes in growth over the cycle? Second, the data can be used to pinpoint where the economy is today relative to past trends and the cycle. Third, a decision maker can use the data to suggest where the company might be going relative to the growth of the economy.

**TABLE 2.2**　Real Gross Domestic Product, Gross National Product, and National Income

| | Billions of Dollars | | |
| --- | --- | --- | --- |
| | 2007 | 2008 | 2009 |
| **Gross Domestic Product** | 14,061.80 | 14,369.10 | 14,119.00 |
| Plus: Income Receipts from the Rest of the World | 871.00 | 839.20 | 629.80 |
| Less: Income Payments to the Rest of the World | 747.70 | 664.70 | 483.60 |
| **Gross National Product** | 14,185.10 | 14,543.60 | 14,285.30 |
| Less: Consumption of Fixed Capital | 1,767.50 | 1,849.20 | 1,861.10 |
| Less: Statistical Discrepancy | 21.10 | 136.60 | 179.10 |
| **Equals: National Income** | 12,396.40 | 12,557.80 | 1,225.00 |
| Compensation of Employees | 7,885.90 | 8,060.80 | 7,811.70 |
| Wage and Salary Accruals | 6,415.50 | 6,554.00 | 6,279.10 |
| Supplements to Wages and Salaries | 1,440.40 | 1,506.80 | 1,532.60 |
| Proprietors' Income with Inventory Valuation and Capital Consumption Adjusted | 1,090.40 | 1,102.00 | 1,011.90 |
| Rental Income of Persons with Capital Consumption Adjusted | 143.70 | 222.00 | 274.00 |
| Corporate Profits with Inventory Valuation and Capital Consumption Adjusted | 1,510.60 | 1,262.80 | 1,258.00 |
| Net Interest and Miscellaneous Payments | 731.60 | 812.80 | 784.30 |
| Taxes on Production and Imports Less Subsidies | 972.60 | 992.30 | 964.40 |
| Business Current Transfer Payments (Net) | 103.30 | 121.70 | 134.00 |
| Current Surplus of Government Enterprises | −11.80 | −16.70 | −13.20 |
| **Addendum** | | | |
| Gross Domestic Income | 14,040.70 | 14,232.50 | 13,939.90 |

*Source:* U.S. Department of Commerce.

By benchmarking key variables, decision makers can generate a forecast of future national economic activity and compare the growth of the economy to the growth of top-line revenue sales of the firm. Finally, this can be used to stress test business plans, income statements, and the balance sheet for changes in the economy.

## Real Final Sales

Real final sales are a useful measure of the underlying momentum of the economy. As illustrated in Figure 2.7, real final sales provide a less volatile

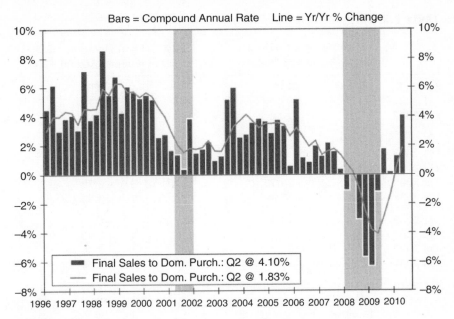

**FIGURE 2.7**  Real Final Sales to Domestic Purchasers
*Source:* U.S. Department of Commerce and Wells Fargo Securities, LLC.

measure of underlying growth and a useful benchmark for the economy. For the decision maker, real final sales provide critical insight into the internal dynamics of the economy. For example during the years 2008 to 2010, real final sales fell dramatically while the GDP was buoyed upward by a sharp gain in unwanted inventories.

Real final sales exclude the effect of inventory changes (increases and decreases) and thereby serve as a more reliable benchmark for gauging underlying demand in the economy. When the balance between this underlying demand and the pace of inventory change gets out of alignment, then sharp movements in production, employment, and prices are needed to reestablish a new balance. This occurs at both the level of the firm and the national economy. Unfortunately, this dynamic process of economic adjustment is not widely examined, but is very critical in examining change and feedback in the economy.

For example, as illustrated in Table 2.3, the years 2008 and 2009 witnessed a sharp decline in real final sales as the Great Recession hit, followed by a big drop in inventories. This accounted for most of the decline in the GDP. By 2010, inventory rebuilding gradually added to growth. Over time,

**TABLE 2.3**   Inventories and Final Sales

|  | Change in Inventories (Billions of Dollars) | Final Sales to Domestic Purchasers (Compound Annual Rate) |
|---|---|---|
| Q1 2007 | 14.5 | 2.00 |
| Q2 2007 | 23.3 | 2.10 |
| Q3 2007 | 29.8 | 1.90 |
| Q4 2007 | 10.3 | 0.40 |
| Q1 2008 | 0.6 | −0.90 |
| Q2 2008 | −37.1 | 0.30 |
| Q3 2008 | −29.7 | −2.70 |
| Q4 2008 | −37.4 | −4.90 |
| Q1 2009 | −113.9 | −6.40 |
| Q2 2009 | −160.2 | −0.90 |
| Q3 2009 | −139.2 | 2.30 |
| Q4 2009 | −19.7 | 1.40 |
| Q1 2010 | 41.2 | 1.60 |

*Source:* U.S. Department of Commerce.

the imbalance of final sales and inventories can last just a few quarters or can be prolonged, as in the current protracted housing correction.

## BENCHMARKING INFLATION: PRICING POWER AND THE COST OF GOODS SOLD

All businesses must seek a balance between output prices and the prices of inputs. The difference is profit, sustained operations, and the avoidance of economic failure. Inflation, which has the dual harsh characteristic that higher inflation tends to be accompanied by volatile inflation, is measured in several different ways. These ways can mislead as well as enlighten.

The term *inflation* is used often in a way that does not accurately represent the real concept of inflation. Inflation is a rise in prices of a large number of goods and services. The price of an individual good may rise, but that is not inflation. There is no inflation in oil or gold prices, there are price increases. For strategic thinking, price increases in individual goods such as oil, gold, and wheat are relative price changes that signal opportunities for the seller and cost increases for the buyer. Relative price changes are market signals and changes that can alter an existing business model. In the late

1970s, the rapid price increase in relative oil and gas prices was a signal to a buyer to use less gas and for the oil company to find more oil. In contrast, a rise in inflation is a signal that the real value of currency or nominal bond yields has diminished and that individual investors would hold less cash, invest in short-term assets like money funds, sell bonds, and buy real assets such as housing, all of which individuals did in the late 1970s. Relative price changes and inflation are distinct phenomena and provide different incentives for very different choices.

Inflation's benchmark has traditionally been the consumer price index (CPI) because this series has a long history. The CPI is used extensively in many contracts today for private sector collective bargaining and payments to Social Security recipients and the military and civilian retirees of the federal government. The CPI measures over time the cost of goods and services purchased by the consumer compared to a base period. CPI measures price changes for a fixed basket of goods, but since no substitution is allowed there is a tendency to overstate price changes over time. An estimate is made of the significance in the typical household budget for each major category in the index. Different major categories have different weights in the CPI. For example, food represents 13.7 percent while movies represent 0.14 percent of the household budget.[3] As in GDP, some items in the consumer budget, particularly owner-occupied housing, are not purchased each period and therefore must be imputed. For decision makers, one advantage with the CPI is the long history and the detail of the breakdowns in the data. There are over 200 subcategories in the CPI. The first CPI index was published in 1921 and took the series back to 1913. The CPI is also available monthly, in contrast to the GDP data. One issue involving the CPI that leads to many complaints is the question of quality adjustment. This issue is often skipped over in many discussions in both the private sector and academia, but is an essential component of understanding of the potential bias in measuring inflation. As quality has improved in products such as automobiles, and services such as medical care, the adjustments for quality can seem quite arbitrary. In effect, a higher price of a good at the store can be eliminated by a quality adjustment. Therefore, while the prices of medical care may rise for the patient, there does not appear to be any increase in the CPI component for this spending. This quality change bias was identified by the Boskin Commission as one of four possible sources of bias in calculating the consumer price index.[4] This bias appears when improvements in the quality of products, such as greater energy efficiency and reliability, are not accounted for adequately in the quality adjustment in the prices of consumer goods. We know consumers are willing to pay a bit more for reliability, so part of the price of a good is for that reliability, but measuring that quality is another matter.

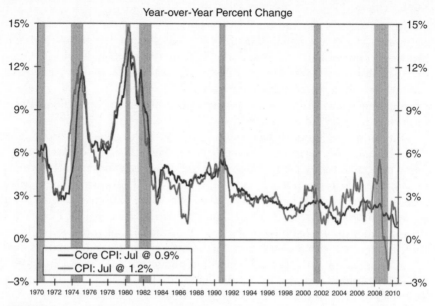

**FIGURE 2.8**   Headline CPI versus Core CPI
*Source:* U.S. Department of Labor and Wells Fargo Securities, LLC.

   In recent years the dramatic decline in home prices has reduced the CPI
index. This is an interesting case of product price declines that have kept
the overall measure of inflation lower. A subset of the CPI is the core CPI
(Figure 2.8), which subtracts from the overall CPI the impact of food and
energy prices. Born out of the inflationary 1970s, this is an attempt to show
the underlying trend in inflation by taking out the more volatile elements of
the CPI. However, in recent years food has not been one of the more volatile
elements in the CPI. In the 1970s, food prices were fluctuating because
of the volatility of the Russian grain harvests. But that is no longer true.
However, energy does remain a volatile component of the consumer price
index and therefore can give off misleading signals on the underlying trend
for inflation. Moreover, both food and energy are core to the consumer's
budget, so taking them out and then comparing them to consumer incomes
gives a misleading picture of the strength of real consumer spending.

## Producer Prices: Business Prices and Some Interesting Detail

Producer prices are prices received by producers. The producer price index is
intended to measure prices of goods traded at the wholesale level. Therefore,

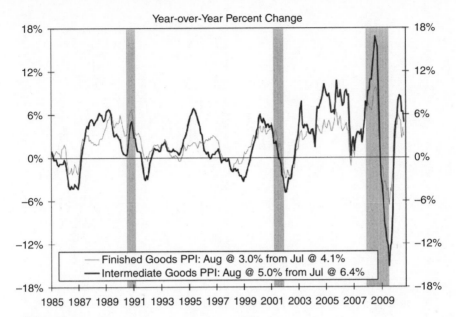

**FIGURE 2.9** Intermediate and Finished Goods PPI
*Source:* U.S. Department of Labor and Wells Fargo Securities, LLC.

business leaders, particularly supply managers, using this index gain an interesting insight into the costs of their inputs as well as the going prices of goods they sell to the next stage of production. What makes this series so interesting is the breakdown in the data by the stage of processing framework that is illustrated in Figure 2.9.

The first stage of processing is the finished goods, which is defined as goods that have completed their manufacturing processing. Crude materials, in contrast, are materials that go directly into the initial stages of the production process such as iron ore and bauxite. Finally, there are the intermediate goods which are items that do not fall in either category. In addition, the PPI index has several sub indices for many sectors so detail is available for further analysis.

## GDP Deflator

Finally, the third measure of inflation is the GDP deflator, which also has immense detail. The GDP deflator is the benchmark price index for the GDP, and therefore has a price index for all the major components of the GDP. Here we focus on the consumer measure of inflation in the GDP accounts, the personal consumption expenditure (PCE) deflator, which allows for the

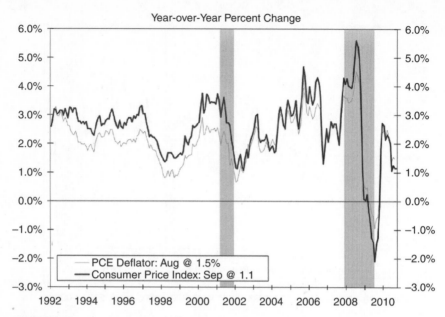

**FIGURE 2.10**   Consumer Price Index versus PCE Deflator
*Source:* U.S. Department of Commerce, U.S. Department of Labor, and Wells
Fargo Securities, LLC.

changes in the market basket for consumers, while the CPI has a fixed basket
of goods and services over time. Also, the GDP deflator includes only those
goods produced domestically. So the prices of imported capital goods or
automobiles, for example, are not included in the GDP calculation. Since
the composition of the basket of goods and services measured by the PCE
deflator changes from time to time, this allows for the substitution by the
buyer of cheaper products over time. In effect, this also produces a measure
of inflation for the consumer, as measured by the GDP deflator for personal
consumption spending, to be generally lower than the CPI over the same
time period as illustrated in Figure 2.10.

The Federal Reserve in recent years has focused more precisely on the
core (food and energy) personal consumption deflator as a benchmark—not
a target—for monetary policy. As illustrated in Figure 2.11, this inflation
benchmark, along with the overall PCE deflator, have hovered around 2 percent for some time and this has given rise to expectations of little change in
Federal Reserve's federal funds rate—the subject of the next section. Also of
interest is that the core PCE deflator is indeed less volatile than the overall
PCE deflator illustrated in Figure 2.11. The oil price spike in 2008 is quite

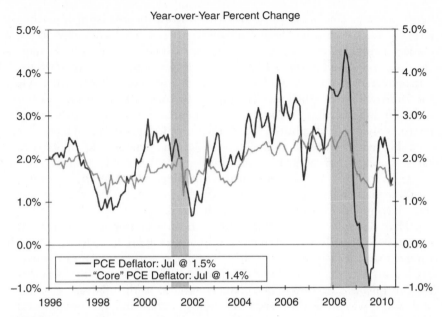

**FIGURE 2.11**  Personal Consumption Price Deflator
*Source:* U.S. Department of Commerce and Wells Fargo Securities, LLC.

noticeable in the jump of the PCE deflator, while the core deflator barely moves at all.

## INTEREST RATES: REAL NOMINAL, THE SHORT AND LONG END OF IT ALL

Imagine you are a member of an investment management team and you are asked to present your observations to a board of trustees on the outlook of the interest rate market. This is a risky proposition. Since the mid-1970s, the volatility in interest rates has been a driving force in some of the most spectacular failures in private (Long-Term Capital Management) and public (Orange County, California) management of interest rate risk. Long-Term Capital Management (LTCM) was a hedge fund management firm based in Connecticut that combined arbitrage strategies with leverage in betting on interest rate moves. Their bets were based upon small discrepancies in bond pricing for different bonds due to differences in liquidity between these bonds. Bonds differ in their liquidity or acceptability in the marketplace and hence when pricing was out of line with historical spreads for liquidity the strategy was to arbitrage these small discrepancies. This strategy worked, of course, as long as price differences remained small. However, the financial shocks of the Asian crisis of 1997 and the Russian debt crisis of 1998 led to large interest rate moves and hastened the downfall of LTCM.[5] Meanwhile, for Orange County, the story is simpler. Robert Citron, Orange County's treasurer, was betting on the decline of interest rates using fairly complex instruments. He chose poorly. In 1994, Orange County declared bankruptcy.

This focus of this section is confined to the benchmarks of short-term rates, characterized by the Fed funds rate, and longer-term, 10-year Treasury rates. This allows a discussion of the fundamentals of interest rate movements while not getting overwhelmed by the complications of the variety of fixed income instruments available in the marketplace.

First, decision makers must distinguish between nominal and real interest rates—especially when financing a home, as many have learned to their sorrow over the last five years. The nominal interest rate is simply the stated rate on a contract. In the 1960s and early 1970s, that was the benchmark used in business frameworks for the economy. With inflation remarkably low, there was little difference between nominal and real interest rates. However, President Nixon decided to take the dollar off the gold standard in 1971, due to the rapid decline in our gold stores. Requests by both Britain and France to convert dollars to gold at the set rate of $35 per ounce would have drained significant gold from the United States and Nixon ended the gold/dollar exchange. The economic model of stable, fixed exchange rates tied to a gold anchor ended and so, therefore, did the security of fixed exchange rates. As inflation rose throughout the 1970s, real, after inflation, interest rates fell sharply. Fluctuations in real interest rates impacted the relative returns to creditors and the real burden to debtors. Rapidly rising, unanticipated inflation produced less-than-expected real interest returns to creditors and a bonus for debtors who could pay off their debts in cheaper dollars. In the late 1970s, creditors, especially banks and savings and loans that held longer-term mortgages, were getting less in real value from their mortgages. In contrast, homeowners were repaying their debts in cheaper dollars and were very happy.

Inflation fell sharply in the early 1980s. Many homeowners, who financed a few years earlier, held very high interest rate mortgages. As inflation fell, creditors were receiving very high real interest payments while debtors were paying their mortgages in much more expensive dollars than they expected. This experience emphasized the distinction between *ex-ante* and *ex-post* interest rates and led to the rapid growth of interest rate hedging to control interest rate risk.

The ex-ante interest rate is the expected interest rate to be paid over the life of the loan at the time the loan is originated and is often expressed more precisely as the ex-ante real interest rate to reflect the anticipated impact of inflation. The ex-ante real interest rate concept can be further refined as the after-tax real interest rate. Here the driving factor is the expectation that is discounted in the interest rate for both inflation and taxes, and most recently in Europe, sovereign debt risk. When analysts design an economic framework they implicitly, if not explicitly, assume an ex-ante real interest rate that incorporates some estimate of future inflation as well as future taxes. As time passes, changes occur in these basic framework assumptions about inflation and taxes. Almost without exception, the after-tax real interest rate that is received ex-post, that is, after the loan is actually paid off, is different from what was anticipated.[6] If decision makers can stand the difference, then they don't hedge their interest rate exposure. However, in most cases, institutions do hedge to reduce the volatility of returns and stabilize cash flow. Some leaders plan on using ex-ante real interest rates, but live with the outcomes of ex-post real interest rates. Others design an interest rate hedge or swap. In every decision involving interest rates there is risk, whether we recognize it or not.

The Federal funds rate and the Treasury rate are the focus here along with the incentives that come from the yield curve—the difference between the yields on 10-year rates less 2-year Treasury yield. The Federal funds rate is the interest rate that banks charge one another for overnight loans. The Federal Reserve sets the rate, which then serves as the benchmark for the cost of funds to the banking industry and, thereby, the rest of the economy. The Federal funds rate, along with its first cousin, the discount rate,[7] is an administered interest rate and thus it is not determined primarily in the open market.

At the long end of the yield curve is the 10-year Treasury rate, illustrated in Figure 2.12. This rate serves as a significant benchmark for pricing other instruments in the bond market both in America and abroad. Differences in the 10-year yield and other financial instruments provide an incentive to move invested capital and therefore real investment over time.

Finally, the steepness of the yield curve as illustrated in Figure 2.13 provides the incentive to investors and private firms issuing debt to alter the maturities of the debt issued. Or they can issue long-term debt and then use interest rate swaps to substitute floating rate short-term debt for fixed long-term debt.

Learning to identify the links between growth, inflation, and interest rates in any well-structured economic framework is what makes economics so exciting. The interrelationships between growth, inflation, and interest

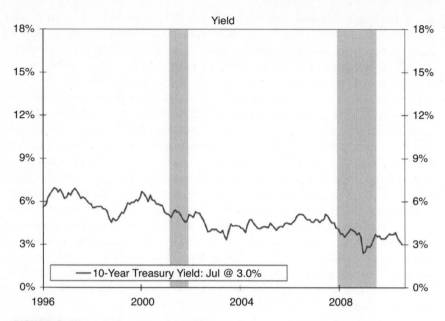

**FIGURE 2.12**   10-Year Treasury Yield
*Source:* Federal Reserve Board and Wells Fargo Securities, LLC.

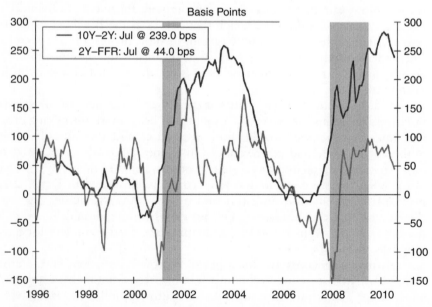

**FIGURE 2.13**   Yield Curve Spread
*Source:* Federal Reserve Board and Wells Fargo Securities, LLC.

rates that can be readily identified are also the same interrelationships that bring into question the approach in graduate education in economics. In the academic realm, the real world is analyzed using linear spreadsheet models that offer neat, incorrect, solutions to complex problems.

## EXCHANGE RATES: A RELATIVE PRICE WITH MANY RELATIVES

Exchange rates, especially the dollar, euro, and yen, have many relatives. The dollar's exchange rate value can be compared to many different currencies and for many businesses these bilateral exchange rates are often of primary importance. Unfortunately, both in the media and in political discussions "the dollar" is represented by a single value in a multinational world. For decision makers who are doing business in many different markets and who are concerned about exchange rate risks, the important exchange rate for the dollar may be the dollar/peso, dollar/Canadian dollar or the dollar/yuan. The "dollar" may be of little value since trade may be conducted primarily with one particular or small set of countries. Imports may come from five or six countries and be sold to a dozen more. Many international companies produce in a dozen countries and sell in 50 more. For these firms there are many dollar exchange rates in an increasingly global trading and capital marketplace. As with interest rate volatility, many firms' exposure to exchange rate risk has led to a significant growth in exchange rate hedging over the past 30 years.

Any institution with international exposure must deal with the "impossible trinity." An economic framework needs to recognize that a nation cannot have free capital flows, a fixed exchange rate, and an independent monetary policy. A country such as the United States chooses to have free capital flows and an independent monetary policy with a flexible, not fixed, exchange rate. Hong Kong, a special administrative region of the People's Republic of China, also chooses to have free capital flows, but has decided on a fixed exchange rate and no independent monetary policy (The Federal Reserve acts as the de facto central bank for countries that fix their currency to the dollar.) Finally, a country like China chooses a fixed exchange rate and an independent monetary policy, but adopts a policy of strict capital controls. (See Figure 2.14.) For any institution, part of any thoughtful framework should be an identification of which option each of its trading partners' countries adopt and what the risks are for each.

Since the United States exchange rates fluctuate, decision makers here need to ask: Can we get our contracts quoted in dollars? And if not, how can we hedge the exchange rate risk if we have significant exposure? For

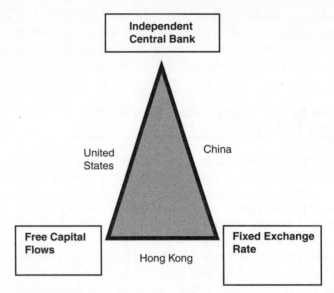

**FIGURE 2.14**   United States, Hong Kong, and China Frameworks
*Source:* Mankiw's *Macroeconomics*, p. 360.

example, what should a manager do when earning in euros? The combination of an independent central bank and free capital flows, even in an advanced economic community, means that there is significant exchange rate risk. If earnings are left unhedged, the euros could, when brought back to the United States, have significantly depreciated real values.

In Hong Kong, there is no independent monetary policy since the Monetary Authority of Hong Kong follows a fixed exchange rate based on the dollar. When a nation fixes its currency to that of another nation, in this case America, it is adopting that other nation's monetary policy. The issue then revolves around these key questions: How committed is that country to the dollar peg? If the commitment is solid, what happens if the country setting monetary policy (the United States) begins to behave badly? In this sense, the problem is that the smaller, pegged country's monetary policy takes on the character of the large country. In the case of the time period from 2008 to 2010, monetary policy in the United States has been very expansionary with a bias toward higher inflation. How tolerant will be the pegging country (Hong Kong) be to an inflation or deflation driven by policy abroad (in the United States)?

During the early 1990s, Argentina implemented an unusual exchange rate scheme labeled the Convertibility Law. On the heels of decades of economic mismanagement, spiraling hyperinflation, and a newly liberalized economy, the Argentine government's primary goal was price stability. A convertibility board managed the amount of pesos in circulation pegged to the exchange rate with the United States dollar. The board promised to exchange pesos indefinitely for dollars at the stated rate. The commitment to full convertibility between the dollar and the peso stabilized demand for the domestic currency by temporarily calming public expectations of future devaluation. But full convertibility means that a monetary authority no longer has discretion to choose output targets or inflation targets; it is restricted to the goal of maintaining the exchange rate. A convertibility board's success is tied to the credibility of its commitment to exchange domestic currency for a given foreign currency. If the public lacks faith in the plan, the demand for foreign currency will deplete the monetary authority's foreign reserves, resulting in a downward adjustment in the exchange rate (devaluation). Argentina's initial success with the convertibility plan was due to largely fortuitous circumstances such as prevalent dollarization and surplus foreign reserves from improving terms of trade. The gradual erosion of these endowments contributed to the short life span of full convertibility.

Finally, China restricts the international flow of capital in and out of the country. Thus, the domestic Chinese interest rate curve is independent of the global capital markets. Interest rates reflect the policies of the central bank as well as the goals of the political leadership. In recent years, this policy mix has allowed the Chinese to maintain a fixed exchange rate to the dollar as well as adjust the peg when they wish to change. This is very unusual. Historically, currency pegs, such as Argentina (2001), Brazil (1999), Vietnam (1996), and Turkey (2001), have led to a failure to maintain the peg and to currency devaluations. In contrast, we have seen China revaluate its currency peg upward. This historical experience has generated what is considered to be a bipolar view of currency regimes where successful pegged regimes, such as the one in China, are truly rare.[8] Some readers may ask about the Japanese appreciation of their currency during the post–World War II period. During this period of Japanese yen appreciation, the yen was not formally pegged against the dollar but followed a "dirty float" policy where the yen traded in the open capital markets. However, the exchange value of the yen was influenced from time to time by market intervention by Japanese authorities.

Once again, the interdependence of economic factors makes good decision making rewarding and linear thinking disastrous. In 2010, the fear of a possible Greek government default on loan repayments led investors to seek higher interest rates to compensate for the risks of default, currency devaluation, and withdrawal from the euro. Moreover, subsequent actual depreciation was followed by a rapid rise in inflation.

Interestingly, the mere expectation that Greece might withdraw from the euro led to a rise in the risk premium on Greek debt and a depreciation of the euro. Expectations in financial and currency markets are enough to alter market prices. To stay ahead of such psychologically induced crises, decision makers need to analyze how changes in expectations can lead to feedback effects and changes in their economic framework. The Mexican meltdown in 1994–1995 was another example of a country that conducted an expansionary domestic fiscal and monetary policy combination that was inconsistent with its commitment to a pegged currency exchange rate to the dollar. This inconsistency led to a breakdown of the peg and the Mexican economy and lead to significant intervention by the United States. Part of this intervention was a currency swap program engineered by the Fed in which they swapped dollars for pesos. In addition, the United States put together a rescue package of loans, emergency credit, and an advance payment for oil. One lesson here is that political risk is an exogenous factor that can alter an economic framework and lead to significant changes in expected growth (recession in Mexico) and higher interest rates and a depreciated currency (euro). In terms of political risk, Mexico had nationalized all the banks in 1982, closed all bank accounts denominated in dollars, and declared a moratorium on principal payments for its debt.

Finally, another exogenous factor is a country's trade policies—usually protecting domestic industries from foreign competition either by imposing a tariff (tax) on goods imported or just outright limiting the supply of goods sold (quota). Trade policies can alter the profit outlook for doing business in a marketplace very quickly. A policy aimed at prohibiting the import of meat or chicken in the name of food safety is a popular action in recent years. As a result, imports of meat or chicken from the United States decline while exports of these products in the newly protected markets also decline. The net result is a general decline in the amount of trade and thereby also in the benefits of trade.

## PROFITS

Three major profit measures are available:

1. Profits as reported for tax purposes.
2. Profits as reported in the National Income and Product Accounts (NIPA).
3. Profits as reported to shareholders.

The focus here is on the last two, which is also the primary focus of all analysts. Profits represent the return to investors in the company and are a factor cost, as are employee compensation (workers), interest (bond investors), and rent (landowner). Each factor has its own set of incentives, rewards, and risk characteristics.

Profits in the NIPA accounts measure the distribution of the earnings of corporations to the shareholders. This distribution is impacted by patterns in economic growth, interest rates, and tax policy. Note, for example, the different pattern of financial and non-financial profits over the business cycle in Fig. 2.15. The NIPA profits data comes primarily from corporate income tax returns, with some adjustments to conform to national income account conventions. Profits are measured before taxes, before deductions for depletion, after the exclusion for capital gains and losses, and net of dividends received from domestic corporations.

Traditionally, profits are adjusted to reflect current-period accounting rather than historical costs. An inventory valuation adjustment (IVA) is made to adjust the usual change in book value of inventories, as reported by business, to reflect instead the change in the physical volume of inventories valued at prices of the current period. This IVA is equal to the excess of

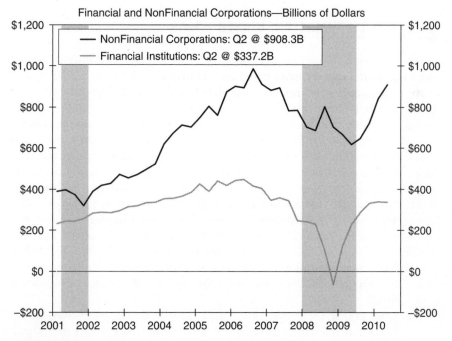

**FIGURE 2.15** Domestic Profits
*Source:* U.S. Department of Commerce and Wells Fargo Securities, LLC.

replacement cost of inventories used up over their historical acquisition cost. The capital consumption adjustment converts tax return–based capital consumption allowances to a replacement cost valuation and to uniform service lives and depreciation formulas.

Profits reported to shareholders reflect management's view of how the company is performing. This is intended to provide investors with the best guidance available to the true operational profitability of the company. These shareholder reports reflect the worldwide consolidation of earnings and assets. Meanwhile, profits, as reported by NIPA, are published quarterly in the second month after the end of the quarter (August for the second quarter, for example). In addition, there is an industry breakdown provided in each quarter along with a breakdown into financial and nonfinancial profits. Also, major industry groupings are subdivided into domestic and "rest of world," which is actually a net number—net inflow of profits from abroad to American corporations and residents. Financial profits include those earned by the Federal Reserve on its interest earnings on its Treasury bond portfolio. Therefore any analysis undertaken to examine financial profits in the NIPA accounts should exclude profits at the Federal Reserve.

## UNBIASED INFORMATION: BIASED USERS

While the measurement of an economic series is relatively straightforward, the uses of the underlying data are not. Unfortunately, analysis often starts with a view and then tortures the data until it yields the proper result. In part, this reflects one of the sources of bias decision makers need to avoid—confirmation bias. Researchers, and especially editorial writers, will search, sometimes for long periods of time, for that one data point that will illustrate their view even when that point is a stretch. If desperate, they will look for anecdotes that prove their point of view. Yet anecdotes are not proof and often one anecdote can be countered with another anecdote. There is another issue with a large amount of research, which is, often, the conclusion of the research will stay the same, but the evidence used to support that conclusion has changed because the first set of data that supports that view failed or simply changed its behavior, thus forcing the researchers and editorial writers to scramble to find new data to support the old view. In such cases, the theme stays the same but the source of supporting data drifts.

Benchmarking the five key economic factors (growth, inflation, interest rates, the dollar exchange rate, and profits) is therefore very important to prevent this intellectual drift. If the GDP data weakens, maybe your initial assumption of strong economic growth is losing its validity. Then, change the assumption and recognize the feedback and choices you need to make to your model. The last 30 years have delivered numerous examples of changing data on economic growth, inflation trends, interest rates, exchange rates, and profit behaviors that all suggest a change in our model assumptions and therefore a call to action.

A second source of decision-making bias is called *group think*. Group think occurs when the decision maker prefers a group consensus view as opposed to considering alterative views. A third bias that the decision maker must avoid is the recency bias, which places undue emphasis on the most recent observations of events and fails to put the data into context or under careful examination. This is especially important with economic data given the volatility of the data in response to seasonal forces (housing starts and employment), weather (retail sales and industrial production), or just unusual factors such as the vagaries of floating holidays (Easter, Thanksgiving) or government processing of Social Security and jobless claims. Some of these effects can persist for some time and the exact timing and size of the effects are unknown until well after the fact.

Complicating the interpretation of the data even further is the mixture of business cycle volatility superimposed on a longer secular change in the socioeconomic makeup of any society. While leaders try to discern the behavior of each of the key five economic inputs, they must also contend with the longer-term changes they see on the economy, such as globalization, the liberalization of capital markets, and the relative rates of return to factors of production, which are the topics we turn to next.

## DISCUSSION QUESTIONS

1. Leading indicators are a key input to business decision making. As a member of your strategic planning committee, how might your advice on the economy respond to these changes?
   a. Initial weekly claims for unemployment insurance have risen over the last three months.
   b. New building permits have risen over the last six months.
   c. Money supply (M2) adjusted for inflation has risen above its trend pace over the last year.
   d. Consumer expectations have been disappointing lately.
   e. Interest rate spreads (10-year less 3-month Treasuries) have declined sharply.
2. You are a member your company's strategic planning group. Your company is in the business equipment sales and services field. You are tasked with the following:

   a. Using the National Income and Product Accounts, develop some benchmark measures of the overall economy and your business in order to provide a standard for judging performance.

   b. Distinguish between CPI and GDP deflator calculations and suggest which might be more appropriate for benchmarking your business-to-business pricing strategy.

   c. Employee recruitment is central to your company's success. Distinguish between structural and cyclical unemployment. Explain how unemployment can vary between demographic groups and how this might influence your recruiting efforts.

   d. Since your company has operations in Europe as well as Asia, please provide some guidance on the differences in European and American labor markets that would impact your decisions on plant location, sales, and labor market hiring policies in these three regions.

3. As the head of your human resources department, you are asked to make some brief comments on the current state of the labor market. You wish to comment on five points:

   a. The distinction between frictional and structural unemployment.

   b. How wage rigidity suggests that labor costs are not as flexible as management might wish in the short run.

   c. How the existence of discouraged workers might distort the view of the real level of unemployment.

   d. How labor force participation rates have varied over time for men and women and might influence the availability of workers in the future.

   e. How an efficiency wage might influence worker productivity.

4. The consumer price index (CPI) is the prominent economic statistic because of its role in cost of living adjustments in the IRS tax code, Social Security, labor contracts, poverty calculations, and the many implicit contracts that account for the cost of the consumer basket. Yet, there are many questions about the accuracy of the CPI. As the CFO of your company, discuss the calculation of the CPI as a fixed-weight price index and distinguish that from the calculation of the consumer expenditure deflator. Discuss the issues of new products and quality adjustments for the CPI. How would your understanding of these shortcomings influence your use of the CPI in contracts?

## NOTES

1. Simon Kuznets, *National Income and Its Composition, 1919–1938* (Cambridge, MA: National Bureau of Economic Research, 1941).

2. www.census.gov/manufacturing/m3/.
3. Source: U.S. Department of Commerce, 2009.
4. Michael Boskin et al., "Consumer Prices, the Consumer Price Index, and the Cost of Living," *Journal of Economic Perspectives*, 12(1)(1998): 3–26.
5. Roger Lowenstein, *When Genius Failed: The Rise and Fall of Long-Term Capital Management* (New York: Random House, 2000).
6. Higher tax rates on interest, as well as dividends and capital gains, will lower the after-tax rate of return and thereby alter the flow of financial capital in society away from the higher-taxed activities to other, lower-taxed, entities. Changes in tax rates are a significant change to any investment framework.
7. The discount rate is the rate set by the Federal Reserve for loans from the Federal Reserve to private banks.
8. See Andrea Bubula and Inci Otker-Robe, "Are Pegged and Intermediate Exchange Rate Regimes More Crisis Prone?" (International Monetary Fund working paper, WP/03/223, November 2003) and Stanley Fischer, "Exchange Rate Regimes: Is the Bipolar View Correct?" *Finance and Development* 38:2 (International Monetary Fund, June 2001).

## RECOMMENDED READING FOR SERIOUS PLAYERS

Carnes, Stansbury, and Stephen D. Slifer. *The Atlas of Economic Indicators*. New York: HarperCollins, 1991.
Mankiw, N. Gregory. *Macroeconomics*. 7th ed. New York: Worth Publishers, 2007.
Tainer, Evelina M. *Using Economic Indicators to Improve Investment Analysis*, 3rd ed. Hoboken, NJ: John Wiley & Sons, 2006.

# CHAPTER 3

# Cyclical and Structural Change

*You can't argue with a hundred years of success.*
—William I. Walsh[1]

**A**ctually, you can argue with success when the environment changes around you. The economic world is changing and success is fleeting. In the early 1950s, A&P, which was then the leading grocery chain in America, ranked only behind General Motors in annual sales. America's tastes changed. They wanted choices, not the limited availability associated with the Great Depression and World War II periods of thrift. A&P stores did not provide the level of variety, nor cleanliness, expected by the new, growing middle class suburban households that began to emerge after the war. America's tastes had changed and the offerings of A&P did not.[2]

## FORCES OF ECONOMIC SUCCESS

Three forces interact to drive economic success: economic activity, historical bias, and the parameters of future success.

1. Economic activity provides the overall flow of information and sets the character of surprises and our decision framework. Yet, in practice, decision makers conduct stress tests, risk assessments, and simulations that do not deal with the cyclical nature of economic behavior. Most business and public policy decision makers are not trained to deal with or think in terms of the business cycle. Forecasting for most consists of straight-line projections from a spreadsheet. Also, dealing with the business cycle demands a set of assumptions and the interaction of those assumptions can require scenario building. The results of these scenarios on the outlook for

growth, inflation, and interest rates, for example, can be more complex than decision makers have the time or willingness to engage. These decision makers feel more comfortable focusing on the business and not forecasting. Even more misleading, over time, their model of the economy does not fundamentally change, and thus retains its original framework despite the evolution of the real economy.

In addition, many simulations are defined in terms of allowing one factor, for example, economic growth, to fluctuate. This is done to simplify the analysis, but with the knowledge that other key variables are likely to change at the same time. There is a trade-off here between simplicity and reality. Often, the comfort of simplicity leads to a misrepresentation of the outlook. Better to deal with the complexity and get a sense of the issues than fall back on simplicity and misrepresent the future outlook. These simulations ignore the reality that other drivers, such as inflation, interest rates, profits, and exchange rates, also move along with changes in growth. Over the last 50 years, the economy has never returned to its prior normal. A new framework always emerges with each business cycle, different from previous frameworks, sometimes in significant ways. The original equilibrium was never restored. Creating economic models as if stability had returned will not make it so.

2. Decision traps limit the leader's ability to deal with cyclical and especially longer-term changes. Decision makers tend to anchor their expectations about the future in the past and to think in terms of their historical investments in their career and in their firm. Our memory of events and decisions tends to be framed in terms of our own experience. Decisions about the future of the firm tend to reflect the firm's existing structure. Seldom do firms break out of character and set a new course; they do not examine the marginal costs and benefits of moving to a new future. In addition, public policy makers are slow to recognize the changing character of competitiveness in industries (automobiles, textiles, and consumer electronics) and thereby subsidize such industries for far too long. This is not only an American tendency, but very much the general case as evidenced by the United Kingdom in the post–World War II period, until Prime Minister Margaret Thatcher took office in 1980 and introduced a market-driven approach regarding subsidization of industries.

3. Decisions on the future of the institution reflect the influence of past decisions (i.e., are path dependent), which sets the parameters for success regarding future decisions. In some cases, decisions cut off options tomorrow while other decisions today open up options for the future. For example, a student who decides to go to one college cuts off the opportunity to go to another college. An athlete decides to play baseball and gives up playing soccer. A business firm decides to pursue project A and set aside project B.

Once we decide on one path, generally we cut off other options and decisions today will reflect our decisions in the past. Business decisions also have this tendency for path dependence, as is shown in several cases in this chapter.

## CYCLICAL PATTERNS, LINEAR PROJECTIONS

Policy makers in both private and public sectors rely on models to project essential decision benchmarks such as sales and tax revenues. Yet, often these projections are based upon linear projections into the future when in fact the world is characterized by cyclical patterns in these same benchmarks. In this section, we review some of these cyclical patterns and point out that often economic and financial benchmarks do not travel in straight lines and that the cycles of acceleration and deceleration characterize both the ups and downs of each series.

### Dealing with Recessions: Too Narrow a Focus

Business and public policy strategies must deal with the reality of recessions and business cycles. Yet such cycles are often expressed solely in terms of economic growth, in part to simplify the analysis. However, the last three economic recoveries have exhibited growth, but with very different patterns in other economic drivers such as inflation and interest rates. Moreover, all these drivers have their own cyclical pattern and these patterns contrast vividly with the linear projections of most business and public policy forecasting exercises. This model is too closed, since it admits of no other driving factors (such as interest rates) and permits only simplistic outcomes (growth, no growth) without the real world complications of rising or falling inflation and interest rates. Cycles are also common in inflation (up in the 1970s, down in the 1980s) and interest rates, as illustrated in Figure 3.1. Cycles in the dollar exchange rate and corporate profits were cited in an earlier chapter.

Decision makers need to learn from the long history of business cycles that there are driving factors that lead to changes in more than one of the five economic factors. For example, the 1970s saw a period of above-average inflation and interest rates combined with below-average economic growth. Meanwhile, the dollar fell sharply in value. Yet, in the 1980s, the economy grew faster than expected, although both inflation and interest rates fell more than expected. During the economic recovery of 2009 and 2010, growth was below expectations while inflation remained very low. Meanwhile, interest rates remained low as the dollar increased in value despite, or perhaps in sympathy with, the lower interest rates.

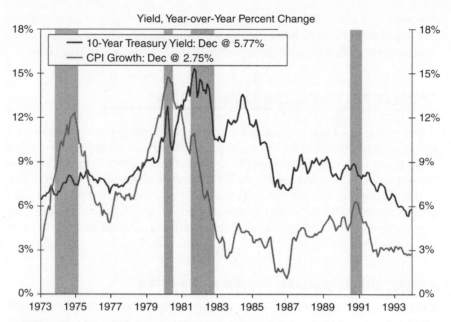

**FIGURE 3.1**    10-Year Treasury versus CPI Growth
*Source:* Federal Reserve Board and Bureau of Labor Statistics.

When decision makers recognize such cyclical patterns they can see the risk of relying solely on simulations of linear spreadsheet projections driven by single-variable changes. These projections are misleading and inadequate to deal with cycles and patterns of change in an economy. Problem solving and business planning done in a static, controlled environment are unlikely to provide a realistic view of the outcome of either cyclical change or the simultaneous, longer-term changes acting on the business environment. Both alter the framework of all economic models. Static models give a false sense of precision in a highly variable world.

In practice, the confluence of cyclical and structural change in our economic models gives rise to the extensive application of add-factors by forecasters to smooth out the results and fit the model to historical experience. These add-factors are simply values added, or subtracted, from the economic time series under study to ensure a smooth forecasting result and avoid any unusual forecast results. These add-factors reflect the judgment of the forecast builder and therefore can also be misleading; the forecaster will use values that might make sense in normal times, but may hide some significant trends that signal that the economy is heading in a different direction. Therefore, on closer inspection, these add-factors should give pause to anyone who adopts a fixed model in a changing world. Add-factors may be a necessary evil, but the extensive application of them should alert us to the truth—real-world observations are drifting away from the original model.

### Identifying Change: How Do We Know When the World Is Changing beneath Our Feet?

Mathematics can enlighten or obscure reality; it can be a lamppost or a crutch. In this section, the focus is on three simple approaches to draw out from the data hints that the economic framework may be changing beneath us and, therefore, we need to question the validity of our view of the economic world. Those approaches are:

1. The indicator approach.
2. The use of a mathematical filter, such as the Hodrick-Prescott filter.
3. The use of 3-month and 12-month moving averages.

Sometimes the underlying behavior of the focus of our outlook changes over time and alters our expectations of what results we should look for in our estimates. These methods identify change that can be applied by decision makers without a complex model and will still generate the type of observations necessary for serious discussion.

## LEADING, COINCIDENT, AND LAGGING ECONOMIC INDICATORS

An economic indicator can be used to predict future financial or economic trends. There are three categories of indicators, classified according to the types of predictions they make.

### Leading

These types of indicators signal future events. That is, leading indicators are economic series that change direction before the overall economy itself changes direction. In addition, there are leading indicators for many individual economic sectors. For example, changes in initial jobless claims tend to lead changes in employment and therefore personal income and consumption. Therefore, for a retail firm, changes in the initial claims for unemployment will tend to lead changes in retail sales and thereby would be a significant economic variable to watch. A familiar economic statistic—housing

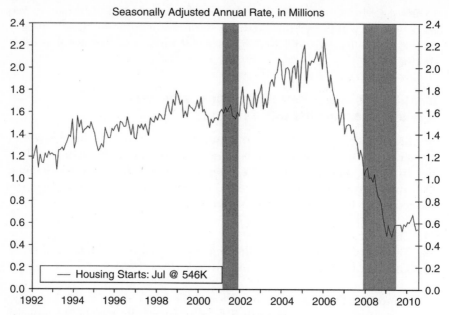

**FIGURE 3.2**   Leading Economic Indicator: Housing Starts
*Source:* U.S. Census Bureau.

starts—acts like a leading indicator and is used by many as such. However, it is the series on building permits that is actually employed as the leading indicator index. For simplicity here, we use housing starts since housing starts are generally used as the headline number in the press releases most recognized by most decision makers. These starts are so frequently commented upon that the use of housing starts here can provide us with some guidance. The pattern of housing starts is shown in Figure 3.2. Leading indicators tend to turn before the overall economic cycle. As shown in Figure 3.2, housing starts peaked in 1999 before the 2001 recession and again peaked in 2007 before the 2008 recession. Housing starts also hit bottom before economic recoveries.

The leading economic indicator index is published by the Conference Board in New York City. This index includes new building permits issued, new orders for consumer goods, the index of stock prices and the University of Michigan index of consumer expectations. For our purposes, several of the indicators relate to the performance of different sectors and thereby can be employed to help forecast performance of these sectors. Housing is reflected in the building permits indicator. Consumer activity is reflected in the initial jobless claims, new orders for consumer goods, and consumer sentiment. The jobless claims indicator picks up the number of initial claims for unemployment each week. Increases in claims are associated with a weaker economy, as more claims imply more job losses and thereby lost income and spending. For the industrial sector, there are indicators such as new orders for nondefense capital goods and vendor performance. This last indicator is a measure of the number of companies receiving slower deliveries from suppliers, that is, the period of time between when an order is given and the product is delivered is lengthened. Longer delivery lags are associated with stronger product demand.

There are also financial indicators: stock prices as measured by the S&P 500 Index, the money supply adjusted for inflation, and the yield spread between the 10-year Treasury and the 3-month Treasury bill. For this last indicator, the larger the spread, the more likely the pace of economic growth in the future since future interest rates are discounting stronger credit demand and therefore interest rates in the future.

## Coincident

These indicators occur at approximately the same time as the conditions they signify. In other words, rather than predicting future events, these types of indicators change at the same time the economy changes. Industrial production is a coincidental indicator for the economy, as seen in Figure 3.3. There are four coincident indicators:

1. Employees on nonfarm payrolls.
2. Personal income less transfer payments.
3. Industrial production.
4. Manufacturing and trade sales.

The dominant statistic is the nonfarm payroll employment statistic, which is generally released on the first Friday of the month and is a focus of the financial markets. Employment gains are associated with income gains and reaffirm consumer confidence. Therefore, employment gains help explain consumer spending, which is the largest component of the GDP (gross domestic product) measure of national output. The second indicator, and the one shown in Figure 3.3, is industrial production, which captures the measure of output of the manufacturing, mining, and utility sectors. As indicated by Figure 3.3, turns in industrial production are coincident with turns in the economic cycle. Another characteristic to note for industrial production is the high variability of the series over the business cycle.

Personal income, less transfer payments, adjusted for inflation, is the third coincident indicator; this series is a measure of consumer spending

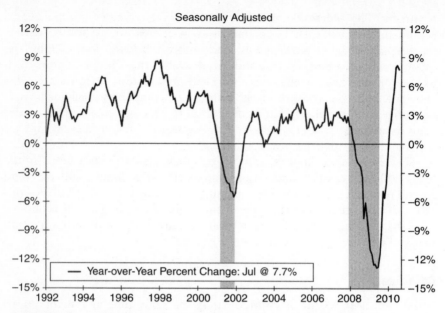

**FIGURE 3.3**   Coincident Economic Indicator: Industrial Production
*Source:* Federal Reserve Board.

power. Finally, the series for manufacturing and trade sales, adjusted for inflation, is an excellent measure of what is being purchased at the manufacturing and wholesale stages of the economy. Increases in sales here are associated with stronger economic growth.

## Lagging

A lagging indicator is one that follows an event. The importance of a lagging indicator is its ability to confirm that a pattern is occurring or about to occur. Unemployment is one of the most popular lagging indicators. Technically, the unemployment rate is not in the index of lagging indicators while the average duration of unemployment actually is in the index, but the public focuses on the unemployment rate because of its political importance and the ease of accessing it since the unemployment rate is widely reported. Unemployment rates generally lag the business cycle and this is important to recognize for two reasons. Many observers still focus on the unemployment rate as an indicator of where the economy is standing, but that is not effective. By definition, unemployment means that one must be both actively looking for a job and be unemployed, so as more people start looking there is a tendency for the unemployment rate to rise as the economy recovers.

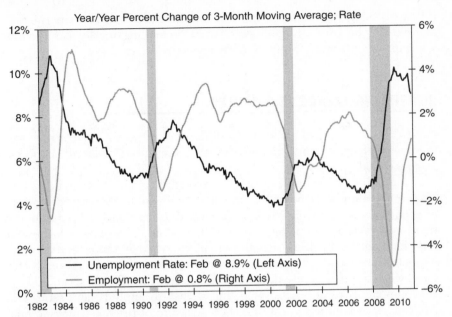

**FIGURE 3.4** Lagging Economic Indicator: Unemployment Rate
*Source:* Bureau of Labor Statistics.

The recovery itself generates optimism and that gets people looking for jobs again. The unemployment rate lags because as the economy improves, some people reenter the labor market to search for jobs. Figure 3.4 illustrates the lag between employment, a coincident indicator that tells us where we are now, and the unemployment rate, which is a lagging indicator. In 1988, employment growth started to decline but the unemployment rate did not start to rise until late 1990. In the latest recession period, employment peaked in late 2006 but the unemployment rate did not begin to rise until late 2007.

Other lagging indicators include bank commercial and industrial loans and the consumer price index for services. Both of these are interesting for their own reasons. Popular wisdom holds that the economy needs banks to lend before the economy gets going. In reality, businesses are cautious about borrowing at the start of the recovery and will invest their own cash first and then borrow at the bank. Meanwhile, the bank is also cautious since it probably has some bad loans it wants to work off from the last recession. As a result, bank lending is a lagging, not leading, indicator of the recovery.

Consumer prices for services are also a lagging indicator. The inflation of consumer prices follows economic growth. This presents an interesting policy problem for the Federal Reserve. One of the mandates to the Fed is to provide inflation stability, and yet one of the primary indicators of inflation is actually a lagging indicator. In this sense there is a basis for criticism that by following inflation as a guidepost, the Fed is looking out the rear window while driving monetary policy and the economy forward.

## IDENTIFYING TRENDS AND CYCLES

How can decision makers identify differences between movements over the business cycle from changes in the long-run trends of economic fundamentals?

Identifying above and below trend growth is often the analytical challenge for economists. Robert J. Hodrick and Edward C. Prescott, professors of economics at Carnegie-Mellon, developed an approach to separate the trend and cyclical components of any time series.[3] The Hodrick-Prescott (HP) filter allows the decision makers to assess whether a time series is moving below the trend growth (slowdown) or above the trend (boom). This filter, when applied to any time series, helps separate out the trend and cycle components of any time series and is easy to apply to any series (see Appendix). In Figure 3.5, the statistical measure of the real domestic final

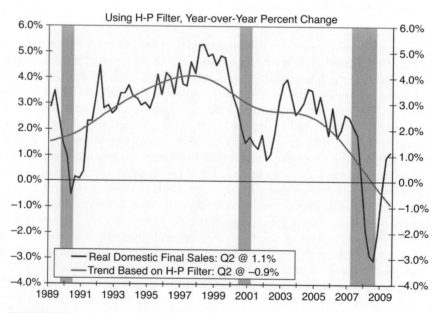

**FIGURE 3.5** Decomposing Real Domestic Final Sales
*Source:* Bureau of Economic Analysis.

sales in the United States economy can be broken down into cycle and trend components. Real domestic final sales is a measure of the underlying true demand in the economy that is not distorted by the volatility of inventories. When the cyclical component breaks below the trend component, the outlook is for weakness in the series, in this example real domestic final sales. As is evident in Figure 3.5, the breakdowns in 2001 and again in mid-2008 denoted a difficult period ahead for the economy. The sharp breakdown in 2008 was a signal that a very difficult recession was ahead.[4]

## Smoothness of a Time Series: Moving Average (MA)

Another simple method of distinguishing trend and cycle is the application of the ratio of the 3-month to 12-month moving averages of any series. Essentially, when decision makers read any set of data they should note the relative position of the 3- and 12-month changes as in Fig. 3.6. In late 2001, the 3-month change for industrial production broke below the 12-month change, thereby hinting at a slowdown in the economy ahead. In the opposite direction, the rise in 3-month above the 12-month moving average in early 2001 signaled the start of an economic recovery.

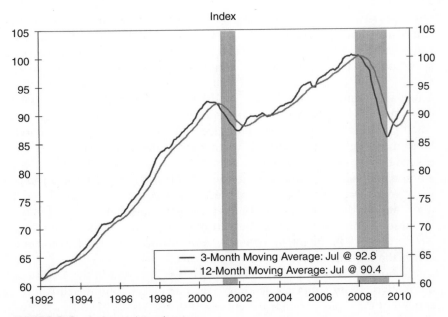

**FIGURE 3.6**   Industrial Production
*Source:* Federal Reserve Board.

Both the Hodrick-Prescott and the 3-month/12-month moving average calculations are very simple, and they do provide the decision maker with tools to capture the character of a turn in any time series and thereby give the decision maker a sense that the economic cycle could be changing and our decision making will have to account for change in economic direction.

## BIAS IN DECISION MAKING

Two aspects of successful decision making in a changing economic world are evident so far. First, a strategy is needed that recognizes the reality of fluctuations in economic growth as well as in the four other economic drivers. Second, this strategy should prevent economic shocks or change from causing business failures. If they apply the three techniques reviewed in the prior section to identify change, decision makers now have observations that suggest the future direction of economic change. But what mental barriers prevent decision makers from accepting such change?[5]

### Normalization of Deviance

Our first decision-making challenge is the normalization of deviance. In this situation we normalize, learn to live with, small deviations in the normal run of affairs. We learn to live with a dripping faucet, a toilet that runs a bit longer, a door that sticks. Diane Vaughan, sociology professor at Columbia University, studied the Challenger space shuttle disaster of 1986.[6] Vaughan's study focused on the gradual development of a set of beliefs that small deviations from the norm in the behavior of the O-rings under cold temperatures were acceptable since no major problems had occurred. Since most flights had occurred with temperatures in a normal range, the overwhelming evidence was that there was no major problem. The small amount of erosion that did occur in some flights was considered an anomaly. Over time, these anomalies became the accepted course, much like the sticky door, and so they were taken for granted as the normal course of action. Deviations from the norm became part of the acceptable risks of any flight. At the time of the flight in 1986 the temperatures at launch were much colder than normal and disaster soon followed.

In business, normalization of deviance was apparent in the credit standards involved in subprime lending—yet borrowers continued to pay, or enough of them paid, so that the entire enterprise was profitable, at least in the short run. The rise in housing prices over the last 20 years provided the underlying rationale of the housing mortgage market. Credit standards were continually eased, often for political purposes, by government-supported enterprises such as Fannie Mae and Freddie Mac. At the same time, capital gains taxes were lowered on housing, taxes on income in general were rising, and interest rate deductions were eliminated for consumer credit and automobile loans. Thus, to meet their desire for consumption, households increasingly took equity from their homes through home equity loans, which further reduced the capital cushion of ownership and thereby the cushion for any possible downslide in home prices. Home equity loans were not responsible for the collapse in housing, but once that collapse began the equity cushion for many owners was not there to limit the decline. Easier credit standards, meanwhile, meant that the purchaser of the home had "less skin in the game"—that is, the homeowner had less invested in the home and therefore less incentive to pay off the mortgage if events turned bad (which they did as house prices fell). As a result, the real credit risk in lending was rising. This ultimately proved to be the undoing of the market. Lower credit standards meant more buyers could qualify. Rising demand for housing initially drove up prices. Eventually, supply caught up. Housing prices slowed and the carrying costs of mortgages could not be justified. Many buyers walked away.

In recent years, the normalization of deviance was evident in the housing market bust of 2008 to 2009 and the deterioration of credit standards that came to be accepted, as shown in Figure 3.7. Mortgage standards eased by 2005 and 2006 such that 60-day-plus delinquencies were rising earlier in the life of adjustable rate mortgages (ARMs), indicating that the risk profile of the borrowers had risen and likely this rise was faster than investors in these loans expected. The rapid rise of delinquencies in 2006 and again in 2007, illustrated by the upward shift in the 60-day-plus delinquency lines in Figure 3.7, suggested that indeed the housing problem was much greater than many had expected.

In short, the mortgage market framework changed and many failed to notice. The fact that home prices were rising justified the increasing deviance of lending standards—until home prices no longer could rise and started to fall dramatically. In fact, in the history of markets, it often takes a substantial change in prices to reveal the underlying deviance of traded prices from their fundamentals. Political choices also play a role. Frequently, political goals are introduced into many aspects of economic life—ethanol subsidies, first-time home buyer credits, and education subsidies—often with the best of intentions and sometimes driven by necessity, given the importance of the activity. However, politics introduces a confusion of purpose to the activity, as it did for housing, and this can often lead to a misallocation of resources and the normalization of market activity away from its true fundamentals. For the policy decision makers in Washington, success under both Democrat

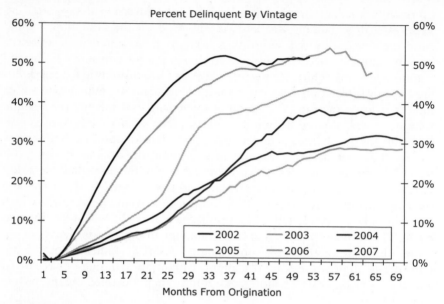

**FIGURE 3.7**   Subprime ARMs 60+ Days Delinquent
*Source:* Intex Solutions Inc.

and Republican presidents was defined in terms of rising home ownership. Yet, the underlying credit quality of the borrower and the appraisal/market value of the house were increasingly suspect. Policy makers normalized the deviance in credit standards as long as home ownership rates went up.

## Recognizing Change as a Process

A second barrier to effective decision making is the failure to recognize change as a process, not an event. Decision makers want to identify one event as the cause of a significant change. Yet, the lesson of the pre–World War I period is that an entire sequence of decisions led to the outbreak of the conflagration—not a single cause such as the shooting of Archduke Ferdinand.[7] Since 1956, three firms have dropped out of the Dow Jones index: Bethlehem Steel, General Motors, and Woolworth. Yet there is not a single event in each of these company histories that caused the companies' relative decline. Instead, changes in the overall economy led to an increasing disconnect between the economy and the framework of decision making in each company.[8] Catastrophic failures such as Johns Manville (asbestos litigation led to bankruptcy filing in 1982) and Enron (irregular accounting

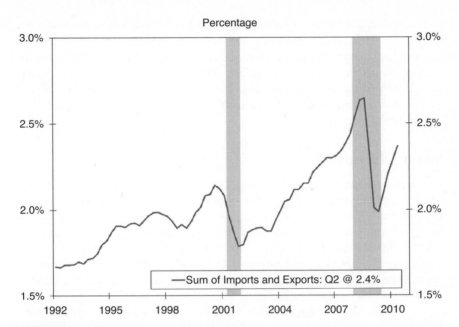

**FIGURE 3.8**   Sum of Imports and Exports as Percentage of GDP
*Source:* U.S. Census Bureau and Bureau of Economic Analysis.

concerns led to bankruptcy in 2001) can be attributed to singular failures over a short period of time.

For business firms, the trend growth in the globalization of trade, as illustrated in Figure 3.8, signifies the process of rising competition that characterizes the economic framework today.

Recent years have also produced a trend of lower inflation and lower interest rates. Lower inflation, on average, connotes a reduction in pricing power with products and services increasingly being perceived by customers as commodities—perfect substitutes in a perfectly competitive marketplace. The challenge for businesses is to create the impression, if not the reality, of product differentiation—imperfect substitutes in a monopolistically competitive environment. For example, in financial services, are the services offered significantly different to justify a pricing for service model or are all the benefits of a financial service firm generated at the back end by reducing back office recordkeeping costs?

There was also a general decline in interest rates even after the Great Recession of 2007 to 2009 was officially declared over. This is odd since perceptions of risk rose with the recession and the associated delinquencies and defaults in the housing sector. Perhaps the lower interest rates reflected risk aversion as investors sought a safe haven in United States Treasury debt. Yet, it also appears there was a change in perceptions of the sustainable growth rate in the global economy, or at least that of the United States and Europe, while there was also a belief that continued low inflation was also more likely in the years ahead. This trio of changes highlights the difficulty of linear simulations of single economic changes in the traditional business model stress testing.

## Illusory Correlation

Another decision-making stumbling block is the illusory correlation. This idea, which is particularly popular when many decision makers are scrambling for simplistic explanations in a very complex environment, is the leap from observing one economic trend and then using that trend as an explanation of another trend without any intervening theory. Certainly odd events happen and there is a tendency to ascribe cause-effect to situations where no real link exists. This illusion is particularly prevalent among financial commentators.

It is also true among decision makers at firms or in state governments who ascribe changes to individual decisions. In fact, national or global trends are the real culprits. American presidents and corporate heads are credited or blamed for every advance or decline on their watch while trends occur totally outside their control.

In the early years of the post–World War II period, some analysts asserted that the economic success of the Soviet Union validated their economic model. In fact, the correlation of economic growth with the Soviet model was purely coincidence. The Soviet Union was living off the resource transfers from other nations and countries that it had conquered, with little regard for the long-run consequences. It did not have the incentives within its economic framework that would ensure continued success over the long run. In economic studies, the appearance of success in the short run may hide underlying problems and those countries, states, and companies may be living off past success with little provision for the future. Flash-in-the pan success in the short run may give the appearance of a new economic model, but often that success is illusory unless supported by long-run-oriented policies.

Another example involves the volatility in the price of gold. Gold prices fluctuate and for each major movement in the price of gold there is an explanation. While many of these explanations (fear, inflation, blood in the streets) appear valid in the short run, over time there are as many explanations as there are movements. Traders and investors in gold, silver, and other commodities will find many correlations between the prices of commodities and economic and political factors in the short run, but unless

## TAKING A FURTHER LOOK

In finance, for example, unsustained models of Penn Square during the early years of the oil boom in the 1980s played the oil card on the way up but had no answer on the way down. Penn Square Bank in Oklahoma failed on July 5, 1982. Penn Square had grown rapidly based on the oil boom and had sold participations to other banks throughout the United States for loans it had made in the oil business. Large money center banks such as Continental Illinois and Chase Manhattan purchased a sizable portfolio of these loans. Major regional banks such as Seafirst in Seattle and Northern Trust in Chicago had also been major buyers. When inflation and oil prices subsided, the profit went out of the loans and the loans became uncollectible. Over 100 credit unions and an additional 100 savings and loans and commercial banks had unsecured deposits at Penn Square and were not rescued by the FDIC. Seafirst was merged with Bank of America. In May of 1984 a run began on Continental Illinois; its investor deposit base had learned the lessons of Penn Square and were not going to stick around in the face of the risk of failure due to nonperforming loans by Continental Illinois to International Harvester and Braniff Airlines. The time lag between Penn Square's demise and the effective FDIC nationalization of Continental Illinois, years later, reveals again how pernicious financial problems can linger in the economy.[9]

there is a fundamental driver of these prices, any correlation is likely to be illusory.[10] Therefore, as in the price of oil and measures of national success, the short-run changes, if not supported by long-run positive fundamentals, will produce cycles of greed and fear rather than prosperity. Analyzing cycles and separating cycles from trends is essential in effective decision making. What may appear as a significant correlation may only be a temporary string of good luck followed quickly by a turn of fate.

### Anchoring Bias

One bias that blinds decision makers to cyclical and structural change is the anchoring bias, in which an initial reference point, the anchor, distorts estimates of the true value of a good or service. For example, an anchoring bias can be the listing price of a home, which a seller sees as a reasonable estimate of value. Yet, as the recent years demonstrate, the real value of a

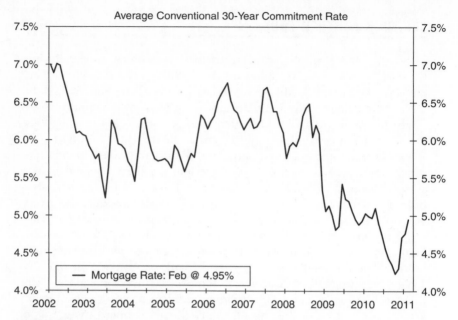

**FIGURE 3.9**   Mortgage Rate–Volatility in the Short Run
*Source:* Federal Home Loan Mortgage Corporation.

home is what someone will pay for the home, not the price at which someone wishes to sell.

In economics and the equity markets, this bias is readily apparent and widely seen in the range and starting points of the many graphs that are presented as unbiased data. In reality, picking a starting point in time and determining the range of values can give an observer a biased anchoring point to begin an analysis. Consider the same series presented in Figures 3.9 and 3.10. Figure 3.9 gives the impression of a very volatile series with very high values. In contrast, Figure 3.10 presents the same commodity over a longer period with a broader range. The conclusions that can be drawn from these two graphs are very different.

In economic or business comparisons, Americans are hampered by their anchoring bias dating back to the early post–World War II period. Japan and Germany had been destroyed by war. China, India, and Russia were not trading partners. Brazil and Mexico were run by military juntas. The United States had a largely closed economy and little global competition. Yet current public policy makers continue to speak in terms of America's leadership in many industries—textiles, furniture, and consumer electronics—that have become global. In fact, the post–World War II period was an exception in

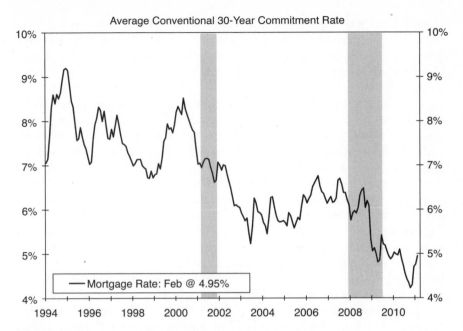

**FIGURE 3.10** Mortgage Rate–Steady Downward Trend over Time
*Source:* Federal Home Loan Mortgage Corporation.

economic leadership with one country—America—holding such a dominant position. The reality is that change is constant and memories of the past are a prescription for failure in most cases.

## CYCLES, STRUCTURAL CHANGE, AND THE EVOLUTION OF A FRAMEWORK

The ability of decision makers to react to cyclical and structural change is hampered by their attachment to sunk costs. These are defined as past, irreversible costs put into a project and they are not altered by the decision to continue or to stop the project. Richard Brealey (professor at the London School of Business) and Stewart Myers (professor at MIT) point out the decision in 1971 to continue with Lockheed's development of the TriStar airplane after $1 billion had already been spent.[11] Whether Lockheed went ahead with the project or scuttled it, the $1 billion was not recoverable. In 1981 Lockheed announced it would stop production of its money-losing L-1011 jetliner. Eventually, Lockheed dropped out entirely from commercial airline production.[12] Decision makers, sometime overly committed to certain activities, doggedly persist with investments that are quickly losing value. They are unable to let go of the past and move on to new opportunities. As a result, these investments lose value. Cyclical and secular change, by its nature, means that old investments become sunk costs and barriers to innovation.

In fact, in many cases decision makers escalate their commitment, believing that just a bit more investment will allow them to achieve their goal.[13] In public policy, this can be seen in the commitment to retain the scale of many industries through protectionism and subsidies beyond any economic justification. While many American firms in the textile, furniture, steel, automobile, and consumer electronics industries are globally competitive, government subsidizes these industries on a scale that allows weak companies to persist. They then can sell products at low prices and thereby hamper the ability of competitive firms to earn a profit and reinvest so as to remain globally competitive. Policy focuses on preserving jobs with little regard to workers and their skills. As a result, there are too many workers in old technology fields when in reality these workers must move into fields where they have a competitive future.

Cheers and relief characterized the fall of the Berlin Wall in 1989. A sense of political freedom spread throughout Eastern Europe, as well as a diminished fear of nuclear war. Another consequence of this turning point in history was greater economic freedom. The product and labor markets of Eastern Europe opened up, thereby shifting the Soviet Union enough so it rekindled trade with the West. This in turn helped Communist China recognize that its future depended on more open trade relations. Developing nations such as Brazil and India were soon following the same path. Many emerging market countries and the United States became part of the North American Free Trade Association (NAFTA) and the World Trade Organization (WTO).

Given all these changes, what were the feedback effects on the then economic model? First, an increase in the available supply of production facilities meant an outward shift in the aggregate supply of many commodities—particularly those produced by low- and medium-skilled labor. This lowered prices and the pace of inflation, on average, in the West. It also brought about lower interest rates, which led to a rise in real investment and in equipment in the West and in emerging markets. The rise in production facilities in emerging countries also put downward pressure on compensation for low- and semi-skilled workers in the West, which has led to more change.

Throughout the world, younger workers have been on the move: from Eastern Europe to the West; from rural Eastern Europe to city factories; from rural China to the coast of the country; and, in the United States, from the industrial cities of the North to the service and transportation opportunities of the South, Mountain West, and the West Coast.

However, labor problems persisted for older workers, who are less mobile than younger workers because of their career status, family obligations, and fixed assets such as home ownership. Since the fall of the Berlin Wall, it is not surprising that economic recoveries in the United States have been slower to regain jobs, as domestic low- and semi-skilled workers in the United States and Western Europe are having trouble finding jobs in once prosperous areas. In addition, lesser-skilled workers who once worked in entry-level positions in factories, find those factories closed or being built abroad closer to the new customers in the emerging markets. This pattern has reached even state and local government workers during the Great Recession, as the loss of revenues has forced retrenchment. In some states such as New Jersey, the move to balance the budgets has meant significant spending cuts as tax revenues declined in response to an economic slowdown and an uncertain pace of recovery ahead.

Structural change in the labor market since the fall of the Berlin Wall delivered a new global production model where capital was mobile and would be combined with low- and semi-skilled workers anywhere in the world. The beneficiaries would be workers in Eastern Europe and Asia on the production side and the consumers in Western Europe and the United States on the buy side. The new global production framework for many goods is one of greater supply elasticity—any given rise in global demand can be met with additional supply without a rise in prices. The sources of global demand and supply are also broader than they were in the earlier framework. United States firms sell into more markets and consumers buy more imports, particularly from China.

In recent years, however, because of the housing correction as well as the equity market decline, there was a shock on the demand side. Households' perceived wealth in their homes and retirement funds and savings fell sharply, causing them to reassess their willingness to buy homes and to improve existing homes. For many, there was no real economic return to investing in home improvements, since the selling price of the home was unlikely to rise very much in the near future. Feedback effects also included a higher consumer savings rate and a slower pace of spending on consumer durables, especially automobiles. Slower consumer spending meant a slower pace of overall growth in the economy. With slower demand growth, but still significant global capacity to produce, inflation rates stayed lower than many expected given the economic recovery. Meanwhile, slower growth and lower inflation generated lower interest rates than would have been expected given the traditional framework of rising inflation and interest rates associated with economic recovery.

Lower housing and equity market prices were a double hit on household wealth and thereby lowered personal consumption through the wealth effect where lower wealth is associated with lower consumer spending. With the wealth effect, lower housing prices meant lower perceived wealth by consumers, which forced consumers to choose more savings and less spending at the margin. The wealth effect refers to changes in consumer spending based on changes in consumer wealth. For example, increases in home values or a rising equity market would be associated with an increase in wealth and thereby consumption. Slower economic growth, lower consumer spending, and inflation have combined to generate lower income and sales tax revenues for state governments and put the crimp on state budgets. Lower home values and a slower pace of home price appreciation meant lower property tax revenues for local governments. Therefore, the hard choices for state and local governments are just beginning.

These two examples of shocks on the supply and demand sides emphasize that apparent cyclical change also generates a change in the underlying economic framework. Decision makers should recognize that each cycle is different, as each shock that appears initially to be a cyclical phenomenon also contains an element or two of a structural change in the prevailing current economic framework.

### Internal Dynamics of Cycles: The Short and Long-Run Responses to Any Change

Volatility in energy prices has been a constant feature of the American economy since the early 1970s. This pattern reflects the nature of an internal dynamic familiar to some as expressed in the traditional "corn-hog" cycles.[14] The planned production of hogs reflects the price of hogs in the previous period and the price of corn in the previous period. Since corn is a principal input to hog production, then changes in its price will alter production plans. Hog prices today depend on corn prices in the previous period. Any change in the price of corn will lead to a change in the supply of hogs, and if the change in the price of corn were to be volatile it would lead to sharp movements in the supply and price of hogs.

Sharp movements in the price of crude oil also generate drastic movements in the price of gasoline as well as sharp movements in products like the automobile that use gasoline as an input. Volatility in the supply of oil leads to abrupt price movements, since the demand for gasoline is very inelastic in the short-run.

However, over time, price volatility generates its own set of responses. Higher prices will provide an incentive to search for more oil. On the demand side, higher prices will lead buyers to shift travel preferences and attempt to find alternative means of transportation over time. The market fluctuations of prices will generate its own cycle of price and output behavior.

As a result, while any shock may generate sharp price rises in the short run, incentives are generated to produce more and thereby moderate the price rises over time. In addition, sharp price rises also diminish some of the quantity demanded so that over time a new balance is found between supply and demand at a price below the shock price but above the original price. The oil shock of the 1970s was on the supply side, while changes in consumer preferences for oat bran, Beanie Babies, yoga exercise, or wine bars generated an initial flurry of price rises and supply increases. This is followed by a moderation in prices and demand and some inevitable decline in supply from recent suppliers with a very high cost structure that can only exist with high prices.

In the short run, supply can be very inelastic as it takes time to organize production. Decision makers must estimate the viability of a successful enterprise at a future price below the initial shock price that originated the interest in entering the business. For example, in recent years, many carpenters turned general contractors to serve the housing boom, while mortgage brokers, real estate agents, and appraisers appeared everywhere. When the Great Recession occurred, many of the positions in these professions were not economically viable.

This internal cyclical dynamic reinforces the emphasis on the value of expectations and imperfect information that often drives economic activity and decision making. The expectations for profit propelled many to enter the housing boom. However, misperceptions on the sustainability of the boom led to mispricing of housing assets and the securitized products that accompanied them. This is simply financial history repeating itself.

In the early eighteenth century, agriculture produced enormous yields, and profits, to initial investors. The British legislature established the South Seas Company to take advantage of such opportunity. Investment in the company rose rapidly; even Isaac Newton, the great mathematician, tossed in money. Prices soared, thereby stimulating the creation of new investment schemes. One of these schemes was for "carrying on an undertaking of great advantage, but nobody to know what it is."[15] Of course, all this overinvestment drove down the realized rate of return for many of these opportunities.

For decision makers, the fashion of the moment sets up its own internal pricing cycle that can lead to significant short-run profits, but much lower prices and profits over time. The challenge is to determine how much the underlying framework has changed, so decision makers can make a profit at the projected, below boom, level of prices after the party is over. Cycles persist, only their names change to beguile the innocent.

Shocks from the supply side have also taken the form of significant changes in technology, and thereby a significant shift in the modeling framework for decision making. While most are familiar with the evolution of computing technology and mobile communication, the telegraph and railroad were a significant advantage for the North in the Civil War and led to a huge increase in transportation technology and the lowering of agricultural prices in the latter half of the nineteenth century. Improvements in roads and automobiles and trucks again reduced the cost of transportation in the early twentieth century as the emergence of the radio improved communications. These types of changes give rise to what we would call real business cycles and are the focus of the next chapter.

## DISCUSSION QUESTIONS

1.  You often hear comments about the economic recovery of 2010 to 2011 taking the shape of a V or U or L, or even the W shape. Using your understanding of the dynamics of cyclical and structural change, how would you distinguish the forces of the cyclical change/structural change? For example, the V-shaped recovery would imply a traditional recovery driven by cyclical forces. An L-shaped recovery suggests that long-term negative structural forces dominate.
2.  Business and public administration graduates are not trained to deal with economic cycles. Moreover, leaders seldom consider the business cycle when projections of future revenues and costs are considered. Spreadsheets are dominated by fixed mathematical relationships that do not vary with economic conditions. The best laid plans of most organizations are squeezed or simply postponed when the business cycle changes. The 1990 recession was associated with a downdraft for financial institutions that had enjoyed a boom in the 1980s. The 2000 to 2001 recession signaled the end of the dot-com boom. The 2008 to 2009 recession signaled the end of the housing boom.
    a.  What patterns do you see in the economic cycles of the past that could serve as warning signs of a turn in the economy?
    b.  How could you introduce these signs into the decision-making process in your organization?
    c.  How might the overconfidence bias and the normalization of deviance impact actual decision making in the organization as signs of an economic downturn begin to accumulate in the next cycle?
    d.  To what extent might the concept of path dependence limit the organization's ability to make changes in the face of economic cycles?
    e.  What means might you apply to limit path dependence and open up your options in the organization?

3. The Hodrick-Prescott filter process is an easy tool to set a baseline for identifying the trend of any economic or financial series and where in the cycle the current set of economic observations sit.
   a. Explain how your organization may be able to apply the H-P filter to distinguish cycle from trend in a series such as your top-line revenues or your input costs.
   b. How can you apply the H-P approach to counter the tendency to accept a normalization of deviance in a series?
   c. How might you use the H-P filter to recognize a change that might be overlooked?
4. Secular growth has certainly been the story in the United States from the period after World War II until the 2008 to 2009 recession. Now it appears that strong secular growth is the story for Asia.
   a. How might the anchoring bias influence expectations by both policy makers and the public about the future given this history of secular growth?
   b. To what extent does growth reflect the application of more labor and capital?
   c. As the CEO of a multinational organization, what are the incentives and disincentives you see in growth in the United States, Europe, and Asia that would influence your allocation of labor and capital across the globe?

# NOTES

1. William I. Walsh, *The Rise and Decline of the Great Atlantic & Pacific Tea Company* (New York: Lyle Stuart, 1986).
2. See Jim Collins, *Good to Great* (New York: HarperBusiness, 2001), 65–69.
3. R. J. Hodrick and E. C. Prescott, "Postwar U.S. Business Cycle: An Empirical Investigation," *Journal of Money, Credit and Banking* 29(1) (1997): 1–16.
4. John E. Silvia, "The Evolution of the Economy, Credit and Economic Policy," paper presented at the Federal Reserve Bank of Atlanta, *Debate & Confirm: 2009, Banking Industry Outlook*, February 19, 2009.
5. For a great read on decision-making biases see Michael Roberto, *Know What You Don't Know: How Great Leaders Prevent Problems Before They Happen* (Upper Saddle River, NJ: Wharton School Publishing, 2009).
6. Diane Vaughan, *The Challenger Launch Decision: Risky Technology, Culture and Deviance at NASA* (Chicago: University of Chicago Press, 1996).
7. Barbara Tuchman, *The Guns of August* (New York: Ballantine, 1962).
8. Jim Collins, *Good to Great*, provides an interesting view on Bethlehem Steel. James O'Toole, in *Leading Change* (San Francisco: Jossey-Bass, 1995), provides a view on the decline of General Motors.

9. See Jerry W. Markham, *A Financial History of the United States, Volume III* (Armonk, NY: M.E. Sharpe, 2002), 76–77.
10. Precious commodities such as gold and silver are frequently the focus of speculative attempts to corner a market, as evidenced by the Hunt brothers' experience with silver in 1979 and 1980 at the height of the inflation fears.
11. Richard A. Brealey and Stewart C. Myers, *Principles of Corporate Finance*, 3rd ed. (New York: McGraw-Hill, 1988), 95.
12. John Greenwald, Jerry Hannifin, and Joseph J. Kane, "Catch a Falling TriStar," *Time*, December 21, 1981.
13. For a real-world example of the sunk-cost effect with tragic consequences, see Jon Krakauer, *Into Thin Air: A Personal Account of the Mount Everest Disaster* (New York: Anchor Books, 1997).
14. James M. Henderson and Richard E. Quandt, *Microeconomic Theory*, 2nd ed. (New York: McGraw-Hill, 1971), 145–149.
15. John Train, *Famous Financial Fiascos*, The South Sea Bubble, Fraser Publishing, 1995, p. 91.

## RECOMMENDED READING FOR SERIOUS PLAYERS

Krakauer, Jon. *Into Thin Air: A Personal Account of the Mount Everest Disaster* New York: Anchor Books, 1997.
Markham, Jerry W. *A Financial History of the United States*. Armonk, NY: M.E. Sharpe, 2002.
Roberto, Michael. *Know What You Don't Know: How Great Leaders Prevent Problems Before They Happen*. Upper Saddle River, NJ: Wharton School Publishing, 2009.
Vaughan, Diane. *The Challenger Launch Decision: Risky Technology, Culture and Deviance at NASA*. Chicago: University of Chicago Press, 1996.

# CHAPTER 4

# Economic Dynamism: Growth and Overcoming the Limits of Geography

In 1453, the Ottoman Empire conquered Constantinople, the ancient capital of the Eastern Roman Empire. From this position of power, Muslim authorities controlled the trade routes to the east and extracted taxes from all who sought to enhance their fortunes. For Western Europe, the trade over the Silk Road[1] had been the path to economic growth and prosperity. How, then, could they overcome the challenge to growth and the barrier the Ottoman Empire presented in terms of geography? The answer, and the unintended consequence of this situation, was the incentive to find a way to avoid these taxes and the beginning of the great age of European exploration. Despite the dangers involved, by the end of the fifteenth century the Portuguese had rounded the Cape of Good Hope at the southern tip of Africa and reached India. By 1510 they had reached the Spice Islands, the source of spices such as pepper that yielded fabulous profits once brought to Europe.[2]

The Portuguese opening of a new trade route in order to make money possesses the elements that still drive trade today. There was a consumer demand for commodities and or services that could not be produced domestically, but could be obtained from abroad. Entrepreneurs took the risks to meet this need, especially because high taxation creates an incentive to circumvent these tolls. Success generated huge returns to the first successful entrepreneur, Portugal, which then led the Dutch and then the English to follow. Over time, the amount of goods and the total flow of trade expanded, and the prosperity of the trading nations improved.

Let's take another example. In the 1600s, the American colonies were an emerging market and England was an established economic power. England passed a series of laws called the Navigation Acts, which, beginning in 1651, regulated trade with the American colonies. The acts restricted the colonies to utilize ships built, owned, and manned by British subjects. The Navigation Acts also required that certain commodities exported by the American colonies could be shipped only to England, while European goods imported to America had to first pass through England. Over time, Britain placed increasing restrictions on American manufacturers. Once again, trade for the Americans was primarily through one port, Britain. American consumers and producers looked for an alternative. Success would generate huge returns. The expected economic returns far outweighed the costs of war and whatever risks would be associated with such a conflict.

Pivotal economic historical events such as the Corn Laws in England after the Napoleonic Wars and tariff laws passed in the United States during the nineteenth and twentieth centuries, culminating in the Fordney-McCumber Tariff Act of 1922 and Smoot-Hawley Tariff Act of 1929, raised tariff barriers and reduced trade. In contrast, the North American Free Trade Agreement (NAFTA) and the World Trade Organization (WTO) had their origins in consumers' desire for more products at lower costs and entrepreneurs' recognition of the opportunity for profits, and thereby lowered tariff barriers.[3]

Effective decision making requires an understanding of the incentives of economic growth and the interaction of growth and trade over time. Economic success reflects the ability of decision makers to overcome barriers of time and space to generate the profits that compensate for the risks involved in each new venture. Along the way, disruptive innovations, growth, and change make for success when decision makers generate a new framework for decision making that helps customers meet their needs.

Incentives under both the English Corn Laws of the early nineteenth century and the Fordney-McCumber Tariff of 1922 were remarkably similar. In both cases, increased war demand had created a high level of domestic demand in England and the United States, respectively, and the tariffs were there to protect the home markets from cheap imports. In both cases, the distributional impacts were similar to expectations. Tariffs raise the price of foreign goods and thereby benefit the domestic producers of goods that would have competed with those goods. Meanwhile, consumers of those goods and firms that may have employed those goods as inputs to production pay higher prices. Evidence suggests that the rising cost of farm equipment put many small farmers out of business in the early 1920s.[4] In England, David Ricardo, the economist, and Sir Robert Peel, British prime minister at the time, both argued against the Corn Laws (which had been put in place in part to prohibit the import of cheaper American corn). In the United States, Henry Ford, in particular, argued against the Fordney-McCumber Tariff along with many farm groups. The high tariffs of the Fordney-McCumber

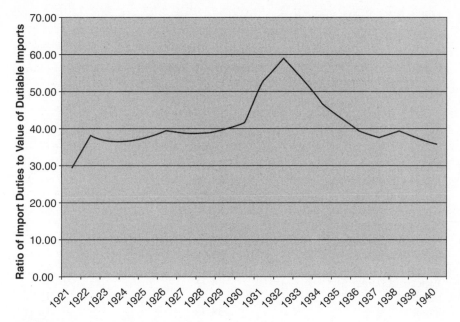

**FIGURE 4.1**    Smoot-Hawley Tariff
*Source:* U.S. Bureau of the Census.

Tariff and the further increase in tariffs under the Smoot-Hawley tariffs (Figure 4.1) put a real crimp on trade, as evidenced in Table 4.1. Escalating tariffs in the United States and Europe have been cited as one of the contributing factors to the beginning of the sustained global depression throughout the 1920s and early 1930s.

## A FRAMEWORK FOR GROWTH

The effective combination of labor (population growth and the quality and quantity of labor), capital, technology, and entrepreneurship—the factors of production—produce what kings wanted in the sixteenth century and what consumers desire today, while creating growth and raising the standard of living for society. Entrepreneurs earn their profits by meeting those needs. Differences in the standard of living within and among countries reflect the ability of the entrepreneurs to combine these factors. Public policy can play an important role in assisting with this process, although, all too often, policy makers exploit growth and trade for short-run political interests rather than long-run economic gains. Often overlooked by policy makers is the set of

**TABLE 4.1**  Tariffs Rates under Fordney-McCumber versus Smoot-Hawley

| | Equivalent ad Valorem Rates | |
| --- | --- | --- |
| Product | Fordney-McCumber | Smoot-Hawley |
| Chemicals | 29.72% | 36.09% |
| Earthenware and Glass | 48.71 | 53.73 |
| Metals | 33.95 | 35.08 |
| Wood | 24.78 | 11.73 |
| Sugar | 67.85 | 77.21 |
| Tobacco | 63.09 | 64.78 |
| Agricultural Products | 22.71 | 35.07 |
| Spirits and Wines | 38.83 | 47.44 |
| Cotton Manufactures | 40.27 | 46.42 |
| Flax, Hemp, and Jute | 18.16 | 19.14 |
| Wool Manufactures | 49.54 | 59.83 |
| Silk Manufactures | 56.56 | 59.13 |
| Rayon Manufactures | 52.33 | 53.62 |
| Paper and Books | 24.74 | 26.06 |
| Sundries | 36.97 | 28.45 |
| Total | 38.48 | 41.14 |

*Source:* U.S. Tariff Commission, *The Tariff Review*, July 1930, Table II, p. 196.

incentives needed to ensure the delivery of these inputs to improving the standard of living.[5]

Our growth model simply assumes that if both capital and labor are multiplied by the same factor, the output of the economy would also rise by the same factor. This is termed *constant returns to scale*. It suggests that the output per worker is a function of the amount of capital per worker. A complementary relationship exists between worker and capital. The extra output for each worker depends on the extra unit of capital, which is termed the *marginal product of capital* (MPK). Of course, MPK diminishes with additional units of capital. If the average worker has only a little capital to work with, the next shovel, for example, is very handy. However, with more shovels, the average worker finds that each additional shovel is not as useful, so the marginal product for additional capital declines.

Decision makers draw on the National Income and Product Accounts published by the Bureau of Economic Analysis in the United States Department of Commerce to measure the trends in savings and investing flows that generate the capital that complements the worker in the production process. In this sense, the rate of saving is also the fraction of output devoted to investment. This is the beginning of a framework for understanding the growth drivers in any market that are examined for possible expansion. For any given capital stock, both public and private, the production function indicates how much output the economy produces, while the saving rate determines the allocation of that output between consumption and investment.

For decision makers, monitoring the growth of the capital stock provides key data in estimating the growth potential of any market. Two primary forces that impact the growth of capital stock are:

1. The pace of investment of new capital.
2. The depreciation of the existing capital.

The amount of investment per worker determines, in part, the marginal production of that worker. As for depreciation, a certain fraction of capital stock wears out each year. The rate of depreciation is subject to the forces of physical wear as well as technological obsolescence (especially in high-tech laptops and personal communications) and these factors themselves vary over time and by type of capital. Whereas a laptop computer might be state of the art for 3 years, many office buildings are still serviceable after 50 years. The net result is that the change in the capital stock equals investment less depreciation. Increases in capital stock leads to greater levels of output and associated investment. The higher the level of the capital stock, the greater the amount of depreciation.

Many cities (Detroit, Cleveland, Buffalo, Baltimore) and regions (industrial Northeast) in the United States grew and benefitted from the significant public and private capital built up in the early post–World War II era, but have not invested new capital in many years, as demographic movements and the evolution toward a service economy have reduced the physical advantages of the old capital in these areas. For many cities and companies the old capital is depreciating faster than new capital is added. Alternatively, some cities such as Shanghai are adding new capital so quickly that the old capital is hard to find. Contrasting these areas leaves an impression, however rough, of growth and decline—and upon such impressions a location decision on new facilities is made by firms both domestic and foreign. For example, the majority of Japanese and German automobile production facilities are located in the South and mid-southern states, and the southern part of some northern states such as Indiana and Ohio.

Decision makers must always look for ways to determine balancing investment and saving in the economy. Countries, cities, regions, states, and businesses must always renew themselves.

Our framework for growth involves the balance of savings and investment that generates just enough investment to offset depreciation in order to keep the level of the capital stock steady. A balance between savings and investment and a balance of investment and depreciation should exist. With both of these relationships in balance, this steady state will persist. If these relationships become unstable, the economy will tend to return to the steady state as long as the underlying relationships have not changed. This is the economy's long-run equilibrium. At less than the steady-state level of capital, investment exceeds depreciation and the capital stock rises to its steady state. When the economy has a capital stock above the steady state, investment is less than depreciation and the capital stock will decline.

So why do some cities, regions, and countries appear to have more capital and invest more than other areas? Saving rates are the core issue. A rise in the saving rate leads to greater investment with a given capital stock and rate of depreciation. Investment exceeds depreciation and the capital stock rises so that a city, region, or country has a higher capital stock and level of output than the prior steady state. The saving rate thus becomes a key determinant of the capital stock and the potential of any city, region, or country to deliver the output public and private decision makers want. A higher saving rate is associated with a larger capital stock and a higher level of output. In contrast, a low saving rate is associated with a small capital stock and a lower level of output at the steady state—not a pleasant steady state indeed.

The low savings rate in the United States prior to the Great Recession led to an underinvestment in certain regions and sectors of the economy. In other areas and industries (construction and commercial real estate), the capital stock depreciated more rapidly than new capital was being built. Around the world, countries that have a high saving rate are receiving significant investment that creates prosperity; in countries where the saving rates are low, investment gains are extremely limited.

### Higher Output—But Not Faster Growth Forever

Our framework for growth also has an internal dynamic that is subtle, but very important for decision makers to understand. A society with a higher saving rate grows faster only during the period in which the capital stock is being built up to reach the higher steady-state level. A higher, maintained, saving rate allows a country to maintain a level of capital stock, but not a higher rate of growth forever. In the early post–World War II period, countries such as Japan and Germany had much of their capital stock destroyed. But if the saving rate is unchanged, the economy has a saving rate that leads to a rapid pace of investment relative to depreciation (there was little left to depreciate after the war). Output grows as more capital is added by investment than is depreciated, until the balance of the savings and investment is reestablished at a rate at which depreciation of the larger capital stock again balances investment in new capital stock. This can be seen in newly emerging countries such as Vietnam and Korea, as well as in China after the Cultural Revolution.

Successful societies are defined by their ability to maintain a high level of output associated with a high saving rate, and their ability to handle a temporary imbalance due to capital destruction where the saving rate is high but depreciation very low. Here savings will go into investment that exceeds the pace of depreciation. For the last 20 years in the United States, the growth of the capital stock has shifted toward states with a high saving rate relative to their capital stock, generally from the Northeast to the South and the Mountain States. However, this is likely to be only short-term as these regions build up their capital stock to a steady state.

Globally, some countries—Japan, South Korea, Brazil, Mexico, and, yes, the United States—have investment that as a percentage of output is very high and is associated with high income per person. These are attractive markets. On the other side, income per person remains low for societies in which savings and investment are limited, such as Sub-Saharan Africa.[6]

### Saving Rates: Signals for Prosperity

With our growth framework, decision makers can identify changes in savings that leads to increases in investment and output that, in turn, causes investment in those markets. In addition, the savings and investment balance reestablishes itself at a new level with a higher level of output, but the same

## TAKING A CLOSER LOOK: POLITICAL STABILITY AND SAVING RATES

Saving rates vary because of tax policy (a perennial debate in the United States), retirement patterns, the development of financial markets, and social and cultural differences. Political stability and the quality of public institutions are also very important. In recent years, increasing political stability and a decline in military takeovers helped some Latin American countries advance economically. For instance, for Latin American countries, the real GDP growth rate increased to 3.8 percent for the 2000 to 2008 time period as compared to 2.9 percent during 1990 to 1999. In addition, national savings as percent of GDP jumped to 21 percent during 2000 to 2008 as compared to 17 percent for the 1990 to 1999 time period.

growth rate of output. What are needed now are indicators of change that move the savings and investment balance and lead investors to be more positive about a particular region.

When saving rates decline for some reason, such as higher taxes on savings, investing slows and consumers substitute spending for savings at the margin. In these circumstances, investment is below depreciation. When this occurs, the capital stock declines, and this is followed by declines in output, future investment, and consumption. At the new steady state, consumption is a larger share of a smaller pie; output and investment are lower as well.

When saving rates rise, investment increases and consumption sees a relative decline (Japan, Germany, and China are good examples here). Increased investment induces a rise in the capital stock; as capital accumulates, output, consumption, and investment rise as well. Over time, the higher level of output allows for both a higher level of consumption and investment. In the short run, consumer spending declines as the society increases its saving rate, but over time consumer spending grows as output increases. For decision makers, the investment horizon becomes significant. The consumer sector, for example, might see slower growth in the short run but outsized gains as the market opens up to consumer purchases. The evolution of Japanese and Chinese consumers illustrates this well.

A high saving rate generates a higher level of output, but not a sustained higher rate of growth once the economy finds its new balance between savings, investment, and depreciation. So how do decision makers identify markets that allow a change in the framework so that the sustained pace of growth remains high for at least some period of time? Looking at the United States in the nineteenth and twentieth centuries, as well as China and India in the first part of this century, shows that an above-average growth rate can be maintained for a sustained period of time.

## POPULATION GROWTH AND THE WESTWARD EXPANSION OF THE UNITED STATES

As shown, capital and labor are complements in the production process and additional capital per worker means additional output at a diminishing rate. The challenge of population growth is that workers are added, but capital is not. That would appear to hurt the growth rates of a society.

Population growth reduces the amount of capital per worker much the same way as depreciation does. Depreciation means the wearing out of capital per worker. Population growth spreads the same amount of capital among a larger number of workers and therefore capital per unit of labor declines and hence so does productivity. The steady state requires that capital per worker remains unchanged, so investment now must balance with depreciation plus population growth. Total capital and total output grow at the rate of population growth, while the output per worker does not change.

Rapid increases in population can outpace the growth of capital. Capital per worker declines, as does the standard of living as a whole. For example, when political refugees pour into a country there is not enough capital to put everyone to work immediately. Refugee camps persist for years, along with poverty. The high rates of population growth in Sub-Saharan Africa are also associated with low levels of income per person. China's one child per family policy is a means of slowing population growth and minimizing the downward effect of lower capital per workers leading to a lower standard of living.

Technology's role in growth is to improve the efficiency of labor. When this occurs, output per worker rises. Both the quantity and quality of the labor force improves over time. New increases in the capital stock compensate for the depreciation of existing equipment, increase the amount of capital available to new workers, and provide for increases in the efficiency of each worker by providing workers with better quality equipment. Capital per the new, more effective worker is constant in the steady state. Technological progress allows for sustained growth in output per worker and a higher standard of living over time. In contrast, a higher rate of saving only leads to faster growth as a society moves to a higher steady state. Technological progress allows for both growth in output per worker and the capital stock per worker, which has been the experience in the United States. Real wages for workers tends to follow the pattern of the real GDP per worker as well. Real wages rise along with the real GDP per worker over the long run.

Our framework for positive economic growth opportunities focuses on economies with above-average saving rates, population rates that fall in line with the growth of capital, and improvement in the quality of the labor force through education and/or the application of labor-enhancing technology. Also important is the quality of public institutions and public policy. Standards of living reflect both the quantity of our factors of production and the efficiency with which we put these factors of production to work.

Flawed policies, such as British nationalization of industries post–World War II, can set a country back for decades, as the uncertainty of property rights becomes a paramount issue when discussions about privatizing public enterprises comes to a public discussion. High inflation, large fiscal deficits, overbearing regulation, and corruption often combine to discourage capital accumulation. This, in turn, can result in slower economic growth in the short run and a decline in the standard of living over time. This is evident in recent years in several Latin American (Cuba and Argentina) and African (Zimbabwe) economies. Within the United States, economic performance among the states reflects, in part, changes in public policy that have discouraged or encouraged growth over time and have led to a change in the relative standards of living among people in different states. For decision makers, what are the signals of change in our framework for growth?

## POLICIES FOR GROWTH: WHERE ARE THE CHALLENGES TO OUR FRAMEWORK?

Every investment made by an individual or firm in a career or location reflects a framework that assumes that the future pace of growth in that career or location will achieve targeted financial goals. But what are the changes to that framework that could alter expectations and would lead to choices that shift our investment model?

## INSTITUTIONS AND THE SAVINGS/ INVESTMENT DECISION

The first step is to gauge the institutional framework of the community at hand. In the United States, property rights, the rule of law, regulations, and taxation differ significantly among the states. When expanded to the global level, this is even more difficult due to the additional complications of national cultures and social mores. For example, corruption that involves payments expected by foreign public officials allowing Americans to do business has become a major issue that must be factored into the framework.

In recent years, tax differences among bordering states have widened to such a degree that some entrepreneurs are incentivized to move to low or no income tax states. Florida, which has no income tax, has benefitted from the migration of retirees and near-retiree baby boomers from the relatively higher taxed Northeast states. Burdens of regulation and the vagaries of legal decisions have also been associated with increasing the cost, or at least the uncertainty of doing business, in some areas. Local zoning restrictions and a sense of antibusiness attitudes have certainly created the impression, if not the reality, of an antigrowth environment.

Many states offer incentives in the form of tax rebates as a means of altering the relative attractiveness of locating a business in a particular area. For any business, the expected after-tax rate of return is the driving factor for investment in equipment and the hiring of workers. Greater regulation, legal uncertainty, and uncertain property rights raise the cost and/or the risk of doing business in any particular area and, thereby, along with taxes, lower the expected, risk-adjusted, rate of return on doing business. Areas with higher taxes on the income from savings and investing discourage these varying activities, so we often see the states with higher taxes and greater regulatory burdens offering incentives to select firms to compensate, in part, for those burdens.

## Corporate Profits Tax

*I'll probably kick myself for having said this, but when are we going to have the courage to point out that in our tax structure, the corporation tax is very hard to justify?*
—Ronald Reagan

Taxes are very important in our framework because they work like incentives. When taxes change, incentives change. Simply put, there is an inverse relationship between higher taxes, which reduce the reward for work, investment, and saving, and the amount of work effort saving and investment that is undertaken. Here we focus on the rise in corporate taxes that reduces the incentive for companies to invest and undertake risk, since higher taxes on profits reduce the reward for this investment/risk taking. Greg Mankiw comments on this disincentive effect that "for this and other reasons, many economists believe that the corporate tax discourages investment."[7]

This discouragement for investment will impact our expectations for economic growth over time. In fact, currently policy makers in Washington are debating the merits of reducing corporate tax rates as a way to encourage more growth and jobs here as our corporate tax burden is estimated to be second only to Japan's among major industrialized nations.[8] Higher taxes reduce the incentive to work, invest, or save, therefore reducing the aggregate supply of goods offered in the marketplace. Taxes may change the long-run path of economic growth because they alter the returns on labor, capital, and land. In other words, taxes have a significant impact on aggregate supply and aggregate demand and the economic dynamism of the United States economy.

The Tax Reform Act of 1978 lowered the capital gains tax rate. The year before the passage of the bill the venture capital industry raised just $39 million; by 1981 the industry raised $1.3 billion.

## Technological Progress

During the last few decades, the demand for investment and capital increased significantly because technological progress—the personal computer, the Internet, for instance—encouraged capital-intensive production techniques and increased the available capital relative to labor employed in production. Consequently, during last three economic recoveries, job gains in the labor market remained depressed even as the recessions ended. Technological progress thus creates a structural change and alters the path of long-run growth and the labor-capital contribution to that growth.

Technology can be labor-augmenting and increases the demand for labor. In the early nineteenth century, textile mills in New England hired many immigrants to work the looms. By the mid-nineteenth century, mega projects such as the transcontinental railroad needed thousands of workers, forcing employers to import Chinese and Irish immigrants to supplement the Civil War veterans.[9] Again, any major change in the production function (from capital intensive to labor intensive or vice versa) will alter both the pace and composition of economic growth and therefore our economic framework. After the transcontinental railroad opened there was a huge boom in agricultural products, lower prices, and the emergence of America as breadbasket for much of Europe.

## WHY DOES CAPITAL NOT FLOW TO POOR COUNTRIES?

Standard neoclassical economic theory rests on three assumptions: Individuals have rational preferences and maximize their utility, firms maximize profits, and individuals and firms act independently on the basis of full and relevant information. Within this framework, capital should flow from capital-rich to capital-poor countries—the rate of return to capital would be greater in the capital-poor country while the return to labor would be greater in the capital-rich/labor-poor country. However, Robert E. Lucas, economist at the University of Chicago, compared the United States and India in 1988 and found that, contrary to the neoclassical model, capital did not flow from United States to India, owing to differences in the fundamentals—technological differences, human capital quality, government policies, and institutional structure affect the production structure of the economy. Furthermore, he discovered that capital may have high return in developing countries but it does not flow there because of market failure or political risk.[10] In the end, it is the risk-adjusted expected rate of return on capital for a new investor that will drive capital flows, and in many emerging markets the risk is simply too high.

## OVERCOMING GEOGRAPHY: STRETCHING THE PRODUCTION POSSIBILITIES CURVE

Consumers have unlimited wants but limited budgets. Faced with this reality, suppliers seek to minimize costs by producing and trading around the globe. Firms export products in which they have a greater advantage compared to foreign competitors, while importing goods that they have a competitive disadvantage in buying or building domestically. Effectively, a firm's opportunity costs to supply its buyers reflect a trade-off between what it pays domestically and what it pays to import. If a firm can produce or buy domestically at a cheaper price than it pays to import goods from abroad, it will do so.

Effectively, the aggregate supply of goods increases to a society and this provides the incentive for firms to seek trading relationships abroad.

Trade also has an interesting impact of factor prices—the returns to labor and capital. Trade tends to bring about the equalization of factor prices. Export of goods produced by an abundant factor, labor for example, increases the demand for its services and thereby its compensation. This has been seen in recent years as the return to labor in China has risen. Meanwhile, importing products that contain large amounts of a scarce domestic factor decreases the value of those scarce factors (American labor for textiles, for example). Exports raise the abundant and inexpensive domestic factor while imports reduce the return to the scarce and expensive factor.

For decision makers, trade impacts both output and input prices. Trade allows a firm to increase its total market if it has a comparative advantage as the low-cost producer and thereby export abroad. At the same time, trade alters factor prices and raises the price of factors employed to produce exports relative to those factors used solely in domestic production.

Alternatively, a firm can import goods from abroad where a foreign producer has a comparative advantage, while also recognizing that certain factors of production will be cheaper if imports of goods produced by that factor are rising rapidly. In recent years, there has been a relative decline in the cost of unskilled and semiskilled labor as imports of goods (textiles, furniture) produced by foreign workers has risen.

For private and public leadership, the challenge is to recognize what their organizations and businesses are good at and what they are not. Unfortunately, this runs counter to the sunk cost bias. Private decision makers are comfortable continuing their investments in human and financial capital. Yet, new producers are always entering markets, often with a comparative advantage in production. Public policy makers also see the businesses in their communities threatened by foreign competition and seek to protect them through tariffs or quotas. In recent years, trade has opened up because of the North American Free Trade Agreement and the World Trade Organization. In addition, India, China, and Russia have become substantial trading partners because of a reorientation in their economic philosophies.

With each of these changes, new markets have opened for export. The numbers of sources for production and competitors who supply goods to the United States have also increased. In turn, increased trade has generated changes in relative prices for both output (goods and services) and inputs.

For American consumers, there is a choice now between established domestic producers and new foreign exporters to the United States. Many Americans buy cheaper foreign goods and shun more expensive domestic items. For domestic producers, there is a choice between competing with new foreign competitors and/or producing abroad. Many American producers have decided to export what they are good at and discontinue producing goods where they are relatively noncompetitive. Meanwhile, labor and capital moves from less competitive to more competitive industries. Change, feedback, and choices reflect the evolving price dynamics of a global trading environment.

Economic choices for consumers and business decision makers are driven by the incentives. In the global trading environment those incentives are expressed as the real exchange rate, or terms of trade. The real exchange rate is the ratio of the price of the domestic good relative to the price of the foreign good. When the domestic price is high relative to the foreign good, consumers buy the foreign good. This relative price, however, must be adjusted by the nominal exchange rate (expressed as the units of the foreign currency traded per one dollar). Therefore, the relative price that drives consumer and business choice reflects the nominal exchange rate and the relative prices of the goods in each country. Effectively, the real exchange rate measures the value of a country's goods against those of another country or group of countries.

If the real exchange rate is high, then foreign goods are cheaper for consumers and business in the United States to buy while domestic goods appear relatively expensive to these same buyers. In contrast, if the real exchange rate is low, then foreign goods appear relatively expensive while domestic goods appear cheaper.

Forces for change develop when the relative prices of a tradable product or service does not line up with the real exchange rate. For example, if the nominal exchange rate between the dollar and the euro is 1.2, a good that costs \$1.20 in the United States would cost 1 euro in France. The real exchange rate is one. But if the price of the good is actually 1.2 euros, the euro is overvalued because the euro has more value in the United States than at home. In this case, there is pressure for the euro to decline in value over time. For a firm it makes sense to buy dollars to purchase the tradable good to export to Europe. Buying dollars drives up the value of the dollar and the nominal exchange rate until the real exchange rate returns to one. Firms that import goods from Europe face an overvalued euro; therefore, their costs are higher than could be justified if the currencies were fairly valued. American consumers, given an undervalued currency, prefer domestic goods relative to foreign goods. This comparison ignores the impact of transportation and trade barriers.

When real exchange rates diverge, then the nominal exchange rate faces pressure to change. For overvalued currencies, such as the dollar during the high-inflation 1970s, there is pressure to depreciate. For undervalued currencies, such as the Chinese yuan during 2008 to 2010, there is pressure to appreciate. As a first approximation, when inflation rises in a country relative to that of another country, there is a tendency for that currency to depreciate. A decline in the real exchange rate makes domestic goods less expensive relative to foreign goods and net exports rise.

For consumers, there is a change in relative prices. For firms, there is a change in the price of inputs and outputs. With a lower real exchange rate—the dollar depreciates versus the euro—American consumers see domestic selling prices as less expensive—for example, California wine gains relative to French wine. If the dollar depreciates versus the Chinese yuan, Chinese buyers would purchase more goods from the United States while American consumers typically buy fewer Chinese goods.

However, a depreciated dollar also means that firms that buy from abroad see higher input costs—the price of Portuguese cork rises for American vineyards and perhaps prompts some firms to move to screw-on caps.

## THE COMPETITIVE IMPLICATIONS OF ALTERING THE EXCHANGE RATE

One common driver of real exchange rates around the world is the adoption of expansionary fiscal policy (as in the early 1980s in the United States, for example). An increase in federal spending and tax cuts stimulates aggregate demand and reduces national savings. Lower national savings means fewer dollars to supply abroad, which induces a rise in the dollar exchange rate, as well as a rise in aggregate demand and consumer spending, more imports, and a larger trade deficit.

In contrast, if fiscal policy expands abroad, these countries' aggregate demand rises, resulting in the appreciation of their currency relative to the dollar. Exports from the United States are likely to rise while the foreign currencies' trade surplus declines, which is also true of the trade deficit in the United States.

Another path that alters the real exchange rate is monetary policy. An expansionary monetary policy is associated with a depreciation in the currency and thereby an increase in exports and reduction in imports for a small, open economy.

In a large, open economy such as the United States, the international flow of capital plays a central role in setting the path for exchange rates and trade. Increases in American interest rates relative to those abroad lead to capital inflows and an appreciation of the dollar. In contrast, in 2010 there was an exogenous change in perceptions of sovereign and counterparty risk. Questions arose about the fiscal budget imbalances in Europe, especially among Southern European countries such as Greece. As a result, the euro depreciated relative to the dollar.

## GROWTH, OPPORTUNITY, AND PRESERVATION

Over the next 20 years, emerging market countries such as Brazil, China, India, Indonesia, and Russia will place greater competitive pressures on private and public decision makers in the United States. In the early post–World War II period, the United States was the preeminent financial power in the world. Japan and Germany had been destroyed. China, India, and the Soviet Union were inward looking economically. The Soviet Union was an expansionary communist power. It wasn't inward looking politically and certainly was still expansionist into Eastern Europe, but its military expansionism did not translate into global economic power. Meanwhile, many Central and South American and African nations were absorbed in military juntas and socialist revolutions, particularly in Africa where several nations were recovering from colonial rule.

In the future, the global economic environment will continue to become more competitive. What does this mean for decision makers? For American consumers, the range of goods offered will likely increase but prices also may rise as the dollar faces downward pressures against Asian currencies. For American producers, competitive pressures will continue to rise, suggesting greater pressures on profit margins for firms that compete on price with foreign exporters. The lower dollar will offer some assistance to American exporters to foreign markets. For factor inputs in America, the likely pattern will be continually downward pressure on low and semiskilled labor that is in abundance on the global scene. At the same time, the return to factor inputs involved in high-tech, medical, financial, and educational sectors will continue to gain on a relative basis.

These patterns face a number of decision-making hurdles. First, the sunk cost problem represents an ongoing concern for private and public decision makers. The benefit of the victorious war-time position of the United States entering into the post–World War II period meant the United States has much older capital than Germany or Japan, for example, and the United States has workers who were paid relatively higher wages and substantial benefits when compared globally. However, these wage/benefit advantages will not be sustained with the open trading markets of the future as we have witnessed over the last thirty years. Since the 1980s, many firms in industries such as textiles and furniture have followed the declining pattern of large industrial companies. The marginal costs of sustaining some of these manufacturers will simply outweigh the benefits. Unfortunately, there will be continued temptation to obtain public subsidies to sustain private competitors for political reasons.

The anchoring bias will also impact policy making. Products, services, skills, and production facilities, such as in textiles, automobiles, consumer electronics, and furniture, that once were profitable have fallen off in recent years. Despite this reality, there is an expectation, in some cases promises by political office seekers, of restoring these products, jobs, and facilities to their former glory. However, technology and trade competitiveness, as the previous discussion of cycles and secular change indicated, cast doubt on this restoration. Greater trade openness over time and improving, long-term competitiveness of emerging countries, and their firms and workers, that are joining the global trading network suggest that previous levels of profitability are unlikely to be repeated in many cases. Anchoring future profitability and competitive success based on past history is unlikely to be correct.

Finally, prospect theory is a practical way to understand much of public decision making on trade in recent years. In prospect theory, if a situation is framed in terms of potential losses rather than potential gains, then it is more likely that decision makers will take fewer risks. In trade policy in the United States, the concern about jobs appears to have overtaken a focus on opportunities. Many free-trade agreements, such as those for Columbia, Panama, and South Korea, are kept on the shelf. This suggests that those consumers/producers that would benefit from trade do not gain. Consumers will probably then continue to pay higher prices for some goods. Producers who would import goods from those countries will have to find more expensive alternatives. Some domestic producers would appear to be protected for some period of time—but not forever.

## DISCUSSION QUESTIONS

1. In 2001, the debate on the new economy appeared to hinge on three factors: innovation, our ability to manage such innovation, and public policies that supported the innovation, its implementation, and the acceptance of the economic implications of that innovation (creative destruction). Innovation also brings change, therefore upsetting the established order and replacing that order with a new set of rules and victors.

One of the most famous Super Bowl ads pictures a young woman approaching a very large picture screen upon which an austere man is speaking to a crowd of uniformly dressed people who appear to be in a trance. The young woman throws a hammer at the screen. The ad is filmed in black and white. Discuss the concept of creative destruction and its application to this situation. How did the unique timing of changing fundamentals of labor, capital, and technology come together to signal the enormous shift in the American society at that time?

2. As a member of your corporate marketing team you are asked to compare the growth prospects of three countries.
   a. What four growth factors would you identify and how might each impact your projections for future growth?
   b. Saving rates differ between countries. Why might that matter?
   c. Population growth patterns differ between countries. Why might there be too little population growth? Why might there be too much population growth?
   d. What is the interaction between trade and growth?
   e. Growth often is accompanied by change. What is the concept of creative destruction? How might we see that today in places such as China, the United States, Brazil, and Russia?
   f. What do you see as the barriers to creative destruction evidenced in countries such as Greece or France in recent years?

3. Trade protectionism and tariffs were a way of protecting the established economic elite in England in the early 1800s (1815 to 1846) as exemplified by the Corn Laws. Meanwhile, movements toward free trade create winners and losers.

   Freer trade increases the size and extent of what was solely a domestic market and therefore increases the advantages of specialization for both companies and labor. Consumers benefit from a greater variety of goods at a lower price. Producers of low cost/high reward goods benefit by exporting abroad. Losers are high cost/low reward domestic producers.
   a. Identify how this trade model has influenced the prospects of the U.S. domestic producers of textiles, furniture, automobiles, and automobile parts since the signing of NAFTA and Chinese ascension to the WTO.
   b. Identify the benefits to the American consumer in terms of lower prices/better quality/broader choices over the last 30 years.
   c. Identify how many of the S&P 500 firms earn over 30 percent of their earnings from abroad. What does that tell you about the globalization of business today? What impact would you see if there was a serious attempt to reduce/limit trade on a global scale by imposing a Smoot-Hawley type of tariff law today?

4. One national debate that continues to arise is the debate around the saving rates in the United States relative to other countries. What is the case in favor of a higher savings rate in the United States in terms of its impact on investment, interest rates, and the standard of living? What is the link between the saving rate and long-term economic growth? Should incentives be used in the United States to increase saving? What incentives might you suggest if you believe that incentives should be employed?

## NOTES

1. Luce Boulnois, *Silk Road, Monks, Warriors and Merchants* (Hong Kong: Odyssey, 2008).
2. John S. Gordon, *An Empire of Wealth: The Epic History of American Economic Power* (New York: HarperCollins, 2004).
3. An excellent case on the Corn Laws is by Kevin Brennan and Matt Gorin, "Free Trade vs. Protectionism: The Great Corn Laws Debate," Harvard Business School No. 701-080 (Boston: Harvard University, 2001).
4. Edward S. Kaplan, *American Trade Policy, 1923–1995* (Westport, CT: Greenwood Press, 1996).
5. N. Gregory Mankiw, *Macroeconomics*, 7th ed., Chapter 7 (New York: Worth Publishers, 2005).
6. Institutions play a key role in economic growth as well; see Daron Acemoglu, Simon Johnson, and James Robinson, "Institutions as a Fundamental Cause of Economic Growth, in *Handbook of Economic Growth*, ed. Phillipe Aghion and Steven Durlauf (Amsterdam: Elsevier, 2005), 385–465.
7. N. Gregory Mankiw, *Macroeconomics*, 532.
8. See "Talks on Corporate Tax Revisions Set to Start," *Wall Street Journal*, January 14, 2011.
9. Stephen E. Ambrose. *Nothing Like It in the World: The Men Who Built the Transcontinental Railroad 1863–1869* (New York: Simon & Schuster, 2000).
10. Robert E. Lucas, "Why Doesn't Capital Flow from Rich to Poor Countries?" *American Economic Review* (May 1990): 92–96.

## RECOMMENDED READING FOR SERIOUS PLAYERS

Ambrose, Stephen E. *Nothing Like It in the World*. New York: Simon & Shuster, 2000.
Grossman, Gene M., and Elhanan Helpman. *Innovation and Growth in the Global Economy*. Cambridge, MA: MIT Press, 1991.
North, Douglass C. *Structure and Change in Economic History*. New York: W.W. Norton, 1981.

# CHAPTER 5

# Information: Competitive Edge in the Twenty-First Century

**I**nformation can make or break the best strategy for any institution. Consider the case exemplified in the movie *Trading Places*. While in a bathroom stall, Billy Ray Valentine (played by Eddie Murphy) overhears the conversation of Randolph and Mortimer Duke (played by Ralph Bellamy and Don Ameche, respectively) who were brothers and partners in a large Philadelphia commodities trading firm. The Dukes are discussing a little wager they had made. Valentine discovers the truth about the switch the Dukes have played on himself and Louis Winthorpe III (played by Dan Aykroyd).The switch in economic and social positions between Billy Ray and Louis occurs as a test of the nature versus nurture debate. The Dukes frame Louis, one of their best employees, and arbitrarily select the beggar Billy Ray and put Billy Ray in Louis's position. After hearing of the switch, Billy Ray then seeks out Louis to inform him of the real story. They decide to join forces to thwart the brothers with the help of Ophelia, a heart-of-gold prostitute (played by Jamie Lee Curtis, who won the Oscar for best actress in a supporting role). Later, while watching television, Billy Ray and Louis learn of a Clarence Beeks, who is transporting a secret report on orange crop forecasts. Beeks is the information source of the Dukes' trading strategies and just happened to be filmed on television. Billy Ray and Louis recall large payments made to Beeks by the Dukes and realize the brothers are attempting to corner the futures market for orange juice. Billy Ray and Louis capture Beeks on a train and the replace the real report with a forgery. Taking it to the Philadelphia stock market floor, Billy Ray and Louis trade on the true information and make a fortune; the Dukes, using the forged information, are ruined. Such is the value of information.[1] Information changes the rules of competition—and can make winners and losers overnight.

Historically, natural resources, labor, capital, and new technology were the weapons of choice for competitive advantage. Now, information has become the new factor of success in the twenty-first century. Yet, information cuts both ways. For many businesses, better information offers a means to improve the competitive edge and lower costs. Wal-Mart, for example, has applied information to better monitor sales and control inventory. However, better information also gives the consumer greater power in bargaining and in purchasing goods and services. In this chapter, we quickly review the context of information in an existing business and then the context of a new growth business.

## INFORMATION IN AN EXISTING BUSINESS

Every business is an information business, either in the creativity of a solo entrepreneur or in the flow of information between departments in a large corporation or government enterprise. Some areas, such as the costs of information gathering, processing, and distribution, represent a large percentage of the enterprise's costs and risks. Information is often the glue that holds together the structure of a business.

For instance, in community banking, knowing your customer is traditionally a competitive advantage. Proprietary information, customers, and their customers' familiarity with financial products are essential for success. For the local community banker, personal knowledge of the community and its people is a tremendous comparative advantage compared to only knowing the high-level economic statistics of population, employment, or tax base of a community. The character of the loan applicant cannot be judged based upon financial information alone.

Moreover, the flow of information is not linear, like the production of a good or service, and travels independently of production or other company activities or people in the enterprise. This independence is a product of our technology. For example, the gathering of inventory and sales information at the point of sale has given Wal-Mart a tremendous competitive advantage and defined Wal-Mart's supplier relationships and the channel of communication between it and its suppliers.

As we have seen in many applications, information, especially its distribution, establishes the relative bargaining power of buyer and seller. In the case of automobile sales, a car that is a lemon highlights the asymmetry of information about the real value of the automobile.[2] George Akerlof's point on the lemon issue is that in car sales, the seller knows much more about the car than the buyer does. Therefore, this information asymmetry can lead to a buyer getting a lemon. This asymmetry also exists in home and boat purchases. The availability of information through the Internet has increased the bargaining power of consumers in purchasing automobiles, books, music, vacations, and airline flights such that prices on many of these goods and services have dropped below the average pace of inflation for some time now.

## INFORMATION AS AN INPUT TO TODAY'S COMPETITIVE ADVANTAGE

How does information fit into the production process of an existing business as well as enter its strategic thinking? First, every step of the production process relies on critical information. Often very little work is started until the paperwork is first reviewed. At business meetings, where information is recorded and reviewed, current results are compared to targets and then action is taken.

Second, information courses through its own channels and has its own hierarchy steps in the command chain of the company. In some cases, information is delivered to one level of the organization without going through all the organization's intermediate stages. Information also flows independently of the path of work in an organization. This is a distinct and growing aspect of today's decision making. Attendees to a meeting arrive at the meeting independent of the information presented, such that there is an asymmetry between attendees in their familiarity with the information, and therefore there are differences in bargaining power. The creators of the information are not the same people who evaluate the information, and the creators have an informational advantage at the meetings. Information conveys a competitive advantage in many settings, similar to what superior resources or technology might in other circumstances. When different economic agents, consumers or businesses, receive the same information but at different times, or if some agents see some information and others see bits of other information on the same subject, their economic behavior will be different and we lose the uniform response assumption underlying so much of business modeling.[3] This is especially important when that information is influential in forming expectations about growth, inflation, interest rates, and the dollar—the economic drivers of markets.

Finally, the flow of information has two characteristics—reach and richness—whose subtlety and significance are often overlooked.[4] Tweeting by celebrities can have enormous reach to many people but its content, its richness, is limited to 140 characters. Alternatively, an instant message of a few words or a picture can be limited in its reach because it is sent only to an individual, a small group, or within a business. In contrast, a detailed document rich in content can be read or reviewed by a few people or hundreds of thousands. Think of anything written by Stephen Hawking.

In many applications, unfortunately, there is a trade-off between reach and richness, but in others there is no trade-off at all, as when we send a broadcast e-mail with an attached report to a subscriber list.[5]

## INFORMATION IN A NEW GROWTH BUSINESS

> *There is no limit to the number of people who can stay away from a bad play.*
>
> —Oscar Hammerstein

In a free, open marketplace information acts as a signal for entrepreneurs to innovate, for savers to invest, and for consumers to spend. However, when market information is not available due to mandates on production, for example, federal mandates on pay for federal projects (Davis-Bacon), wage-price ceilings, capital or rent controls (New York City), then businesses and households cannot respond completely to market forces. Where market signals are not available, economic resources may be overused (the tragedy of the commons) or never built (nuclear power and other major industrial facilities in the United States). The tragedy of the commons occurs when property is owned in common by everyone, but is overused and therefore deteriorates over time. In other cases, market demands for energy may dictate building a nuclear power plant, but a federal prohibition on nuclear power development prevents any new construction. In other instances, unavailable information about true customer demand can generate the production by monopolies in both capitalist and socialist economies of too many products (the Trabant, an East German automobile) or not enough (think of bread lines in Poland). In contrast, over the last five years, market responses from both entrepreneurs and consumers to smart phones have been a signal for innovation and for producing more of the given product.

How does information create a new-growth enterprise that responds to changes in opportunities in the United States economy or the global economy? There are many examples, but here we focus on two that are most closely tied to the application of information in economic decisions, following consumer innovations and disruptive technologies for business itself.

Customer service is essential to business success. And consumer access to information is central to that service. Over the last 30 years, traditional businesses such as newspapers, travel agencies, and consumer product sales have been disrupted by new means of communicating information entirely independent of delivery of a physical product or service at the same time. Such disruptive innovations induced what famed economist Joseph Schumpeter called creative destruction. Now commonplace, they force decision makers to carefully examine information gathering, interpretation, and delivery on the basic business models in many sectors of the economy.[6]

Owing to disruptive innovations such as the Internet, newspapers, and broadcast television news, for example, have been significantly impacted in the ability to deliver reach without richness on one hand, and the ability to combine speed with richness and reach on the other. Disruptive innovations are new products, new distribution methods, or new production methods that alter the nature of the marketplace. New products such as the telegraph, telephone, radio, and broadcast television each altered the market for information and news. Canals, railroads, and then highways altered the distribution of goods. New production methods, from Ford's automobiles to Ray Kroc's fast food, altered the marketplace for their products. Personal computers altered the way we process information. In contrast, a sustaining innovation would not alter the marketplace, but would more likely improve the quality of what is being done in a marketplace.[7] Newspapers have traditionally offered one physical location for a breadth of information (news, sports, book reviews, lifestyle, television listings, etc.) that could satisfy a well-read person. If someone were only interested in one aspect of the news, perhaps just sports, for example, the reader faced the dilemma of buying the whole newspaper for just one section, or going without the sports news entirely. The paper could not be unbundled. But now, with newspaper web sites providing free information, the reader can just click on the desired section and ignore the rest.

The dramatic changes in the newspaper business are an excellent representation of the dynamic, decision-making model seen so often in economic life and discussed in prior chapters. Historically, the newspaper business emphasized broad content, economies of scale from large printing presses that could produce large runs of the newspaper, and distribution across a national or regional marketplace in a timely manner. For many decades, there were few true substitutes for the newspaper's breadth and depth of coverage.[8] It remained the prime vehicle for local business to advertise their goods and services. With the advent of television news, an uneasy balance existed as long as the number of stations (and therefore content) was limited and the news and weather and sports were neatly packaged at only one time in the evening.

Gradually, cable television with its many channels could compete with the newspaper's economies of distribution to a wide audience. By the middle and late 1990s, cable and the Internet were beginning to destroy the timeliness of newspaper content by offering constant updates on a wide variety of content including news, weather, and sports. Advertisers began to flee to these newer media. The traditional model of newspapers was now in jeopardy. But what choices remained for those who headed these businesses?

When the market for music changed, the management of Tower Records simply closed their stores. When the market for movies and video games changed, Blockbuster closed stores and altered its delivery system.[9]

Over time, more changes occurred in the news industry. By the first decade of the twenty-first century, sports radio stations, including ones on satellite radio, sprang up throughout the country. Entire channels on cable television targeted subscribers with interests in the weather, food and cooking, music, sports, and many other specific areas. The newspaper lost its content advantage in all of these areas. Consumers now had little reason to buy the whole paper.

At the same time, the emergence of the Internet and smart phones spearheaded a significant decline in the marginal cost of gathering and processing information. Once the information was gathered, the transaction costs for any decision were also lowered dramatically. Consumers could shop around for the best service or good at the lowest price. This had a huge impact on newspaper advertising. Beyond destroying old models, the flow of information through the Internet also opened the door to new models of information for new markets and new means of gathering and processing information. For example, households and businesses often searched online for travel information before any customer contact was made with a traditional travel agent. More and more, no contact was made at all with any person. Instead, consumers communicate directly with vendors' computers.

## INFORMATION AS INPUT TO THE DECISION PROCESS FOR FIRMS AND HOUSEHOLDS

Trading off between the reach and richness of information has changed in recent years. Reach refers to the number of people, and the evolution of the Internet and e-mail has meant that documents and messages can reach a vast audience in seconds, unlike postal mail deliveries. Richness means bandwidth, or the amount of information that can be moved from sender to receiver. Over time, the capacity for the size and type of messages that can be moved on the Internet has increased dramatically. Information via the Internet provides for efficiency gains through lower search and transaction costs, and a richer menu of consumer and business options than could be gathered physically by visiting traditional information outlets. A broadcast television ad is less customized than personal sales pitch. Yet, over the last 20 years, ads on cable television, for example, have become more targeted to the interests of viewers. During the ads for many national shows there are ads for local automobile dealerships. In other cases the national ad is tweaked to fit the local market for a certain Internet service or television viewing option aimed at that local audience.

In a small group, information can be exchanged interactively through verbal and physical clues that give the information meaning. In contrast, broadcast and cable television or Internet messages can reach millions, but lack the clues available through conversation. E-mails can have a very different tone from what their author intended. In the past, communication of rich information required proximity and dedicated channels whose costs or physical constraints limited the size of the intended audience. Today, that is no longer true. Communication of information via the Internet to a large audience offers both reach and richness, and thereby alters the framework of the business models in fields such as newspapers, consumer advertising, and communication and public notices.

## THREE STEPS OF INFORMATION PROCESSING FOR DECISION MAKERS

For decision makers, there are three steps to processing information—gather it, interpret it, and distribute it. Within each of these steps, however, lurk potential mental biases that have prompted legendary failures in the past. Often the decision maker's inability to overcome bias is the barrier to success.

### Step One: Gathering Economic and Business Information

For decision makers, problems present themselves here in the gathering of information. The availability bias predisposes those gathering data to select the most easily available information. For Nathan Rothschild (not the baron of wine fame, although he was part of the famed Rothschild banking family), the cost of gathering information on the outcome of Waterloo, where the Duke of Wellington defeated Napoleon, was very expensive. Nathan Rothschild and his four brothers developed a network of information gatherers throughout Europe. While it is likely he did know of Napoleon's defeat a day ahead of the British government, his fortune had been made long before the event, as Nathan was a contractor with the British government in the war campaigns in Portugal and Spain. There is evidence that Nathan had bet on a protracted war, so while he made some money on the bond trade, he did lose money on his holdings of supplies intended for a long war. Nathan and his brothers were in the business of trading off information and that made them wealthy over time—not the luck of a single trade.[10]

Gathering information is a trade-off of the marginal cost of gathering the information and the marginal benefit of what that information reveals. In essence, there are search costs involved and decision makers must exercise judgment in how aggressively to pursue new information. In business, it costs little to sit at the headquarters and gather reams of information, but it is costly to get on an airplane and see what is happening out in the field. In other situations, a decision maker may learn more from telling an anecdote than reciting a series of numbers about a situation. Unfortunately, graduate business education tends to significantly overweight quantitative information and methods relative to the value of qualitative approaches. Moreover, complexity is prized in quantitative models; simple models, while practical, are not deemed elegant enough to illustrate the sophistication of the analysis. Few decision makers go by the old maxim of using the simplest means to explain situations. Instead, those with the requisite background want to show off their mathematical virtuosity—often with disastrous results. For evidence, we have the history of complicated financial trading of Long-Term Capital Management, Enron, and the complicated mathematical models that created securitization and trading schemes during the 2005 to 2008 period in residential real estate that helped intensify the Great Recession.

Limiting an information search is said to exhibit bounded rationality. In other words, people limit the search for truth because they judge that further investigation is not likely to improve their decision making.[11] This "calling it quits" is a judgment call. We all make it and sometimes we regret it. When people call it quits they are implicitly saying that the marginal cost of continued information search exceeds their expected future benefit. Unfortunately, some search only for confirmation of existing beliefs. They don't wish to examine countervailing evidence or seek different views from their own.[12] For example, a senior manager requests that a subordinate "find me a graph that supports my point." This will not likely result in either a good decision on the part of management or in career advancement for the subordinate. Yet the Columbia shuttle disaster in 2003 showed that the culture of an institution or its leadership may not allow for constructive dissent or real independent search for the best result.[13] In this case, foam had broken off in earlier shuttle flights causing little damage. Yet the same managers who signed off on the launch were responsible for determining whether the foam strikes were a flight risk. NASA showed evidence of not seeking evidence that the foam was a risk. Launch cameras were not maintained properly and provided grainy photos. The mission manager did not speak to those who were concerned—only to those who believed that the foam strikes were not a concern.

The recency effect is a particular form of the availability bias. It occurs often due to the pervasive utilization of a spreadsheet to summarize the history of phenomena. Spreadsheets are physically limited when they are printed out at meetings for presentation purposes. Owing to this, the analyst employing the spreadsheet frequently presents only the most recent data and information that will fit conveniently on a printed page. Prior historical data is ignored. As the business cycle ages, only the recent periods of economic growth appear in the spreadsheet. Downside risks are never apparent on a spreadsheet that only shows a growing economy.

In 1961, President John F. Kennedy approved an attempted invasion of Cuba that resulted in the Bay of Pigs fiasco.[14] The information gathered for the plan and the evaluation of the plan were both provided by the Central Intelligence Agency (CIA). The CIA filled a dual role as the advocate for the plan as well as the evaluator of the plan. Other experts in the Kennedy administration were not aware of the plan due to the secrecy constraint—an extreme example of asymmetric information. Asymmetric information refers to the situation where one party to the transaction has more or better information than the other. Information conveys power, and in these cases the balance of negotiating power accrues to those with the better information.[15] There was no evaluation of alternatives—it was a go/no go decision. The CIA felt they had to go forward, given all their invested time in the project (sunk cost effect). The result was a disaster for the soldiers involved and the president.

### Step Two: Interpreting the Information

For over 40 years, Tycho Brahe, the Danish astronomer, gathered observations of the planets, but it was up to Johannes Kepler to process and interpret this data and generate his three laws of planetary motion.[16] While Tycho Brahe had the data, he did not know how to interpret it. Processing and interpreting data by decision makers in business and other institutions is subject to the same biases of other human beings.

As every aficionado of detective shows knows, before interpretation, information needs to be processed, evidence goes to the lab. The few first clues usually turn out to be the deciding factor, at least in Hollywood, but in the real world a closer look at the evidence renders the real verdict. A word of caution is needed on economic data and particularly the issue of seasonal adjustment. In 2010, many economic observers hoped for a housing rebound, and in fact prices rose in the spring. A housing recovery seemed a reality. Unfortunately, housing starts, sales, and prices always tend to improve with spring owing to the strong seasonal influence on that market. Seasonal adjustment is needed for particular time series of data such as housing and retail sales, although most economic and business information includes a seasonal factor. Students of housing starts and sales in the United

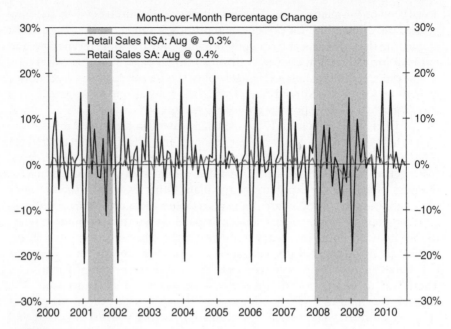

**FIGURE 5.1**    Retail Sales
*Source:* U.S. Department of Commerce.

States know they pick up in the spring, peak around midyear, and then decelerate all the way to winter. As shown in Figure 5.1, retail sales, when not seasonally adjusted (termed *NSA* in the figure), have a huge rise toward Christmas and then again around Easter, as well as during back-to-school time in the late summer. The spikes in retail sales at holidays and back-to-school are very pronounced; therefore, the raw NSA data needs to be seasonally adjusted (SA).

Unfortunately, not all data is seasonally adjusted and many series that are adjusted have different adjustment factors. Decision makers must exercise caution when comparing seasonally and not-seasonally adjusted series, and even seasonally adjusted series with different seasonal adjustment factors. For example, many unwary financial commentators note that for the birth-death adjustment of new firms, and the associated assumption of newly created or destroyed jobs, can account for an unusually large share of jobs created in any particular month.[17] Yet the birth-death adjustment is a not-seasonally adjusted series while the jobs data are seasonally adjusted. Also, seasonal adjustments have their own quirks. Two major holidays, Easter and Thanksgiving, do not occur on the same day each year, yet both significantly influence retail sales. In addition, seasonal adjustment can also be thrown off if in the prior year there was a significant snowstorm or hurricane that the seasonal adjustment process interprets as a new seasonal adjustment pattern.

## TAKING A CLOSER LOOK: INTERPRETING INFORMATION

Interpreting information is fraught with its own biases and opportunities. By 1933, Cadillac sales were down dramatically. Selling a prestige car in the Great Depression was very difficult—and perhaps not worth the effort. General Motors (GM) senior management thought about discontinuing the brand. At the time, Cadillac was not sold to black people as a matter of GM policy. Yet Nicholas Dreystadt, a German immigrant who worked at GM, discovered that blacks were often customers in the service department of dealerships. Upon investigation, Dreystadt found that black people would pay white people to buy Cadillacs for them. Many of these people were boxers, singers, and other elites of the black community. Dreystadt urged the GM senior management to pursue the black market. They did, and Cadillac sales jumped between 1933 and 1934 at a rate almost double of that of other GM cars. Dreystadt was made head of the Cadillac division and Cadillac has sold at luxury prices ever since.[18] Dreystadt had correctly interpreted the data. (It should be noted that GM was not the only automobile manufacturer that was not selling to blacks in 1933.)

Interpreting data is subject to many biases. Only a few are reviewed in this chapter, but they are very common. Longer explanations of these biases can be found in Chapter 3. And sometimes these biases can be very costly. These biases are: the confirmation bias, the anchoring bias, the illusory correlation, and framing.

The confirmation bias refers to the tendency of people to interpret information in a way that confirms their prior beliefs. People read information the way they wish to read it, not as objective observers. People select information that reinforces their expectations. In late 2009 and early 2010, real growth in the United States economy picked up, as illustrated in Figure 5.2. Those people who believed in the stimulus program initiated by the administration of President Barack Obama asserted that it was the beginning of a sustained, V-shaped economic recovery. Others thought it was a

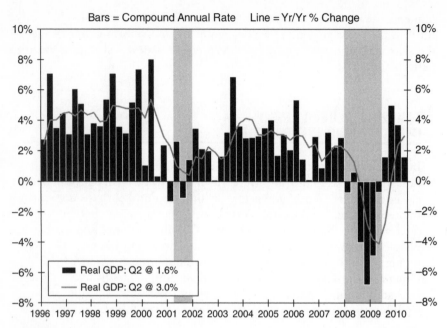

**FIGURE 5.2**   Real GDP
*Source:* U.S. Department of Commerce.

temporary blip driven by an inventory rebound and federal spending, but was not sustainable.

For many decision makers, the reality is that much of the widely disseminated economic information is volatile. Strings of strong or weak data are common and can lead to incorrect interpretations of longer-run trends. Mistakes can occur when decision makers jump on a short series of improvements as an indicator of lasting economic strength. In 2009 to 2010, the temporary improvement in the gross domestic product did not ultimately result in a strong economic recovery.

An anchoring bias refers to the tendency of people to let an arbitrary starting point influence their view of the phenomenon they are studying. During 2008, the pattern of crude oil prices, shown in Figure 5.3, set the base for price expectations going forward. Each new price could be explained, no matter how tenuously, by some set of economic factors. Equity analyst valuations and monthly economic indicator forecasts tend to anchor themselves to the most recent data. They drift over time. When the true market value or economic trend is revealed, it is often a nasty surprise.

**FIGURE 5.3**   Crude Oil
*Source:* U.S. Department of Energy.

The illusory correlation is a favorite of investors, frequently shown every day on cable business networks. Two lines on a graph are displayed and, ipso facto, a correlation is presented that demonstrates the wisdom of an investment strategy. Only later do viewers discover that the link is very tenuous and subject to many other conditions. The whole process was an illusion. In another example, a correlation that is very useful for short periods, but then fades away over time, is illustrated in Figure 5.4.

Framing refers to the tendency for analysts and decision makers to look at information through rose-colored glasses or, in other cases, green eyeshades. This attitude colors, literally, their view of the information they receive as either favoring or discouraging an activity. Does the information we receive favor opportunity or portend risk? Alexander Graham Bell, after successfully demonstrating the operation of his telephone, tried to sell the rights to Western Union. The company, which dominated the telegraph business, saw no potential in the telephone. Many decisions on mergers and acquisitions are framed in terms of risk or opportunity. Where one firm moves ahead, another firm with the same information will not take the

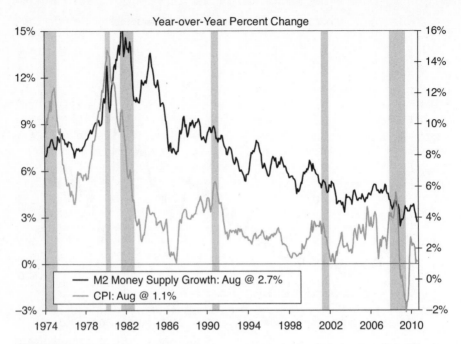

**FIGURE 5.4**  M2 Money Supply Growth and Inflation
*Source:* Federal Reserve Board, U.S. Department of Labor and Wells Fargo
Securities, LLC.

plunge. Venture capital decision making is the essence of framing decisions
as opportunities to succeed or to fail. Each venture capital decision reflects a
balance of risk and opportunity. Where one venture capitalist might see risk
the other sees opportunity. Where Portugal saw Columbus's adventure as
too risky, Spain saw it as opportunity. Creating what might be involves a lot
more effort than staying with what is. Fortunes are made, or lost, in being
there at the beginning and framing decisions as opportunities or flops. Low
initial public offering prices of stock in software and high-tech companies
have often turned out to be great investments.

## Step Three: Distribute Information

How information is distributed is often as important as the information
itself. Do we have the right target audience for our message? Queen Elizabeth
I, in preparing for the Spanish Armada, had men stationed along the cliffs
of England and Wales who built bonfires throughout southern England to

announce the arrival of the ships. Therefore she was alerted sooner than she could have been by a man on a horse, and so her troops and the city were ready for any intended Spanish landing. The failure to communicate is often the source of friendly fire on the battlefield.[19]

In the past 20 years, the model for distributing information both in offices and in homes has changed dramatically. Mail, phone, and the fax have given way to electronic messages. Phillip Evans and Thomas S. Wurster detail how the distribution of information altered the economics of the distribution of the Encyclopedia Britannica, which was sold primarily by individuals door to door.[20] Now the Britannica is online, making this form of selling obsolete. This type of intensive personal selling was also characteristic of some types of insurance, many personal products, travel, and the buying and selling of automobiles and real estate—all of which are now sold more extensively on the Internet than in the door-to-door model, as information is distributed to potential customers on the Internet on a 24/7 basis.

Today, information is increasingly distributed via the Internet and so are many of our financial and personal transactions. People buy insurance, pay their bills, and get paid for their work in electronic transactions. Internet advertising has substituted for other forms of ads for many companies. Once again, the model for seller and buyer information exchange about services and products has changed. Moreover, customers expect to communicate with companies electronically as well.

Likewise, economic research today is broadly distributed by many different formats such as via the Internet, podcasts, and digital tapings that are available through online streaming of conferences and meetings. Beyond this breadth of distribution through several formats, electronic distribution by the Internet, for example, can be with a brief message or an extended document with accompanying attachments. In other cases, short bits of information can be sent out by an instant messenger or Twitter. Just 10 years ago, fax and regular mail were the common means of transmitting information to clients. Today, e-mail, Twitter, and text are the means of quick communication of timely economic information.

What has happened is that the marginal benefit of faster information delivery has speeded up since the days of Waterloo, but the principle of the value of timely information continues. The value of fast, accurate information has risen dramatically for many investors and decision makers. This is best exemplified by the rise of hedge fund and electronic trading strategies that trade off the differences in expected versus actual numbers and program their trading based on such differences. Web sites provide a library of recently published data available to review at any time and many brokerage firms supply trading web sites for the individual investor. Here the marginal benefit of timely information has risen while the marginal cost of electronic delivery has declined. As a result, the investment professional has more information at a lower cost.

## INFORMATION IN THE DECISION MAKER'S FRAMEWORK

Our model stresses three steps regarding information that have value in decision making—gathering, interpretation, and distribution. This sequence suggests implications for breaking down or building on the business model structure. In some cases, the framework can be fragmented to split the delivery of information from a product. In other cases, a business or institution may want to bundle its offerings to customers around a core franchise and grow market share by offering a combination of product and information. Some companies will distinguish their brand by the information content (book reviews in Amazon) while others will see their identity disappear (Tower Records). On the downside are the choke points in the distribution channels, network, and local distribution of a product as witnessed in the Fox/Cablevision dispute in Philadelphia in 2010. The distribution of content must sometimes pass through a single or limited number or capacity of the delivery system so that the content can be limited or, in the case of Philadelphia cable viewers, not available at all.

Most businesses have stressed that their product and their information about their product are tied together. The best source of information about the product is the seller. But over the last 20 years, the advice industry (magazines, newspapers, CNBC, Angie's List, blogs, etc.) has provided an alternative source of information about products and services independent of the primary provider of the good or service. This is especially true for economic and business information. Federal and state agencies produce most of the economic information. Yet, as a matter of policy, these agencies do not comment on the implications, economic or political, of the data. Many private agencies also produce economic information and, generally, are very careful about commenting on such information. For consumer products, product evaluation (*Consumer Reports*) and automobile reports (*Edmunds*) have been around for years. For economic and business information, there are multiple sources of commentary on each statistical release.

With the Internet and various information networks, the amount and quality of information on products and commentary about their value has risen dramatically. Economics is one of those products. Economic information is available on a number of government and private web sites and many blogs are more than happy to indicate the importance or irrelevance of any piece of information.

## INFORMATION AS PART OF THE BUSINESS MODEL

In our dynamic decision-making framework, information sits astride any specification of supply and demand fundamentals. Information enters the decision-making chain by providing confirmation or challenging observations to any business framework. Information often represents change. Decision makers then must see the implications and feedback effects of that information on their business plan or framework.

For example, the demand to buy an automobile is also a demand for information from the customer. Moreover, many customers are skeptical of the salesperson's claims and the manufacturer's suggested retail price. So there is a market demand for information about the car and a supply of car information. When the information supply increases, the ability of the buyer to bargain increases and the profit margins on the car are likely to narrow. Where product information is readily available online (e.g., on automobiles, books, hotels, and airlines), pricing margins become very thin. In other areas (health care providers, attorneys), pricing margins are still very wide because information on price and quality are difficult to obtain. The demand elasticity in products and services is directly impacted by the availability of information about that product.

In other cases, the delivery of the product or service has become separated from the payment. Except for fast-food and convenience stores, the direct exchange of cash for product is being broken down—often with the assistance of the Internet. PayPal and other vendors now fragment the transaction model of many businesses. The financing of car and furniture purchases as well as many forms of business equipment investment are increasingly being separated from the actual seller of the good. The buyer pays one vendor while obtaining the product from another vendor. Each actor in the transaction process benefits from his or her source of competitive advantage.

Networks have developed to share information on economic issues, creating greater knowledge about economic conditions and the risks and opportunities in the marketplace. Suppliers of economic information, such as blogs, build their market shares by developing network economies of scale that offer a greater opportunity to distribute information and interpretation of economic events. The more individuals are on the network, the greater the value of being connected, as evident in the case of Facebook, Twitter, and other social networks. These networks offer economies of scale and the interchange of information offers a self-enforcing incentive to maintain connectivity to share information.

Almost every restaurant, supermarket, or shopping outlet has its own web site and asks customers to join its e-mail list for deals and steals. Any financial service company worth its balance sheet also has a web site for the exchange of information. Well-designed and easy to use web sites (that is, where the gathering of information is clear to the user) gain market share for their companies. A successful financial web site reflects the elements of content, function, design, and usability. Content should reflect the expectations of the potential user. Moreover, content must be updated to reflect the interests of the user. Function refers to the tasks the web site wishes to make available to the user. In the twenty-first century, users want to access many functions of the financial services web sites; therefore, firms are challenged to provide the broad set of functions customers expect. Design, like fashion, should be eye-catching and appealing. Placement of the content along with the images is a source of balance in design. Finally, usability reflects the ability of the user to navigate the web site with ease.

As market share grows through web site usage, many company sites can reach a critical mass to become desired sites. Google and Yahoo! compete to be the desired search engine for many users. Amazon and Barnes & Noble compete as the primary source for book lovers. But being first with scale does not guarantee a perpetual or even temporary monopoly, as seen with AOL and then Yahoo!. Each rose to the top, but lost that position in a constantly evolving competitive landscape.

The impact of new forms of information delivery can be seen in many other areas. In real estate, the multiple listing service (MLS) books were a unique choke point since the customer had to go through a broker to see the MLS listings for information for both real estate agents and home buyers. The choke point in any information system is the point in the system that acts as a filter through which all information must pass. The choke point can be an office, a person, or a location. The admissions office in a hospital is the choke point for gathering and processing all new patient information. The MLS book was the source for data about homes, came only in printed form, and was guarded very carefully by real estate agents. With the growth of online real estate information, the advantage of the MLS book fell by the wayside as brokers sought to compete for customers and realized that customers wanted the access to the information at times that were convenient to them. In banking, the competitive advantage was the bank's extensive knowledge of its customers and the dominance of check writing as a means of payment. Financial transactions often required a trip to a branch bank for deposits and withdrawals. Today, customers do not need the physical structure to accept or deliver cash, transfer funds, or perform many other routine tasks. Paying bills has become an increasingly electronic, not physical, function. Meanwhile, for many customers, financial switching costs have dropped, so changing banks and getting automobile loans or home loans from different institutions is very common. Because of this, banks have to develop new ways of generating customer loyalty. Reluctance to change a past winning formula that no longer applies has cost many a bank its profitability and sometimes its very existence. This pattern will continue in the future.

## CHOICES AND INFORMATION CHOKE POINTS

Ad revenues are a driving force on the Internet and the bargaining power of Internet sites will shift as a result of changes in the ability of a web site to dominate its product category. Perceptions of an informational advantage certainly helped the Drudge Report, an online news service, in its search for a market niche. Business models compete on the quality of information. This is especially true of web sites that offer product and service evaluations for readers. Once a web site business model is established, changes occur in the competitive viability of that model, which affects on the firm's model as well as its competitors. Choices then have to be made and a new framework develops. Information remains a very dynamic factor in determining competitive advantage—not only in terms of the traditional form of corporate secrets, but also the means of communication between buyers and sellers. Information gathering, processing, and distribution are also essential in the process of assessing risk, and it is that subject we turn to in the next chapter.

## DISCUSSION QUESTIONS

1. Asymmetric information is characteristic of many economic exchange actions in the economy. Akerlof focuses on the buying and selling of used automobiles in his article on lemons.

    Buying a home is another example of asymmetric information. The seller of the home knows far better than the buyer the character of the home.

    a. What is the role of the listing in the home buying situation?
    b. What types of information not on the listing would the buyer wish to know that the seller may know given the seller's experience of living in the home?
    c. How does this asymmetric information case influence the potential to buy/sell and its associated risks from the buyer's point of view?

    d. To paraphrase Oscar Hammerstein, there is no limit to the number of people that turn away from a badly written listing. Would it also be true about the number of people drawn to a good listing? Given your experience, compare the representation of the house in the listing and your impressions when you actually saw the property.

2. Social networking has become an issue where individuals reveal too much about themselves or sometimes distort their real picture. How might social networking reflect the asymmetric problem of information?

3. For many years newspapers were famous for their global network of correspondents (gathering information), their writing and commentary on events (interpretation), and their ability to deliver the news in the morning (distribution). However, in recent years newspapers have fallen on hard times. In April 2010, The Tribune Company (*Chicago Tribune, Los Angeles Tribune*) filed for bankruptcy.

    a. How have newspapers today been challenged on all three fronts: gathering, interpretation, and distribution of the news?

    b. Ads for automobiles, and jobs were large revenue generators for the newspapers. What changed to drive down those sources?

    c. Television did not appear to be the driving factor in the demise of the newspaper, but the Internet did. Why was the distribution of information on the Internet so much more devastating to the newspaper model than television was?

    d. In 2010, Bloomberg L.P. took over *Business Week*. What does that say about the weekly business and news magazine business and how they distribute information?

    e. Does content trump distribution?

4. Reach and richness were two characteristics of information that were considered in a trade-off for the audience. Radio and television had reach, but the richness of the programming was not up to what people expected. Even with 300 channels many people complain there is nothing to watch. Books have richness, but nobody reads anymore. However, the Internet appears to provide both richness and reach.

    a. In what ways does the Internet overcome the problems of both reach and richness when we compare it to radio and television?

    b. Unlike radio, the Internet provides pictures. Unlike television, the Internet provides text. How has this duality altered the use of advertising by companies to reach their clients?

    c. Today, every company has an Internet site that provides information about their products, services, and often the prices of their wares. This all makes the consumer a better shopper, but what are the advantages for the company?

    d. What reach/richness do the social networking channels offer relative to the Internet?

# NOTES

1. *Trading Places*, Paramount Pictures, 1983.
2. George A. Akerlof, "The Market for 'Lemons': Quality Uncertainty and the Market Mechanism," *Quarterly Journal of Economics* 84(3) (August 1970): 488–500.
3. N. Gregory Mankiw and Ricardo Reis, "Sticky Information versus Sticky Prices: A Proposal to Replace the New Keynesian Phillips Curve," *Quarterly Journal of Economics* 107(4) (2002): 1295–1328.
4. Philip B. Evans and Thomas S. Wurster, "Strategy and the New Economics of Information," *Harvard Business Review* (September–October, 1997).
5. Yochai Benkler expands on this point with his concept of a "networked information economy" in *The Wealth of Networks* (New Haven: Yale University Press, 2006).
6. Joseph Schumpeter, *Capitalism, Socialism and Democracy* (New York: Harper & Row 1975, originally published 1942).
7. Joseph L. Bower and Clayton M. Christensen, "Disruptive Technologies: Catching the Wave," *Harvard Business Review* (January–February, 1995).
8. Evans and Wurster above provide a review of the production and distribution economies of scale in newspapers.
9. On September 23, 2010, Blockbuster filed for bankruptcy.
10. Niall Ferguson, *The Ascent of Money* (New York: Penguin, 2008).
11. See Herbert Simon, *Reason in Human Affairs* (Palo Alto, CA: Stanford University Press, 1983).
12. Arthur Schlesinger Jr., *A Thousand Days* (Boston: Houghton Mifflin, 1965). Schlesinger provides an interesting account of the Bay of Pigs and the tragic results of seeking only confirming information and counsel.
13. Columbia Accident Investigation Board, Columbia Accident Investigation Board Report (Washington, DC: Government Printing Office, 2003).
14. Irving L. Janis, *Victims of Groupthink*, 2nd ed. (Boston: Houghton Mifflin, 1982).
15. In 2001, the Nobel Prize was awarded to George Akerlof and Michael Spence for their analysis of decision making in markets with asymmetric information.
16. Max Casper, *Kepler*, trans. and ed. C. Doris Hellman (New York: Dover, 1993).
17. The birth-death adjustment attempts to control for the start and end of business firms as these births/deaths will impact the number of jobs being created each month in the U.S. economy. See the Bureau of Labor Statistics web site, www.bls.gov/web/empsit/cesbd.htm.
18. John Steele Gordon, "The Man Who Saved Cadillac," in *The Business of America* (New York: Walker and Co., 2001).
19. Scott A. Snook, *Friendly Fire: The Accidental Shootdown of U.S. Black Hawks over Northern Iraq* (Princeton, NJ: Princeton University Press, 2000).
20. Phillip Evans and Thomas S. Wurster, *Blown to Bits: How the New Economics of Information Transforms Strategy* (Cambridge, MA: Harvard Business School Press, 2000).

## RECOMMENDED READING FOR SERIOUS PLAYERS

Benkler, Yochai. *The Wealth of Networks*. New Haven: Yale University Press, 2006.

Evans, Phillip, and Thomas S. Wurster. *Blown to Bits: How the New Economics of Information Transforms Strategy*. Cambridge, MA: Harvard Business School Press, 2000.

Gordon, John Steele. *The Business of America*. New York: Walker and Co., 2001.

# CHAPTER 6

# Risk Modeling and Assessment

I n June 1863, the Confederate States of America issued the Seven Percent Cotton Loan. The principal amount was not paid in Confederate dollars or payable at the Confederate capital of Richmond. Instead, the payments were set in sterling or French francs, in 40 installments to be paid in Paris, London, Amsterdam, or Frankfurt at the option of the bondholder. In addition, payment could be received in cotton, instead of currency, at the option of the bondholder at any time not later than six months after the ratification of a treaty of peace after the war.[1]

This bond structure reflects a keen sense by the issuer of the risks for the investor. The risk of devaluation was covered by payment in sterling or francs. The payment in cotton was a hedge against inflation. The option to convert at any time was a hedge against the fortunes of war and sovereign and political risk.

In this case the elements of risk can be seen, especially the information asymmetry about the state of the war. Clearly, European investors could not monitor how the war was going as well as the bond issuer, the Confederacy, could. In addition, the changing fortunes of the war over the period of the bond's lifetime suggest the dynamic character of risk and the constant need for updating of the decision framework and monitoring by the bond investor. In June 1863, the Confederate army at Vicksburg was still holding out against General Grant and General Robert E. Lee had just entered Pennsylvania on his invasion of the North. By the end of 1864, Sherman was at the doors of Savannah.

Economic growth does not proceed in a straight line. Top line sales, input costs, and profitability vary as well. In fact, macroeconomic risk and volatility is an ongoing character of economic life. Economic risk is never eliminated, perfectly hedged, or perfectly transferred, as was seen with the latest variant of the free lunch, subprime lending and credit default swaps. In recent years, risk may have given the appearance of being transferred away to others with respect to subprime lending. However, many contracts actually allowed the owners of securitized products to put the burden of the risk back to the originator of these products. These so-called claw backs reflect the reality that risk can be transferred, but it never goes away. At the end of the day somebody retains the risk. In the capital markets, reputation is paramount to getting deals done with the least expense and maintaining the trust of clients, which unfortunately has not been done well in recent years, but that's another story. When the inevitable economic shock appears, as it always does, the discovery begins of who is left without a chair to sit on when the music ends.

Risk is also dynamic, changing as the business cycle matures. Interest in risk control is highly correlated with shocks to the financial system. Long periods of financial stability tend to produce amnesia on the part of investors and senior management, as every opportunity for investment appears risk-free. Only recent history matters and everyone forgets the distant past.[2] This decision to overweight the recent past gives way to the recency bias in decision making.

In this chapter, the economic modeling and framework are covered, as well as the surrounding risk and the decision-making problems that assessing risk presents. As discussed before, the economic factors influencing the performance of any institution, private or public, can be the driving force. And biases in decision making can occur anywhere along the dynamic and interactive path toward decisions, and can drive the best-intentioned leaders off track.

## ECONOMICS AND THE RISK MODELING PROCESS

The focus here is on economic risk: What is the probability that a decision maker's view of the economic model of the world or the changes in the five economic factors we have focused on—growth, inflation, rates, dollar, and profits—is different from what was expected. Moreover, what is the difference between what a decision maker expects and what he gets? It is that difference that drives economic behavior.

There are two sources of economic risk:

1. A business leader's framework for how the economy works could be wrong.
2. How a business leader measures and evaluates changes within that framework could be askew.

Unlike the physical models in the hard sciences, modeling errors in economics are fairly common due to the unpredictable nature of people.

Economic models are simplifications of real experience and as such do not capture every type of behavior, only the most typical behavior given the assumptions made. During the 1970s, the model of the Phillips Curve postulated a trade-off between inflation and unemployment. Higher levels of inflation were associated with lower levels of unemployment. From 2009 to 2010, a model of the national economy was employed to project the job response to a stimulus program. Unfortunately, unemployment rose instead of declining once the fiscal stimulus program was put into place. The fiscal stimulus acted as a finger in the dike that stopped the flooding. Unfortunately, though, it was not enough to accomplish the cleanup, which has been hindered by all the credit/financial barriers to recovery that came along with the recession.

The Phillips Curve incorporates three aspects of the dynamic character of the economic system:

1. The expected level of inflation has an independent influence on the actual level of inflation.
2. The difference between actual employment and the perceived full employment rate is a driver of the actual inflation rate.
3. Economic shocks, particularly supply shocks in this case, have an independent impact on inflation as exemplified by the oil price crisis of the 1970s. In the short run, supply shocks and frictional unemployment have an influence on inflation. The real economy and inflation are not independent factors in the economy. In addition, inflation has inertia in the sense that past inflation influences expectations of future inflation.

Unexpected inflation brings its own risks as it redistributes wealth arbitrarily between lenders and creditors, between savers and fixed-income pensioners and speculators. Higher than expected inflation, typical of the 1970s, allows debtors to repay their debts in cheaper dollars than when the original debt was assumed. In contrast, if inflation declines faster than expected, as in the early 1980s, the debtor pays back in more expensive dollars than was assumed when the original loan was made. Variable inflation introduces uncertainty and individuals and investors become increasingly risk-averse. During the late 1970s, high inflation was associated with a bull market in short-term investing, as in money market funds.

The following are two cases in which the Phillips Curve model failed to account for the actual outcomes. In the first case, the response of workers to inflation changed over time. When inflation was a surprise in the early post–World War II period, workers interpreted a nominal wage increase as enhanced reward for work, as an increase in the real wage. But over time, workers began to anticipate inflation and an increase in the nominal wage did not elicit an increase in labor supply. On the contrary, workers were less willing to supply labor at any given wage unless wage gains compensated for expected future inflation. The inner workings of the labor market were changing. Simply put, the model specification missed the response that workers anticipated as opposed to not anticipating inflation.

In the second case, the model itself failed to anticipate all the simultaneous changes that were going on in the labor market and economy at the time. Factors that influenced the labor market were not properly represented in the original model. A number of variables were simply missing from it.

The model decision makers apply may also suffer from the absence of a critical variable or the inclusion of an irrelevant variable. Both of these shortcomings are, no doubt, familiar to investors. On the one hand, the absence of a critical variable such as accurate knowledge of the true state of Greek sovereign finances was a telling issue in setting yield spreads and bank risk credit default swap spreads. On the other, many decision makers have followed a false indicator of success too far down a road only to find themselves on a path to failure.

The second source of economic risk comes from the simple difference between what leaders expect and what they actually observe in the marketplace. Each month on a Friday morning, private sector economists and the business and financial media wait with great anticipation for the employment report issued by the Bureau of Labor Statistics. Statistical work supports the view that differences of the actual from the expected employment release generates the greatest single movement in financial asset prices of any regular piece of economic information.

What is significant here is that difference between actual and anticipated economic information is actually the norm rather than the exception.[3] In Figure 6.1, the inherent volatility of the gross domestic product (GDP) rate of growth for the United States economy over recent years can be seen. In Figure 6.2, the range has been drawn, as measured, as two standard deviations, around the average growth rate of the GDP. In Table 6.1, the volatility of growth in the GDP suggests a significant level of risk of disappointment or surprise for decision makers who often rely on straight-line projections of future growth in the economy.

Moreover, the more variable the economic time series, such as inflation, the more uncertain its future path and thereby the greater the risk aversion of any decision maker. When assessing risk, the role of the law of large numbers comes into play. That is, increasing a sample size will increase the probability that the observed sample probability will vary from the true probability by some stated amount, no matter how small. However, there is still no guarantee that the right answer has been obtained, only that it is closer as the sample increases.

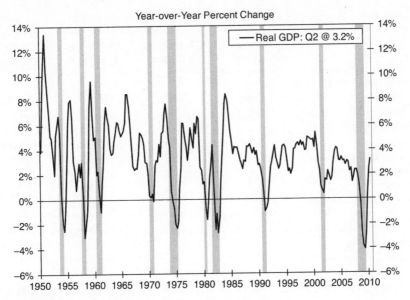

**FIGURE 6.1** Real GDP
*Source:* U.S. Department of Commerce and Wells Fargo Securities, LLC.

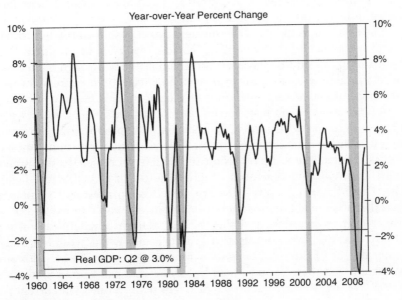

**FIGURE 6.2** Real GDP (Volume Growth)
*Source:* U.S. Department of Commerce and Wells Fargo Securities, LLC.

**TABLE 6.1**  Volatility of Past Business Cycles

|  | Q3-1982 to Q1-1991 | Q2-1991 to Q3-2001 | Q3-2001 to Q2-2009 | Q3-1982 to Q2-2009 |
|---|---|---|---|---|
| **Gross Domestic Product** | | | | |
| Mean | 3.86 | 3.30 | 1.81 | 3.10 |
| Standard Deviation | (1.97) | (1.5) | (2.1) | (1.98) |
| **Consumer Price Index** | | | | |
| Mean | 3.90 | 2.75 | 2.61 | 3.10 |
| Standard Deviation | (1.14) | (0.67) | (1.31) | (1.17) |
| **Corporate Profits** | | | | |
| Mean | 10.48 | 5.78 | 6.50 | 7.44 |
| Standard Deviation | (13.12) | (8.22) | (15.33) | (12.19) |

*Source:* U.S. Department of Commerce, U.S. Department of Labor, and Wells Fargo Securities, LLC.

Expectations of future financial activity also have an influence on interest rates today. A major source of risk today is the high levels of sovereign debt outstanding and expected in the future relative to the ability of countries to pay that debt. In his paper, Thomas Laubach (then economist at the Federal Reserve) presented evidence that future United States fiscal deficits have a modest influence on current interest rates.[4]

Moreover, during 2010, there was a possible shift in the link between federal spending and the economy. The administration of President Barack Obama utilized traditional Keynesian stimulus policy through higher spending to stimulate growth. However, concerns have been expressed that the financing burden of such spending in the future is actually contradictory to growth. Some economists have argued that real interest rates will rise in response to the debt burden. In addition, they propose that current low interest rates have hidden this impact. Slow economic growth has increased worries about a double dip recession and thereby increased the risk premium on private credit and generated a flight to safety to United States Treasury debt. These flights to safety reflect the reaction of investors to rising fears of weaker economic growth. Such weaker growth would be associated with weaker corporate profits and thereby less margin of safety on corporate debt. In this case, investors shift to Treasury debt which would represent a greater degree of safety of consistent interest payments. Other economists have countered these propositions by saying that the United States is not Greece. We are a larger country that issues debt in our own currency and have stronger economic prospects over time, and therefore, we do not face the same debt challenge as does Greece. But risk premiums are not black and white. There are gradations that, over time, can increasingly, and sometimes very rapidly, deteriorate. The nonlinear movement of risk premiums in response to unexpected news is a singular aspect of the challenges faced by decision makers.

In business models, analysts frequently hypothesize small changes in an independent factor and calculate modest changes in their dependent variable. Yet, in the real world, small continued, regular changes in any independent variable of interest are likely to generate uneven changes in the dependent variable. And, at some point, it may lead to an explosive movement in results. Remember, low probability events occurring 5 percent of the time still occur 5 out of 100 times and would appear outside the 95 percent confidence interval. These types of events are unlikely, but still possible.

Differences between expected and actual inflation also drive the movements of both demand and supply in the aggregate economy over time. In the late 1970s and early 1980s, an unwelcome upswing for inflation altered household wealth assessments and led to changes in saving and consumption patterns. On the supply side, the experience of the oil price shocks of the 1970s and 1980s is illustrative. In the 1970s, higher than expected oil prices led to a decline in output and a rise for inflation (a condition termed *stagflation*) in the short run. During the mid-1980s, oil prices fell sharply, thereby lowering inflation and leading to a shift outward in aggregate supply, and therefore output. For decision makers, the focus should remain on the difference between expected and realized inflation that drives the supply and demand forces for the macroeconomy, not simply the inflation rate itself.

## HOUSING PRICES: DEFLATION AND THE SHOCK TO THE AMERICAN PSYCHE

Since World War II, home prices in the United States, on average, have recorded a long string of successive increases. In fact, rising home prices were taken as a given; in other words, they were expected to rise on a regular basis. Two aspects of this should have given pause to decision makers. While prices had risen, a fundamental question should have been: Why are these price increases occurring? What were the fundamental reasons for such a long streak of price increases? Without answers to these questions, many decision makers and homeowners were shocked by the home price correction of recent years. Homeowners had a significant amount of their wealth in their homes (Figure 6.3). Second, decision makers needed to ask: Were the expectations of home price increases self-fulfilling such that lenders

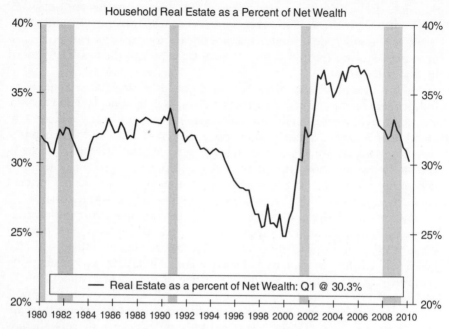

**FIGURE 6.3**   Household Real Estate as a Percent of Net Wealth
*Source:* Federal Reserve Board and Wells Fargo Securities, LLC.

offered credit and buyers took credit not on the basis of the borrower's credit but upon the expected appreciation of the property itself? For home buyers the long-held assumption was that home prices, despite some dips, always trended up over time. In fact, they did, as illustrated in Figure 6.4. For a decision-making framework, however, there was a failure to recognize a systematic risk in lending that was reinforced over time by the presence of the illusory correlation that home prices always went up with time. This does not reflect the real model of home prices based on income, interest rates, and credit quality. When these factors changed, they drove home prices down despite the march of time. In 2010, the housing correction continued as home sales remained weak and a persistent excess inventory of housing existed. These patterns continue to test the basic assumptions of homeowners.

Finally, there was a fundamental challenge to the home finance model that represented a risk to lenders that was overlooked. Over time, the social stigma for defaulting on debt has declined with so much credit available and with reduced penalties for default.[5] Therefore, for some groups of

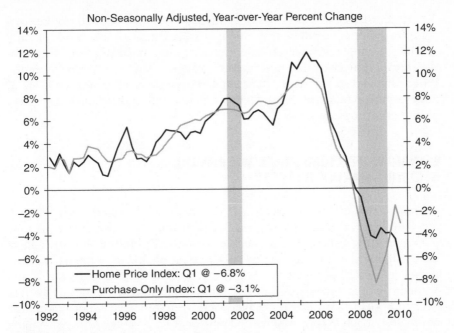

**FIGURE 6.4**   FHFA Home Price Indexes
*Source:* Federal Housing Finance Agency and Wells Fargo Securities, LLC.

households the commitment to pay off debts declined and this, along with reduced information costs, has been associated with a rise in bankruptcies.[6] Over the years, this commitment by borrowers to pay off debt appears to have diminished as the memories and stories on the Great Depression have faded. As a result, borrowers are more willing to walk away from a mortgage than before, which again reflects a change in the model of risk in the housing market. Of course, the willingness of borrowers to walk away from mortgage payments raises the risk of lending, which alters the distribution of risk and reward in the credit markets. All these changes imply a structural change in the relationship between risk and reward in household lending that, in part, was overlooked by many before the Great Recession.

One other important source of risk in economic affairs is the political risk involved when public policy makers raise the risk profile of any activity. There is a time inconsistency problem in decision making between public and private decision makers. Private policy makers have a time horizon much longer than does the political official who is looking at the next election.

Major turns in the elections of 1932, 1980, 2008, and 2010 resulted in a major turn in public policy while many private decision makers had already had long-term plans in place. Discretionary policy at the public level reflects the shifting power of different interest groups at different times. Since the Progressive era in the early twentieth century, we have seen a sequence of policy turns on taxes, trade, and regulation that reflect the changing fortunes of interest groups over time.[7]

## MANAGING ECONOMIC RISK WITHIN THE DECISION-MAKING PROCESS

Economic risk offers two challenges to any decision maker. First, there is a definite cyclical character to risk. Society's tolerance of risk rises as time passes since the last crisis. Most people drive very carefully after witnessing a car crash, but the next day they go back to their old habits. Similarly, as time passes since the last recession, people are more willing to take risks again. Second, there is an evolution of risk taking that, like the economy, evolves over time such that risk taking/aversion has its own cycle, but risk-taking never ends back where it started. For example, leverage and risk taking have risen since World War II despite recessions and sharp financial corrections. People appear to learn from each recession, but what they learn to do is better structure their risk taking, not to avoid risk altogether. Financial products such as commercial paper (Penn Central Railroad) and high-yield bonds (Drexel Burnham) were an integral part of earlier financial corrections, yet today they are seen as part of the fabric of a normal operating financial system.

The foremost challenge for decision makers is to shift to rewarding problem prevention as well as problem solving. Using an effective model to define their risks and then monitoring the changes to their model is the most effective approach to defining risk exposure.

### The Initial Framework: Specifying a Useful Risk Model

History only allows one sample of the economy and the capital markets. With thousands of separate and randomly distributed numbers, a model of the economy and of risk reflects what people have experienced now, not what they can observe from hundreds of experiments. Economic risk can be represented by volatility in three areas; growth (recessions and booms), interest rates (savings and loan association crisis of the early 1980s), and exchange rate risk (Franklin National in 1974, the euro in 2010, and possibly the American dollar and yuan in the near future). For asset prices, housing price volatility in recent years and the dot-com boom of the late 1990s represent risk in a way that was not anticipated by earlier model makers.

Traditionally, risk is modeled based on the behavior of the mean and standard deviation of any economic series. For example, in Figure 6.2, the mean and one standard deviation of economic growth are readily apparent. Risk modeling assumes that any model that is developed depends on just two numbers, the mean and standard deviation. This is acceptable if security returns for equities and bonds, for example, are normally distributed. But with evidence of a variable standard deviation, the distribution of errors is not symmetrically distributed, about the mean and outliers are likely present. Sometimes economic models are developed on poor sampling, as evidenced by the polling conducted for the magazine *Literary Digest*. In the 1936 presidential election, the magazine surveyed people selected from telephone directories and automobile registrations. The results suggested that Alfred Landon would defeat President Franklin Roosevelt. However, this procedure did not yield a representative sample of voters, since at that time people who had a telephone and/or a car were upper middle/upper income and certainly above average in income and would have more likely been Republican than Democrat at the time. In fact, Roosevelt won in a landslide. Moreover, new economic information arrives in a random fashion. The economy moves in unpredictable ways even though a well-designed model tries to track it. In models, changes in economic factors are arrayed according to normal distribution, but such changes are likely to arrive in non-normal ways. Finally, when analysts develop models we assume that changes in economic factors occur much more often than extreme influences, both good and bad.

Bennett W. Golub and Leo M. Tilman (managing director and director of risk management respectively at BlackRock, Inc.) provide a practical taxonomy of risk management.[8] They reinforce the view that there must be a fundamental model around risk assessment if risk is to be properly analyzed. Golub and Tilman suggest that first an analyst must "identify the relevant systematic risk factors." This can be broadened to say that analysts must speculate on the relationship of these risk factors to their target measure of risk and be aware of any interrelationships between the variables under discussion. There must be a model of what variables drive an analyst's risk assessment, how these variables relate to his objective measure of risk, and, finally, what relationships lurk between his independent drivers of risk such that any of these relationships could upset the analyst's valuation. Golub and Tilman identify the failure of missing knowledge or overlooked variables. For example, an analyst could look at the sovereign debt crisis in Europe and suggest that failure to account for the debt overhanging in Greece misled many investors to underprice risk. In an economic model, these missing variables are a typical problem in research. They lead to accepting the statistical significance of other risk factors, although those factors might not be as significant if the missing factors were included in the model.[9]

In any attempt to identify relevant systematic risk factors, it is clear that some risk factors are not observable with the same history and consistency of measurement. For example, growth rates in many emerging economies, such as China, are rough guesses at best. Measured inflation is very sensitive to what is included in the market basket. Exchange rates have their own history of political management for economic gain. In some areas, there aren't enough data available in a timely manner to estimate risk. State and local income and employment data would be very useful in estimating household delinquency patterns. But such data is slow in coming and often of only rough accuracy. When analysts deal with such omitted economic variables, they find themselves with biased estimates of the significance of other risk factors to the extent that the correlation coefficient between omitted and included variables is very high.[10]

When analysts measure risk exposure they employ various independent risk factors. They also recognize, however, that economic risk factors seldom move in isolation, all else the same, ceteris paribus. So the estimated change in risk exposure may reflect the pattern of multiple factors moving together. This is the statistical problem termed *multicolinearity*. Also, as seen in financial shocks such as the failure of Lehman Brothers, economic models may be helpful for small changes in exogenous risk factors, but when changes are large, the path of risk exposure is very hard to anticipate. Finally, analysts have a problem with the simultaneous change in several risk factors in an open market economy once they take their model out of the test tube. Most risk models are tested by changing one economic factor at a time, for example, growth or interest rates. However, once out of the test tube and into the real world we get multiple independent changes and a multitude of outcomes.

## Biases in Decision Making and Building the Framework

At each stage in an analyst's decision-making process, biases will divert her from her goal of designing a successful decision-making model. In building a model framework, analysts gather information and then figure out a model that defines how they see the world. Three issues face analysts when developing a framework for any business model. The first is anchoring bias. The economic outlook is often anchored with reference to the current state of the world. If it is an economic boom time, the model starts with the assumption of a continued boom. Many decision makers get caught up in the current enthusiasm and overpay for optimistic assessments of the future, with little consideration of the possible downside to the current boom. In contrast, during a recession, an economic recovery appears a long way away. The challenge here is to not get caught up in the enthusiasm of the moment, but rather to maintain a longer-term view of risk and reward in the economy and financial markets.

Anchoring biases limit choices. They cause business leaders to make choices based on the path with which they are familiar. They become comfortable with their spreadsheet models, the linear relationships of the models, and even the precise solutions that are generated by those relationships. For example, Avery Sewell of Montgomery Ward was so mentally fixated on the experience of the past that he failed to anticipate the growth and diversity of consumer spending in the post–WWII period. In 1946, Montgomery Ward was as large as Sears. By 2001 it was closed by its then owner General Electric. Such is the price of opportunity lost because of an anchoring bias.[11]

The second issue facing analysts is as any analyst builds a model, there is a tendency to seek information that confirms the analyst's prior beliefs—how he would like the world to be—rather than seeking a balanced assessment of the world as it is. This is the confirmation bias. Later in this chapter, this bias is explored as it pertains to the subprime mortgage market.

The third issue in building models is the tendency to find a relationship that analysts believe exists, foregoing a look at the actual data. Analysts find that two factors are related, but the relationship, or correlation, is an illusion. In doing research, analysts often overlook certain factors, known as *missing variables*, that are the true driving factors of a risk that analysts seek to control. In this case, analysts are more focused on another factor that appears related but is not the underlying driving factor. This illusory correlation leads to the problem of autocorrelation in analysts' estimates; that is, they find that their errors today are related to their statistical errors of yesterday.[12]

Finally, in risk assessment there is a tendency for risk decisions to reflect how analysts frame the risk and reward trade-off. A risk-averse organization tends to bias each decision in a way that will avoid risk. A risk-seeking organization tends to downplay the risk in favor of the possibility of expected rewards. Framing decisions tends to limit choices in favor of or biased against risk where a more objective assessment of the risk in the economy is needed.

## Interdependencies among Risks in the Framework

Golub and Tilman's work argues that one major failing of risk assessment is the lack of a model for assessing risk. An economic model *is* essential to effective business decision making. While Golub and Tilman focus strictly on risk taking, the application can be broadened to all aspects of decision making. Or, in everyday parlance: What were they thinking? That is: What was their model of risk assessment when they attempted to do something? Often, there was not a model of risk assessment. From a study of military history, it can be asked: Did Hitler think about the risk of an invasion of Russia after having knowledge of Napoleon's earlier failure? Thoughtful risk assessment was no match for the overconfidence bias Hitler demonstrated, and his soldiers paid for, with the invasion. In marketing, the case of New Coke illustrates the lack of thought regarding the risk and rewards of introducing a new product. The original Coke brand had a very loyal following that, similar to the love of Fenway Park and Wrigley Field, goes beyond just price and taste. Coca-Cola management's oversight of the nature of the brand loyalty tipped the introduction into the high-risk category. In business, Henry Ford's attempt to extend his production and market savvy to the Fordson tractor failed, even in the face of years of experience in the same business, against International Harvester.[13] Years later, Ford introduced the Edsel, which was marketed as a brand-new design. Yet the design was conventional, its pricing was confusing with other models, and it met the 1957 recession at its inaugural year.

Economic activities reflect two or more risk factors, but risk factors do not represent the same level of risk. Moreover, economists are interested in the possible movements of two risk factors together—in other words, their joint probability distribution. Often, slower economic growth accompanies higher unemployment while higher inflation often accompanies higher interest rates. The challenge, among many, in gauging economic risks is to recognize that often changes in economic factors move together.

Change can occur in more than one risk factor at a time, happen in different sizes for each factor, and have significantly different costs and loss implications for each factor. For example, America has experienced recessions and periods of job losses in the past, but what made the Great Recession so difficult was the surprise drop in home prices. Moreover, what makes risk modeling so difficult is that different risk factors have significantly different costs and significantly different probabilities of occurrence, with very unlikely (and often completely unanticipated) events having the greatest cost simply because they are considered very unlikely. In risk assessment, planning follows the principle of focusing on frequent, small risks, but the greatest threat to the organization is often the problem of large-scale shocks associated with very unlikely events.

In financial services, risk assessment is often based on a scenario of modest changes in the federal funds rate, the Fed's main policy tool over the last 30 years; these changes are what management has seen most often and what management knows how to deal with (the frequent, small principle). However, the real shocks of the last 30 years to the existence of many financial firms have been the large-scale, unanticipated changes: sharp, unanticipated shifts in liquidity premiums, surprise increases and declines in oil prices, changes in tax laws, and large-scale alterations in home prices and securitization values. Each of these could be argued as outside the comfort zone of most forecasters' expertise, but are exactly the problems that most threaten the enterprise.

Changes in the funds rate tends to follow other changes in the economy, such as growth and inflation. It is another example of the joint probability distribution among economic factors, with different economic implications for any decision maker. Changes in the federal funds rate, by themselves, would have significantly different implications compared to a situation in which easier federal funds follow a slowdown in the GDP, or a higher funds rate is adopted by the Fed after inflation concerns have started to rise. Moreover, changes in the funds rate would suggest movements in the yield curve that would be quite different under different economic environments. There will always be recessions—yet some recessions come with rising inflation and interest rates, and others with falling inflation and interest rates. In modeling risks, the real challenges to decision makers are not the modest changes decision makers are familiar with but rather the big changes that are the surprises and threats to the central thesis of their business model.

For example, economists often face complex time series, such as corporate profits, and yet are asked to provide understanding and forecasts of time series behavior to non-economists, especially investors. One technique that can be applied to analyze a time series would be to subdivide the series into multiple parts instead of simply looking at the deviation from the long-run average of the series.[14] In other words, a more accurate assessment of the volatility, and thus risk, can be gained through understanding the volatility as it pertains to a specific time period, such as a business cycle, as opposed comparing the volatility to the long run average of the time series. The idea behind this technique is that for specific periods of time there may be structural changes in the time series that result in different means and standard deviations. Thus, the volatility may be higher or lower as a result of these differences in mean values. These structural changes can take the form of federal policy changes or a corporate restructuring that may affect profitability after implementation.

Understanding the volatility of a specific period of time, such as a boom period during which corporate profits are far above average for the business cycle period, may indicate that a bust period is on the horizon. This period-specific insight allows the decision maker the opportunity to prepare for this transition to a lower level of profitability. This technique can be applied to any basic time series of data but can be most helpful in the context of econometric models.

## ASSESSING RISKS USING ECONOMETRIC MODELS

Although the preceding comments apply to the spreadsheet models that are typically the purview of business leaders and senior committees, these comments can also be applied to risk assessments undertaken with econometric models. Additional issues on the application of econometric models are important to understand.

Models reflect the historical data employed to estimate the model. Models developed in the low-inflation 1960s would, and did, fall apart with the high-inflation 1970s. Simulation models used to estimate the drop in unemployment associated with the American Recovery and Reinvestment Act (commonly referred to as the stimulus) of 2009 completely failed to pick up the changes at the micro level of the labor market. These changes included the rising cost of health insurance and the pending regulations, a higher minimum wage, and a mismatch of worker skills and employer needs in sectors such as construction and manufacturing. Why did these projections of a decline in unemployment fail to materialize? First, in economic frameworks, economists assume that they have information about all the relevant factors that drive behavior. Like any good scientist, they wish to confine their problems to something they can identify. Second, economists expect that all their observations of the phenomenon they study are independent trials, that is, what they see today for selected factors and results is independent from what they saw a month ago or in a different sample group.

However, economic models may not capture all the information needed to make an accurate forecast, because economists may have missed a significant factor or the manner in which a factor enters the model may have changed substantially over time. When a variable is missing there is a tendency for forecast errors, in the same direction, to persist over time; the influence of the missing variable will tend to alter the behavior of the framework. In recent years, unemployment rate forecasts have tended to be too low and housing starts forecasts not low enough. It would appear that some variable is missing or that there is a new way that the variables in the economy are influencing the model.

For example, the decline in home prices during the Great Recession has meant a drop in household wealth for homeowners. For some homeowners, this has meant that these homeowners are "under water"—that is, they owe more on their mortgage than what the property is worth and they would incur a capital loss on their property if they were to sell their home. This may be only one of several new relationships between economic factors. It suggests that the structure of the economy has changed and therefore so would predictions of key economic variables in any risk assessment.

Changes in the economic structure would also suggest that old reliable relationships have been altered. Lower home prices have certainly thrown a twist into the traditional thinking of the economy. For example, home affordability calculations based upon home prices, mortgage rates and income are very high and yet home sales are very disappointing. What has changed for many households is the expectation of home price appreciation; the fear of continued deflation, rather than appreciation, is keeping home buying in check. Models of housing demand that did not include the risk of home price deflation would lead to misleading estimations. Models that fail to include all the relevant variables would generate biased coefficient estimates of the impact of economic factors on our risk assessment. Moreover, the covariance between the value of the house and the rate of the variable rate mortgage and the homeowner's income would generate a set of housing estimates that would be unbiased relative to an estimate that did not include the expected value of the house in the equation.

In the risk modeling process, the exactitude of small changes in obvious factors leads to the impression of exactitude, whereas inexactitude is the more likely outcome, and significant, large changes remain lurking in the darkness.

Economists must be testing a model that is falsifiable or testable and not counterfactual when building a framework or model. They must be able to show that their model is capable of predictions, and then they must test that model. Frequently, econometric models provide comfortable results to management when the model is stressed just enough but not enough for a real test. But the real world provides a stress test beyond what we model, and that test often leads to failure and bankruptcy.

## Learning along a Path

Along these lines, risk assessments need to recognize that learning takes place among economic agents in the marketplace. This learning alters the response of the market to any given change in the independent factors. The framework itself changes as economic actors respond to change and learn from it. With inflation, workers came to understand and to anticipate inflation. Therefore, the trade-off that was the Phillips Curve in the 1950s and 1960s fell apart in the 1970s.

In a risk management model, economists should be able to distinguish those areas in which they have a high level of confidence over the outcome from those areas—often the human element—in which they have much less control over the outcome. Engineers can design safer highways, but the final link in the safety chain is the driver himself.

Also, risk assessments from any econometric model rely on the assumptions employed for the key independent variables. In the most recent period, assumptions about home prices and employment and income gains have fallen far short of the actual outcomes. Therefore, any predictions concerning delinquencies and foreclosures were far short of the mark.

Econometric and spreadsheet models are unable to account for paradigm shifts or the sudden emergence of selected economic factors as driving forces in economic activity. Models are built upon evidence of the past and so are ill-equipped to deal with paradigm shifts of the type cited by Kuhn. Economic factors, such as oil prices in the 1970s and the emergence of developing Asia today, were not important before the models were being developed in the 1960s for inflation and in the 1990s for trade. For example, the globalization of trade has altered pricing activity for many consumer goods as well as the response of employment in the United States to the nation's growth. Increasingly for the American economy, an increase in domestic demand is met with increasing supply from abroad, not from domestic sources. In economic terms this would be described as America's import elasticity to income is very high. Import elasticity refers to the increase in import purchases as growth and income increases in the United States. In this case, imports rise quickly and faster than economic growth and income rises and hence reflects the high import elasticity in the United States with respect to economic growth. In other words, increases in household income in the United States are associated with a very high propensity to buy imported goods as one can observe by a weekend trip to any shopping mall.

Conversely, influential risk factors that may appear unimportant, but still appear periodically, like a hint of problems or discrepancies in a detective show, may prove to be far more significant at a later point. In the late 1970s and early 1980s the money supply was the driving factor for inflation, and thereby for the conduct of monetary policy. However, in recent years the money supply is hardly noticed and plays little role in policy deliberations at the Federal Reserve. The end of the Cold War was seen as a major break in the allocation of the federal budget for military spending and the opening up of trade into Eastern Europe, as well as a general sense of relief for the individual household around the world. Yet, at the same time, the end of the Cold War brought a renewed expression of ancient ethnic hatreds in Eastern Europe. The threat of nuclear war appeared to have diminished, but that of Balkan conflicts reappeared. Over time, military spending increased once more due to the Islamic threat (The Soviets left Afghanistan and the United States entered) as well as increased fear of nuclear war.

Finally, econometric models remain subject to unexpected exogenous events that are, by their nature, not forecastable: Russian or Argentine defaults, surprise sovereign debt revelations, chicanery with corporate balance sheets, and that perennial favorite, the John Law/Charles Ponzi/Bernie Madoff blind pool funds that fail to deliver what many thought was a sure thing. Blind pool investments are simply very opaque investment schemes, in which no one knows how the returns are being generated, yet people are willing to invest for the realized returns for the early investors today and the guaranteed returns promised in the future.

Increasingly subjective judgment must be introduced into risk management models flexible enough to allow for the addition of qualitative risk factors, the addition of new risk factors, and the deletion of those risk factors that are no longer applicable even where there is limited measurement capability. In addition, there is a need to recognize the importance of knowing or not knowing the model that drives policy maker actions, especially monetary policy. In cases where the policy maker targets are known, the behavior of the market is altered compared to when policy maker intentions are not known.

Even with a model of risk assessment, there remains the need to monitor the changing dynamics of the economy and to provide the correct oversight for the risk assessment process. The great failure of the housing boom and bust cycle of the previous decade was not the lack of regulations and rules, but rather the failure of all involved to monitor the changing dynamics of the housing market and make the decision to stop lending. Too often, decision makers are drawn into complacency once a model is in place. There is a tendency to not monitor the process or ensure that the process of risk assessment is achieving its goals. For many mortgage lenders, there was a credit review process for lending in the 2005 to 2009 period. The problem became the inability to monitor that process and stop the erosion of lending standards in the face of ever-increasing demands for top-line revenue growth and market share.

Risk assessment runs both ways. Decision makers can take too many risks and they can also take too few. Polaroid first looked at digital camera technology, decided not to enter the market, and then saw its film and camera market disappear. The attack on Pearl Harbor is an example of a risk successfully taken by the Japanese and the failure of the United States to check out the clues that indicated an attack was possible.

## IDENTIFYING CHANGE

Change is a fundamental character of all economic models. In the classroom, economics professors set aside many factors and those that they examine are assumed to remain in character for the purpose of their lectures. Yet, household, business, and government preferences continue to evolve. Moreover,

over time, the impact of nature on agricultural production and shipping has given way to the variations in human behavior. Engineers can build better airports, highways, and railroads, but the person in control has become the single most important factor determining the project's success or failure. Risk is now a question of people rather than the weather or luck.

The challenge in creating econometric models is to recognize change and give its magnitude and character a quantitative value so as to assess its impact on the assessment of risk. The failure to monitor change and changing risk implications has been very evident over the years in foreign and economic policy. For example, in foreign policy, Fidel Castro was once America's ally and then became the country's enemy, much to the surprise of American political leadership. America provided weapons to the rebels in Afghanistan to fight the Soviets, but later had to invade the country to defeat the Taliban. In economics, the breakdown of the inflation/unemployment trade-off gave rise to the decade of stagflation. Today, the rapid rise in the duration of unemployment has introduced questions about the functioning of the labor market in the United States and the problem of long-term unemployment.

The problem when making decisions is that economists and business leaders have incentives, personal and professional, to ignore change since that change could be interpreted as a failure in the original design of the framework. For Thomas Edison, 1,000 ways not to build a lightbulb did not dissuade him from believing in the lightbulb framework he had developed. Unfortunately, economists and business leaders think the need to make corrections and adjustments to their model is a sign of failure rather than a sign of flexibility and innovation. Yet, in fact, most great success stories involved adjustments to the original model—from the Egyptian pyramids to the space shuttle program.

Risk aversion can and often does vary over the economic cycle. People, investors, and business leaders are very risk-averse during a recession and the early phase of an economic recovery but then lower their guard as an economic expansion takes hold. This is illustrated in Figure 6.7, as credit spreads can be seen to have a very procyclical pattern. Spreads are very high between AA (Aaa) corporate bonds (Figure 6.5) and BB (Baa) corporate bonds (Figure 6.6) and Treasury bond rates during the early phase of the recovery, but then decline steadily as the recovery proceeds. In banking, the worst loans are usually made at the best times and the best loans are made at the worst times.

To effectively monitor change, decision makers must be proactive and constantly watch their credit standards as a recovery proceeds. Unless they do, they can be caught in what is called a *practical drift*. Risk standards drift into easier modes as the business cycle proceeds. When the economy is hit with a major shock or a recession, decision makers overreact and

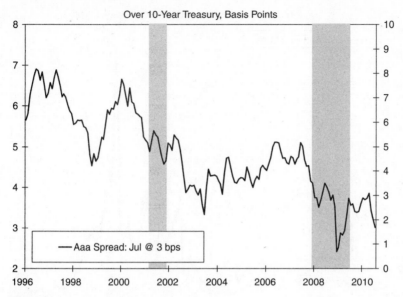

**FIGURE 6.5** Aaa Corporate Bond Spreads
*Source:* Federal Reserve Board and Wells Fargo Securities, LLC.

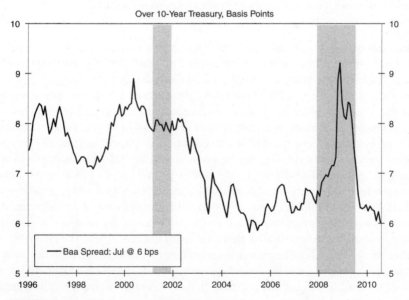

**FIGURE 6.6** Baa Corporate Bond Spreads
*Source:* Federal Reserve Board and Wells Fargo Securities, LLC.

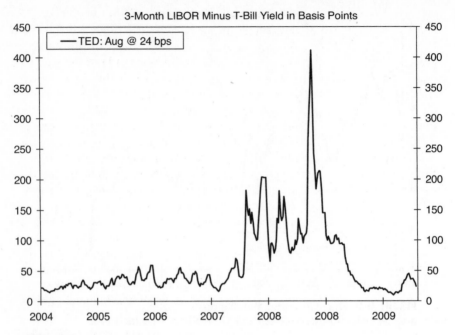

**FIGURE 6.7**  TED Spread
*Source:* Federal Reserve Board and Wells Fargo Securities, LLC.

shut down the credit process entirely. Such a process can be seen in Figure 6.7—the spread between Treasury bill rates and the euro rate before and after the initial credit shocks of 2007 to 2010. Beginning in 2007 and escalating sharply in 2008 and 2009, the euro rate rose sharply compared to the Treasury bill rate. This spread reflected the increasing risk concerns of investors. The shift to Treasury bills and away from private market credit instruments such as euro dollar and commercial paper instruments is typical of the credit cycle over every cycle since World War II. Similar patterns were seen in high-yield and high-grade bonds as well as in bank credit default swaps. In California, Orange County's experience in 1994 with the leveraged risks it took with its portfolio reflects another case of inadequate monitoring and measurement. The county took positions with its investments that became increasingly disconnected from the realities of the economy and interest rate trends. The portfolio managers were betting on lower interest rates in the face of the Federal Reserve's monetary policy of raising interest rates to head off an inflation threat. This is another example of the adage of John Maynard Keynes—markets can remain irrational longer than you can remain solvent.[15]

Change can come in two forms, a sharp break or a slow deterioration. The sharp break is illustrated nicely in the collapse of bridges, such as "Galloping Gurdy" in Washington State and the I-35W Bridge in Minneapolis, or dramatic turns in political elections, such the elections of Franklin Roosevelt and Ronald Reagan. However, one can argue that it is the slow deterioration that leads to the sharp break of most bridges. Market dislocations, widening credit spreads, a collapse in liquidity, and the lack of credit support all followed the rapid deterioration of the housing credit market from 2007 to 2010. In this case, the failure to monitor changing risks followed decisions to accept a decline in credit quality for the benefit of continued revenue growth, even though that growth was being bought by the rising risks to lending. Short-run profits were emphasized at the cost of long-run sustainability, with risk standards the casualty.

Another subtlety in risk assessment is to recognize that such assessment may vary over the business cycle. But there are also secular changes, that is, changes that evolve over a long period of time, particularly demographics that subject a model to change from non-economic factors, independent of the business cycle. The post–World War II baby boom placed pressure on educational spending during the 1960s and early 1970s. Today, aging baby boomers and their looming retirement suggests rising public spending for retiree entitlements despite the poor state of the American economy.

## What Is the Character of Change?

In economics, it is recognized that deviations from the norm do not all cluster symmetrically about the norm and that the deviations of the independent factors influencing risk assessment do not occur with the same frequency. Shocks can be a discontinuity that may not be an abrupt break with the past, but the logical consequence of preceding events. World War I was a surprise to most observers, but not to Winston Churchill. After the horrors of World War I, statesmen like British Prime Minister Neville Chamberlain could not see that issues about war reparations and the collapse of the German economy would lead to Adolph Hitler, his takeover of neighboring countries, and ultimately to another world war. Wars, it seems, come and go but always enter as surprises. In a similar way, the inevitable issue of entitlements and how to pay for them has been a perennial one that many politicians have recognized for years, yet few have done much about it.

In the real economy as well as financial markets, wildness is always waiting to show itself, although there is seldom warning when the exact moment will be forthcoming. Yet, there is also a tendency to pay excessive attention to low-probability events accompanied by high drama and overlook events that happen in routine fashion. The stock market crashes of

1929 and 1987 are recognized, but most problems in financial markets have a long incubation period.[16] In assessing risk, decision makers need to be aware when information is enough, too much, too little, or just right to take action. Unfortunately, events change expectations rapidly in many cases, leading to hockey-stick-type movements where changes in economic factors such as growth, inflation, and interest rates lead to sharp reassessments of risk and thereby create massive dislocations for both the supply and demand for credit. A prime example was the recent reassessment of sovereign risk in Europe in 2010.

## Modeling Change

How do analysts and business leaders model or anticipate change when they conduct their quarterly risk assessments? Modeling will be misleading when a framework and the changes that are introduced are not consistent with the issues that need to be faced. The typical pattern is that what-if scenarios introduce spot changes in the pace of growth, or interest rates that happen instantaneously or over some specified horizon in discrete equal increments. The risk model is then run and the results are certified as an adequate stress test. Unfortunately, such a risk assessment is very unlikely to compare well with real world changes. Many risk assessments are treated as base cases but then also as the most likely or the only test of the organization's risk assessment. Such a test should only be the first step. Moreover, the changes introduced are frequently mild adjustments, which would be neither fitting for small changes but not the changes of the Great Recession nor consistent with the sharp movements we have in the capital markets in 1998, 2000, or 2007 to 2009.

In addition, economic risk factors such as growth, inflation, interest rates, the dollar, and corporate profits are not perfectly correlated, do not exhibit similar volatilities, and do not change at the same time over the business cycle. Moreover, as risk factors, changes in each of these factors can occur as random events and are not perfectly correlated and equally volatile or of equal significance over the economic cycle. And the likelihood of any given event and the event's degree of significance are not equivalent. For example, hurricanes are more likely in Louisiana than Kansas, but tornadoes are more common in Kansas than hurricanes. The impact significance of each is significantly different by differences in location and intensity.

## Evolution of Feedback in the Framework

With each change comes the problem of estimating the feedback anticipated and how that will lead decision makers to make changes in their behavior and eventually their model. Any change is considered new information. How do analysts estimate the feedback of the economy and competitors to that change?

Several issues face analysts in making an assessment of the feedback of any change beyond the simple model simulations. There is the challenge of recognizing the uncertainty that lies in estimating the intentions of the others—how they will respond to change as well as any adjustment they will make to any actions we may take. Different economic actors may respond to change in many different ways. Some respond immediately to change, while others wait to see how significant that change is and how sustainable it will be over time. Some firms try to maintain market share while others want to preserve earnings and a targeted rate of return.

In some cases, decision making will be impacted by a recency bias. Recency bias implies that a change represents the new world, or the opposite view—that what is new is really old again and the world will return to the old model. In the late 1970s the rise of inflation meant that firms and individuals could either adopt the view that inflation was here to stay, along with very high nominal interest rates, or that the world would return quickly, or eventually, to an environment of low inflation and interest rates. As it turned out, memories of inflation persisted for policy makers and the public itself. The majority of investors and decision makers, both public and private, took the new inflation framework as new information for their models and began to plan accordingly.

In contrast, the models of the competitive environment adopted by General Motors, for example, did not anticipate sustained competition from foreign manufacturers and they did not adjust their business model as quickly as some suggested.[17] Given the view that the economic model continually evolves over time, the concept of a regression to the mean as a tool for anticipating a return to the old ways is more of a false benchmark than an effective strategy and not viewed as a certainty in economics. Reversion to the mean may be appropriate for individual height and physical laws but not for financial markets, interest rates, or stock prices.

Expectations for a quick and complete return to the mean in any economic activity will often be disappointed. In recent years, the decline in unemployment and the response to the 2009 fiscal stimulus were far slower than the experience of the fiscal stimulus embarked on by presidents Kennedy and Johnson in the early and mid-1960s and by President Reagan in the early 1980s. The underlying structure of the economy has changed over the last 50 years.

Returning to normal is often interrupted by another shock to the economy. The return to normal during the 1970s was interrupted by oil, inflation, and the foreign policy shock of the Iranian embassy takeover. The end of

**TABLE 6.2**   Volatility of Past Business Cycles

| | Q3-1982 to Q1-1991 | Q2-1991 to Q3-2001 | Q3-2001 to Q2-2009 | Q3-1982 to Q2-2009 |
|---|---|---|---|---|
| **Unemployment Rate** | | | | |
| Mean | 6.73 | 5.49 | 5.57 | 5.90 |
| Standard Deviation | (1.38) | (1.17) | (1.1) | (1.32) |
| **Fed Funds Rate** | | | | |
| Mean | 8.10 | 4.80 | 2.60 | 5.19 |
| Standard Deviation | (1.33) | (1.12) | (1.71) | (2.54) |

*Source:* U.S. Department of Commerce, U.S. Department of Labor, and Wells Fargo Securities, LLC.

2008 and early 2009 also saw a sequence of surprises—the near collapse of the economy, wild gyrations of the stock market, the fall of major financial institutions—that meant returning to normal, or the mean, was constantly interrupted. Finally, the mean or normal itself may be constantly changing. The economic history of the 1950s was significantly different from that of the 1960s; the 1960s was very different from the 1970s, and on and on. Table 6.2 illustrates the volatility of business cycles beginning in 1982 and ending in 2009. In fact, looking at the average pace of growth, inflation, and interest rates for each decade since World War II, it is hard to imagine that the pattern of mean reversion or a return to normal was ever a reliable paradigm.

Instead of a return to normal, the economy is constantly evolving on a secular basis with the additional twist of a business cycle thrown in for good measure. In some cases, the secular trends may amplify the business cycle turns (recession and globalization have probably boosted unemployment in the 2008 to 2010 period), while in other cases the secular forces of globalization of trade have moderated the cycle patterns of inflation.

Meanwhile, changes in economic factors can, and do, create correlations among asset classes that would be fundamentally uncorrelated otherwise. In part, corrections in financial markets lead to a search for liquidity that prompts many investors to sell what they can. Therefore, sales of liquid assets, such as United States Treasury bonds, agency debt and high-grade corporate bonds are such that all their asset prices move together. In addition, there is a trend to measure economic reactions in risk benchmarks as a linear relationship, while often the response of risk premia to economic change is nonlinear. Correlations among risk factors also change over the business cycle, thereby altering the supposedly linear relationship that is the base assumption of many risk models. All these issues feed into the choices business leaders make in addressing the risks they face.

When observation becomes a call to action, the choices business leaders make cut off the option of waiting until new information comes along and creates, often, an alternative path for future options. For Caesar it was crossing the Rubicon, for Eisenhower it was landing in Normandy. Not acting has value, as does acting, and so the choices that are made are based on probabilities, not certainties. The history of fiscal and monetary decisions of public policy makers, as well as those in the private sector, has given testimony to the uncertainty of outcomes.

For decision makers there are three types of choices as responses to biases in response to the evolution of economic risks over time:

1. There is the acceptance of deviance without any change in their framework. Here increasing risks are not met with a reassessment of the model but with the belief that decision makers can overcome them.
2. Risks are deviating, often rising from an original assessment. An increase in risks prompts some decision makers to quickly drop the project, while others aggressively pursue the project. This is based on the decision maker's predisposition toward (risk-loving) or away from (risk-averse) risk.
3. There is a belief that risks are not rising and, in fact, the original model still works if carried out long enough.

## Normalization of Deviance

Normalization of deviance refers to the way we initially rationalize any behavior that deviates a bit from normal as a one-time event or that any deviation really doesn't alter our belief that the system we are operating is still operating as normal. Our car is hard to start, but we believe it is just due to the weather today. Over time we treat the deviation as normal until, at some point, the car doesn't start at all.

In the non-financial realm we have reviewed three cases that illustrate the normalization of deviance. As portrayed by the experiences of adventurer Jon Krakauer in *Into Thin Air*[18] and by sociologist Diane Vaughan in *The Challenger Launch Decision*,[19] many decision makers will recognize the increasing risks in a situation, but they do not see a fundamental change in their circumstances and so a fatal change in the framework underlying their decisions arises. Yet they continue to pursue an increasingly risky strategy. For Jon Krakauer, climbing Mount Everest was a challenge in itself, but the climbing team with him was facing a change in the weather as a blizzard struck. Moreover, the team had violated a rule on timing the climb which dictated a turnaround-time rule. That is, if you cannot reach the top by one or two o'clock in the afternoon, you should turn around because you do not want to be climbing down in the darkness. Yet the hiking team began their ascent to the top too late in the day. As a result of these decisions, five expedition members died on the mountain.[20] For Diane Vaughan, the NASA program increased its acceptance of problems in launching the space shuttle such that it had pushed the boundaries of accepted behavior too far. The overconfidence bias on the part of the Everest climbers, for example, is often the downfall of many entrepreneurs, especially in commercial and residential real estate. Often their careers have been a string of successes, but then their push for bigger, more lavish projects leads to failure. For example, we see this in Ferdinand De Lesseps, the builder of the Suez Canal who failed in Panama.

In the financial realm we have witnessed several cases where small differences between expected and actual outcomes in growth, inflation, and interest rates were initially ignored with eventual catastrophic consequences. The initial stock market corrections of 1928–1929 were initially discounted as one-off events with no lasting value. During the 1970s, growth was lower and inflation higher than many expected and was initially treated as temporary anomalies relative to the strong growth/low inflation of earlier post-WWII decades. The initial rise in interest rates during 1994 was discounted by the likes of Gibson Greetings and Orange County, California, with eventual disastrous results.[21]

Nor has the normalization of deviance completely been a phenomenon of the past. Over the last decade, subprime lending has led to the downfall of many mortgage lenders and builders alike. As illustrated in Figure 6.8, during the decade there had been a clear deterioration of credit quality in subprime lending. For each new, annual vintage of loans, the rise in 60-day-plus delinquencies had been faster and sharper beginning in 2005 compared to 2004.

Initially, rising delinquencies were probably disappointing and unexpected, but the deviation from the past did not appear to be threatening. Increasing deviations came to be expected and then accepted. A wider range of deviations became accepted simply because past deviations were not met with disaster. Current deviations would not lead to catastrophe, decision makers believed, because they had supreme confidence in their abilities to control events. Moreover, there was the belief that the financial markets had the ability to correct themselves and therefore any problems would be corrected in the markets. They were wrong.

Unfortunately for the United States economy, a pyramid of decision makers—individual home buyers, appraisers, real estate agents, closing attorneys, lenders, and insurers of mortgage-backed securities—altered their view, in harmony, of what were acceptable real estate values and, in harmony, they were all wrong. Such a harmony in accepting such deviance is the driving force on the Nifty-Fifty stocks of the 1970s (a period when investors

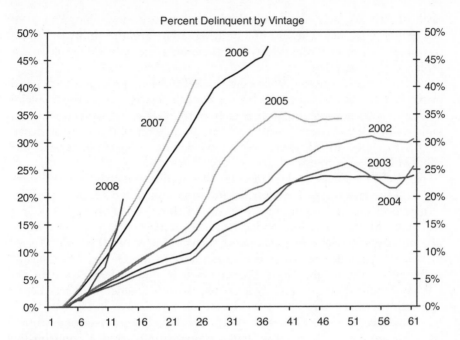

**FIGURE 6.8** Subprime ARMS 60+ Delinquencies
*Source:* Wells Fargo Securities, LLC.

bought the concept stocks, that is, stocks that had a story of long-term out-performance no matter what the economy was doing), the oil boom of the 1980s, and the dot-com boom of the 1990s. The unexpected became the expected, the expected became the accepted, and a long pattern of decisions created a gradual normalization of deviance.

In public finance, the prosperity of certain states, such as Florida and California, had become the conventional wisdom. Real estate and other developers saw every project as a moneymaker. Risks were increasingly discounted in the face of apparent endless prosperity. For many states and real estate developers, the national housing boom had a long incubation period. There were secular forces, the oncoming retirement of the baby boomers, that supported the housing gains in the short run and did make sense in the context of a richer, prosperous aging demographic, but over time the credit quality envelope continued to be pushed until the breaking point was reached.[22]

In some decision models, the influence of sunk costs drives decision makers to stick with their plans even though over time the risk and reward of any project is becoming increasingly dismal. Poorly placed or designed casinos, airports, and real estate condo projects are the lifeblood of local newspaper headlines. The fear of admitting failure and the ability to call on someone else's money (the taxpayer) has kept many a political development project on life support.

Consider this contrast. We recognize that there are economic cycles and therefore the risk/reward ratio changes over the cycle. Yet, in the financial markets, investors will often characterize themselves as either long-term bulls or bears; their gut instinct is that the market will go up or down despite the latest bit of news. Our knowledge of cycles conflicts with our belief of long-term trends.

Daniel Kahneman, Nobel laureate in economics and professor at Princeton, and the late Amos Tresky from Stanford, conducted research that described decision makers in terms of prospect theory where different people will make different decisions under the same circumstances.[23] The responses of contestants on television game shows such as *Deal or No Deal* or *A Minute to Win It*[24] provide them with the opportunity to stretch their winnings or go home with what they have accumulated. In financial markets, for every buyer who thinks a stock is going up there is a seller who sees better opportunities elsewhere.

For decision makers, there is a trade-off that changes over time so that even the most bearish investors will see opportunity at one point on the scale, but their basic frame of reference is to avoid risk. For the adventurer there is, in contrast, always opportunity. For most decision makers, there comes a point of diminishing marginal utility where the disutility associated with a loss will always exceed the positive utility provided by a gain of equal size.

The problem of framing also impacts decisions made under ambiguous threats. Here, decision makers either tend to downplay risks or to overemphasize the problems. There are bulls and bears in the governor's mansion and in the corporate board of directors. A culture of risk taking or risk avoidance permeates each organization. In the high-tech industry there is a culture of risk taking. In contrast, insurance companies, local governments, and colleges have traditionally exhibited a culture of risk avoidance, although the spectacular failures in recent years of AIG, Orange County, and the Harvard endowment bring into question whether risk avoidance remains the dominant culture.

There is a belief that risks are not rising and, in fact, the original model still works if carried out long enough. This belief follows the pattern of the famous Donner-Reed wagon train party. The group suffered several critical delays, but instead of reevaluating their timing, they pushed ahead and were trapped by an early snowfall and subsequently half the travelers died.[25]

The essence of any investment program gone wrong is when, in an attempt to cover the losses, bad money follows good. In the 1920s, it was the Ponzi scheme, in the late twentieth century it was Nick Leeson at Barings, and in the latest version it was escalation of bulls in the housing market on the belief that housing prices never fall.[26]

Leaders become rigid in their thinking—convinced that their original model is correct—and they escalate their commitment to a failing enterprise. They double down on a bad hand. The problem is that the risk and reward for an activity has changed due to economic fundamentals. There is an unwillingness to accept the change since such a change would suggest that the original decision was a mistake. A loss taken is an acknowledgment of error. Decision makers cling to the original mistake. They hope that someday the economy or events will vindicate their judgment and lead to investment or military success. Yet, circumstances change and decisions do need to change in the face of new information.

Pearl Harbor stands out as a singular case of the stubborn attachment to existing beliefs. Information was gathered in a biased manner due to the presence of a confirmatory bias on the part of decision makers. On a strategic level, American intelligence believed Japan would not attack because Americans believed the Japanese could not expect to win the subsequent war. The Philippines, not Pearl Harbor, was the expected focus of an attack. Although intelligence gathered lots of data, the irrelevant data swamped the relevant data and the analysts, not expecting an attack, could not draw out the relevant data. Simply put, their prior belief was that no attack would come and therefore they did not find the signals of the attack in the data they reviewed.[27] Decision makers gather and rely on information that confirms their existing beliefs and they avoid or downplay information that disconfirms their preexisting hypotheses.

Good decision making in a changing economic environment must couple risk with consequence. Moreover, in a dynamic world, there is no single answer under conditions of uncertainty, since information about a situation changes over time. In making choices, life's situations are a spectrum of similar but not identical situations, and discerning the correct lesson of the past is the biggest challenge to decision makers.[28]

## PRINCIPLES FOR A NEW MODEL

Four principles will help influence the choice of a new framework for the economic world decision makers see going forward within the context of risk. First, path dependency reflects both a past framework and a past form of leadership. It also reflects any framework adopted in the future and how that framework will influence leadership within that framework. President Ronald Reagan altered the debate on tax policy and economic growth. Paul Volcker and Alan Greenspan solidified the commitment to inflation control for monetary policy. Today, Ben Bernanke has the reputation as anti-deflation.

Second, there is continuous learning and reaction in the marketplace, even if not by the political leadership. The economy moves on, and the economic factors of growth, inflation, interest rates, profits, and the exchange value of the dollar all change over time. Their average values and variability influence both public and private decision makers.

Financial markets constitute a complex, dynamic, self-learning system, although the lessons learned in the short run might work against long-term interests. Truth changes as market participants learn—recall the learning about inflation in the 1970s. And financial markets change as knowledge about them is assimilated into practice. Therefore there must be frequent reality checks to verify that the forecasts of risk models are still consistent with actual market behavior.

When business leaders adopt any framework that revolves around one economic factor—for example, interest rates—the framework shapes the outlook and decision making on every component of the economic framework. Using monetary policy to target inflation is expected to provide the best framework for good economic decision making over the long run. But monetary policy cannot then be employed to target employment as well.

In the 1970s and 1980s, the framework for risk assessment certainly changed for savings and loan associations and for every investor in general with the emergence of inflation. S&Ls faced unrecognized risks in their yield curve bet. They borrowed short and lent long. Yet, rising inflation drove up short rates and their cost of funds rose faster than the returns on long-term loans. The rise of inflation was outside their inflation experience or their expectations. The rapid flattening of the yield curve altered their business model.

Third, there remains a decision-making bias that is a high hurdle for business leaders in developing a new framework—the anchoring bias. Effectively, a decision maker's initial reference point limits her choices unnecessarily. She tends to stay on the original decision path with only minor and often insufficient changes in her framework. In addition, decision makers also must watch the framing they adopt on the risk-and-reward trade-off. The frame will often drift back in favor of risk avoidance and thereby back to accepting the original and more emotionally comfortable model.

Finally, decision makers can also be susceptible to practical drift. Their changes are half-steps that do not deal with the fundamental changes needed in their framework, but open them up to the risk of overreacting when they fail to reach their targets. People learn early on not to oversteer a car. In monetary policy, there have been several instances where policy adjusts slowly, only to then speed up and make bigger adjustments as inflation or growth targets remain elusive.

While risk assessments and a framework for recognizing those risks is a necessary first step, the next step is to tackle the question of how decision makers frame a strategy under conditions of uncertainty. This is the topic of the next chapter.

## DISCUSSION QUESTIONS

1. Surprise always appears to be on the menu for the economy. Inflation during the 1970s and 1980s surprised decision makers first with inflation on the upside and then on the downside. Growth was stronger than expected in the 1980s and 1990s, but the past few years have brought a string of disappointing GDP numbers.
   a. Risk represents the price of getting the unexpected. Identify periods over the last 30 years when growth, inflation, interest rates, dollar exchange rates, and profits came in very different from expectations.
   b. For each of these periods identify what assumptions in the marketplace gave rise to expectations that would be nullified by the data.
   c. In each case identify elements of the marketplace that would explain how they developed those expectations.
   d. Based upon your review in questions a, b, and c, how would you rewrite the history of the housing collapse from 2007 to 2010 as a surprise that upset the expectations of market participants, and what elements gave rise to those expectations for housing?
   e. Most surprises in the economic/business arena can be viewed as a three-part sequence. Identify another shock in the economic environment that you can use to break down the surprise/assumptions/ elements that provide the understanding of a situation where risk is present.
2. The models we construct on how the world works influence our assessment of risk. Models represent how the world works and incorporate our assumptions and yet, we know that these assumptions can be biased based on our education, upbringing, or current professional position. This is particularly true in the field of investing.

a. The absence of a critical variable or the inclusion of an irrelevant variable will create a misrepresentation of the outlook for investment returns.

How might a currency trader miss the downdraft and then recovery of the euro in 2010 if the Greek sovereign debt situation had been overlooked?

b. Framing an investment in terms of risk/reward is the essence of the investment decision. Where one investor sees risk another investor will see rewards. Where some saw economic recovery, others saw continued recession in mid-2009.

How might this framing set the investment strategy for an investor for 2010?

c. The anchoring bias is the tendency to build a model based on the present situation that overweights the present and fails to allow for change over time. Yet we always experience change.

How might an investor with a model that suggested a traditional V-shaped recovery have been misled by events in the 2009 to 2010 recovery? Why might an investor overweight historical trends in developing her view of the future?

d. Investors have a tendency to focus on a concept that often has very little staying power over time. This tendency to jump at an illusory correlation tends to lead many investors astray. What are your thoughts on the focus on commodity prices, particularly gold, copper, or oil, as a signal of both growth and inflation over time? How well do these three indicators actually work over the entire economic cycle?

3. Three characteristics for risk are that risks are interdependent, they evolve over the business cycle, and their appearance can be very uneven over the cycle. These characteristics continue to appear business cycle after business cycle, yet we are constantly surprised. The latest version of this was the housing boom and bust.

a. Liquidity, marketability, and the value of the underlying asset (housing) were assumed to be independent risks. Yet, during the housing correction everything appeared to fall apart. Explain why.

b. How did the success of the early home buyers and mortgage lenders give rise to the increase in risks over the cycle and why might such risks be overlooked by the market?

c. Early in the cycle the perceptions of risk were minimal. Over time, the delinquency rates on subprime lending kept rising with little apparent concern until, all of a sudden, risk perceptions skyrocketed. This pattern repeated earlier cycles most recently seen in the dot-com and high-yield bond corrections. Why might such a process of uneven risk perceptions and then a sudden break be so regular in the behavior of investors?

# NOTES

1. Jerry W. Markham, *A Financial History of the United States,* Vol. I (Armonk, NY: M.E. Sharpe, 2002), 232–234.
2. Bennett W. Golub and Leo M. Tilman, *Risk Management* (New York: John Wiley & Sons, 2000), 1.
3. Robert Barro, "Unanticipated Money Growth and Economic Activity in the U.S.," in *Money, Expectations and Business Cycles*, ed. Robert J. Barro (New York: Academic Press, 1981).
4. Thomas Laubach, *New Evidence on the Interest Rate Effects of Budget Deficits and Debt* (Federal Reserve Board, Finance and Economics Discussion Series, 2003–12, May 2003).
5. Susan Bies, *Business Financial Conditions and Relationships with Bankers Remarks at the Financial Executives International Chicago Chapter Dinner, Chicago, Illinois* (Federal Reserve System, July 15, 2004). This is available on the Federal Reserve Board website, www.federalreserve.gov/boarddocs/speeches/2004/20040715/default.htm.
6. Ethan Cohen-Cole and Burcu Duygen-Bumo, *Household Bankruptcy Decision: The Role of Social Stigma vs. Information Sharing* (Federal Reserve Bank of Boston, working paper no. QAU08–6).
7. For an introduction to the models of political action see Mancur Olson, *The Logic of Collective Action: Public Goods and the Theory of Groups* (Cambridge, MA: Harvard University Press, 1971).
8. Bennett Golub and Leo Tilman, *Risk Management* (New York: John Wiley & Sons, 2000).
9. A. H. Studenmund, *Using Econometrics* (Reading, MA: Addison-Wesley, 2006), 176.
10. Ibid., 176–179.
11. John Steele Gordon, *The Business of America, The Perils of Success* (New York: Walker and Co., 2001), 192–195.
12. A. H. Studenmund, *Using Econometrics*, 337–341.
13. John Steele Gordon, *The Business of America: Henry Ford's Horseless Horse* (New York: Walker Publishing, 2001), 105–109.
14. John E. Silvia and Azhar Iqbal, "Three Simple Techniques to Analyze a Complex Economic Phenomenon: The Case of Profits," *Business Economics* 45, no. 2 (2010).
15. As quoted by Roger Lowenstein, *When Genius Failed* (New York: Random House, 2000).
16. Barry Turner, *Man-Made Disasters* (London: Wykeham, 1978).
17. James O'Toole, *Leading Change: Overcoming the Ideology of Comfort and the Tyranny of Custom* (San Francisco: Jossey-Bass, 1995).
18. Jon Krakauer, *Into Thin Air: A Personal Account of the Mount Everest Disaster* (New York: Anchor Books, 1997).
19. Diane Vaughan, *The Challenger Launch Decision: Risky Technology, Culture, and Deviance at NASA* (Chicago: University of Chicago Press, 1996).

20. This summary reflects the presentation by Michael A. Roberto, *The Art of Critical Decision Making* (Chantilly, VA: The Teaching Company, 2009).
21. Jerry W. Markham, *A Financial History of the United States*, Vol. III, 109–202.
22. Barry Turner, *Man-Made Disasters* (London: Wykeham, 1978).
23. Daniel Kahneman and Amos Tresky, *Choices, Values and Frames* (Cambridge: Cambridge University Press, 2000).
24. Both shows aired on NBC.
25. Ethan Rarick, *Desperate Passage: The Donner Party's Perilous Journey West* (New York: Oxford University Press, 2008).
26. Nick Leeson was a derivatives broker at Barings. He made unauthorized trades and hid his trading losses in an error account. His losses exceeded $1.4 billion and resulted in Barings being declared insolvent in February 1995. This was the same Barings firm that helped finance the young American republic.
27. Roberta Wohlstetter, *Pearl Harbor: Warning and Decision* (Stanford, CA: Stanford University Press, 1962).
28. Richard E. Neustadt and Ernest R. May, *Thinking in Time: The Uses of History for Decision-Makers* (New York: Free Press, 1986).

## RECOMMENDED READING FOR SERIOUS PLAYERS

Bernstein, Peter L. *Against the Gods: The Remarkable Story of Risk*. New York: John Wiley & Sons, 1996.

Golub, Bennett W., and Leo M. Tilman. *Risk Management*. New York: John Wiley & Sons, 2000.

Kahneman, Daniel, and Amos Tresky. *Choices, Values and Frames*. Cambridge: Cambridge University Press, 2000.

Krakauer, Jon. *Into Thin Air: A Personal Account of the Mount Everest Disaster*. New York: Anchor Books, 1997.

Neustadt, Richard E., and Ernest R. May, *Thinking in Time: The Uses of History for Decision-Makers*. New York: Free Press, 1986.

O'Toole, James, *Leading Change: Overcoming the Ideology of Comfort and the Tyranny of Custom*. San Francisco: Jossey-Bass, 1995.

# CHAPTER 7

# Money, Interest Rates, and Financial Markets

**C** onstant change and the evolution of our decision-making framework have been most obvious in private financial markets and public monetary policy. In the 1970s, unexpected inflation, volatility in interest rates, and a subsequent double dip recession were the combination of economic surprises and shocks that led to significant changes in the framework of the economy and mandated alterations in how to make decisions. Three questions face decision makers: How has the model of financial behavior changed over the years and where are we now? What are the barriers to effective decision making? What do the trends in financial markets tell us about our risks and opportunities going forward?

In 1958, A. W. Phillips, a New Zealand economist working at the London School of Economics, presented data showing a negative relationship between the unemployment rate and wage inflation in the United Kingdom.[1] At that time, Phillips observed that periods of rising wage inflation were associated with lower unemployment and vice versa. By the mid-1970s, the traditional model of the Phillips Curve, which postulated a trade-off between inflation and unemployment, was breaking down. Today we associate periods of stronger real economic growth in the economy with higher inflation and lower unemployment.

Over time, however, during the 1960s and 1970s, the rise in inflation gave rise to rising inflation expectations and the trade-off between inflation and unemployment appeared to disappear. Two lessons became paramount. First, the framework for the inflation-unemployment trade-off was changing. Second, expectations matter, and as expectations in the economy on economic drivers such as inflation were changing, so did fundamental economic relationships such as the Phillips Curve.

For example, the traditional monetary policy target of steady interest rates did not appear to work and market rates rose sharply in 1973 and

1975. Industrial production fell over 20 percent between 1974 and 1975. Unemployment rose to 9 percent, with consumer prices up more than 12 percent during the period. The economic framework based on the inflation-unemployment trade-off model faltered and the search was on for a new model.

In 1974, the price of oil rose over 60 percent and then jumped again from 1979 to 1981, such that double-digit inflation hit in 1974 and then again from 1979 to 1982. Short-term prime commercial paper rates, which had begun to rise consistently since mid-1977, spiked even faster in the second half of 1979. Investors took every new bit of inflation news as a major concern. Inflationary expectations soared, and as a consequence, drove nominal interest rates further upward. Money market funds became the investment of choice. The global economy again interrupted our domestic bliss. The effective dollar exchange rate fell from 1977 to early 1979, adding further to inflationary pressures and perceptions of heightened risk in the markets.

President Jimmy Carter, facing political problems of declining popularity and a difficult reelection campaign, offered the job of Federal Reserve Chairman in July 1979 to Paul Volcker. At the time, Volcker had been president of the Federal Reserve Bank of New York from 1975 to 1979 and had served as under-secretary of the Treasury for international monetary affairs. Volcker's background at the Treasury and as head of the New York Fed had given him the international exposure needed, as President Carter saw the rapidly escalating problems of the dollar and inflation. However, it was not until Volcker faced the distrust of foreign central bankers at the International Monetary Fund meetings in Belgrade that the tide turned on American monetary policy and its approach to inflation.[2] At those meetings, foreign central bankers questioned the Fed's commitment to getting inflation under control given the rapid increase in the money supply and credit in the United States. In addition, the weak dollar was framed in the context of rising inflation and negative real interest rates (nominal interest rates were below the rate of inflation). Money growth in the U.S. exceeded the 1979 targets. This suggested further inflation ahead and very limited commitment to dollar exchange rate stability on the part of the American government.

In response, in October 1979, Volcker dramatically altered monetary policy and thereby the role of money growth, inflation, and real interest rates. The Fed would hit its money targets and allow interest rates to fluctuate—which they did a lot during this period, as seen in Figure 7.1. In the short run, interest rates and the dollar rose while inflation and growth continued to move ahead. Over time, inflation abated and the wisdom of controlling inflation by slower money growth proved correct. By 1982, real interest rates on commercial paper were just 4 percent while inflation, measured by the CPI, had fallen from over 12 percent in 1980 to just 6 percent.

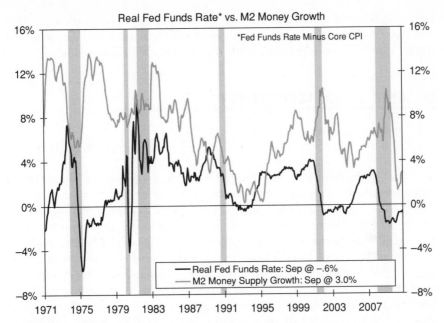

**FIGURE 7.1** Real Interest Rates and Monetary Growth
*Source:* Federal Reserve Board and Bureau of Labor Statistics.

During this latter period, unemployment rose sharply to over 9 percent. By late 1979, the economic landscape had deteriorated further as a second oil shock (the first was in 1974) was accompanied by double-digit inflation over the first six months of the year.

Yet, despite the success of the Volcker policy, the framework of money and capital markets continued to evolve; therefore, the targets and instruments of policy continued to change. By the mid-1990s, the pattern was stronger growth in the money aggregates (again, see Figure 7.1), but the inflation data continued to remain modest. Contrary to expectations, rapid inflation did not follow the rapid growth in the money supply. As a result, monetary aggregates diminished in importance as a focus for the Fed and eventually were discontinued as a formal target. The link between oil prices and inflation had diminished since the 1970s, along with the decline in the apparent money-inflation link. Inflation began a long-term, gradual slowdown with the globalization of trade and the approach of inflation control among many foreign central banks. Talk of a "Great Moderation" in economic volatility became the fashion. Meanwhile, monetary policy influenced the micro patterns of credit and interest rates over the business cycle, which took on greater importance, in turn, by setting the parameters for financing domestic real growth. Understanding monetary policy and credit conditions and their implications for financing growth in the national economy as well as the individual enterprise are critical to successful decision making.

## MARKETS BEFORE INSTITUTIONS

*I will pay cash or pay nothing.*

—Napoleon Bonaparte[3]

The establishment of the Federal Reserve as the central bank of the United States is a recent development. It is not even 100 years old. Unfortunately, there is a tendency for some writers to overemphasize the role of the Fed as the driver of all changes or shocks to the economy, when the complexity of the economic system certainly gives the Fed a significant but not all-powerful role.[4] However, as is obvious from the recent experience of 2007 to 2010, financial markets are independent entities with their own influence on growth, interest rates, inflation, and foreign exchange rates. Private markets exist for credit, goods, and foreign exchange. Each market has its own set of supply and demand factors, prices, and exogenous forces. These market factors evolve and so do their influence on any business—private or public—and their economic activity. Changes in these factors alter market prices for interest rates independent of any action of the Fed, and drive economic growth, inflation, and exchange rates. A primary focus on the Fed as an institution fosters a tendency to focus on the Fed for a solution. In fact, the resolution of the most recent financial crisis depended on the actions of many private market participants, not just the actions of the Federal Reserve.

## MARKETS: INTERDEPENDENCE AND THE DRIVING FORCE OF UNEXPECTED EVENTS

Many students are exposed to a course of study in economics where the national economy is treated as a single market in which changes in fiscal and monetary policy produce changes in economic output. Here the framework emphasizes change in the financial markets that involves movement in three distinct markets: goods, money, and credit. This framework can be expanded to equity markets as well, but for now, we will focus on these three markets. Rather than the partial equilibrium of a single market, we will assume a more general equilibrium view of the economic world, with the actions of three distinct markets impacting the decision making facing every private or public sector leader.

The supply or output of goods is a function of the amount of capital and labor for a given level of technology. Improvements in technology lead to greater output for any given amount of capital and labor. Improving technology is the result of innovation, which is covered in a later chapter. The production function is characterized by constant returns to scale. That is, equal percentage increases in all factors of production (capital and labor) leads to an increase in output of the same percentage. Firms maximize profit by hiring each factor of production up to the point where the marginal product of the factor equals its real factor price.

There are three sources of aggregate demand for goods: consumption, investment spending, and government spending. Consumption spending depends on consumer attitudes, wealth, and income. In this chapter, the focus is on capital investment owing to the critical link to the role of credit and interest rates that have traditionally driven investment spending. The quantity of capital employed by firms depends on the interest rate, which measures the cost of funds utilized to finance investment, as well as future expected sales.

Real investment spending is the link in this simple economic model between the real economy and financial markets and the most active link over the past 20 years. The balancing act is between the cost of funds (the interest rate) and the rate of return on the increased output produced by the new capital investment. When the cost of funds is greater than the return on the investment, the project is not undertaken and vice versa.

In the money market, the value of goods exchanged is expressed in the monetary unit. Changes in the value of money (inflation or deflation) reflect changes in the overall economy, which is a signal to alter investment strategy for pension funds, mutual funds, and the individual investors and their 401(k) plans. Households and businesses hold money primarily for two reasons. First, as very evident in 2007 to 2010, there is a precautionary demand for money as a safe, liquid asset with little principal risk. Second, money demand reflects a transactional demand and is related to income. Increases in income are associated with increases in the demand for transactions balances, which are the amounts of cash that households have in their checking and savings accounts. However, large transactions balances have an opportunity cost—they earn a very low rate of return. As short-term interest rates rise, the willingness to hold non-interest-bearing money declines.

In this way, the demand for money reflects the transaction demand for money that is related to income in the economy. In normal times, the speed of the turnover of the money supply—velocity—is constant. Of course, it is in abnormal times that the impact of changes in velocity produces sudden shifts in economic behavior and is a challenge to decision makers—but more about that later.

Economic activity, such as investment spending and money demand, is predicated on the ex-ante interest rate, that is, the interest rate at the time of the transaction. This rate reflects the expected return on investment, given anticipated inflation and tax policy over the life of the loan. Yet the world is full of surprises. In our decision making model, surprise changes in inflation and in tax policy lead to changes in investment strategy, which will alter the pace and direction of economic growth. Gold discoveries in California and Alaska, money printing in the Weimar Republic, and volatility in American tax policy all led to significant changes in ex-ante and ex-post interest rates and thereby to alterations in both the economic and political frameworks.

Our third market is the market for loanable funds, or credit. In this market, demand and supply drive the quantity and price of credit in the economy. As a result of the global economic downturn from 2007 to 2009, there was a dramatic decline in both the quantity and price of credit. The interest rate is the cost to borrow funds as well as the return for lending those funds in the marketplace. The supply of credit comes from savings—domestic and foreign, private and public. U.S. domestic saving has been augmented recently by foreign financial capital. Foreign investors have invested in the full range of financial assets in the United States, including United States Treasury debt, high-grade and high-yield debt, and agencies such as the government-sponsored enterprises, Fannie Mae and Freddie Mac, as well as mortgage-backed securities (see Figure 7.2). Private savings comes from households and private businesses, while the federal government sector has been primarily a dissaver, a net borrower rather than saver, in recent years.

Demand for loanable funds reflects the decision by households and private businesses to invest, and therefore their expectation that the return on that investment will exceed the cost of the investment. In our model, the ex-ante real interest rate balances decisions to save and invest. In periods of optimism, the demand for credit to conduct investment picks up relative to savings in the economy, so that the ex-ante real interest rate rises. Periods of rapid technological gains and real capital investment reflect this increase in investment demand. Alternatively, when savings exceed investment, the ex-ante real interest rate will decline. In recent years, fear of the recession increased savings and discouraged investment.

## Inflation Trends and the Changing Framework for Inflation Expectations

Expectations and their formation are therefore central to the understanding of the allocation of credit and the evolution of the credit markets. In the period of the 1950s and 1960s, inflation was low and the Federal Reserve focused on interest rate targets without a concern for inflation. In this environment, the framework for modeling expectations viewed expectations as adaptive—they reflected past information, with a greater weight on the most recent past.

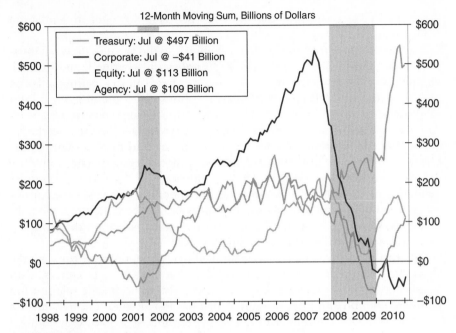

**FIGURE 7.2**  Foreign Private Purchases of U.S. Securities
*Source:* U.S. Treasury Department.

However, in the 1970s, inflation trends responded to changes in monetary growth. During the period from 1979 to 1982, with the very public pronouncements of Federal Reserve policy, market expectations incorporated a view of how the economy would work moving forward. Expectations were no longer just adaptive, but "rational" in the sense that market participants incorporated all available economic information in forming their beliefs about the future.

As market participants began to discount current monetary policy actions and their impact on the future, the lags previously associated with policy diminished and the model of the economy changed radically. First, changes in current money growth were associated with future changes in inflation. Investors and savers were no longer subject to the money illusion; they were not fooled by a nominal increase in incomes to induce increased spending when real incomes had not improved. Second, the framework for inflation and its influence on the economy also changed the characteristic of the relationship described by the Phillips Curve. In this case, workers no longer based their inflation expectations on the past, but rather on their model of how inflation would be formed in the future. They were no longer surprised by inflation, and the trade-off of unemployment and inflation faded away.

As the formation of expectations changed, so did the link between inflation trends and money growth. The Fed's policy of lowering money growth was perceived by investors and savers as a commitment to lowering inflation over time and was reflected in a quicker response of nominal interest rates to a change in money growth. Such rational expectations took time to form. Among savers and investors there may always be a residual uncertainty about the true economic model for the economy and how committed the central bank is to inflation control and using monetary aggregates to reduce inflation. However, during the 1980s, confidence in the Federal Reserve's commitment to fighting inflation rose. The model of rational expectations gained credibility with investors and businesses. At the same time, the public's understanding of the implications of monetary policy on the economy became far more widespread than in prior years.

As this model was increasingly applied over time, the time between the short run and the long run in economic activity began to compress, with significant implications for economic activity. In addition, the relationship between inflation and interest rates, called the Fisher equation, tightened in the short run. Irving Fisher, Yale University economist, argued that nominal interest rates can move for two reasons: the change in the real interest rate and the inflation rate.[5] As such, the framework of the economy also changed. Success against inflation allowed the Federal Reserve to achieve better economic growth with lower interest rates sooner than in the past, since lower inflation expectations led to lower nominal interest rates faster than they would have if inflation expectations had remained high. The old model of liquidity preference, where slower money growth led to higher interest rates, gave way to a model where slower money growth was interpreted as tighter policy that would lower inflation and therefore lower nominal interest rates sooner than earlier models would have allowed. Once again the framework of decision making evolved over time in response to learning by individuals and decision makers about the character of the modern economy and the structure of the economy adjusted as we learned.

## CHANGE AND PUTTING OUR FRAMEWORK THROUGH ITS PACES

Recent financial history provides another example of changes in the operations of our framework. From the period of 2004 to 2007, there was an increase in the demand for credit to finance investment in commercial and residential real estate. Investors believed that the return on such investment far exceeded the cost of funds as measured by the perceived low level of nominal interest rates at the time. Inflation was rather low and mortgage rates were very low relative to the expected rate of return on an investment in housing. Economic growth was moderate. Consumer and business spending continued with the gains in personal income and expectations of final demand.

However, beginning in early 2007 and increasingly through 2008, expectations of profit from further investment in commercial and residential real estate fell. The perceived high ratio of reward to risk fell dramatically. In some markets, home prices plateaued and in others declined as supply outpaced demand. For lenders, the appraisal values of the homes and the credit quality of the borrowers signaled deterioration in the quality of the credits. With this change in perceived risk and reward, the demand for credit fell sharply, while the supply of credit also declined as lenders turned cautious.

With a heightened sense of caution and growing fears of recession, the demand for cash rose for both households and businesses despite an easing in monetary policy through the money supply. Prices did not accelerate and, in fact, inflation moderated over the next two years more so than it had during the low inflation period of 2002 to 2004 (Figure 7.3).

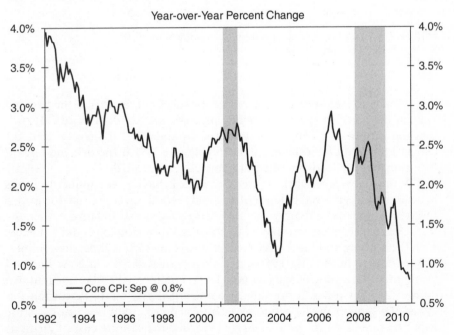

**FIGURE 7.3**  U.S. Core Consumer Price Index
*Source:* Bureau of Labor Statistics.

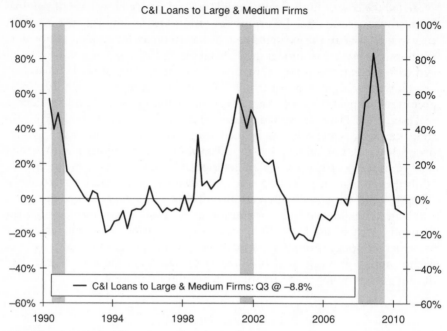

**FIGURE 7.4**   Net Percentage of Banks Tightening Standards
*Source:* Federal Reserve Board.

While the Federal Reserve increased the supply of reserves to the banking system, the banking system tightened its credit standards (Figure 7.4) such that the supply of credit at the old credit standards fell sharply. Yet, the demand for credit fell even more sharply (Figure 7.5) as the risk and reward for using credit effectively tilted dramatically toward risk.

Within our framework of credit market behavior, economic decisions depend on the perceived balance of risk and reward. Over the last 40 years, a series of happy and unhappy surprises have altered that balance. Often, the real value of the assets that served as collateral for many loans did not exist, as in the housing and farm price corrections of the early 1980s, the commercial real estate in the mid-1980s, and the regional shocks in New England (1990 to 1992), and Orange County (1994) commercial and residential real estate. At other times, a housing or commercial real estate expansion followed the growth of the economy or an easing of credit conditions as the expected rate of return on real estate exceeded the ex-ante cost of credit as represented by the market interest rate.

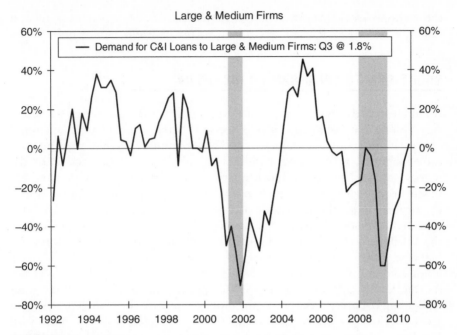

**FIGURE 7.5** Net Percentage of Banks Reporting Stronger Demand
*Source:* Federal Reserve Board.

With each shock, the ex-ante expected rate of return fell short of or exceeded expectations when economic growth rose or declined relative to expectations. In other cases, tax laws that raised the tax burden on interest, dividends, capital gains, and work effort altered the expected rate of return of an activity. In some time periods interest rates rose sharply, such as in 1994 to 1995, and financial market returns evaporated. In the Tax Reform Act of 1986, tax support for real estate fell dramatically so that ex-ante expected real returns disappeared. As the value of the real estate fell, so did the value of the collateral behind the loans issued by banks. The correction to the real estate market and the subsequent savings and loan crisis is emblematic of the link between financial surprises and consequent financial problems.

Unfortunately, this link between the financial and the real economy is often forgotten and so bears reemphasis here. Shocks to the economy and alterations in our decision-making framework can come from many sources—tax changes being one of them. The framework exercised for the economy and for decision making is a constantly evolving model of how the economy works. Sudden changes in monetary policy or changes in fiscal policy, which are reviewed later, are always possible and, in fact, quite likely.

## SHORT-RUN TO LONG-RUN ADJUSTMENT

An interesting dynamic element of the economy is the transition from short-run to long-run behaviors. While decision makers can identify an initial change in an economic framework, that preliminary change may be reinforced or even reversed over time. The imbalance of the growth of the money supply, however defined, relative to the growth of the demand for money leads to a sequence of changes. Historically, periods of rapid money expansion, under the gold standard, led to a rapid rise in inflation. This was characteristic of Spain after the gold discoveries were brought back in the 1500s and reinforced, although the gold did not initiate the period of higher inflation.[6] In the United States, monetary growth after the discoveries of gold in California in the 1849, silver in Colorado and Nevada (1859 to 1862), and gold in Alaska (1898) supplied the liquidity needed for an expanding country. A decline in the money supply in the United States from 1931 to 1933 prolonged the Great Depression. Under Fed chairman Paul Volcker, a slower growth in the money supply accompanied a slowdown in inflation.[7]

The liquidity effect would in the short run be associated with a decline in short-term interest rates—yet, over time, the impact of rising inflation would be associated with higher interest rates over time.

As for credit, changes in the demand and supply of credit set the tone for changes in interest rates across all markets. The pattern of interest rates reflects the influence of liquidity, credit, inflation, and concerns and expectations of growth over time. Credit has two aspects—price and quantity. For example, in 2009 to 2010, credit was relatively cheap, as interest rates were fairly low. But credit was not widely available, because even though the supply of credit fell relative to earlier periods (2005 to 2007), the demand for credit fell even more. Hence, lower rates and less lending occurred at the same time. As the economy recovers, the cost and availability of credit should improve. While conventional wisdom holds that rising credit rates lead to less credit availability, the pattern over time is that credit and its price move together with the business cycle.

During the height of the Great Recession of 2008 to 2009, the Federal Reserve increased the supply of credit through the purchase of Treasury securities and mortgage-backed securities (Figure 7.6). This effort was stymied, in part, by the risk aversion at banks that kept much of these additional reserves as excess reserves. Simply, excess reserves are defined as extra cash

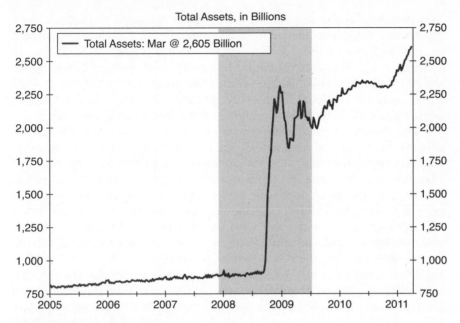

**FIGURE 7.6**   Federal Reserve Balance Sheet
*Source:* Federal Reserve Board.

on hand in excess of that required as reserve requirements to back up the bank's deposits. In a way, the Federal Reserve was pushing on a string. With higher capital requirements and greater uncertainty due to the impacts of new financial regulations and a stagnant economy, lending institutions had kept a higher level of reserves consistent with higher levels of uncertainty. Meanwhile, many households and firms were also concerned that they could not pay back any loans given the uncertainty surrounding revenues for firms and jobs for households. The Fed continued to supply reserves to lending institutions in the hope that as confidence improved, credit would become more available.

Credit spreads and yield curves also have their own supply and demand dynamics. Changes in perceptions of economic growth, inflation concerns, and credit quality alter the shape of a yield curve over time. For example, in the spring of 1907 a stock market correction was accompanied by the failure of the city of New York to sell a $29 million bond issue—only $2 million was sold. Call money interest rates had risen from 25 percent in 1905 to 60 percent in 1906, to 125 percent in 1907. By the fall of 1907, the city of San Francisco could not place a loan in New York City, that is, the city of

San Francisco could not sell its debt in the financial markets in New York City. Adding to the signs of economic stress, U.S. Steel reported a drop in earnings as the recession led to reduced liquidity and profits. In October 1907, the National Bank of Commerce discontinued clearing for the Knickerbocker Trust Company, the third largest trust company in New York, since the National Bank could no longer be sure that the Knickerbocker Trust could meet its obligations. The Panic of 1907 was on.[8]

The shape of a yield curve reflects its own dynamic, where the relative demand for short and long dated, fixed-income instruments changes over time relative to its supply. That may sound simple, but the patterns of factors that influence the shape of the yield curve are anything but simple. At the short end of the curve, investors are lending funds for only a brief period of time, so liquidity is fairly high and the risks associated with reinvestment and inflation remain fairly low. Yet, as we move out the curve, inflation and reinvestment risks increase. Future interest rates may rise or fall relative to current rates. So, there is a risk of reinvesting the invested capital at higher or lower rates compared to current rates. There is also the risk that inflation may rise over time relative to what is currently discounted and that the real value of the interest earned will be less than originally expected. We certainly saw this dramatically illustrated in the case of the rapid rise of inflation during the 1970s, which wiped out the real returns on fixed-income bonds issued earlier in the late 1960s and early 1970s. The ex-ante (expected) real rate of return was far less than the actual inflation-adjusted rate of return.

## QUALITY SPREADS, THE ECONOMIC CYCLE, AND ACCOUNTING FOR RISK

The historical cyclical pattern of the spread of Aa corporate bond rates over the 10-year Treasury rate is illustrated in Figure 7.6. This pattern imparts information on the market's assessment of risk. As the spread rises, the market's perception is that the risk of investing in corporate bonds has risen relative to investing in default-free Treasury bonds. As illustrated in Figure 7.7, spreads tend to rise ahead of recessions as seen in 2000 to 2001 and 2008 to 2009, and then decline during expansions, as illustrated by the decline from 2003 to 2007.

For decision makers, the lesson to learn is that the price of risk varies over the business cycle. Therefore, the process of issuing and buying debt must recognize the variation in risk and opportunity that happens over the cycle.

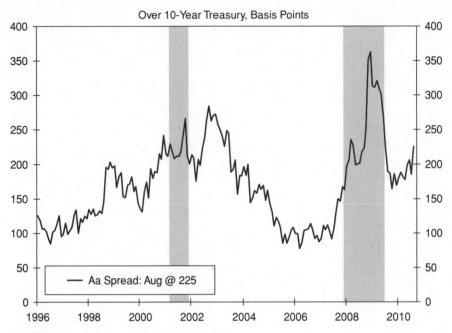

**FIGURE 7.7**   Aa Corporate Bond Spread
*Source:* Federal Reserve Board and Moody's Investors.

## EVOLUTION OF THE MONEY, INFLATION, AND INTEREST RATE FRAMEWORK

For decision makers, our framework on money, inflation, and interest rates has been kept simple to aid in the focus on dealing with real world changes. These challenges include realizing that:

- The framework of money and its relationship to inflation and interest rates has evolved over time.
- Current monetary policy is aimed at easing the problems of recession and slow growth.
- What policy makers perceive as inflation is at a level that is too low to be consistent with price stability.

Yet, when the economy returns to normal, monetary policy will reverse, signaling a change in the direction of interest rates and possibly credit availability.

In the early 1960s, the framework of money, inflation, and interest rates was fairly simple and the challenge for many financial market participants and bankers appeared fairly simple as well. Changes in the money supply, in the short run, led to changes in short-term interest rates through the liquidity effect. Over the long run, a sustained increase in money growth would lead to higher inflation and, through the Fisher effect, higher interest rates—particularly long-term rates. The lag between current money growth and future inflation over time reflected the way many workers and savers were initially unaware that a sustained rise in inflation was under way. Economic model builders modeled inflation expectations upon past low inflation periods. Since inflation expectations were considered to be adaptive at the time, today's inflation expectation reflected yesterday's inflation rate not upon a model of the inflation-driving power of higher than expected inflation. A second aspect of the framework was that over time, money growth would be neutral in its effect on economic growth. Changes in the money supply over time do not alter real economic activity, such as investment or consumer spending, but only influence the rate of inflation.

By the late 1960s and early 1970s, the framework for money and inflation began to change. Strong real growth over the years had diminished the spare capacity of the economy in the early post–World War II years. In addition, inflation had started to rise, from 1 to 2 percent in the early 1960s, to 5 to 6 percent by the end of the decade. People began to notice and commentators noted the intellectual link from money growth to inflation. The framework for policy makers and investors now telescoped the lag from money growth to inflation so that the short run became the long run very quickly. Interest rate volatility rose and the choices made reflected a model where interest rates could and did move further and quicker than earlier thought. The age of the bond fund manager was at hand.

With the rise of inflation, monetary policy shifted to a monetary aggregate target, so the framework for policy monitoring changed as well. The focus of information gathering became the weekly release of the Fed's balance sheet and the measure of the monetary aggregates. Risk now became framed in terms of the weekly volatility of interest rates. The distinction between nominal and real interest rates became paramount in defining the impact of interest rates on the economy. At this time, the conduct of monetary policy became defined in terms of targets, instruments, and methods. During the Volcker era, the target of policy became stabilizing the growth of the money supply in line with the Fed's intermediate targets for monetary growth. The instrument for policy became the monetary base to achieve the money growth targets. The methods of the Fed were open market operations.

What is important for decision makers is that the pattern for the conduct of monetary policy then changed over time. During the 1980s, the link between money growth and nominal economic growth and inflation diminished to the point that monetary targets eventually were dropped. Meanwhile, the Fed, especially under Chairman Alan Greenspan, increasingly came to rely on judgment rather than numerical money targets or selected interest rate targets.

Moreover, the link between inflation and the unemployment rate appeared to diminish as well. This further weakened the economic signals that decision makers could rely on to gauge future moves in monetary policy and interest rates.

In recent years, the Taylor rule, named after John B. Taylor, professor of economics at Stanford University, came to be accepted as a reasonable gauge for the conduct of monetary policy and interest rates.[9] The Taylor rule postulates that the real federal funds rate, nominal interest rate less the rate of inflation, responds to deviations of inflation and growth from their desired target levels. Essentially, the nominal federal funds rate is set equal to the rate of inflation plus 2 percent plus 0.5 of the difference of inflation, less 2 percent plus 0.5 times the difference of actual economic growth, less the estimate of its trend rate. Increases of inflation above 2 percent call for a rise in the federal funds rate. Meanwhile, if growth rises above its trend rate, the real funds rate is expected to rise as well. From 1987 to 2007 this rule helped explain the pattern of the federal funds rate, but since 2007 the rule has totally broken down since the rule attached equal weights to inflation and the output gap. With equal weights, the implied federal funds rate would be a negative 2 percent or a bit more.

## LESSONS FOR DECISION MAKERS

The first lesson for decision makers is that the framework of monetary policy has changed significantly, altering its impact on the economy. So decision makers need to be aware of the anchoring bias—the bias that allows an initial reference point to distort estimates—and how it impacts their analysis of trends in monetary policy. This is especially true now owing to the unusual economic circumstances of the Great Recession that greatly altered the traditional approach of monetary policy.

The second lesson is that the timing of the Fed's recovery window—the period of time between when an ambiguous threat occurs and a large-scale failure occurs—has also changed. This makes it more difficult to anticipate when the Federal Reserve might respond to changes in the economy. During the early period of the housing correction, the Federal Reserve appeared to treat this ambiguous threat as not a significant problem and one that was contained. Clearly the Fed was wrong. When the scale of the problem finally was recognized, the Federal Reserve acted quickly. But the economy slowed again and inflation remained very low. The Federal Reserve reacted cautiously once again.

A third lesson is that the history of money, inflation, and interest rates always involves a search for clues. Clues to the next move seem to appear in each and every economic release, every public statement by a Federal Reserve official, or even in the movements of the financial markets themselves. Unfortunately, the available list of indicators, as well as the number of "expert" Fed watchers, far outnumbers the possible number of Fed policy moves.

In 2010, the Federal Reserve engaged in a new policy called "quantitative easing" that involved purchasing Treasury, Fannie Mae, Freddie Mac, and mortgage-backed securities to promote faster economic growth. Quantitative easing immediately involves the problem of framing. Given this untested policy, the challenge for private decision makers is whether this new policy represents an opportunity (going for economic growth) or increased risk (in terms of higher inflation and interest rates) over the next few years. How decision makers frame the Fed's policy moves will define the success or failure of this untested monetary policy framework. As Bernanke and Reinhart stated when dealing with the low interest rate environment of the 2003 to 2005 period, "However, it is also true that policymakers' inexperience with these alternative measures (Japanese style quantitative easing) makes the calibration of policy actions more difficult."[10]

Now, we turn to the issue of the conduct of business strategy under conditions of uncertainty especially given the continued policy calibrations we have witnessed.

## DISCUSSION QUESTIONS

1. Although the recession began in December of 2007, the reaction of the economy to both monetary and fiscal policies has been very modest compared to the promises of policy makers of the impact of the stimulus.
   a. Discuss your thoughts on the inside lag.
   b. Discuss your thoughts on the outside lag.
   c. Going into this recent recession there was a belief that the modern economy had exhibited remarkable stability, capsulated in the concept of the Great Moderation. What do you think went wrong?
   d. Using the models of aggregate supply and demand, how might the economy have reacted to:
      - Increased consumer concern on house prices.
      - Decrease in credit supplied as risk perceptions rose.
      - A change in the financial market's assessments of liquidity and marketability in housing-related instruments.

    e. How might the other policy changes have altered the framework for financial markets, employment, and housing?

2. Paul Volcker is often given credit for defeating the inflation dragon. Discuss how Volcker's actions influenced perceptions of:

    a. The role of money versus the funds rate as a target for policy.

    b. The role of inflation and the dollar as signals of the effectiveness of policy.

    c. The importance of the independence of the Fed.

    d. The importance of presidential support for the Fed's independence.

    e. The perceived limit on policy due to the Phillips Curve in the short run and the problem of stagflation in the late 1970s.

3. As a member of your investment management team you are asked to present your observations on the market outlook on the interest rate market. You wish to make comments on five points:

    a. The distinction between real and nominal interest rates.

    b. The potential impact of unexpected inflation on your bond position.

    c. The implications from the Quantity Theory of Money of recent rapid growth of money on future inflation.

    d. Implications for your investment position of higher taxes on dividends and capital gains taxes on your expected rate of return on investment.

    e. Recent declines in consumer confidence that suggest that consumer saving is likely to rise quickly in the year ahead.

4. Over the short run the belief is that monetary policy can move the economy forward and thereby can lower unemployment and accept the trade-off of higher inflation. Yet, there is also the belief that over a longer period, growth of the money supply will determine inflation but not alter the rate of unemployment.

    a. Given the thrust of monetary policy toward quantitative easing in 2010, how might the impacts of such a policy play out over time?

    b. What are the assumptions of an economic model that would allow such easing to work? Fail?

## NOTES

1. A. W. Phillips, "The Relationship Between Unemployment and the Rate of Change of Money Wages in the United Kingdom, 1861–1957," *Economica* 25 (November 1958): 283–299.
2. D. E. Lindsey, A. Orphanides, and R. H. Rasche, "The Reform of October 1979: How It Happened and Why" (prepared for the Conference on Reflections of Monetary Policy 25 Years after October 1979, Federal Reserve Bank of St. Louis, October 2004).

3. Spoken at his first cabinet meeting after becoming consul, in response to the burst of inflation following the printing of money under the prior Revolutionary government.

4. Two critiques of the Federal Reserve come from: William Greider, *Secrets of the Temple: How the Federal Reserve Runs the Country* (New York: Touchstone Books, 1987) and Paul Krugman, "Paralysis at the Fed," *New York Times*, August 12, 2010.

5. Irving Fisher, *The Theory of Interest* (New York: A. M. Kelly, Publishers, 1967 reprint of the 1930 edition).

6. David Hackett Fischer, *The Great Wave* (New York: Oxford University Press, 1996), 77–85.

7. N. Gregory Mankiw, *Macroeconomics*, 7th ed. (New York: Worth Publishers), 393.

8. Jerry W. Markham, *A Financial History of the United States*, Vol. II (Armonk, NY: M.E. Sharpe, 2002), 29–33. The inability to clear payments due to counterparty risk revisited financial markets in the United States during the fall of 2008.

9. John B. Taylor, "Discretion Versus Policy Rules in Practice," Carnegie-Rochester Conference Series on Public Policy 39 (1993): 195–214.

10. Ben S. Bernanke and Vincent R. Reinhart, "Conducting Monetary Policy at Very Low Short-Term Interest Rates," *American Economic Review* (May 2004): 85–90.

## RECOMMENDED READING FOR SERIOUS PLAYERS

Fischer, David Hackett. *The Great Wave*. New York: Oxford University Press, 1996, 77–85.

Markham, Jerry W. *A Financial History of the United States*, Armonk, NY: M.E. Sharpe, 2002.

# CHAPTER 8

# Strategy, Risk, Uncertainty, and the Role of Information

The builders of the Transcontinental Railroad in the 1860s faced a trio of strategy challenges that can serve as a framework for thinking about strategy today. First, there was the immediate problem of planning and provisioning for the next day to be sure the men, horses, and supplies are all ready to lay down track. Second, alternative paths needed to be explored by the scouts and surveyors who would decide the path for the railroad over the vast Western landscape. Finally, there was the strategic vision of the California Big Four, Abraham Lincoln, Doc Durant, Grenville Dodge, and Theodore Judah.

The day-by-day decisions of how the railroad was built fell to the workers, many of who were Chinese who spoke very little English, and to the road bosses. Their job was extending the end of the line by another mile each day, and often by several miles each day. When they finished at the end of the day, surveyors and construction and supply managers came into camp each night, and looked over the horizon and planned the road for the next day. For the Union Pacific, the team work bosses were men like Jack and Dan Casement, each a general during the Civil War and now the heads of the construction crews on the line. Financial support came from Doc Durant, a financier from Wall Street, and Oakes and Oliver Ames: Oakes a congressman from Massachusetts and Oliver the acting president of Union Pacific. Grenville Dodge, a former Union general, was chief engineer for Union Pacific.

For the Central Pacific, the California Big Four of Leland Stanford, Collis Huntington, Charles Crocker and Mark Hopkins, four storekeepers in Sacramento, were the financiers, suppliers, and political connections for the Central Pacific. They oversaw the organizational and managerial problems. President Abraham Lincoln, a railroad lawyer himself, having represented the Rock Island Bridge Company and the Illinois Central, saw his long-run strategic goal as the unification of the country—East to West—via the railroad. Yet Lincoln wisely limited the government's involvement. Lincoln told Grenville Dodge, the head of Union Pacific, that the government could support the building of the railroad but not build it. For the Central Pacific Railroad, the strategic vision was that of surveyor Theodore Judah. He saw a way through the Sierra Madre Mountains and was the Central Pacific's first advocate in Washington. Building that railroad in the face of uncertainty, at a time of the Civil War and with challenges that required that new technologies be developed and put into place on the spot, serves as a backdrop to a discussion on the development of strategy under uncertainty.[1]

Dealing with uncertainty and risk is a fundamental challenge to decision makers. The multiple levels of uncertainty over time dictate different approaches given the variations in risk and uncertainty and the differing time horizons involved for each strategy choice.[2]

## FOUR LEVELS OF STRATEGIC THINKING

There are four levels to strategic thinking:

1. Short-run planning.
2. Considering alternative paths using current resources.
3. Changing the vision.
4. Applying new thinking under difficult circumstances.

At the first level, the very short run, the strategic focus is on the year ahead and the range of possibilities is purposely very limited. Such a strategic horizon is very familiar to those charged with developing annual outlook plans. At the second level, the stereotypical off-site meeting tends to focus on alternative paths, but these paths are projections that assume that the resources of the organization have not altered and new outputs can be produced from current given resources. At the third level, the focus is on the range of possible alterations of the culture and vision of the basic organization into new output areas with the assumption of a new set of resources. Finally, at the fourth level, decision makers face blue sky/dark night alternatives when the world turns upside down and new thinking is required because the fundamental fabric of the organization is under question. For each of these alternatives there is an interesting progression of the mix of risk and uncertainty along with changes in the time horizon.

Dealing with uncertainty and risk is a fundamental challenge to decision makers. In this chapter, the focus is on the multiple combinations of the mix of risk and uncertainty that dictate different approaches for different time horizons, and decision makers must also recognize that economic change drives strategy over different horizons. For every level of planning there is a specific mix of uncertainty and risk involved in each option. Moreover, shocks or innovation by a competitor could take a situation from Level One (short-run strategy) and make it Level Two (the risk of pursuing alternative paths); and in some cases, as seen in recent years, most visibly in regard to September 11th, decision makers move quickly from Level One–to Level Four–type planning.

## Level One: Short-Run Planning

Short-run planning for the day workers and the field bosses was focused on laying the tracks for the Transcontinental Railroad for the next day. Planning was done each evening only for the day ahead—not any farther. For them, the way forward was clear—with a given amount of rail, a given number of workers, and the design and technology of the track laid out for them, they knew what they had to do and intended on doing that for the day ahead. They were very short-run in orientation—the next day was their time horizon. The level of risk and uncertainty about the day ahead was very limited.

For the modern decision maker, the very simple, short-term orientation of the railroad workers and field bosses is similar to the traditional pattern of year-ahead planning. This pattern operates on the implicit assumption that the business or institutional model is unchanged and that there are no planned or anticipated changes in that model. Moreover, decision makers assume that all the information that is needed to plan for the year ahead is available.

Yet, as the assumptions underlying this approach are reviewed, the vulnerability of this type of planning is obvious. Economic history teaches that changes in the pace of growth, inflation, and interest rates are quite common and that corporate profits and the value of the dollar vary greatly. The economic model itself also changes over time—the relationship of unemployment and inflation, and the link between money and inflation, also evolve. In recent years, the globalization of trade and finance has altered the pattern of exchange rates and interest rates.

When analysts do year-end planning, they are at the very beginning of their dynamic decision-making model where no change is anticipated nor planned. There is no risk and all information is available. Year-end planning develops a single forecast of the future that is precise enough for strategic business development and is consistent with behavior in the mid-recovery expansion period of the business cycle. Supply and demand factors are very stable in the marketplace. The range of options and outcomes is narrow enough to point to a single strategic direction. Unfortunately, when assumptions of the model are not examined or reviewed carefully, then the outlook for the year ahead does not allow for exogenous economic shocks, technological changes, and/or any initiatives on the part of competitors.

## Level Two: Considering Alternative Paths

*Truth springs from argument among friends.*

—David Hume

Offsite exercises for business leaders typically focus on a limited number of alternate paths for the firm. Here the time horizons are typically a bit longer than just the year ahead and the risk of pursuing alternate paths is greater than in the year-ahead plan. Real uncertainty enters the picture as some of the alternative paths that are discussed are new fields the firm might enter, for which the firm might have little practical experience.

In some cases, the alternative paths may represent a choice or may be forced by competitors or new government initiatives. In these cases, change now acts on the basic economic model and business leaders enter the world of the dynamic decision-making model. These leaders must allow for change—either by evolution or major shifts—where surprises and the character of those changes (expected/unexpected, large, modest, or small) differ and thereby require different scenarios. In many cases, the offsite exercises allow for surprises. Surprises do drive change, and yet, more often than not, offsite alternatives are small, timid, and seldom challenge the core interests of senior management or whoever is leading the offsite discussion.

In addition, modest alternatives can quickly go far afield. A calm day can become a catastrophe, as evidenced by September 11th, or by the quickness of a tornado or by the surprising strength of a Katrina-type hurricane. Catastrophe drills are the norm for hospitals and fire departments, but seldom for private sector institutions.

Alternative paths may also mean different markets—either in terms of geographical or product diversification. Diversified apparel (Gap stores) or restaurant (Brinker's) companies provide slightly different offerings in price and selection. Apparel companies, for example, appeal to very different markets—women, teenagers, tweeners, often with different price points. In addition, the same firm can have different horizons for different product areas. There are often different products with different implementation dates, and therefore the risks for each initiative will be different. In some cases, like Coke and New Coke, the initiative can quickly go astray. In other cases, such as the iPhone, the new initiative can find quick consumer acceptance and overturn the established marketplace.

Each level of strategic thinking corresponds to different levels of risk and uncertainty and the quality of information available to decision makers. The same set of analytical tools for each level can not be employed because the level of risk and uncertainty differs for each level. For example, in Level One, those assumptions of perfect information and no change in the basic business model allow for the spreadsheet projections that are frequently used. Unfortunately, many strategic plans are developed around the spreadsheet approach without the planners recognizing the implicit assumptions they are making with respect to information, risk, and uncertainty.

**Probability and Risk**    For Level Two, the existence of discrete scenarios commands the assignment of probabilities and therefore assessments of the risks involved in planning. Moreover, alternatives also suggest that the information and models are not deterministic. Better information may deliver better decision making. Yet, what is the probability of each outcome from these discrete scenarios? What is the path to each outcome? How will your institution implement change to achieve each alternative outcome?

Alternative paths for a firm represent the attempt to build a better mousetrap, a new and improved version of the original mousetrap. Still, it is a mousetrap. The firm has not yet ventured into truly new territory. Often, this is the downfall of the offsite, as it seldom explores new ground. The offsite agenda avoids introducing debates that might prove too uncomfortable, that might dig too deep into the microeconomic challenges of pursuing a competitive evaluation of alternatives or of appraising the opportunities and challenges of future alternatives.[3]

Information, risk assessment, and the degree of confidence attached to alternative evaluations are vital for an effective offsite experience. At this stage, choices of alternative paths are not critical to the ongoing future of the institution. Alternative paths are generally small moves away from its core competency.

Yet, at the next step, the challenge before an institution can quickly escalate in a global trading and financial environment with the additional challenges of rapidly evolving technology. Unfortunately, the potential role of the offsite as an opportunity to challenge basic explicit and implicit assumptions is missed in favor of social gatherings and polite, if ineffective, thinking about the core mission and methods of the organization. Institutions often face multiple alternatives with several changes in economic factors happening at once, and often a range of probabilities of alternative paths for the organization. Finally, strategy will also be affected by a competitor's strategy, including both product and pricing changes. The American automobile industry again serves as an example of an industry that followed a successful path of innovation as evidenced by the Ford Mustang and the Chrysler minivan. Yet, its biggest challenges came not from pursuing the alternative path of successful models, but from the greater challenge of a significant change in the entire automobile industry environment that came from the smaller, more gas-efficient and reliable Japanese invasion that began in the late 1970s.

**Limiting Choice: Bias in Choosing among Evaluated Alternatives** Framing biases are the biggest challenge to effective decision making at Level Two since there are often two alternatives analyzed, one of which is to continue along the current path. As a result, the balance of gains versus losses favors keeping to the current path, since the risks and returns of such a path are well known to the decision makers. Meanwhile, the risks of the alternative path are considered more dangerous. The mental model that business leaders apply to frame their decision making will bias them against a new alternative as the risks will appear greater and the rewards less certain. One bird in the hand is worth two in the bush. Whereas Level One takes the current model as given and tests no other, the effect of the framing bias in Level Two also favors the existing business model.

Anchoring bias is another roadblock to effective decision making. When decision leaders evaluate alternatives, there is a bias in favor of the familiar path, the path they have been using, since they are comfortable with its risks and opportunities. This is especially true in the offsite context. Intellectually, the offsite is often an exercise in comfortable discussion rather than hard-nose decision making.

**Level Three: Altering the Vision**

For each individual and for every private or public institution, there is a point in time when the need arises for exploring the option of altering the vision of the firm. In the automobile industry, a firm becomes a credit company as well. A dominant competitor in some field decides to pursue vertical integration. In another case, thinking pursues a vision of the long term rather than just the short-run horizon. Finally, the risk and uncertainty mix leans more toward uncertainty and less toward risk as the institution ventures into areas where it has limited experience and limited information. This level distinguishes itself by the change in the active pursuit of alternatives, a change in the time horizon for strategy, and finally the recognition that business leaders have moved further out on the limb with greater uncertainty and less information to support their decisions.

At this level of planning, the focus is often on developing a new product outside the firm's historical field of expertise (Apple's iPod). Alternatively, there is the attempt to take traditional products and move into new geographical areas (Burt's Bees). In the international arena, cross-border expansions represent several challenges different from conducting domestic-only business. Yet, the economics of entry and exit are the same, although the playing field may be different.

McDonald's up-tiering their menu with premium salads and coffees reflects an attempt to develop the new product line outside the traditional expertise of the company. Given the popularity of Starbucks coffeehouses and the evolving healthful lifestyle of many consumers who wanted fresh salads and sandwiches, McDonald's decided to enter the market. Margins at this level are considerably higher than at the hamburger and fries level. Given McDonald's geographical reach and its tremendous number of stores, McDonald's realized it could make an impact. That has proved to be the case as McDonald's gained market share in both salads and coffee. Recently, we have seen Starbucks begin to offer wine in their coffee shops in the evening—another attempt to develop a second line of business.

In the building of the transcontinental railroad, the changes required in labor, capital, and technology broke new ground for railroad construction. On the labor front, the addition of Chinese workers was critical for the Central Pacific. In addition, crew bosses' prejudices had to be overcome, since these bosses believed that the Chinese were too small to do the job.

As for physical capital, the application of black powder, dynamite, and nitroglycerine was a choice among types of capital in different phases of mountain excavations. As for technology, the transcontinental railroad was built with speed and that allowed little time for innovation in the technology of the railroad itself. However, the success of the railroad did provide the incentive for a host of innovations—air brakes, automatic couplers, steels rails, and ten-wheel locomotives—in the following years as engineers put their efforts and financiers put in the money to build the railroads across America.[4]

Strategic visions can change successfully over time. The year 1981 was considered the beginning of personal computing. The IBM PC was built on August 12, 1981, and while not a spectacular machine by today's standards, it did bring together a lot of the desirable features of a computer into one small machine. IBM's biggest mistake during this early period was to contract the PC components to outside companies like Intel and Microsoft. Until that point, IBM implemented a vertically integrated strategy, building the key components itself. Instead of retaining ownership of the operating systems and the processor architecture (the true power and value), it gave away all that market value. Today, IBM has moved further up the ladder in the services business to generate work that requires more specialized skills. This strategy has proved to be very successful—as evidenced in their market cap and stock price.

When conducting strategic planning, business leaders often adopt Level One and Level Two as their standard strategy framework. Yet the more frequent short-run reality is that Level Three, with its multiple choices and techniques required to get to each choice, is what is needed. Moreover, actual strategy options lie along a continuum. It is not simply a choice between options one or two as would be suggested by Level Two planning, or even the three or more choices examined under Level Three. When considering strategic options, business leaders' biases come into play and limit their choices so that certain favored groups are not upset or that the existing production technology of the firm is not overturned. The options for companies in emerging industries and new geographic markets that are thinking at Level Three are both numerous and varied in design and often do require upsetting the corporate political apple cart. What economic factors influence the choices that institutions decide to pursue at this level of strategic thinking?

The focus here is on the economics behind entry and exit in the marketplace. The Level Three strategy approach is one of testing new markets for the firm, and so a competitive strategy assessing the actions and reactions of competitive firms is appropriate.

**Entry and Exit for Firms**   For most firms entering any field of endeavor, other institutions already exist in that market space. As the new entrant, the challenge is to assess the firm's competitive advantage or its strategy vis-à-vis the other companies. The study of entry and exit in economics has a long history and is the means for assessing competitiveness at this level.[5] Whereas Level One thinking relies on the spreadsheet, Level Three relies on the assessment of the economics of entry and exit. There are several caveats here. First, institutions tend to have a comparative advantage in the field in which they already practice. When they venture into new fields a different strategy mix is appropriate for each new segment of the institution.

This strategy mix will reflect the different combinations of risk and uncertainty and the quality of information gathered for each new initiative that the institution wishes to pursue. Unlike the certainty of Level One, the confidence range for each potential option will have to be estimated. In addition, the quality of the model will reflect an analyst's ability to assess the limited number of independent variables that will drive the estimated outcomes. In statistically driven models, this challenge is often more difficult than developing the model itself. Finally, these estimates for alternative paths will likely have a broad range of values and those values and their ranges will differ between alternative paths. Leaders must be cognizant of a framing bias as they examine alternative paths. This bias can prejudice their decisions in favor of or against risk taking.

Three other characteristics for Level Three must be recognized. First, decision makers commonly examine a limited number of alternatives; they are bounded by time and their imagination to a small set of all possible options. Second, when leaders examine alternatives they need to be aware of redundant scenarios that are not distinct options. For example, a transportation company can examine alternative routes to deliver a product, but if each route has to pass over a certain bridge any problem on that bridge is a problem for the company. The transportation company has no real alternative option to crossing that bridge. Finally, decision makers must be aware that different options will most likely be driven by different trigger events, that is, different events may impact alternative transportation routes.

An accident on one road will not affect traffic on another, while construction may impact the other route. For Abraham Lincoln, there were three routes to the West Coast and each route offered different risks and rewards.[6] So the time to implement different options may be a function of the timing of trigger events rather than a time of one's own choosing. For New Orleans, the time to think about options in a hurricane would have been before the hurricane hit—not while or after. Leaders may also suffer from an overconfidence bias. They underestimate uncertainty and focus on strategies that neither defend against threats nor take advantage of opportunities. In business, the copyright was left unprotected for the movie *It's a Wonderful Life*. This failure to defend against copyright infringement allowed anyone to replay the movie without paying a royalty.

**Economies of Scale and Scope**    For any institution or entrepreneur evaluating a set of alternative strategic moves, the economics of scale and scope will determine the future success of any endeavor.[7] Economies of scale exist when average costs decline as output increases, that is, the marginal cost of the next unit of production is below the average cost. Bigger is better, in other words. The challenge for leaders is to estimate over what range of output existing firms have economies of scale and then to estimate their firm's ability to compete at that level of output. In contrast, diseconomies of scale exist when marginal cost exceeds average costs.

Economies of scope occur when an institution achieves savings as it increases the variety of goods and services it produces. In effect, the institution achieves cost savings as it increases the variety of goods and services it produces at a cost below what could be done in two or more firms. In Levels One and Two, the implicit assumption is that there is no entry competition and no cost to continue current operations or enter a new area.

Scale economies reflect several forces including: indivisibilities and spreading of fixed costs, increased productivity of variable inputs, and the scale of inventories and their link to final sales. Indivisible economies arise from spreading fixed costs over an ever-greater volume of output. However, inputs cannot be scaled down below a minimum size due to high fixed costs.

Economies of scale result from the spreading of product-specific fixed costs over a greater number of units. If, however, unit production declines, then fixed costs can be a very heavy burden.

Any firm contemplating entering a new field, but with heavy fixed costs, will find that output below a certain level will result in high fixed costs. Unless the firm can be assured of a very large initial level of output, then at least initially there will be a loss in operations. This situation is to be expected for capital-intensive production, like steel and cement. But it also occurs in operations requiring high levels of research costs such as pharmaceuticals, high-tech equipment, and industrial equipment.

For many of the alternative paths a firm may explore under Level Three, the ability to achieve efficient operations and post entry profits will be limited by the extent of the market and therefore the institution's ability to achieve scale. Smaller markets limit the ability to capture economies of scale and the ability to specialize in any new endeavor. Scale will vary by the intended industry target and not by the current scale of the existing firm. While the existing firm may be large, the size of the intended new market may be too small to achieve economies of scale and be an effective competitor. For example, over the years, many otherwise successful fast-food/casual-dining chains have attempted to enter the breakfast wars only to fail (Wendy's).

Finally, inventories and their financing will be easier and at a lower cost if the firm is doing a high volume of business. The institution can usually maintain a lower ratio of inventory-to-sales while achieving the same risk of running out of inventories. Therefore, inventories behave as if there are scale economies. A new entrant into a sector may not achieve the scale to be competitive with existing firms given the extant firms' ability to manage inventories in a leaner manner and therefore save on financing costs.

**Diseconomies of Scale**    In this situation, the institution finds that its variable costs rise with production. Larger firms generally pay higher wages and provide greater benefits. As a management problem, the specialized resources and talent of the firm are spread too thin and have difficulty keeping all the corporate balls in the air. While talent may be able to run the current scale of the firm, when considering expansion, the leadership is unable to bring success to a new proposed initiative.

Incentive and coordination effects also are a challenge to decision makers considering expansion into new fields. Any institution that grows in size finds it more difficult to link the individual worker's compensation with the firm's profit. The individual worker also finds it difficult to link her performance to the success of the large firm. The institution will also find that it is more difficult to monitor and communicate to workers and thereby find it hard to promote effective worker performance.

Organizational efficiencies may also be brought to bear as an institution acquires new resources to pursue opportunities. An organization can spread its resources—particularly management expertise—over a wider range of activities. The ability to bring management expertise to an organization is a core competency of private equity investors. Organizational efficiencies also arise with a firm's ability to reduce both transaction costs and coordination barriers across firms. Essentially, leadership can better coordinate activities across the platform and thereby lower average costs. Finally, a larger firm can operate efficient, internal capital markets. It can thus allocate financial capital to the various divisions within the firm without having to go to the capital markets or borrow through banks. Smaller enterprises have less bargaining power.

## TAKING A CLOSER LOOK: FAILURE OF ECONOMIES OF SCOPE—AOL AND TIME WARNER

When AOL and Time Warner announced their merger in January 2000 the deal was considered a new-era breakthrough—a massive company was formed with 90,000 employees. AOL actually bought Time-Warner for $164 billion. However, by the time the merger was completed in 2001 the size of the company and its different cultures proved difficult to manage—especially with the rapid changes occurring in the Internet environment for an Internet service provider (ISP) firm such as AOL. The market value of these firms collapsed with the end of the tech bubble. While the faltering economy/recession of 2000 to 2001 was partially to blame for the new firm's inability to deliver on the 12 to 15 percent annual growth that was promised, it was quite apparent both firms were highly overvalued in the dot-com bubble era, which led to unrealistic financial expectations over time. The competitive position of AOL did not hold up and its market value sank. In 2002, the company wrote off $99 billion for the merger and in 2003 the name AOL was dropped from the corporate title.

Moreover, cultural issues became very apparent between high-tech AOL and media conglomerate Time Warner. The new company was never able to achieve economies of scope, for example, the addition of AOL to Time Warner did not add to the distribution network as originally anticipated. Consumers preferred the freedom to download whatever content they desired, rather than be forced-fed what a service provider (like AOL Time Warner) offered. A great example of this was music downloads.

**Stepping Outside the Organization: Vertical Integration and Diversification**
Vertical integration is one way to explore new options for a firm. Vertical integration can work for two reasons—technical and agency efficiency. Technical efficiency refers to the ability of a firm to lower production costs through the implementation of a lower cost production process. Agency efficiency refers to the benefits of more effective organization of the existing production/distribution process for the exchange of goods and services in the vertical integration process.

Diversification offers an institution a range of options to reach the same customers in more ways, or to reach new customers with the original set of products. Brinker International reaches new customers by adapting new restaurant types (Maggiano's Little Italy and Romano's Macaroni Grille) while Yum! Brands (Kentucky Fried Chicken) and McDonald's take their reliable restaurant models to new markets such as China. Costs to diversification are similar in character to the diseconomies of scale for the expansion of the existing enterprise. The diversified firm's management has the problem of coordinating incentives and rewards for workers who perceive that their individual effort is further and further unrelated to the performance of the overall firm. Diversification of the enterprise into related but distinct enterprises may actually inhibit the internal capital market of the firm, as transfers of resources among distinct units would be more obvious and encounter resistance at the corporate unit.

There is also the famous "winner's curse," where the firm with the most optimistic assessment wins, pays the most, and likely overpays, since the other bidders did not project value at the higher price.[8] Oil field auctions and spectrum auctions are two areas in which the winner is likely to bid too much for the item in question. This happens most often when there is a single winner and that winner overestimates the value of the property in question. Today, we can ask whether Hewlett-Packard paid too much for data storage company 3Par in its bidding against Dell Computer.

**Biases Leading to Subpar Level Three Results**    Three biases limit the ability of decision makers to evaluate alternatives. First, there is the framing problem—mental models that are utilized to simplify an understanding of the complex world. While leaders may not be wedded to their original business model, their ability to evaluate alternatives may be biased by willingness to take or avoid risk. Where teams of evaluators are involved, as is often the case in many organizations, these evaluators need to be challenged to constantly update their mental models so as to build collective awareness of the risks and rewards for each alternative.

Second, confirmation bias leads some evaluators to gather and rely on information that confirms existing views and to avoid or downplay information that disconfirms preexisting hypotheses. No matter how evaluators try to be neutral, certain prejudices crop up. Many evaluators of strategic options find data to support their view and downplay contrary indicators. In economics this can be seen in forecasters who find a straw man piece of data to support their increasingly out-of-touch view.

Finally, the anchoring bias allows an initial reference point to distort an evaluation of alternatives. There is the inherent bias in favor of the initial starting point. We are familiar with it and know its pluses and minuses. We love our old car since we are familiar with its quirks. We tend to stay with restaurants we know. For enterprises, we stay with programs and products we have now and do not switch paths unless the evidence is overwhelming.

Since many evaluations of alternative paths are frequently a group decision, sense making plays a key role.[9] Sense making is a shared recognition process—not simply what is going on in one person's head—but a shared recognition of a similar set of issues and problems. In sports, in a winning game, pitchers and catchers are on the same page, as are quarterbacks and wide receivers. In business, conflicts between the CEO and the corporate board or the CFO tend to make front page news. In cases such as Enron, the leadership team was clearly not on the same page as shareholders and employees in terms of corporate strategy and goals. In contrast, effective sense making derives from a clear philosophy known throughout the organization while in other cases it is the members of the small team working together over time toward a shared goal.

In 1949, 12 smoke jumpers/firefighters died in Mann Gulch in the Helena National Forest, Montana, in what they originally thought to be a routine fire when they arrived on the scene.[10] However, in a few hours, their initial assumptions about a routine fire began to unravel. Their early actions, including taking photographs and an apparent casual dinner enjoyed by their leader Wag Dodge, indicated their comfort with what they thought was a routine fire. Later, Dodge's assessment of the fire changed suddenly when he saw a pattern of billowing smoke. Unfortunately, by that time, the threat imposed by the fire was no longer routine and, in fact, led to the death of many of the smoke jumpers. There were four issues. First, the crew and Dodge had not trained together and so the crew could not reconcile the sudden turn in Dodge's attitude with his earlier actions. Second, Dodge told his crew to drop their tools and, for the crew, their tools were their identity as firefighters. Third, Dodge lit an escape fire and lay in the ashes since he judged they could not outrun the fire. For most of the crew, their intuition told them to run. Finally, the crew was not trained together as an operational team. They were trained as smoke jumpers and forest firefighters, but not as a unit. Theirs was not a shared experience. Much like the rookie pitcher and the experienced catcher, sometimes signals get crossed.

**Barriers to Entry**   Barriers to entry are factors that allow incumbent firms to earn positive economic profits while making it unprofitable for newcomers to enter the industry. There is a central role to be played by information and risk assessments in setting up barriers to entry. Both the entrant into a new market and the incumbent must recognize the asymmetry of information, as neither firm is entirely sure of the other firm's capabilities and strategies. This increases the risk assessments required by both firms. This asymmetry impacts the assessments of the strategies available to incumbents and entrants. In essence, the incumbent has sunk costs in meeting its perceived needs of the marketplace. The newcomer, meanwhile, has incremental costs to enter the marketplace and faces the challenge of achieving enough scale to register acceptable post-entry profits. The entry of a new firm and the reaction of the incumbent introduce a set of actions that cannot simply be projected with high confidence based on historical relationships, since no history of the entrant's strategy exists.

Barriers to entry can be either structural or strategic. Structural barriers include favorable regulations, natural cost or marketing advantages. A strategic barrier reflects the decisions of the incumbent to aggressively deter entry. These barriers include limit pricing, predatory pricing, and the ability to expand output capacity. Structural barriers can be so high that the incumbent does nothing, yet the potential entrant firm still does not attempt to enter the business. Alternatively, structural barriers can be so low that attempts to deter entry will be ineffective. or the cost to deter a potential entrant exceeds benefits. Low structural benefits are typical in markets with growing demand and rapid technology improvements.

Control of essential resources is a familiar structural entry barrier, exemplified by the DeBeers diamond monopoly, the fight for water rights in the West (as in the case of Los Angeles drawing water from Mono Lake), and that between Mexico and the United States over the waters of the Colorado River. In addition, there are barriers that reflect accumulated knowledge, investments in technology, and trade relationships. In much of the European expansion of the sixteenth and seventeenth centuries, the Dutch, English, and Spanish nations fought for control of trade routes for spice trading, for example. Many actions took the form of limiting the possibility of competition from other countries that came later to the global trading race.

**Strategic Barriers**   When an incumbent firm tries to keep an entrant firm out by employing an entry-deterring strategy, it must make an assessment of current information and the level of risk. Once that is done, employing this strategy should boost the incumbent's profits through certain actions. Yet, nothing is guaranteed. Economies of scale and scope provide an economic basis for strategic barriers. Firms that operate beyond a minimum efficient scale have a substantial cost advantage. This allows a firm to set a market price that is greater than or equal to average costs. For the potential entrant, the challenge is to assess, with limited information, the ability and amount to spend to overcome the incumbent's cost advantage.

The information asymmetry here is that the incumbent does not know what price the entrant will charge if it enters the marketplace. In addition, the incumbent has an established brand. Therefore, it can retain market share without the same level and expense of advertising required by the entrant to achieve the incumbent's brand awareness. The incumbent also has a cost advantage. The new entrant must spend a considerable amount to achieve a certain level of production that minimizes the average cost of production in order to reach the profit goal associated with the decision to enter. Yet, the total market size may not allow both the entrant and the existing firm to achieve enough scale to experience economies of scale.

This is especially true if the strategy of the established firm is to not back away. Here the issue of sunk costs comes into play.[11] Since the incumbent faces fixed costs, it has an incentive to lower prices to retain market share, thereby increasing output if necessary. This makes it more difficult for the entrant firm to achieve enough scale of output to generate the lower average costs needed to achieve its profit goals. This problem of scale is particularly associated with large-scale entry into capital-intensive industries.

The leading company in any industry can alter the entrants' expectations about the nature of post-entry competition by limiting the price margin over average costs, thereby limiting the incentive of any firm to consider entering the marketplace. Effectively, the incumbent firm, by limiting pricing, attempts to avoid the emergence of a contestable market that would allow enough margins for the firm contemplating entering the market to initiate such entry.

Limit pricing is simply the practice where an incumbent firm discourages entry by charging a low price before entry occurs. There are two forms of limit pricing that reflect the different risk and the asymmetry of information in the marketplace. First, the incumbent firm has rising marginal costs and is unable to meet all the market demand, yet sets a price below the estimated marginal cost of the entrant, with the expectation that the price will discourage entry. The incumbent firm believes that low pricing would deter an entrant. The price suggests to the potential entrant that the post entry price would be as low or lower going forward. Therefore, any post-entry profits for the entrant would be less than would be acceptable if the entrant decides to enter the marketplace. In this case, the entrant is unsure about the demand for its product or service at the going price and whether the entrant can cover the costs of production given the uncertainty of the price.

Second, limit pricing may take the form of a potential entrant that decides to fight for market share and long-run profits by forcing the incumbent to set limit pricing indefinitely. The entrant thereby accepts lower profits over time that would be less than the incumbent estimated when first adopting the limit pricing strategy and expecting the entrant to quickly withdraw. The strategic move of the incumbent to limit pricing is based on the assumption that the entrant can be influenced by expectations about post-entry pricing and competition and will drop any interest in entering the market. There is a risk here. The incumbent may be required to accept a permanent decline in profit margins to sustain the entry deterrence. The role of asymmetric information is crucial here because the potential entrant does not know the real average costs of the incumbent. At the same time, the incumbent does not know how long the potential entrant will accept minimal profits and losses in the short run to achieve a long-run entry to the marketplace.

As an alternative to limit pricing would be predatory pricing which occurs when a large incumbent sets a low price to drive smaller rivals from the market and this low price also deters future rivals from entering the marketplace. For the incumbent, any short-run losses due to low pricing are expected to be made up in the long run since there will be no competing firms if the low-price strategy is successful. The role of asymmetric information is crucial here. Predatory actions may be profitable if incumbent firms have information about their own costs or market demand that entrants or potential entrants lack. Therefore, any potential entrant faces a significant risk. The potential entrant does not know the incumbent firm's true average costs and how willing it is to lower prices in the short run to undercut any initiatives by the potential entrant firm. Therefore, the entrant firm faces a significant risk that the incumbent firm has both the ability and the willingness to set a price that will make the potential entrant's market entry unprofitable.

The asymmetry of information between the knowledge of the market by the incumbent and the estimates of the market by the entrant are significant and act as a barrier to entry. The incumbent wants the entrant to believe that post-entry prices will be low. If the entrant is uncertain about the post-entry price, and thereby profits, then the incumbent's pricing strategy could affect an entrant's expectations. The entrant is likely to know less about the incumbent's costs than the incumbent does. So, engaging in limit pricing makes it appear that the incumbent has low costs. This lowers the entrant's expectations for post-entry profits and deters it from entering. In addition to being unable to perfectly infer the incumbent's cost, the entrant is also unsure about the level of post-entry demand. Entrants are also unsure about the incumbent's willingness to slash prices to maintain market share and thereby limit the entrant's profits. Incumbents that have a reputation for toughness will discourage entry. The existence of a group of potential entrants will require the incumbent firm to have deep pockets to ward off all potential newcomers.

A firm may carry excess capacity that will affect how potential entrants view post-entry competition. For the incumbent, the sunk cost is a natural asymmetry. The incumbent can expand output at a relatively low cost. Therefore, an expansion of output by the incumbent will reduce the entrant's post-entry profits, perhaps below sunk costs of entry, and the potential entrant stays out. The idle capacity stands as a credible commitment to expand output to limit entry. Excess capacity will deter entry if the capacity is a sustainable cost advantage where the excess capacity is serviceable, efficient capacity. In addition, the entrant will be discouraged if the perception is that the growth in market demand should be slow—otherwise, rapid demand growth will quickly outstrip capacity and allow for the entry of a new firm. In sum, decision makers must be able to intelligently estimate the entry and exit conditions of their businesses just like generals must estimate the break point of an opposition army.

Successful strategy results from applying consistent principles to constantly changing business conditions. Therefore, strategies are adaptive but principled responses of firms to their surroundings and to the economic forces acting on the franchise. Conditions change and, therefore, so do strategies. In our next section, we shift the focus from strategy that begins inside the firm in a thoughtful process to strategy that must react to radically altered, often externally driven, circumstances.

## Level Four: Applying New Thinking

At this level, uncertainty dominates risk, information is limited and the vision and commitment of leadership is the crucial factor—certainly this was the case for the transcontinental railroad. In contrast to earlier levels, the comfort of a gradually lengthening time horizon or an offsite meeting no longer exists. Decision makers are faced with a situation in which the world appeared to be Level One and now is turned upside down. One minute leaders have Level One, and then they face Level Four. Here the time horizon collapses rapidly—action and decisions need to be taken rapidly and without a clear vision of the future. Situations such as Apollo 13 (re-entry to the earth with a dying space capsule), September 11th, and the Miracle on the Hudson (the crash landing by Chesley "Sully" Sullenberger) require a rapid response. In business, the Tylenol scare (the recall of millions of suspected tainted pills) and the failure of Lehman Brothers exemplify Level Four.

When a case has no precedent, as was true of Apollo 13, the world turns upside down. In such situations, the old framework is immediately suspended. Goals are switched—from profits to survival in business and from landing on the moon to getting the Apollo 13 crew back safely. In these situations, leaders cannot rely on a historical record—there is none. We create a new database as we go along—recall how Ken Mattingly, the astronaut who was scratched from the flight, had to create a way to conserve energy on the spacecraft to keep the capsule in the air and the astronauts alive. Leaders are also operating along multiple dimensions of uncertainty— with people, equipment, and technology. Once the basic model is broken, the environment is virtually impossible to predict. The range of possible outcomes cannot be precisely identified. Nor is it easy to determine all the relevant variables that could drive the outcomes. For example, it was impossible to know the results of German unification on the balance of the European economy. The collapse of the Soviet Union created a new Eastern Europe and many new relationships available in foreign policy. The opening of Chinese and Indian economies to trade and finance has certainly altered the competitive economic environment for all.

The four levels of strategy options respond to a different balances between risk and uncertainty, information quality, and time horizons. In a famous exchange as Apollo 13 began its reentry, one senior NASA official commented that this could be the worst disaster NASA had ever faced, to which, the flight director, Gene Kranz, replied, "With all due respect, sir, I believe this is going to be our finest hour."

For decision makers, this is a classic example of framing. When a problem is framed in terms of risk one person can see the downside, while another person sees the same situation as opportunity. The mental model exercised by the mission leader was one of the ways to find success rather than anticipating disaster. Framing allows people to simplify their understanding of the complex world.

Framing also becomes important when people are tempted to view the problem only in the framework of the old model. Instead, people must constantly update their mental models to build collective awareness. The old model of how to bring the crew back from lunar orbit was gone. The mission was no longer going to the moon, but getting back to earth. In response to the collapse of Lehman Brothers, the Federal Reserve's vigilance against a resurgence of inflation was over; the new challenge was to provide financial stability and prevent the downdraft of the economy into another 1930s Great Depression.

Sense-making also plays a critical role in addressing the world turned upside down. The shared recognition process becomes vital in these situations. It took a team approach to build a filter to maintain air supply on Apollo 13. In the aftermath of the Lehman Brothers failure, it was the response of both private and public institutions that helped stabilize the financial system.

In the twenty-first century, the central role of capital markets in driving economic growth becomes apparent given the surprisingly wide, to some, impact of the failure of Lehman Brothers. Alternatively, the capital markets can be viewed as an aid but also a hindrance to the best-laid strategy options for any institution. Finance represents its own set of information challenges and risk/uncertainty/reward trade-offs, as has been apply demonstrated throughout the recent turmoil. This is the story that unfolds next.

## DISCUSSION QUESTIONS

1. You are the strategic adviser to a major public utility company.

   Please explain the underlying economic structure of the demand and supply for electricity in the region today. This structure should also reflect the demographics of the region.

   Given the likelihood of environmental and energy regulation in the future, as well as the changing demographics of the region, please provide your views on the three strategic postures your firm should adopt to deal with three different horizons (one year ahead, 10 years ahead, and 30 years ahead) for your strategic vision for your firm.

   Each strategic posture should reflect your assumption on the driving economic and political patterns that influence your strategic vision of the firm going forward. Consider the impact inflation, real growth, oil/coal/natural gas prices, interest rates, and the exchange rate may have for each of your postures.

2. In 2010, continued slow economic growth, low inflation, low interest rates, and the rapid disappearance of investor interest in certain financial products have forced your firm to rethink its future profitability and competitive performance. As a strategic adviser to your firm, discuss how these changes in growth, interest rates, liquidity, and thereby sales assumptions would impact your management goals, product choices, and financial goals for the year ahead.

   Over the longer run, how would the economic and regulatory changes of this period impact your firm's strategy for growth and expected returns in different product areas? How would recent changes alter your view of domestic and international expansion?

3. Mergers and acquisitions are often justified on the basis of future opportunities as well as immediately adding to shareholder value. Yet, often such justification fails to pan out.

   How would the influence of considerations of entry and exit drive expectations of success on a merger? In recent years, Chinese firms have sought mergers to enter new markets. What are the pluses and minuses that face the Chinese as they attempt to expand?

Mergers also promise economies of scale and scope. Explain how such promises could deliver shareholder value. How would such promises fail to deliver value? How would you evaluate the AOL Time Warner merger in terms of economies of scale/scope?

## NOTES

1. *Nothing Like It in the World,* written by Stephen Ambrose (New York: Simon & Schuster, 2000), is one of the best books on strategic thinking in action, and is the source of the discussion of the transcontinental railroad.
2. The importance of uncertainty and trade-offs is presented in a very useful case study, *The Decision Process: Five Key Steps.* Excerpted from *Decision Making: 5 Steps to Better Results* (Cambridge, MA: Harvard Business School Press, 2006).
3. From my professional experience, I have reformulated the academic approach to decision making presented in a very good case study presented in "Strategy Under Uncertainty" by Hugh Courtney, Jane Kirkland, and Patrick Viguerie, *Harvard Business Review* (On Point Article, November–December 1997).
4. Ambrose, *Nothing Like It in the World,* 268.
5. Joan Robinson, *The Economics of Imperfect Competition* (London: Macmillan & Co. Ltd., 1933) and Fritz Machlup, *The Economics of Sellers' Competition* (Baltimore: Johns Hopkins Press, 1952).
6. Ambrose, *Nothing Like It in the World,* 23–41.
7. This section draws on the exposition in *Economics of Strategy* by David Besanko et al., 5th ed. (Hoboken, NJ: John Wiley & Sons, 2010).
8. Richard Thaler, "Anomalies, The Winner's Curse," *Journal of Economic Perspectives* (Winter 1988).
9. K. Weick, *Sensemaking in Organizations* (Thousand Oaks, CA: Sage, 1995).
10. Karl Weick, "Sensemaking in Organization: The Mann Gulch Disaster," *Administrative Science Quarterly* 38 (1993): 628–652.
11. Sunk costs have had a long history in economic debates. For a recent contribution, see R. Preston McAfee, Hugo M. Mialon, and Michael A. Williams, "When Are Sunk Costs Barriers to Entry? Entry Barriers in Economic and Antitrust Analysis," *American Economic Review* (May 2004): 461–465.

## RECOMMENDED READING FOR SERIOUS PLAYERS

Besanko, David, David Drano, Mark Stanley, and Scott Schaefer. *Economics of Strategy,* 5th ed., John Wiley & Sons, 2010.
Collins, Jim. *Good to Great.* New York: Harper Business, 2001.
Gordon, John Steele. *The Business of America.* New York: Walker and Co., 2001.

# CHAPTER 9

# Capital Markets: Financing Operations and Growth

Every high school textbook on American history proclaims the Louisiana Purchase from Napoleon as the crowning achievement of Thomas Jefferson's two terms as president of the United States, and an accomplishment almost entirely of his own doing. Reality is a bit different, however. And this difference highlights the importance of capital markets in supporting economic growth. While bankers are frequently portrayed as evil by politicians and the popular press, the Barings Bank of England came to the rescue several times as the republic came of age.

In the early nineteenth century the rapid growth of the West depended on the Mississippi River to reach global markets. Jefferson, along with Madison, was the leader of the Democratic-Republican Party. Jefferson relied on the western rural states for political support in his battles with the Federalist Party, whose strength lay in the eastern states. Therefore Jefferson sought expansion into the Mississippi River region and he was very concerned about the future of the Louisiana territory. Meanwhile, a weakened Spain ceded the Louisiana territories to France. England offered to step in to ease Jefferson's fears about the French, but Jefferson was more concerned about having the English at his back door than he was worried about the French. Jefferson, in fact, a former ambassador to France, had been the one person in Washington's cabinet who wanted to help France during its revolution. For Jefferson, it was England, not France, that posed the greater threat. Jefferson sent his friend, James Monroe, past minister to France and future president, to France to help the American minister at that time, Robert Livingston, to negotiate.

There was significant domestic opposition to the deal from those who complained that the United States already had too much land and not enough money. Yet, at the negotiation table, it was Barings Bank that provided their good name and financing, and that was credited with lowering the price of the purchase by providing the funds—putting up 60 percent of the capital needed to complete the deal. Barings profited from the deal, which is the nature of capital markets to this day. A major merchant banker based in Amsterdam, Henry Hope, supplied the other 40 percent. Napoleon thus actually sold Louisiana to Barings and Henry Hope, not the United States, since their credit was better than that of the country's at the time. Barings later turned over title to the United States in exchange for 6 percent United States bonds, since Barings and Hope were investment bankers, not landlords or farmers, and had no long-run interest in the land. Moreover, this was not the first time that Barings had helped support the United States. Barings had financed the growing cloth trade in the colonies as well as performing the typical banker magic of transforming early republic bonds, which were of questionable value, into silver—an international currency of choice—to pay off the Barbary pirates who had harassed American merchant shipping.[1]

## ENGINE OF ANALYSIS: THE MARKET FOR REAL CAPITAL AND THE MARKET FOR FUNDS

The Louisiana Purchase, cloth manufacture, and the Barbary pirates illustrate a central principle: Actions in the real economy have their counterpart within the financial sector. The economic framework for decision makers must reflect the interaction of two markets—the market for real capital (investment) and the market for funds to finance that real capital investment.

For the market for real capital, entrepreneurs must estimate their expected rate of return, after taxes, for every given investment opportunity. First, the real rental price of capital depends on the stock of capital, the amount of labor, the pace of technological improvement, and the expected pace of economic growth. With limited capital stock, the real return on any additional new capital stock would be high. Second, as more labor becomes available then any firm can put more capital to work. In contrast, if labor is very limited then a firm is limited in how much the firm can produce even if plenty of capital is available while being left unused. Immigration has often supplied the needed labor as we know from the history of the textile mills in New England and the building of the American railroads. Third, improvements in technology that are embedded in a new investment would suggest a higher return from such investment and thereby an increased demand for real capital. Finally, the higher the expected pace of economic growth, the greater the incentive to invest. At the national level, the demand for investment capital comes from the sense of opportunity for growth in the national economy. Such opportunities can be characterized in economic terms as the opportunity for profit. Profits represent the difference between revenues and costs where the revenues reflect the productivity of capital to produce a product that sells compared to the cost of that capital reflected in its rental cost which, in turn, reflects its price and its rate of depreciation. Profits also represent the return on risk capital in an economic framework, and thereby bring in the aspect of risk previously discussed. Returns on investment also reflect the impact of taxes and depreciation schedules that are based on public policy decisions.

Meanwhile, the economy also generates a flow of real savings from both the consumer and household sectors to help finance growth. This interaction between national investment and saving generates equilibrium in loanable funds at a given interest rate. That interest rate adjusts to balance out the desires of firms to invest with the amount other firms or households wish to save. If interest rates rise from that equilibrium point, savings will rise but investment opportunities will not meet the required rate of return. In contrast, if interest rates decline from the equilibrium level, savings will fall short of the desired amount of financing for the increased amount of investment projects that appear profitable.

So how do those savings get to the intended investment project? That, along with incorporating the aspect of reliable information on risks and setting investor and borrower expectations consistent with the risk/rewards of any project that is so critical to thoughtful decision making, is the job of the financial capital market. Moreover, the evolution of options for savers and for those firms that want to put those savings to work has been truly remarkable over the past 40 years. Savers originally saw their options as being of three primary types, savings accounts, bonds—often savings bonds, and direct investment in equity markets. Over time, however, the changing nature of the economy has provided the incentives to savers to seek alternative savings channels (ergo the boom in mutual funds in the 1970s and the growth in exchange traded funds in recent years) and for financial intermediaries to provide those channels. Changes in the values of five key economic factors (growth, inflation, interest rates, the dollar exchange rate, and profits), relative to expectations, have been driving forces for innovation in capital markets to meet the needs of both savers and investors. In the meanwhile, financial intermediation has been the conduit for transferring financial resources from savers to borrowers—with sometimes very uneven results.

## PERSPECTIVE OF CHANGE OVER TIME

Over the past 30 years, the interactions of capital markets and the real economy have come to define the patterns of the business cycle, the development of a high-tech service economy and the globally competitive manufacturing economy that emerged in the post–World War II period. Both the economy and financial system have and will move ahead, evolve, and achieve greater prosperity over time. Economic and financial recoveries appear after each recession; depressions do not. Each recovery brings with it opportunities. The longer trend for the economy is positive growth, not inevitable decline. In part, it is the flexibility of capital markets to support that growth that makes a difference.

Dynamic change and adjustment are the essence of capital markets. Therefore the success of any decision maker will reflect their ability to take advantage of opportunities as they arise. There is an engine of economic and decision-making analysis, a process of opportunity and innovation that characterizes the American economy and thereby provides signals to entrepreneurs as to when to act. While each decade since the 1970s appears to begin with a given framework for capital markets, by the end of the decade unexpected shocks have altered that framework. A new framework then becomes evident.

A thoughtful analysis of financial developments reveals a history of crises, resolutions, and the emergence of new opportunities in areas such as commercial paper, money market funds, high yield bonds, high-tech equity finance, and mortgage finance. Moreover, this history demonstrates the interaction of monetary policy, fiscal policy, and financial markets. Public policy and private markets do not operate independently—they are very much interrelated in both the ups and downs in credit cycles.

The integration of global financial developments in recent years has re-emerged, reminiscent of the pre–World War I period. Surprising to many observers today perhaps is that the period of the late 1800s into WWI was characterized by extensive global capital flows as investors in Europe, for example, helped finance the expansion of railroads in both North and South America. Between the world wars, however, global finance had declined as emerging political philosophies of capitalism, fascism, and communism were in competition. The exchange of financial capital was difficult and diminished entirely during the Great Depression. Financial regulation during that time in the United States, and elsewhere, severely limited the capabilities of domestic financial markets while imposing tighter regulation and prohibiting some activities outright.[2] In contrast, today's global integration has produced significant impacts on many areas, such as labor markets, that would have not been previously associated with globalization. Once again, this globalization of capital markets has altered the framework for decision makers in many businesses and economic applications. Today, excess savings flows from Asia to help finance investment spending in North America and many emerging markets.

# ECONOMIC CHANGE AS DRIVER OF AN EVOLVING CAPITAL MARKET FRAMEWORK

Economic change has been the driving force in providing the incentives for both savers and investors. Each economic expansion in growth has been accompanied by an expansion of credit in the economy. Yet, over each cycle the risk assumed by borrowers and lenders has also increased until that point when a macroeconomic or credit market change alters the perceived risk/reward trade-off. That change generates feedback effects that force choices on borrowers and lenders as they devise a new economic and credit market framework. This process repeats itself in each cycle, as we shall now see.[3]

By the mid-1960s, the pace of economic growth in the economy had exceeded the expectations of many and the fears of some that there would be a repeat of the Great Depression. Savers began to see a distinct strength in equity markets relative to their expectations and the concept of mutual funds investing gathered momentum. Meanwhile, for investors, tax cuts and economic growth raised the expected rate of return on capital. The number of shareholders in America more than tripled between 1952 and 1965. McDonald's went public in 1965, signifying the emergence of the consumer market in the United States as well as the acceptability of consumer stocks as an investment alternative to the big industrial steel, automobile, and railroad stocks. Meanwhile, the 1960s became an era of mergers and the growth of conglomerates as old industrial structures were being remade to fit the modern era.

At this time, two of the great drivers of capital markets and dynamic decision making appeared. First, inflation, a central economic factor, became a major concern as the society's output began to run up against supply constraints not seen since before the Great Depression. Unemployment, not inflation, was expected to be the problem of the post–World War II era, but just when it appears that the economy is in for a smooth ride, changes happen. Second, the internal dynamics of the capital markets created a momentum to continue doing what is successful until the breaking point was reached. By the late 1960s, the conglomerates of Ling-Temco-Vought (LTV) and International Telephone & Telegraph (ITT) had stretched the capabilities of management—the diseconomies of scale and scope that we reviewed earlier began to overcome the skills of managers. Meanwhile, many corporations began to extensively utilize the commercial paper market for their short-term financing. Commercial paper is an unsecured (not linked to a specific asset as collateral) note issued by a corporation for a short time period, usually less than six months, but it can be longer. Yet, in 1970, the Penn Central Railroad, the largest nonfinancial company in the country, filed for bankruptcy and at the time had a significant outstanding debt in commercial paper. Since commercial paper was perceived to be issued by only the best companies, with very short maturities, the paper was considered very safe. The economics of railroads in the northeast United States were negative since the railroads depended upon labor-intensive, short-haul services that were vulnerable to the emergence of the interstate highway system that began in the mid-1950s. In addition, railroads were burdened by the heavy regulation at the Interstate Commerce Commission that limited the rates, output prices, and charges for freight and passenger traffic. Cost reductions were also limited by government regulations and labor union contracts.

Although the economic framework of the American economy was very dynamic in the post–World War II period, Penn Central's bankruptcy brought into question the viability of the commercial paper market that had been a primary source of capital for major business. This situation highlighted two elements of the changing economy. First, it showed the changing nature of the traditional business model for railroads in the face of alternative modes of transportation such as the interstate highway system and the airlines. Second, as shall be seen again and again, the viability of a new financial asset class, commercial paper, would be redefined and reconstructed to emerge as a core element in the financial markets. Financial assets such as mutual funds, high-yield bonds, and securitized assets each have their own life cycle of booming, busting, and then reappearing like the phoenix in a different but more viable financial form.

By the 1970s, oil shocks and the continued rise in inflation at a rate much greater than expected gave impetus to the growth of money market funds, which rose from $3 billion in 1976 to over $80 billion in 1980. For savers, the need to seek a rate of return on savings to compensate for inflation drove the search for the higher nominal returns available in money market funds. The obvious underperformer while this was occurring was the bond market; passbook savings and United States savings bonds also declined significantly. By 1980, Congress authorized national banks to offer negotiable order of withdrawal (NOW) accounts, that is, a checking account that pays interest.

During this same period, the Nixon administration dropped the link of the dollar to gold. The dollar/gold parity at the time could not be maintained, as the gold supply was being drained too rapidly by foreign governments in exchange for dollars. The break in the fixed dollar/gold exchange rate opened the era of floating exchange rates. The dollar, another fundamental factor, was allowed to float and that generated the opportunity—and risk—of hedging this foreign exchange rate exposure. Unfortunately, for the Franklin National Bank in the United States and for the Bankhaus Herstatt in Germany, the risks of exchange rate fluctuations became all too real and both banks failed in 1974—both banks had speculated on changes in exchange rates and had bet wrong. Here again, economic change forces a revaluation of the framework and, in some cases, such a revaluation does not take place quickly enough or completely enough to avoid catastrophe.

## COMPLEX INTERACTIONS: ECONOMICS, EXPECTATIONS, AND INFORMATION

The experience during the years 1973 and 1974 illustrates the central role of expectations and information in setting the right framework for decision making as well as the changes and shocks of economic factors that drive those expectations. Higher inflation, higher oil prices, the unlinking of the dollar to gold, and finally the recession all generated a series of shocks that should have prompted many decision makers to reevaluate their basic economic model. Higher inflation combined with higher unemployment created what was called *stagflation*. This situation generated an intellectual challenge to the accepted wisdom of the prior decades. Finally, the links between capital and real economy markets enhanced the challenge for decision makers and reduced the reliability of simple spreadsheet models as a means of capturing the complexities of the national economy.

Capital markets are informationally efficient, that is, the capital market reflects all available information about the value of an asset. Price changes are reflections of information changes that impact expectations of future economic fundamentals and thereby the future value of financial and real assets.[4] New information is constantly coming before decision makers. The values of new information can be quite different from expectations and therefore lead to a rapid change in asset prices, which can be both volatile and informationally efficient at the same time. Such volatility is not necessarily a sign of market manipulation. Rather, it can be more a result of new information that differs from prior expectations. Volatility, then, is actually a rational reaction to new information. The history of market manipulation claims is very long, as evidenced by the 1923 investigation of farm commodity prices by Henry C. Wallace, the agricultural secretary, who could not establish that the lower prices were the result of manipulative activities. Over the very short run, price manipulation is possible, but as evidenced in the Hunt brothers' (Herbert and Nelson) attempt to corner the silver market, such manipulation is impossible over the long run without government sanction. In the short run, the Hunt brothers had bought ounces of silver directly, as well as over 10,000 silver futures contracts. In early 1980, regulators and the Commodity Exchange altered the rules on trading and margin levels, prices plunged, and the Hunt brothers' attempt failed. On average, however, price volatility over time reflects the fundamentals of economic developments, not the sustained manipulation of market prices by a few rogue traders.

Rationality does not mean there are no mistakes, bad investments, or financial crises. Markets are rational in the sense that they incorporate all available information under the conditions that define rationality. That is, the market price of any financial instrument is equal to the expected present value of the future cash flows available for distribution to that financial asset and the quality of information embedded in that expectation is greater than the information available to any one individual. This framework serves as a good approximation of the behavior of real-world financial markets. The model is not consistent in cases in which prices depend in an important way on factors other than the fundamentals of the cash flows or the discount rate applied to those cash flows. In some cases, also, market prices may not reflect the information associated with the fundamental value such that investors can systematically identify differences in market prices and fundamental values. These principles do not eliminate the impact of fear and panic or the fact that sometimes investors can beat the market and sometimes they lose money. These, however, are the exceptions and are not expected to persist over time.

Here the important point is that people and markets make the best guess on an investment given the information they have. Of course, when new information comes along, then the prior decisions can be proven wrong and market prices will change. Markets don't fail in the sense that rapid, violent changes in asset prices happen. Instead, markets reinvent themselves with new information. Straw man characterizations of financial markets that rely on rapid, violent price adjustments as a signal of market failure are no more valid than a claim that election surprises mean that the political and electoral process fails. New information that is radically different from what is expected will lead to rapid adjustments, no matter what the field of study.

Part of internal adjustment to new economic information is the reaction of business firms to the changing opportunities for investment alternatives. These changing opportunities are reflected in the expression termed *Tobin's Q*, which is covered in many economics textbooks and has special meaning to the internal dynamics of capital markets.[5] The Q ratio simply compares the market value of installed capital relative to the replacement cost of installed capital where the market value is the value of the economy's capital as determined by the stock market. The denominator of the ratio is the price of that capital if it were purchased today. In cases where Q is greater than one, the market value is greater than the replacement cost and the firm has the incentive to buy more capital. However, when Q is less than one, the market value is below replacement cost and the firm does not have an incentive to invest.

Looking at the issue from a different angle, if the expected marginal product of capital is greater than the cost of capital, the firm can expect to make a profit, so investment is likely to increase the firm's market value—this would be associated with the case of a high Q value. In contrast, if the marginal product of capital is below the cost of capital, the firm would be losing money with further investment and so reduce its market value and be represented by a low Q ratio. Several points are interesting here. First, the values of the expected marginal product of capital and the cost of capital will change over the business cycle. Second, policy moves, such as changes in tax rates, depreciation schedules, and easier monetary policy will alter the character of the trade-off driving business investment decisions.

Profits expectations also are characterized by a cyclical pattern. Hence, the decisions made to pursue investment and strategic options will also change over the cycle even though the characterization of a recovery would still fit the stage of the economic cycle. This pattern provides an internal dynamic to the profit cycle independent of the overall economic cycle. At the early stage of an economic recovery, revenue tends to rise faster than costs; hence, year-over-year profit growth usually spikes upward and peaks early in the cycle. Firms have rationalized their operations during recession and therefore are operating at very low fixed costs. Gains in revenue are over a very low cost base and thereby generate strong profit gains. These surprising profit gains generate improvements in equity prices and generate some of the best gains in equity prices for the cycle. Meanwhile, firms sense a new set of opportunities and therefore pursue greater real investment and merger opportunities and thereby draw on credit availability in capital markets. Although corporate profits are frequently portrayed as a negative aspect of America's economic system, these profits are the incentive for investment and further growth in the economy. Meanwhile, profits contribute to household wealth as investors and workers begin to tally up the value of their investment and pension portfolios. For the health of the macroeconomy over the long run, equity investors are the owners of the firm. Their historic role has been to allocate their capital in a way that maximizes economic returns. This incentive also drives the way society moves capital to maximize economic growth. The patterns of equity flows, dividends, and price-earnings ratios provide information on the success of a company and the economy.

The framework for resource allocation through the capital markets constantly evolves. From the time that the joint stock company first evolved in England and the Netherlands in the sixteenth and seventeenth centuries, the allocation of capital through the private markets has been vastly superior to the allocation of capital by political dictate. Allocation by the government plagued Spain in the sixteenth and seventeenth centuries and limited the long-run rate of growth of the country.[6] Looking ahead, the evolution of global capital markets will represent a new challenge to the entrepreneur, as global capital flows will reflect the multitude of economic forces (growth, inflation, interest rates, public policy, taxes, and regulation) that are associated with domestic policy. (This global influence is covered later in this book.) In the years ahead, the continued evolution of capital markets will take on a greater international character.

## THE 1980s: ANOTHER DECADE, ANOTHER NEW NORMAL FOR THE FINANCIAL MARKETS, AND THE CRITICAL ROLE OF THE RECENCY BIAS

Each decade since the end of World War II has presented decision makers with a different economic context for the financial markets. There is no old normal, new normal, or just normal. Evolution and change are the proper appellation for each decade.

For the 1980s, the major intellectual challenge was the recognition that the difference between expected and actual historical patterns and a new direction were the defining characteristics for successful decision making. Entering the present decade, the character of decision making would best be defined by the recency bias. Decision makers placed too much emphasis on the recent economic history of a double dip recession (repeat of 1980 to 1982), high inflation, and high short-term interest rates. Building on the earlier analysis of the confluence of cyclical and structural factors, the turn of the decades from the 1970s to the 1980s represented a significant shift in economic behavior that would have been totally missed by those whose thinking was dominated by the recency bias.

With the strong commitment by the Federal Reserve under Chairman Paul Volcker to defeat inflation, it should have been clear to decision makers that the path of future inflation would be far below that of the 1970s. Nominal interest rates should follow the inflation path and decline as well. Investors who bought high short-term interest rate credit default swaps (CDS) in the early 1980s had missed the opportunity for capital gains in the equity and bond markets. Meanwhile, lower tax rates provided the incentive to work and invest and reinforced the incentive for economic growth that further boosted the equity markets, profit growth, and the sense of economic prosperity.

Yet, these changes in economic forces also caught many by surprise. The shocks of lower inflation, in particular, meant that nominal mortgage rates and many business loan rates became very high ex post and therefore led to further economic adjustments. The shock of lower oil prices caught institutions such as Penn Square Bank in Oklahoma by surprise—the value of its loans depended on high oil prices to generate the revenues to pay off the loans and the loan participations they sold to other investors. The oil shocks also created insurmountable problems at Seafirst Bank in Seattle which had bought several hundred million dollars worth of these loan participations. Continental Illinois Bank had also purchased loan participations, which compounded other problems associated with a large portfolio of nonperforming loans to firms such as International Harvester and Braniff Airlines. By mid-1984, Continental Illinois Bank was effectively nationalized by the FDIC, renamed the Continental Bank, and eventually bought by Bank of America in 1994. Meanwhile during the first half of the 1980s, lower interest rates prompted many savings and loan institutions to seek higher yields by taking on riskier assets. Unfortunately, this strategy took many firms into unfamiliar territory and led to the failure of many thrifts in the mid- and late 1980s.

The experience of the 1980s reinforces the necessity to treat an economic shock and surprise as new information and then to evaluate how that change will impact the economic model and make choices that result in a new model of the capital markets. This decision-making approach recognizes that capital markets, as is true of other economic markets, evolve over time and that each decade since the 1950s has been different. Unfortunately, models of how the world works are often cast in concrete more in the minds of decision makers than in the real world. Leaders give lip service to the argument that change is constant, but their business models are rigid to change. In the early 1980s, inflation fears dominated the minds of decision makers despite the apparent commitment by the Federal Reserve to fight inflation. Slower inflation created problems in the commodity markets and, at the same time, higher real interest rates increased the debt burdens of many borrowers. The value of the dollar rose quickly in the early 1980s and then fell in the latter years of the decade. Failure to modify the economic framework led many financial and non-financial firms to ruin as strategy failed to match the new regime of lower inflation and interest rates as well as exchange rate volatility.

The 1980s also reinforced the significant economic distinction between real and nominal interest rates and ex ante and ex post interest rates, which would come back to haunt financial markets some 30 years later. With inflation high and Fed policy tight, nominal interest rates, those usually reported daily in the marketplace, were very high. Many of these rates appeared on long-term obligations such as mortgages and corporate debt, for example. Yet, as inflation fell faster than many expected, the real interest rate, the nominal rate adjusted for inflation, rose sharply and therefore drove upward the real cost of debt. As a result, the real burden of the debt was greater than many had expected and was a continuous source of stress on many firms and households. In a similar way, the same process appears to have followed the experience of the Great Recession. Ex ante interest rates reflected the expected high pace of future inflation. Yet, ex post, inflation fell sharply and the ex post interest rate burden was higher than many firms expected. The 1980s reinforced the distinction that the real interest rate borrowers and lenders expect to pay when the loan is made is the ex ante real interest rate. The interest rate actually realized is the ex-post real interest rate.

In the 1990s, the driving force was the maturation of technological change—the evolution of personal communication and Internet access. In addition, the growing globalization of trade after the North American Free Trade Agreement led to a sustained period of moderate inflation. Finally, political developments led to limits on federal spending and a cut in capital gains tax rates in 1997, which helped, in part, to strengthen the venture capital and high-tech boom of the 1998 to 2000 period. Within this environment there was a shift toward greater equity investing, especially in the dot-com sectors. Effectively, there was a change in expected equity returns relative to risk. Once again, the framework for capital markets had changed as investors sought greater returns while accepting, at least in the short run, less risk.

## INTERNAL CYCLICAL CHANGES IN CAPITAL MARKETS AND THE OVERCONFIDENCE BIAS

Yet, the distinction between expected and actual risk evolved over the cycle in a pattern reminiscent of the internal dynamics seen over prior cycles. In essence, the challenge for decision makers is that within each economic cycle there is a tendency for risk to be increasingly discounted and rewards overly emphasized such that even with the overall continued growth in the economy, the internal pricing dynamics of capital markets will change.

Moreover, the pattern of steady economic expansion and low inflation leads to an attitude of complacency at both the private and public sector levels that generates problems in the future. Such an attitude of complacency gives rise to the overconfidence bias. With the passage of time, the data entered into any mathematical spreadsheet model is likely to trend toward greater stability and, as a result, the apparent level of risk declines and the steadiness in rewards appears assured. Private investors tend to overplay this apparent, more than real, increase in the ratio of reward to risk, as is evident in the experience of Long-Term Capital Management (LTCM) in 1998.[7] The essential trading strategy for this hedge fund was to build complex mathematical models to take advantage of convergence trades, that is, the convergence of bond prices for different sovereign debt issuers due to differences in liquidity. However, as LTCM's asset base grew, the company pursued even more aggressive strategies and took on leverage to achieve expected investor returns.

These complex trading strategies for LTCM fell apart with the economic shocks of the 1997 East Asia financial crisis associated with the currency collapses in Thailand and Indonesia and the 1998 Russian government default, reflecting in part the decline in the prices of commodities, including oil. As panic set in, similar to what would be seen in 2007 to 2010, investors sold European and Japanese bonds to buy United States Treasury bonds. The value of the bonds diverged, contrary to LTCM's strategy, and the convergence trades generated huge losses. In September 1998, representatives of the New York Federal Reserve Bank and the United States Treasury visited LTCM. As a result of the meeting, they decided to pursue a program of support. The Federal Reserve Bank of New York organized a rescue package with contributions by major Wall Street creditors to avoid a wider collapse in the financial markets.

## TWO UNDERAPPRECIATED FORCES IN FINANCIAL MARKETS ARE IRONY AND PARADOX

For decision makers, the lesson should be clear by now. Each framework they adopt is dependent on the macroeconomic environment for success. Trading for small price differences only makes sense when the markets are highly stable and price volatility is extremely low. While this certainly can be true over short time periods, the history of much of the post–World War II financial span has been full of surprises, change, and the constant evolution of a new financial framework. Overreliance on precise mathematical models, without recognition of macroeconomic volatility, is often the downfall of most elaborate economic and asset pricing models. Precision is the purview of the physical sciences, not of the investing fancies of investors.

Public policy is also not immune to the surprises of the real and financial economy. Early in the 2000s, complacency arose among both the investor community and policy makers due to the growing belief about the "Great Moderation" in macroeconomic volatility in both the rate of economic growth and inflation.[8] Various explanations of such moderation were advanced, including structural change, improved macroeconomic policies and good luck. By 2007, obviously, the good luck ran out. Unconventional macroeconomic policies were called for since the "improved" macroeconomic policies did not work. And, of course, structural change in capital markets occurred again in response to these changes. Public policy makers, as well as private investors, appeared to suffer from a case of the overconfidence bias. Wall Street and Washington now had to engage in explaining new-era economics to millions of Americans who did not happen to work in the brokerage houses or live inside the Beltway.

# THE GREAT RECESSION OF 2007 TO 2010: UNDER THE HEADING THAT FACTS DON'T MATTER UNTIL THEY DO

> ...*while the preponderance of economic and public policy commentary focuses on traditional macroeconomic measures—growth, jobs and inflation—the role of the financial system, outside the Federal Reserve, in fostering those activities is often overlooked.... In contrast to the media portrayal of irrational exuberance and the madness of crowds, there is a surprisingly logical process in the financial marketplace that drives economic behavior.*
>
> —John Silvia[9]

Credit cycles follow a pattern. This pattern can be expressed as first a period of caution, then better-than-expected profits that draw in new financial capital seeking profits and a growing optimism about the possibility of future profits. This optimism leads to a period of overbidding on the profit opportunities, but at some point the optimism on profits is disappointed, followed by a market correction and possibly collapse in the previously profitable market followed by an initiation of another period of caution.

The Great Recession of 2007 to 2010 (and certainly longer in some localities and industrial sectors of the United States and the global economy) exhibits behaviors seen before in the post–World War II period. While the magnitude of the correction has been the most significant since the Great Depression, the logical process is much the same as prior adjustments. Change, however radical, calls forth choices and the construction of a new framework to deal with the altered reality. From the dot-com bust to the housing price crash, it appears that speculation is a social activity carried on in groups.

America's latest credit cycle, subprime lending, is not a unique experience but rather the latest variation of a traditional cycle of innovation, excess, and correction compounded by public policy laxity followed by overreaction. Indeed there is very little that is new or creative in the whole subprime saga. This is disappointing because the subprime credit patterns we observe are so typical that they suggest much of the recent experience could have been avoided. In the end, the whole experience brings forth several core public policy issues that are more often avoided than faced.

## Subprime Lending: Just Another Market

Little is unique about the market for subprime loans. There is both a demand and supply. Opportunity and risk are compared and a price is assigned to credit. This simple framework highlights that first, in any decision-making network, it is important to recognize that there is an underlying structure of the economy and that the structure is dynamic and thereby reflects the interaction of finance and economics over time. The structure of the credit markets, for example, reflects the forces behind the supply and demand for credit and does not exist in a vacuum.

How does our decision-making model apply to the subprime experience of today? The housing market model is quite simple, with a buyer, take, for example, a young married couple, with a given credit history and income. Contrary to popular myth, speculators, also termed *investors*, make up only 10 to 15 percent of housing market purchases. On the supply side, we have a builder. In between, we have a mortgage broker who qualifies the borrower for the purchase.

Expectations drive all parties' behavior. From 2006 to 2010, what were their expectations? Buyers expected home price appreciation, in some markets very big appreciation, and often expected their personal income to also rise over time to cover their future payments. Builders saw a healthy housing market and were willing to build many homes that were expected to sell at a profit in a very short time. The mortgage brokers also anticipated a healthy market and expected an active market for the ultimate holders of the mortgages.

## ECONOMIC EVOLUTION AND THE CHANGING RISK/REWARD CALCULATION

We often know, but more often forget, that the structure of the economy changes over time, and therefore, neither today's public economic policy nor private sector strategies will always be suitable for the economy ahead.[10] Moreover, perceived problems are never fixed in perpetuity; this is especially evident in public experience with highway construction. How often have we asked ourselves when they will ever finish this highway? Yet, we know the highway will never really be finished, since as the economy grows and work/traffic patterns change, modifications to the transportation system will always be required. So it is for housing and its associated credit cycle.

For the housing market, public policy had developed along the path that the role of government was to provide financing, or at least a seal of approval, in the guise of the Federal Housing Administration, as well as secondary market liquidity in the form of several government-sponsored enterprises. This framework was developed in the pre-globalization era of the 1960s through 1980s. At that time, standardization and liquidity were major issues for the housing market. However, since the early 1980s, global capital markets evolved to provide more than adequate liquidity and securitization of mortgage loans.[11] Unfortunately, as the economy evolved, public policy did not adjust with the rise of private secondary markets. The net result is that liquidity became overwhelming and financing was no longer a constraint on home purchases. In fact, it may be said that too much liquidity helped overexpand the home-buying possibilities in recent years. This is a case of too much credit chasing too few homes.

Cyclical recovery in the housing market, in typical credit cycle fashion, gave way to a boom period (Figure 9.1). Positive fundamentals of rising household incomes and low mortgage rates in the early recovery period of 2003 to 2005 were supported by rising liquidity in financial markets as rising housing demand led to a period of rapidly rising home prices (2004 to 2006). As households began to count their paper gains on housing, speculative fever began to build with ultimately disastrous results. The dynamics of home pricing started to change as household expectations of paper capital gains rose sharply to increase investor housing demand relative to the demand for actual owner occupation.

Home prices began to reflect the rapidly rising shortage of land rather than the quality of the structure, further complicating the process. Meanwhile, demographics began to favor certain regions (retirement and

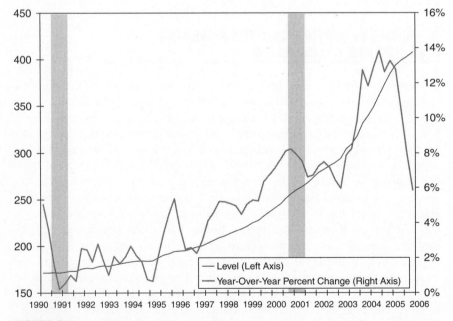

**FIGURE 9.1**   OFHEO House Price Index
*Source:* Office of Federal Housing Enterprise Oversight.

seashore) as well as property types (townhouses and condos) relative to the traditional single-family home.

The globalization of housing demand and mortgage financial instruments for American homes/mortgages reflected capital flight from Latin America and retirement alternatives for Europeans. In this respect, housing prices reflected the influences of investment interests, a shortage of land and globalization of demand that were not typically present in prior business cycles.

At the margin, housing evolved from owner-occupied living quarters to speculative land acquisition by absentee investors. Combined with the oversupply of liquidity, this evolution of buyer motivations led to rapidly rising home prices that further altered the perceived risk/reward trade-off for buyers. House-flipping, not occupation, became the rationale for the marginal buyer.

For builders, rising prices were the incentive needed to buy land and anticipate the easy pass-through of higher prices to willing homeowners (or speculators). Lenders, with federal guarantees and global liquidity in hand, found the financing of such home purchases fast and easy. This housing/credit cycle built on itself. It is very important to note that at the margin many failed to realize significant profits. Most homeowners or speculators only perceived price increases. On average, they did not realize the scale of home price appreciation reported in the media.

## PRICE DICHOTOMY: TRADED AND NON-TRADED GOODS

As home prices accelerated, when a shortage of homes was perceived, all builders and homeowners perceived that their homes, which were not on the market at that time, were also appreciating at the same rate. As a result, owners of previously off-the-market homes decided to trade up in some cases and boosted the supply of new and existing homes. The supply of homes rose sharply, such that no perceived shortage of homes persisted for the available demand from new buyers. Price dichotomy is a classic trap in the typical credit cycle disconnect where transactions prices, for actually traded goods, at the margin are confused with market prices for all goods in existence.

Effective supply of homes overwhelmed the effective demand at the highly inflated prices that builders and homeowners had perceived to be market prices. Yet these perceived inflated market prices existed only at the margin when a perceived shortage existed. Rising prices fed on themselves, in the short run, as in the typical credit cycle of prior American business cycle experience. As long as everyone expects to be able to sell at a higher price to "the greater fool" sometime in the future, the feeding frenzy continues. Buyers turned into speculators and bought based on expected investment returns, not affordability over the long haul. Builders provided the type of home to suit the needs of buyers and creditors. Mortgage brokers focused on transactions processing and mortgage marketability rather than long-run buyer affordability. All this activity was based on the confusion of traded and non-traded goods prices.

There was, and is, plenty of blame to go around. More to the point, this entire process is not unique but rather follows a very traditional pattern of prior credit cycles. What begins as fundamentally sound decision making becomes, in the context of the available institutions, speculation and misunderstood pricing, a speculative excess that leads to gluts and credit revulsion.

## INTRODUCING THE WAKE-UP CALL

With the evolution of the economic structure and the progression of ever more optimistic assessments of returns relative to risk, market pricing increasingly becomes disassociated from the long-run fundamentals of the marketplace. At some point, the housing market no longer clears at the continually rising inflated prices and the wake-up call is issued. In the past, these wake-up calls were associated often with the failures of financial institutions (Penn Square, Continental Illinois, Barings) or a particular deal (the United Airlines buyout of 1989) or strategy (convergence trading for Long-Term Capital Management).

In what appears to be a New York minute, market participants engage in a deliberative attempt to alter the existing incentive structure that some observers believe no longer generates the economic outcomes these same observers desire. Simply put, greed turns into fear. Speculators who attempt to realize their perceived paper capital gains find that their actual returns are far more disappointing. The economy still works and markets do function, and yet their outcomes no longer suit the preferences of buyers and sellers as well as policy makers.

In the scramble that follows, market actions send the economic and financial process off in very uncertain directions that increase market risk, decrease expected returns, and ultimately are unlikely to return markets to anything like their prior equilibrium. We can see this in Figure 9.2, where credit spreads on the ABX.HE index rise as the expected value of the home equity cash flows decline due, in part, to rising fears of mortgage delinquencies.

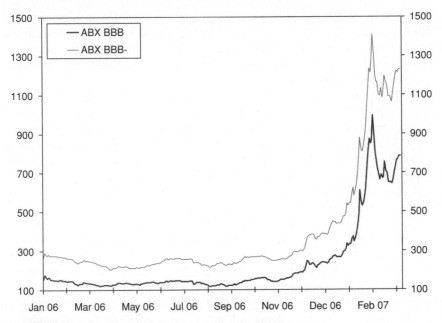

**FIGURE 9.2**   ABX Synthetic Spreads BBB and BBB–
*Source:* Wachovia Securities.

## PRECISE MATHEMATICS GIVES WAY TO IMPRECISE REALITY: WHAT HAPPENS TO MARKETS WHEN THE AVERAGE EXPECTED RETURN AND THE VARIABILITY OF RETURNS BECOME UNCERTAIN?

To complicate matters, as buyers and sellers alter their price expectations, their behavior will affect not only the pace and distribution of economic events but also increase the degree of uncertainty of economic outcomes from the current environment. The blowout in market pricing radically alters the average expected rate of return, and its variability, over time. Change brings greater uncertainty to all economic agents. Greater uncertainty confounds existing institutional barriers for some whose tolerance of risk rises significantly compared to the sure thing that they had expected in home buying and mortgage origination. Prospective delinquencies and capital losses represent significant challenges to private capital and public policy expectations.

Why is this critical? The problem is that pricing models for investors that balance risk and reward depend on small changes in one variable, such as price, to generate understood valuations. But what happens when both the expected price and its variability change over time? In this case, uncertainty rises significantly and investors are far less willing to invest, given the higher level of uncertainty. The market freezes up and trading halts. We have seen instances of this in the stock market crash of 1987 and the high-yield bond collapse in the early 1990s.

Moreover, financial and economic regulations have had their own cycles over the past 100 years. These cycles have consistently altered the trade-off of reward and risk for market participants. The creation of the Federal Reserve in 1913 occurred in response to the Panic of 1907, yet many economists argue that the Fed made the Great Depression deeper and longer than would otherwise have been possible.[12] Geographic banking restrictions, originally intended to reduce the risk of bank failure, actually increased the risk of failure with the onset of accelerating inflation and higher interest rates in the late 1970s and early 1980s. In this latest cycle, we are already beginning to see the increase in regulatory oversight as negative outcomes of the downside of the credit cycle are being revealed.

As for economic fundamentals, from 2007 to 2010, we have seen short-term interest rates rise and, over the past year, a slowdown in the overall economy (slower employment growth and, thereby, fewer home buyers who might qualify). These fundamental factors were clearly moving counter to the market expectations where the psychology of favorable home price expectations fed the demand for homes. Moreover, beneath the rise in credit extensions there was also a weakening of credit quality as mortgage brokers attempted, by lowering credit standards, to maintain transaction flow to meet sales goals while also accommodating an increasingly capital gains–oriented investor group. As housing speculation developed during 2004, subprime adjustable rate mortgages rose from 6 to 9 percent of the total mortgages originated.

This conflict of weakening fundamentals, exemplified by diminishing housing affordability as home prices rose from 2004 to 2006 (Figure 9.3), combined with the price shock to speculators who could no longer find the greater fool, led to a subsequent quick unraveling of the credit cycle beginning in mid-2006 and a subsequent sharp downturn in home prices and a sudden break in prior confidence in the inevitability of home price appreciation. For speculators and investors, decelerating transaction prices were a shock to market expectations. Recall that speculators had built their investment strategy on perceived marginal transaction prices. These prices were not sustainable once the overwhelming increase in supply met a more limited demand. Buyers are less willing to buy as home price appreciation becomes less certain. Further, lower employment numbers suggest fewer home buyers and fewer mortgage applications.

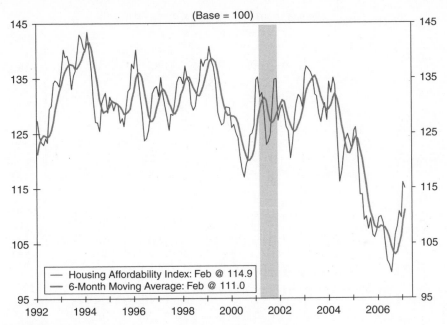

**FIGURE 9.3** Housing Affordability, NAR-Home Sales
*Source:* National Association of Realtors.

At some point, as sellers attempted to realize paper profits, they found that actual market prices were far less than the expected paper prices they had built into their evaluations. Realized prices no longer justified the investment prices paid for real estate. The distinction between prices on traded homes and non-traded homes became despairingly clear. A house that sells at a specific price does not indicate that all houses will sell at the same price—if only one house is listed, that house is exclusive, but if all houses are listed for sale, then there is nothing special about any of them.[13]

## Feedback from Slowed Housing Demand

Slower economic growth engenders less income growth and, as mortgage payments reset due to higher interest rates on teaser loans, many buyers found that the payment increase was greater than their income gain. Delinquencies started to rise, as illustrated in Figure 9.4 Yet, builders still had inventory to sell. As the demand for housing slowed, builders reacted by offering discounts on new homes, which effectively fed back into lowering

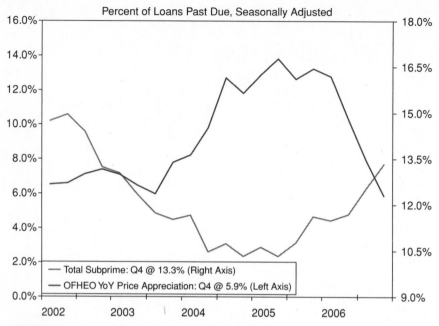

**FIGURE 9.4** Conventional Mortgage Loan Delinquency
*Source:* Mortgage Bankers Association, Office of Federal Housing Enterprise Oversight.

the appreciation of existing homes, which is also illustrated in Figure 9.4. The vise in the housing market quickly turned as buyers found that home prices started to decline, thereby wiping out their equity. Meanwhile, lenders saw a dramatic rise in delinquencies. A slower housing demand meant price declines as well as rising delinquencies.

Rising delinquencies and falling house prices reflected a new process of modifications—how does the public make economic decisions on housing and mortgage commitments? The framework for decision making in the housing market has changed. A second point that has emerged about the housing/mortgage markets is that movement in prices and sales were not small changes along a stable set of demand and supply relationships. In contrast to most models of economic activity, the housing/mortgage markets have not moved from one stable equilibrium to another, but, rather, to a new equilibrium with a matrix of much lower prices, housing starts, and credit restraint which is quite different from what was conceivable prior to the breakdown of subprime lending just a few years ago. In the subprime lending case before us, feedback from institutions and decision makers will likely generate results that were unanticipated just a few months ago. This is often called the law of unintended consequences in other contexts. While many of our financial models are often made in a static vision of the world, the real-world actions of the economy and financial systems are dynamic. Policy often neither anticipates nor models the feedback loop.

In contrast, when policy makers fail to adapt to changing circumstances, the financial and economic systems will likely end in ruin in short order.[14] In the most spectacular of examples, the failure of the Whig party to come to grips with slavery in the antebellum years led to its ultimate demise. Today, regulatory and tax burdens at the state level (particularly in the Northeast) have exacerbated the national migration of population and jobs over the past 30 years. Failure to adapt by business and political leaders has defined the failure of many companies and communities.

Meanwhile, too much flexibility in policy, particularly tax rates, can lead to adjustment costs and higher risks associated with tax-favored and then tax-penalized activities. This is apparent in the history of commercial real estate during the 1980s, when tax cuts put in place in the early period of the decade were quickly reversed mid-decade, leading to a significant real estate slump and financial failures. In a similar way, the taxation of capital, particularly investment capital, which is highly mobile, has exhibited a volatile pattern in the United States over the past 40 years and a repeat of this volatility may be seen in the years ahead.

## CHOICES: REACTING TO FEEDBACK—THE MOST DANGEROUS PHASE OF THE CREDIT CYCLE

Why would decisions made in reaction to the feedback process represent the riskiest stage of the credit process? In the current subprime lending situation, we would recognize the process as being very fluid, with many actors attempting to resolve the risk/reward trade-off and the appropriate pricing for real assets (houses) and financial assets (mortgages and mortgage-backed securities). Private and policy actions taken at this time could either amplify or dampen the volatility of the market process.

Economics is a discipline of choice. Economic choices occur within a specific institutional structure that is itself changing with the economy. Feedback from economic developments provides decision makers with information. Leaders can decide to react, or not, to that information and alter their earlier decisions or the earlier framework for decision making. The decision not to change is also a choice. When the economy evolves, but institutions do not, the outcome is often stagnation (European and Japanese growth in recent years) or major upheaval (the Soviet Union).

For subprime lending, private actors have a decision to make with respect to lending standards and the price of credit to allow for variations in the riskiness for subprime loans. Public policy makers have a choice about how to set standards on the quality and quantity of loans they will accept for federal forms of insurance or their portfolios. Change is a choice, but to choose not to change is also a choice—and often a fatal one. If federal policy makers and private lenders do not alter the prior rules on subprime lending that led to the current problems, then another credit cycle in housing is likely to be repeated. However, if policy makers overcompensate and lending guidelines are tightened too much (Figure 9.5) then a true credit crunch becomes more likely and the downdraft in the housing cycle will be amplified. Credit constraints will generate even greater rates of delinquencies and foreclosures. This credit reign of terror was the pattern for the high-yield bond market during the 1990 to 1992 period. In the 2000s, we can see that the rapid rise in the net percentage of banks tightening standards sets up the preconditions for a rout if public policy amplifies the call for the exits.

The ranking of credit risks is exemplified in Figure 9.6. Once again, the market is moved quickly to ration credit. For housing and mortgage markets,

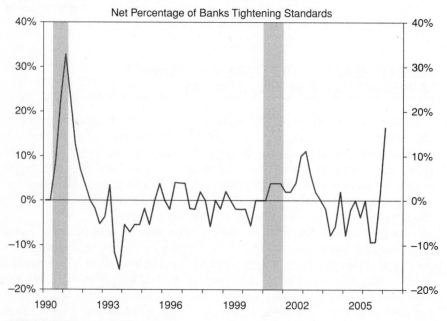

**FIGURE 9.5**  Mortgage Loans
*Source:* Federal Reserve Board.

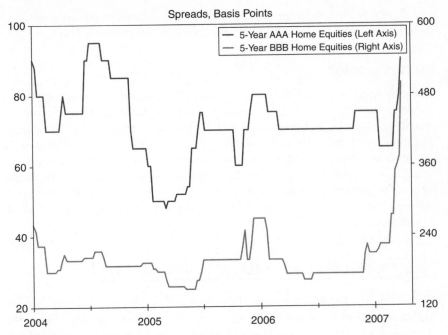

**FIGURE 9.6** *5-Year AAA versus BBB Home Equities*
*Source:* Wells Fargo Securities.

the credit dynamic can be further complicated by policy makers. Federal authorities issued guidance to tighten mortgage lending standards. Moreover, Freddie Mac issued tighter guidelines on the mortgages it will accept. Unfortunately, this happened after the horse left the barn. Tighter standards will make it more difficult for future buyers to qualify, thereby reducing the demand for homes. This accentuates the downward price momentum and, thereby, the upward swing in delinquencies. How much and how quickly do regulators raise credit standards to where they "should have been" without shutting out all transactions that might clear the existing overbuilt market? All this suggests that policy makers need to tread carefully given the modest pace of economic growth seen in early 2011.

Some policy makers in Washington suggested bailing out the delinquent borrowers. This creates a risky set of incentives and a hopelessly complicated set of regulations. How will government determine the truly unfortunate as compared to the simply speculative borrowers? Many subprime mortgage brokers are headed for failure, but then who will make up the payments to investors? Will future taxpayers be asked to pay interest on bonds to fund current speculators? If no new credit is forthcoming, then many homes and developments will not be finished, neighborhoods will take years to complete, and community and personal stress will remain elevated.

## Lessons Learned

Interaction between finance and economics is a dynamic process with many unanticipated twists in the course of market adjustments. Too often, both private and public policy makers fail to heed the implications of change. Moreover, too much decision making only considers the very first step in the process. Effective leadership must look down the road to anticipate the second and third turns in order to judge the effect of current decisions. Subprime lending is simply the latest example in a long history of such dynamic economic processes with uncertain outcomes and unanticipated, sometimes crushing results.

## CREDIT CRUNCHES: WHEN MARKETS DON'T CLEAR

Underlying the modern vision of credit markets is the assumption that the price (interest rates) and the quantity of credit are free to move given the stimulus of changing economic fundamentals. The Banking Acts of 1933 and 1935 prohibited the payment of interest on demand deposits and authorized the Federal Reserve to set up interest rate ceilings on time and savings deposits paid by commercial banks. Regulation Q limited the interest rates paid on time deposits by national banks as a way to limit competition for deposits and, in part, to limit the movement of deposits between banks and lead to illiquidity in the marketplace. This kind of regulation was possible in a low inflation environment where many households vividly remembered the bank failures of the Great Depression and World War II rationing. The return of principal mattered more than the return on principal. Consumer options for saving and investing were also very limited at that time. Meanwhile, for bankers, taking in deposits at 3 percent and lending at 6 percent was a guarantee for steady profits—as long as the economic framework did not change.

However, the framework was changing as inflation began rising consistently in the early and mid-1960s. Regulation Q ceilings were raised four times between 1962 and 1965. In response, the negotiable certificate of deposit came into existence in the early 1960s. This instrument offered savers with $100,000-plus to earn a market rate on their funds while offering banks a means to attract such funds. The fundamental problem remained, however, that federally mandated interest rate ceilings, in the face of rising inflation, were an ineffective means of allocating credit. Regulation Q, like all wage-price control ceilings or floors, creates a distortion in the allocation of resources.

As the economy grew in the 1960s and inflation rose as well, the demand for credit rose faster than the available credit at many banking institutions. Banks were limited by interest rate ceilings from competing for funds in the open marketplace. As banks attempted to compete for funds with thrift institutions, which did not face interest rate ceilings, the banks were squeezed by the rising cost of funds at the short end of the yield curve and by what they were earning on long-term assets, which reflected interest rate levels of the past. The credit crunch of 1966 began, and the recession ensued, especially in the housing sector.

In response, the federal government limited interest rate competition through the Interest Rate Control Act of 1966, which imposed ceilings on the interest rate that thrifts could pay on deposits and set that rate slightly above that of banks. Such interest rate controls were clearly anticompetitive and anticonsumer and saver, and led to a generation of bankers and savers attempting to find ways around the arbitrary rules.

## High-Yield Bonds and the 1990 to 1992 Credit Crunch

By the late 1980s, high market interest rates presented a challenge to many savings and loan associations, as the cost of deposits was very high relative to traditional returns for consumer lending. As a result, these institutions began to widen their investment options, but often entered fields where they had very little experience. As a result, many thrifts, such as Vernon Savings and Loan Association in Texas, invested in high-risk projects that subsequently failed. In response, Congress passed the Financial Institutions Reform, Recovery and Enforcement Act in 1989. The legislation mandated that 70 percent of thrift assets be held in residential mortgages and mortgage-backed securities. In addition, the legislation prohibited junk bonds, bonds issued by corporations with a credit rating considered below investment grade, in thrift portfolios. This led to a sharp drop in high-yield bond prices and further sales of these bonds by other institutions. In addition, with the recession of 1990 to 1991, commercial real estate in the Boston and New York regions fell off dramatically, leading to further cuts in bank capital and lending.

What distinguished this credit crunch was the sudden break in credit availability for commercial real estate and the high-yield bonds that reflected the federal government's mandate to make thrift lending independent of any risk and reward trade-off available in the marketplace. This mandate was a response to the lack of oversight in the mid- to late 1980s over thrifts and the subsequent deterioration of the thrifts' portfolio credit quality. This same pattern of lack of oversight was repeated in the 2005 to 2010 period. In each credit cycle the optimism phase will extend itself, no matter what the asset class, such that we appear to repeat the same mistake, but each time with a new type of asset.

These credit crunch periods—times when credit allocation does not function by interest rate rationing, but rather by a discontinuity in credit availability—represent a challenge to decision makers. The spreadsheet approach to long-run planning assumes a smooth pattern to the economy, with the implicit assumption that smooth access to credit exists to finance the growth of the institutions associated with a trajectory of long-run economic growth. Credit crunches disprove that assumption.

In a period when an institution faces a financing constraint, the ability to borrow is limited by current cash flow rather than expected long-run profitability. A recession, or even periods of disappointing growth (2009 to 2010) means slower current profits (current cash flow) and reduces investment spending, even if the long-run outlook remains unchanged. Here, then, investment is more sensitive to current economic conditions than long-run prospects. For consumers facing borrowing constraints today, current income is far more valuable than their lifetime expected earnings. This has certainly been true in the period from 2008 to 2010. For state (California), local (Harrisburg, PA), and sovereign (Greece) debt markets, illiquidity in the short run was the foremost issue trumping any consideration of the long-run performance of the economy. For lenders, such as many banks, the ability to carry out the intermediary function was severely hampered. Some institutions were thus forced to forgo potentially profitable investment projects.

## CAPITAL MARKETS AND THE LIFE CYCLE OF AN INSTITUTION

Independent of the economic cycle, the financing challenges and growth opportunities of any private or public institution will vary over the different stages of growth for that institution. Here the focus will be on a business.

When starting up, most businesses rely on an entrepreneur's personal savings as well as contributions from friends and family. In some types of businesses, trade credit from suppliers is also available. At this point, the source of funding reflects a history of saving by an entrepreneur and friends and family. There is, however, a close positive correlation between the number and success of start-ups and the overall economy. Business success at an individual small firm is much easier in a growing economy with a growing economic pie than in a shrinking or slow-growth environment.

Stage two for most firms when seeking credit is the bank loan. Small firms pursue bank lending for a variety of reasons. First, firms need to finance inventory to deal with seasonal sales cycles. The inventory financing requires a firm to estimate funding requirements over a period of time, usually very short-run (recall Level One of the strategic planning process from an earlier chapter). For some firms, a longer-term loan may be an option. Such loans have a maturity greater than one year with the intention to repay the loan out of future cash flow, not short-term liquidation of assets as in the selling of inventory. Some long-term loans can also be relied on to purchase fixed assets. Revolving credit allows a business to borrow from a bank up to maximum commitment level over the life of the credit line and this revolving credit is also utilized to finance permanent working capital needs.

For decision makers, the challenge is to recognize the variation in the economic cycle and the availability of credit that might occur over the period of the loan—especially if there is an expectation that the loan may have to be refinanced sometime in the future at a very inopportune moment, when interest rates are higher and credit availability reduced. The lessons of past credit crunches are vivid here. For lenders, the risk of nonpayment is very large given the illiquidity that can be associated with any assets that a small firm may possess and the difficulty of recouping value during the very time, a recession, that a small firm is most likely to default on its loans. Moreover, lenders balance the rewards of lending (expected profits) with the risk of lending.

As seen with the thrifts in the 1980s and with bank lending to emerging markets in most of the post–World War II period, the resources and capability of lenders will be tested when lending drifts outside their original field of expertise. For borrowers, too, there is a caution. While their state of financial health may be fine, their lending institution may be credit constrained at the very moment that the firm may need them most (a vital lesson from the 2008 to 2010 period).

Evaluating creditworthiness, therefore, runs both ways. While traditionally a lender evaluates the borrower's ability to repay, the borrower has a strong self-interest in monitoring his lending institution. At minimum, borrowers can monitor earnings reports and credit ratings of their lenders. In addition, a personal visit and asking questions are also parts of a minimalist strategy. Changes in expectations for growth, inflation, interest rates, and regulations will have a significant impact on the ability of any lending institution to meet the credit needs of its customers.

Risk assessments—for both the borrower and lender—will change over the business cycle, as will the ability of the bank to lend and the individual firm to borrow. Trends in growth and inflation will impact revenues and costs and thereby influence the success of business plans associated with the original credit agreement. Economic factors will also influence the collateral values of vehicles, buildings, equipment, and inventory that stand behind those loans.

Venture capital or the private sale of shares is often the next stage of financing for many firms.[15] What is intriguing about this step is that the firm is now moving on to a path to eventually selling part of its ownership to the public or to another institution. This reflects the desire of the venture capitalists and private owners who will, at some point, wish to get a return on their investment. This path suggests a longer-term time horizon and an entrepreneur must build the firm's structure in a way that will satisfy the vision of the marketplace in the future. Venture and private capital fills the void between friends and family financing and the eventual initial public offering or the purchase by a larger company down the road. Yet, an entrepreneur must recognize that venture capital is not long-term money, but rather a step on the path to eventually selling part ownership of the company.

At this stage, the strategic horizon of the firm becomes more long-term with financing in the future in an economic environment that could be friendly or hostile to that financing. Growth, inflation, interest rates, or regulatory conditions could be quite different from those that exist today, as was seen in the equity and public finance markets over the period from 2007 to 2010. The strategic vision of the institution's leadership has shifted toward commercialization of its product or service in a way easily understood by other senior managers and investors, with high expectations of profitability for investors in the future. Decision makers will build the infrastructure required to grow the business along a path that will interest future buyers in much the same way that one might remodel a kitchen or paint some walls to make a home more attractive to sell. This stage of financing is an inherently risky business. Economic cycles, as well as cycles of innovation in many sectors, such as green energy, health care, high-tech, and personal communications, could rapidly make a new initiative obsolete even before an initial public offering.

For both lenders and borrowers of credit, the path ahead represents an alternative path for the firm as it follows the strategic options covered earlier. The risk and uncertainty mix is much more open to uncertainty than the straight-line projections of continuing past yet familiar patterns of business operations which implicitly assume an outlook of very low uncertainty. For a small firm, the objectives are usually profitability and sustainability. Over time, the objectives are widened to include salability and realization of capital gains at a time not too distant. The value of market information in planning the terms and timing of the sale are critical. Buyers will be looking for a bargain to fit their objectives as well. Leaders of the firm no longer operate just to meet their needs, but also the goals of an undetermined buyer sometime down the road.

Going public is the next step for many firms. It certainly benefits, in terms of increased personal wealth, the owners, private investors, and venture capitalists who have backed the business over time. New financial capital from the initial public offering can be employed to pay off interest-bearing debt, as well as increase the financial capability to develop and sell new products. An entrepreneur, however, now has the challenge of public scrutiny over his decision making, and there is a dilution of ownership where gains to the firm do not accrue almost exclusively to the entrepreneur. Moreover, the goals of the entrepreneur have shifted to provide more short-term financial gain to shareholders, not only to himself.

From the economic viewpoint, increased importance is attached to evidence of economic growth, and how the firm's offerings will link up to that growth. What is the strategy for the firm and how does that fit into the outlook for growth in the overall economy and the demand within the niche the firm's product or service is trying to meet? What is evident here is the degree of uncertainty introduced into the process due to the switch in the firm's leadership—often entrepreneurial in culture—and the demands of the public marketplace. In addition, any new initiative undertaken by this firm is likely to create a response by existing firms. This brings about a second level of strategy, reviewed earlier, that focuses on the interactions and incentives of new entrants and established firms in any line of business.

Further up the ladder on financing the enterprise is the choice of external financing in the debt markets between short-term debt, such as commercial paper, which is unsecured paper and long-term debt, such as corporate debt. For large corporations with high credit ratings, commercial paper is often a lower-cost alternative to bank financing. In addition, given a traditionally positively sloped yield curve, commercial paper financing is also less expensive than corporate bond financing. The choice between commercial paper and longer-term debt would also reflect the firm's ability to match assets and financing options.

For short-term commitments, financing current assets with current liabilities, such as commercial paper, would appear appropriate. Yet, there is the risk that it will not be possible to roll over such financing at maturity (credit crunch) or that the new interest rate at rollover may be significantly higher than current short rates or even current longer-term rates. Meanwhile, longer-term bond finance would be consistent with financing longer-term assets such as a building or infrastructure improvements and long-lived equipment. Once again, there is refinancing risk in any decision to sell bonds, as well as the possibility that interest rates may decline in the near future and that selling shorter-term debt would have reduced interest rate costs over the life of the asset being financed. One caution here is that long-term financing could be relied upon to meet short-term financial commitments, yet this reliance could present problems down the road for the owners of the firm when short-run fluctuations in revenues would make debt service difficult to meet.

## CAPITAL MARKETS AND THE ALLOCATION OF CAPITAL

Michael Porter, a professor at the Harvard Business School, wrote an essay entitled "Capital Disadvantage: America's Failing Capital Investment System" in the *Harvard Business Review* nearly 20 years ago that is still pertinent to a number of issues on the allocation of capital.[16] In light of the dot-com boom and bust, the subprime housing collapse and yet the continued resiliency of the American economy, what can be said about the allocation of capital through the markets?

Porter identifies three virtues in the allocation of capital—efficiency, flexibility, and responsiveness. Opportunities in the dot-com era were seized on very quickly, and while the focus on the very short-run returns was a shortcoming, the thrust of financing for innovation was there. Markets allocate capital efficiently as investors seek the highest risk-adjusted returns for each investment horizon. For the United States, flexibility reflects the ability of capital markets to reallocate capital from failing to good prospects and in funding fairly quickly emerging fields such as biotechnology that find ways to deal in increasingly complex and intangible forms. Responsiveness reflects the ability of the system to find ways to finance investment in increasingly flexible, but sometimes also more complex, forms to fit the financing needs of a project.

On the negative side, there are several drawbacks to the current capital markets. First, there is the divergence of interests among shareholders and corporate managements, between investment advisers and the investor, between investment firms and their customers. This all falls under the rubric of the principal and agent problem.

From the investor's point of view, the differences between the roles of principal from that of an agent are critical to understanding the many problems in housing and mortgage markets. The private firm is usually the principal in any financing, as in the issuance of a corporate bond or of equity. The agent is usually the investment bank. As a result, there is a tendency for the agent to focus on the short-run transaction payout rather than the long-run returns that are the focus of the principal investor. A second drawback of the capital markets is that American investor investment horizons are often too short to sustain the needed breakthroughs required in longer, more complex product development cycles. The failure to develop digital camera technology by Polaroid is an example of this problem.

American owners are viewed as transient owners whose goals are primarily financial. In contrast, investors in Germany and Japan are considered as dedicated investors where the owners are principals, not agents. Moreover, many of these investors have long-term relationships, not just a financial interest as suppliers and customers, which solidify their long-term commitment to the success of both firms and their relationship.

But there is also another side to this issue. Where support for some projects may be too short, alternatively, some firms stay too long on a losing project. In America, losses will be recognized quickly and cut loose. In this way, the pattern of the Japanese banks and their exposure to failing real estate in their country is not likely to be repeated in the United States.

There are also some trade-offs in the capital allocation system in the United States. On economic grounds there is a fairly close alignment of the interests of investors and corporations and the national economy when there are few externalities to the production process. However, in the presence of externalities, there may be too much allocation of capital to the production of goods that, for example, generate too much pollution, or too little to the production of goods that create a social benefit. However, when the public sector gets involved in allocating capital for political gains, there is often even greater misallocation of capital and resources in such areas as crop subsidies, housing supports, the Erie railway of the nineteenth century, or the government's armor plate plant in the twentieth century.[17] The Erie railway and the armor plate plant constitute examples of the misallocation of capital by political interests that decision makers must recognize in both the public and private sectors. Federal regulation, more often in the interest of political and not economic gain, will deliver losses from public regulation greater than the supposed benefits.

Two points should be stated here. First, economic competition and globalization make the efficient allocation of capital for investment a critical determinant of competitive advantage over the long run. Innovation via sustained investment is important. Yet, what is often seen is a stop-and-go public policy of investment incentives and tax changes that appear to be at the whim of political interest groups rather than for the benefit of long-term growth. Second, macroeconomic factors provide the context for investment spending. A stable and growing economy tends to encourage investment, reassuring investors that returns will persist over the long term. However, the recent rapid rise of federal deficits, combined with low national savings and sporadic and unpredictable changes in tax policy, suggest that future returns to investments will face a greater tax burden. This reduces the time horizon for investment returns and thereby reinforces the bias investors have for short-term gains. Both these topics are covered more later in this book.

Over time, and with greater emphasis over the last few years, the conventional wisdom on capital markets is one of collapse and financial catastrophe. Such hype has never served the long-run interests of public or private decision makers or of society at large. Instead, innovation greets each challenge, and change brings new innovations. There are cycles in finance and innovations in the financial markets in which problems arise, potential solutions are pursued, and new problems arise. Yet, the financial and economic system moves ahead; it does not collapse in any way reminiscent of the empires of the past. Old frameworks give way to new as the capital markets evolve along with the economy. On the road to economic progress there are many bumps, but history finds its future in innovation, not in resignation to a doomsday scenario. In fact, the pattern of finance and economics is one of challenge, innovation, experimentation, and occasional excesses, but the overwhelming expansion of opportunity. Within the umbrella of capital markets, there is an emphasis on the utilization of financial ratios as guideposts to the performance of institutions and the overall economy. This is the next subject to which we turn.

## DISCUSSION QUESTIONS

1. You chair your company's pension plan committee. Global capital markets are the benchmark today for determining the value of financial assets. Please explain the underlying economic structure of the demand and supply for financial assets on a global scale. This structure must reflect a global nature of the capital markets and the saving/investment balance reflected in the GDP accounts.

   Change: Expectations have shifted in favor of more rapid economic growth in selected emerging markets relative to mature industrialized countries.
   a. What is your expected feedback from such a change?
   b. What are then the choices for your investment allocation?
   c. How might this change alter your new investment allocation framework going forward?
2. You are the assistant to the CFO of a major non-financial corporation. The CFO wants your guidance on the pros and cons of issuing debt and/or equity to raise capital in 2012.

What is your guidance on this issue given the following five possible policy changes in the year ahead?

a. Increased income taxes on dividends and capital gains.

b. The Fed expands its balance sheet by purchasing more Treasury notes and bonds.

c. Dollar depreciation is expected along with a decline by foreign investors willing to buy U.S. dollar–denominated fixed-income products.

d. The increasing risk that inflation concerns will rise in the year ahead.

e. Slower overall economic growth is expected and in recent months this has driven down P/E ratios.

3. You are financial advisor to the U.S. Secretary of the Treasury.

Explain the underlying economic framework for the demand and supply for Treasury securities. This framework should reflect the global nature of the capital markets. Be sure to include dynamic and geographic elements in your model.

Change: Foreign investors have expressed concern on the policy mix in the United States of large fiscal deficits and quantitative easing by the central bank. They are preparing to pursue a policy of greater diversification away from Treasury debt.

Explain your expected feedback from such a change and your expectations on interest rates to the Treasury Secretary. Recall that the United States is going to have a consistent and large budget deficit that will require financing over the long term. How might the Treasury Secretary structure his financing along the maturity spectrum, given your expectations for interest rates?

# NOTES

1. John Steele Gordon, "We Banked on Them," in *The Business of America* (New York: Walker and Co., 2001).

2. For more discussion, read Michael Mussa, "Factors Driving Global Economic Integration" (presentation at a symposium sponsored by the Federal Reserve Bank of Kansas City, August 2000).

3. For a note on macroeconomic externalities and the credit cycles, see Javier Bianchi, "Credit Externalities: Macroeconomic Effects and Policy Implications," *American Economic Review* (May 2010): 398–402.

4. Eugene Fama, "Efficient Capital Markets: A Review of Theory and Empirical Work," *Journal of Finance* 25 (1970): 383–417.

5. N. Gregory Mankiw, Macroeconomics, 7th ed. (New York: Worth Publishers, 2010): 533–534.

6. Daviken Studnicki-Gizbert, *A Nation Upon the Ocean Sea: Portugal's Atlantic Diaspora and the Crisis of the Spanish Empire, 1492–1640* (New York: Oxford University Press, 2007).

7. For an extensive review of the Long-Term Capital Management case, see Roger Lowenstein, *When Genius Failed: The Rise and Fall of Long-Term Capital Management* (New York: Random House, 2000).

8. Ben Bernanke, *"The Great Moderation"* (remarks at the Eastern Economic Association, February 20, 2004).

9. John Silvia, "Economic Outlook: The Role of Finance" (presentation to the Federal Reserve Bank of Atlanta, 2007; *Banking Industry Outlook*, February 21, 2007).

10. Joseph Schumpeter, *Business Cycles* (New York: McGraw-Hill, 1964) cited the role of innovations in business cycles, but here we are more focused on both apparent and real changes in the economic structure or outcomes to which decision makers wish to respond, regardless of whether there is a real fundamental innovation to the economy.

11. The role of securitization and the quality of the issuer, which became one of the core issues in the Great Recession, is covered nicely by Oliver Faltin-Traeger, Kathleen W. Johnson, and Christopher Mayer, "Issuer Credit Quality and the Price of Asset-Backed Securities," *American Economic Review* (May 2010): 501–505.

12. See N. Gregory Mankiw, *Macroeconomics*, pages 329–330 for his view on the debt-deflation theory and its responsibility for the severity of the Great Depression.

13. One interesting cut on the household financial situation broadens the credit risk issues beyond the house value/mortgage debt imbalance to the broader household balance sheet. See Nicholas S. Ronel et al., "What Triggers Mortgage Default," *American Economic Review* (May 2010): 490–494.

14. See Joseph E. Stiglitz, *Globalization and Its Discontents* (New York: W.W. Norton, 2002) for a critique (in Chapter 9 especially) of the failure of international institutions such as the IMF and the World Bank to adapt to change.

15. For more on the role of venture capital, see Bob Zider, "How Venture Capital Works," *Harvard Business Review* (November–December 1998).

16. Michael E. Porter, "Capital Disadvantage: America's Failing Capital Investment System," *Harvard Business Review* (September–October 1992).

17. See John Steele Gordon, *The Business of America*, pages 91–95 and 157–161. The Erie Railway was the payoff to the southern tier in New York State for its support of the building of the Erie Canal up north. However, the canal interests that controlled the Albany legislature set both the east and west terminuses of the railroad in small communities and thereby built a railroad from nowhere to nowhere. Under Woodrow Wilson, the government appropriated money to build an armor plate factory to produce armor plate for the Navy. The factory was completed three years after the end of World War I, and millions over budget, and could not produce armor for less than nearly double what the steel companies charged. The plant shut down after one batch of armor plates was produced and never reopened.

## RECOMMENDED READING FOR SERIOUS PLAYERS

Gordon, John Steele. *The Business of America*. New York: Walker and Co., 2001.

Grant, Jim. *Money of the Mind: Borrowing and Lending in America from the Civil War to Michael Milken*. New York: Farrar Straus and Giroux, 1992.

Lowenstein, Roger. *When Genius Failed: The Rise and Fall of Long-Term Capital Management*. New York: Random House, 2000.

# CHAPTER 10

# Financial Ratios: The Intersection of Economics and Finance

**S**tudents of finance, business managers, and private investors rely on financial ratios as indicators of economic and financial success. Financial ratios are not completely under management's control—there is the influence of broader economic forces on each of the critical ratios. Ratios can, unfortunately, also be a crutch and barrier to good decision making. Surprisingly, the role of financial ratios in decision making for the investment analyst and the business leader is far more interesting and crucial to success than the sterile reporting of a number often conveys.

## FINANCIAL RATIOS

Often, analysts of financial data tend to immediately make judgments based on a financial ratio: The P/E (price/earnings) ratio is too high; interest expense is in line with income; the return on assets is too low. However, it is important to consider three boxes to check off before getting too involved in the trees and losing sight of the forest.

### Targets, Indicators, or Instruments

What do we mean by the three boxes labeled targets, indicators, and instruments? Many financial ratios act as targets for decision makers much in the way that the Federal Reserve targets price stability. As a target, the financial ratio, earnings per share, is a good example, and is the goal of the leaders of many companies. Second, a financial ratio can also be an indicator of financial performance such as the return on equity. Finally, a financial ratio can also be an instrument, such as the debt-to-equity ratio that is used to alter perceptions of financial responsibility and the quality of the company's operations. Problems arise when analysts use a financial ratio, such as earnings per share, as an indicator of performance while a company is manipulating this same ratio to alter the analysts' perceptions of the company's financial quality. In this sense, financial ratios, as well as many other economic and financial data, are not independent of the actions of those being observed. Our approach here reflects the observer effect, or Hawthorne effect, known in psychology.

Financial ratios such as price/earnings or earnings per share are not simply indicators of financial performance; they are also targets for management conduct. This problem has a rich history in economics with respect to monetary policy. Policy directed at interest rate or money growth targeting will lose its effectiveness over time since the markets will alter their behavior in reaction to the targeting of policy makers. This is the so-called Goodhart's Law, named after Charles A. E. Goodhart, who was an adviser at the Bank of England when he wrote his "law."[1] For analysts, the research problem derives from the behavioral response where both the observation of the behavior (by the analyst) and the public reporting of it can change the behavior observed. The intervention of researchers can change the nature of the relationships being studied. This behavioral pattern was observed.

Any attempt to apply a framework for evaluating any financial ratio needs to account for the difference in the degrees of autonomy for financial ratios. For example, the laws of physics and chemistry are autonomous of the actions of the analysts. But in the behavioral sciences, the actions that influence the pattern of financial ratios are not independent of the researcher's actions or opinions. In both the private and public sectors, the process of choosing and evaluating financial ratios has an effect on the pattern of financial ratios itself. Financial ratios are not invariant to analyst evaluations or the public policy rules adopted by regulators. Therefore, the invariance or lack of it needs to be accounted for in each financial ratio to variations in the broader economy and in the regulatory framework being adopted today.

Another challenge is that the framework for evaluating financial ratios adopted for decision making is not invariant to the different policy and regulatory regimes. As observed by Trygve Haavelmo,[2] professor in economics and statistics at the University of Oslo from 1948 to 1979, target variables in economic activity are not invariant to an analyst's observations or management's behavior. This is particularly true for financial ratios given the very public nature of the reviews of such ratios and the emphasis given them in asset valuation. For this review, then, the behavior of analysts and those being analyzed can alter the behavior of the financial ratio being analyzed. Many financial ratios are modeled as statistical relationships, but a statistical relationship has a tendency to break down when it ceases to be an ex post observation of related variables (given private sector behavior) and becomes instead the ex ante rule.

Statistical models assume that, as an essential feature, the dependent variable (here the financial ratio) is invariant to the modeler and the observer's interventions. In this way, the financial ratio can be used as an accurate indicator of the economic behavior analysts are monitoring. But when the indicator becomes a target and an objective of policy or management control, then the indicator is no longer invariant to the behavior of the actors analysts are trying to monitor. Management manages a financial ratio to the expectations of the monitors—public or private—and the financial ratio loses its invariance characteristic. The ex post summary of behavior characterized by the financial ratio becomes the ex ante guide for management and analysts to target.

In the economic framework, the role of expectations also comes to the fore. Analysts expect that a company or industry or, in some cases, a country will track a certain financial ratio. Deviations from those expectations lead to sharp movements in asset prices, as evidenced at the national level by the deviations from budget targets of countries such as Greece or Ireland in 2010.

Different indicators are also likely to exhibit different degrees of autonomy in any framework. High profile ratios, such as earnings per share, are likely to be managed by corporate leaders more than other financial ratios are, given the high visibility of such ratios. At the national level, debt to GDP is likely to be more closely managed by governments subject to the Maastricht Treaty than by other nations outside of Europe. The Maastricht treaty is one of the two principal treaties between the European Union (EU) member countries that set up the EU's constitutional basis and institutions.

A second issue in developing a framework is that a financial ratio is likely to be a dependent variable of a broad array of factors beyond that of management or the company's/industry's fortunes. The broader economic factors of growth, inflation, interest rates, and the dollar exchange rate are likely to impact financial ratios such as the return on capital or interest expense relative to cash flow. Therefore, financial ratios are more likely endogenous, not exogenous, variables to economic activity and can change independently of any action by the company's management.

Any statistical model of financial ratios needs to consider the impact of the broader economy, which raises the modeling problem of the missing variable. Simply stated, the micro focus on company and industry behavior in determining the pattern of any financial ratio will miss the influence of macroeconomic factors. When a key variable is missing, the estimates of the values of the independent variables in the model are biased and not likely to be good estimates of the true value of the impact of the independent variables.[3]

In dealing with financial ratios, there is also the issue of how we wish to identify change in the ratio itself. For example, the numerator and denominator of any ratio may be changing over time at different rates. Therefore, for any ratio, both the numerator and denominator may change in the same direction, but when one changes more than the other, the value of ratio will change and impart new information to the marketplace.

## DEVELOPING A FRAMEWORK WITHIN A BROADER ECONOMIC SETTING

There are two other issues of concern for financial ratios and their interaction with economic activity. These two issues are the interaction of cyclical and secular (longer-term) patterns and the role of broader economic change that alters the financial ratios.

First, the patterns of many financial ratios have a cyclical component tied to the business cycle, as well as a secular component that reflects a long-run pattern. Therefore, it is important to distinguish cyclical and secular patterns with each financial ratio. In examining the behavior of any ratio across time, the role of time series analysis comes into play. As analysts look at the behavior of any series over time, they want to judge whether the movements in the series suggest cyclical motion around a series that has no trend (stationary) or cyclical motion around a changing trend (non-stationary), as the statistical properties and therefore the degree of confidence in their modeling will be different in each instance.

Second, the patterns in financial ratios may reflect a more generalized pattern of economic change; therefore, each financial ratio is not an independent indicator of the financial or economic health of an institution. Putting two ratios in a model to forecast behavior when both ratios may reflect a third, unaccounted-for, economic factor may lead to statistical problems in estimation that are discussed later. Ratios are indicators of some other factor—efficiency, liquidity, leverage, market value, which are the true interests of the analyst. And yet while different ratios may both be inputs to a model, they may also be the dependent variable of other economic factors. Table 10.1 highlights the strong correlation factors between selected financial ratios and basic economic drivers. The correlations for the financial ratios show a statistically significant value in relationship to a number of economic drivers. For example, the P/E ratio is highly correlated to growth and inflation. Taking another cut at the data, the 10-year Treasury rate is negatively linked to the P/E ratio, as would be expected. The dollar is positively correlated with the price/earnings ratio as well, and this would be expected as both would be linked to a growing economy.

**TABLE 10.1** Pearson Correlation Coefficients

| | P/E Consumer Staples | P/E Industrial | P/E Total | Inventory/ Shipments | Debt/ Equity | Debt/Net Worth | Current Assets/ Liabilities |
|---|---|---|---|---|---|---|---|
| CPI | **−0.62195** | **−0.62060** | **−0.70717** | −0.11559 | **0.52268** | −0.26328 | −0.15670 |
| 10YT | **−0.62116** | **−0.41003** | **−0.66132** | **0.65527** | **0.71260** | 0.10726 | −0.37316 |
| Dollar | **0.71837** | **0.55085** | **0.81814** | **−0.55407** | **−0.75412** | 0.06986 | **−0.75467** |
| 5YT | **−0.58854** | **−0.41159** | **−0.65479** | **0.54865** | **0.67816** | 0.07427 | −0.24982† |
| Growth | 0.22747 | 0.27501 | 0.08012 | 0.04771 | −0.15927 | −0.02690 | −0.15655 |
| Profits | −0.05558 | 0.08742 | −0.03973 | −0.19025* | −0.02736 | −0.09628 | 0.23440‡ |

Data dates back until at least 1972, with the exception of Inventory/ Shipments (1992) and Current Assets/Liabilities (2001).
Bold indicates statistical significance at the .0001% level.
*Statistical significance at the 10 percent level.
†Statistical significance at the 12 percent level.
‡Statistical significance at the 15 percent level.

*Source:* Compustat, Factset, U.S. Census Bureau, Federal Reserve Board, and Bureau of Economic Analysis.

## Theory

Financial ratios provide the basis for many investor decisions. These ratios also provide guidance to leaders who want to monitor the progress of their own institutions. Each ratio is linked to economic factors, particularly the economic cycle, which will influence how decision makers interpret any change in the observed values of the ratio. Ratios are endogenous to the economic cycle, impacted by a number of economic factors and yet also show a secular pattern over time. In models that estimate changes in financial ratios, such as the P/E ratio, over time, there is a challenge to choosing the independent variables that influence the behavior of any financial ratio. The focus in this chapter is on the five economic factors of growth, inflation, interest rates, the dollar, and profits.[4]

The principles for information also apply here. The role of financial ratios is to provide information to decision makers —helping them forecast important turns in factors such as liquidity, leverage, operating efficiency, and market valuation of how well firm management is doing. A change in a critical financial ratio is a signal of change in the economic landscape, and that will lead decision makers to reevaluate the implications for whatever purpose they are using their ratio.

## Decision Making and Its Biases

The information decision makers derive from the patterns of the financial ratios that they study introduced, unfortunately, into an imperfectly specified decision-making process. As outlined earlier, in real world decision-making patterns, analysts focus on a few plausible outcomes and assign a probability to each. In some cases, they search for only a limited number of equities or bonds, perhaps for a limited number of countries. Analysts are limited in time and so they often proscribe the number of outcomes they examine. This reflects their judgment and, in some cases, their judgment can be very unrealistic about the range of options. During the Great Recession of 2007 to 2009, assumptions about liquidity, marketability of financial assets, and the real market value of real assets such as homes were quite unrealistic at the start of the recession. Moreover, the damage of the recession was far greater than policy makers at the time anticipated. Information provides data for assessment and revision of the probabilities of various outcomes—it does not provide certainty. Analysts draw upon their experience to suggest what their initial assumptions will be on the models they build and the changes and feedback they anticipate.

Drawing upon their experience and their initial read of the data, analysts will assign their expected probabilities to possible outcomes. These outcomes, such as estimates of the feedback effects of any given change in the framework, cover a range of possibilities. For example, analysts estimate the feedback from any change in oil prices upon a company's earnings, given the analysts' reading of its history. In other cases, analysts, and investors in general, will assign probabilities to the range of possible outcomes for the P/E ratio and earnings per share given any change in oil prices, regulations, or tax rates. As you might suspect, these probabilities are highly subjective at times and often reflect certain biases such as the anchoring bias in decision making, which we will discuss further.

Finally, analysts make choices that reflect the values they bring to the whole process. Their values influence their view on the feedback of any change, their choices in response to the feedback, and the construction of a new framework to go forward. Since the Great Recession, investors and business leaders have clearly chosen to be more conservative in their spending. Their new framework for many consumers and businesses emphasizes caution, not speculation.

Over the past 20 years, there have been three instances where the estimates of a new model drifted away from the values underlying the prior model and in each case the results were disastrous. With the dot-com boom in full swing in the early twenty-first century, many investors—individual and institutional—drifted away from their disciplined models, caught dot-com fever, and bought more high P/E stocks (and in some cases no E for earnings stocks) for their portfolios.[5] In the latter half of the 1990s, formerly standard benchmarks for consumer mortgage lending were thrown overboard on the assumption that any mortgage, no matter what the underlying credit terms, could be securitized and sold in the marketplace. Further, it was assumed that homeowners would never walk away from their homes, no matter how little they put down, if anything, on the houses. From 2005 to 2010, a number of countries in the European Union violated their debt-to-GDP and deficit-to-GDP ratios. The outstanding debt-to-GDP ratio is the ratio of the central government debt, the obligations to be paid, compared to the GDP, as a proxy for the ability of the economy to pay that debt. In a similar way, the deficit is simply this year's addition to debt and that is compared to the additional growth of the economy this year as measured by the GDP. Higher debt- or deficit-to-GDP ratios are signals that indicate the ability of any government to pay its debt. Finally, countries like Greece, whose debt-to-GDP ratio rose sharply in recent years, could no longer finance debt at market terms and had to get help from various other European countries and international institutions. Our initial priors, beliefs, on credit and investment ratios exist for a reason. While economies and credit markets evolve, the challenge is to make good choices that fit a new model, but a sensible model as well.

What is sensible, then? How far can financial ratios deviate from the past before they indicate something more than random noise? In any review of financial ratios, analysts can start by simply focusing on the basic characteristics of the mean and standard deviation of the series. For example, many trading systems for financial assets compared the pattern of the 30- and 120-day moving averages of the series. Alternatively, analysts want to know how far the current observation of a series is from the average and whether that deviation is more or less than one, two, or three standard deviations away. The greater the distance, the more likely it is that they are seeing a significant change in the behavior of the financial ratio.

Correlations among ratios produce a problem when ratios are employed as independent variables in a multiple regression model. Any statistically significant correlation would suggest that the model cannot distinguish the separate effects of the independent ratio inputs on the dependent variable of interest. Likewise, when a number of financial ratios are correlated to economic changes, then economy-wide changes and shocks will affect a number of financial ratios all at once and, more broadly, may be affecting the same financial ratios across a number of firms in an industry, as well as many industries.

## Decision-Making Biases to Watch

As scientific and precise as we may wish the discipline of financial analysis and investing to be, decisions are often reflective of the same biases in decision making that we have witnessed in other fields of policy making at the public and private sector levels. Here we review the availability and anchoring biases that influence our most treasured beliefs of unbiased financial analysis.

**Setting Up a Framework: Availability Bias**   First and foremost, the greatest bias to decision making is that so many of the popular financial ratios are, indeed, so popular. Students learn them; television and radio commentators employ them easily. As a result, students, viewers, and listeners quickly brush over them without analyzing the details of what is driving the underlying trends in the ratios themselves.

The second bias is that of anchoring. Analysts are comfortable with the current set of financial ratios they review. Therefore, they assume that those ratios are the true values that all institutions should follow. Yet, the history of the post–World War II period has been that liquidity and leverage values have changed and that such ratios are likely to continue to alter with changing economic and regulatory changes. Values should be analyzed in the context of the overall economic outlook and the regulatory environment. While this chapter focuses on financial ratios within the context of the

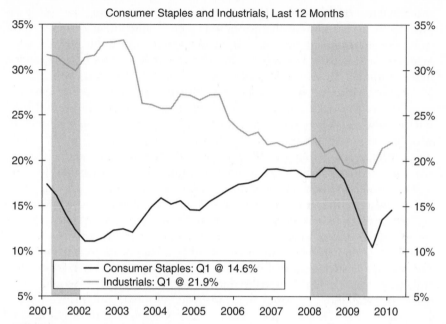

**FIGURE 10.1** Return on Equity
*Source:* Compustat and Factset.

macroeconomic environment, in other reviews, comparisons to other firms and industries would reveal that appropriate financial ratios probably have a wider range of preferred values than prior expectations would allow.

In Figure 10.1, for example, the return on equity for consumer staples stocks is significantly different, and persistently so, than the same ratio for industrial stocks. Therefore, financial ratios do require discretion when employed—specific levels do not fit all situations—and judgment still prevails. In addition, analysts should not focus on the ratio itself but rather its value in context with the economy. Finally, analysts should recognize that changes in economic factors will certainly alter their assessment of the appropriate values of financial ratios that they would consider as standards of economic heath for the corporation.

## Evaluating Change

When analysts move from their framework to evaluating change, three biases challenge them. First is the availability bias. Whenever analysts examine a change they first react to whatever data or research capabilities are at hand. They go with what is comfortable. However, it often pays to dig a little deeper and examine what is driving the ratio they are looking at and how this ratio relates to the object of their study. Did earnings per share decline due to an accounting change, or was there a fundamental change in the economic environment? In much of the academic work published, the standard data sets, such as Standard & Poor's, are often used while only modest effort, especially by students, is exercised to seek out new data sources.

Second, the confirmation bias may distort decision making. Analysts have a bias toward using information that favors their traditional view and framework. Therefore, they must work against this bias by seeking information outside the traditional published sources or taking an alternative view of the issues, getting outside the box, to better understand the problem and seek the best solution, given the broad range of choices available to us. In the famous case of the Cuban missile crisis, President Kennedy purposely set up a group called ExCom that met outside the White House.[6] Kennedy did not attend the meetings. Two options were discussed by two separate subsets of the group. This process allowed each side to bring its best case to the president and ensured that there would be an advocate for each option.[7] The two options were a naval blockade or a military airstrike. The president argued against a military airstrike since he felt that the Soviets would attack Berlin in retaliation. A naval blockade was adopted, and through secret negotiations the crisis was resolved, as the Soviets agreed to dismantle and remove their weapons and the United States, secretly, agreed to remove its missiles from Turkey. The Cuban missile crisis gave rise to the hotline between the Soviet Union and Washington. Today, the Cuban missile crisis is an excellent example of one approach to dealing with the confirmation bias so common in many organizations.

Third, analysts are also biased by the illusory correlation, which is the tendency to bias any evaluation or study because there is a bias to judgment by the appearance of a correlation between economic factors—although there is, in fact, no relationship. This takes two paths. First, they may be quick to judge what appears to be the obvious cause in any movement of a financial ratio. Second, they may jump to the conclusion about the movement of the variable they wish to study, for example, delinquencies or bond downgrades, in response to the financial ratio they have identified. In both cases, analysts may move too quickly because they have seen this problem before, or so they think, or they are lazy and "round up the usual suspects."[8]

## Feedback

The first reaction in evaluating the feedback from any change is to search the latest news for the direction that financial ratios or the economy might take. In finance or in management, the first movement in the markets, the short run, may in fact be very different from the long-run movement. The recency bias puts undue weight on the latest news—what's hot and where the market is moving today. The directions of the trends analysts should be interested in are often not correlated with the first, immediate movement in the data in reaction to a change in the economic data. As traders would say, there is a countertrend move in the short run as traders who are caught on the wrong side of the market when new economic data come in quickly cover their position. But once the short-covering is done, the market reveals the real trend in the data in response to changing economic fundamentals.

Analysts also recognize that risk and opportunity vary over the business cycle. Credit quality evolves. One of the most frequent failings of decision making in any institution is that management only looks at the most recent period, perhaps the last two years, and extrapolates only the most recent experience into the future without any thought of the more distant past. This occurred during the housing boom from 2002 to 2007 where the most recent home sales and housing price data were extrapolated into the future. As a result, ever-rising home prices were expected while the risk of a business cycle downturn was ignored, even though the American economy had always been characterized by such downturns.

As evidenced in Figure 10.2, corporate profits have a clear cyclical pattern to them. Yet, investors are frequently caught up in the moment of recent

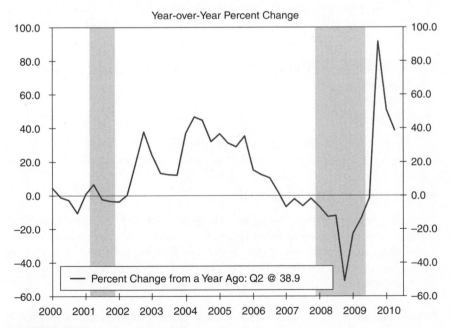

**FIGURE 10.2** Corporate Profits
*Source:* Bureau of Economic Analysis.

success and thereby tend to project the latest results into the future. This can be seen in the spreadsheets in many an investment prospectus where revenues and earnings are presented only for the most recent past, with seldom a mention of the patterns seen in the last recession.

### Choices

Decision makers' willingness to make innovative choices is often limited by the sunk cost bias. Here a leader has a tendency to weigh his existing investment in his career, his financial assets, or the existing structure of his business, and is then hesitant to choose to change the framework of how we view the economic and financial landscape. In the investment field, there are perennial bulls and bears. Henry Ford would produce a car in any color as long as it was black. Newspapers have been slow to adapt to the challenge of the Internet.

## FINANCIAL RATIOS AS INFORMATION

Four different types of financial ratios help provide some guidance on four different questions that economists frequently ask about the financial character of the economy and the institutions—primarily private nonfarm corporate business—that they analyze over time. They break these ratios into indicators of

1. Profitability or efficiency
2. Liquidity
3. Leverage
4. Market value

Their focus remains at the macroeconomic levels of analysis—not firm or industry level; economists leave that to the equity and credit analysts.[9]

### Profitability or Efficiency Ratios

How efficient is the operation of the company/institution we are examining? In this section we review three measures (funny how there always seems to be three of everything) of efficiency. The first two are financial and the third focuses more on the actual operation of production and sales within the operation.

**Return on Equity** One question that economists often ask is, how efficiently are companies using their assets? Traditionally, economists look to the return on equity, which simply relates the net income of the corporation to the amount invested by stockholders. This is an attempt to gauge the efficiency of investing the stockholders' capital. The numerator of net income reflects the economic forces of growth, inflation, and interest rates, as evidenced in Table 10.1. Growth, for example, has a statistically significant positive correlation with net income.[10]

This is consistent with economists' expectation that improvements in the economy would be associated with rising returns to capital over time. Net income reflects the growth in the economy as well as the improvement in pricing power, proxied by inflation, for the corporation. In addition, with assets valued on the basis of their original cost (less any depreciation) there would be a tendency for the return on assets to rise over the cycle as current income is being compared to a historical asset price. Also, the higher return on older assets does not suggest that buying new assets today would generate the same returns, since a new cost basis is associated with the newer assets. Moreover, unlike the price/earnings ratio, the return on assets does not reflect the emotional roller coaster of expected future earnings that is embedded in the market price for assets.

**Return on Assets** Return on assets, another measure of the efficiency of using corporate assets, is also very positively correlated with economic growth, as evidenced in Table 10.2. Once again, during periods of inflation this ratio could be biased upward as current net income is being compared to assets usually priced at historical prices.[11] The return on assets indicates the effectiveness of resource utilization of the assets without regard to how those resources have been obtained and financed. In this case, the cost of the same physical capital can be quite different for different firms if the capital was

**TABLE 10.2** Pearson Correlation Coefficients

|        | Return on Earnings | Return on Assets | Interest Expense/ Cash Flow |
|--------|--------------------|------------------|-----------------------------|
| CPI    | 0.50951            | 0.61052          | 0.34298                     |
| 10YT   | 0.33636            | 0.53069          | 0.58093                     |
| Dollar | −0.07841           | −0.20444         | −0.42166                    |
| 5YT    | 0.44910            | 0.63803          | 0.58325                     |
| Growth | 0.66346            | 0.80333          | −0.26035                    |
| Profits| 0.07713            | 0.46229          | −0.45835                    |

Data dates back until at least 1985, with the exception of RoA (2001).
Bold indicates statistical significance at the 1 percent level.
*Source:* Compustat, Factset, U.S. Census Bureau, and Bureau of Economic Analysis.

purchased and financed at different times. Global competition over the past 20 years has also had an influence, since competition will limit the pricing power of any industry and therefore the net income and the return on assets of any firm and industry.

Contrary to conventional wisdom, interest rates and economic growth move together over the period studied. The usual premise is that when interest rates rise, economic growth, and thereby net income, will slow. That should lower the return on assets and equity. This would work in a world where nothing else changes. Yet, the pattern, surprisingly, is that the return on assets is positively correlated to the 5- and 10-year Treasury rate. The reason is that both the return on assets and interest rates tend to rise with the business cycle, as evidenced in Figure 10.3. Often, financial markets react to news of changes in interest rates and the economic outlook as if they are separate events. But it is the combined impact of both that sets the tone for the path for financial ratios such as the return on assets. As evidenced by the recency bias, decision makers tend to take the latest information

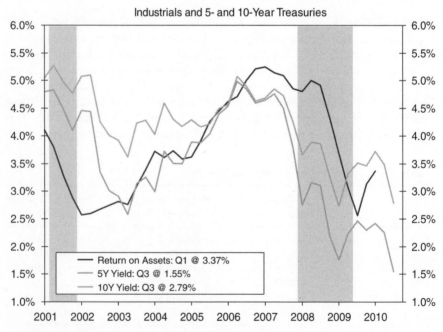

**FIGURE 10.3**   Return on Assets and Treasury Yields
*Source:* Compustat, Factset, and Federal Reserve Board.

(or rumor) as the driving factor for asset prices without an adequate framework that puts economic changes into context.

**Inventory-to-Sales Ratios**   How efficiently does the firm utilize its inventories? How well balanced are inventories and sales in the national economy? Historically, excess inventory relative to sales has led to a slowdown in production and therefore the economy. Yet, the inventory-to-sales ratio illustrates an earlier point: Analysts must understand why a ratio changes and what are the different implications for the enterprise if the numerator or denominator of the series is the driving factor.

Inventory changes can be intended or unintended. As the economy grows, a firm may want to increase its inventories and its inventories relative to sales to ensure that product is available to potential customers, especially in a hot market. Alternatively, a slowdown in sales would likely signal a weak economy and be accompanied by a rise in the inventory-to-sales ratio. Therefore, a business can have an increase in the inventory-to-sales ratio for two very different reasons indicating two very different outlooks for the economy, but in both cases this ratio is very much endogenous, not exogenous, to the economic cycle.

Following on the precept advanced by Baruch Lev, professor at the Stern School of Business, New York University, there should be an economically meaningful relationship between the numerator and denominator in any ratio.[12] The intent here is that this ratio indicates the efficiency of the firm's inventory management. The lower the inventory-to-sales ratio, the better the inventory has been managed. Yet, over short periods of time, this ratio may react more to macroeconomic factors than the microeconomic actions at the firm level. In Figure 10.4, the efficiency gains for firms can be traced by noting the general decline in the inventory-to-sales ratio in recent years. Over time, a general downturn in the inventory-to-sales ratio suggests that the lessons of inventory management have been well learned by many businesses in America. However, there are spikes in this series associated with changes in the patterns of economic growth. Inflation and interest rates also play a role in determining the optimum level of inventories relative to sales. Higher inflation, and therefore higher prices for inventory in stock, has historically been associated with higher ratios of inventory to sales. Higher interest rates meant higher financing costs for inventories and thereby led to a reduction in the inventory-to-sales ratio.

There are costs associated with both too high and too low an inventory-to-sales ratio. Too high a ratio means excess carrying costs and, potentially inventory that must be sold at deep discounts to clear the sales floor. In addition, excess inventory may also suggest that inventory on the floor is

**FIGURE 10.4** Inventory to Shipments Ratio
*Source:* U.S. Census Bureau.

becoming stale and may not move at all at current prices. Alternatively, too low an inventory-to-sales ratio means lost sales and a disappointed customer who may be less likely to return.

Inventory turnover can also function as a liquidity measure. The turnover of the inventory—the number of times inventory is sold—measures the liquidity and the ability of the company to convert inventories to cash. Slower inventory turnover suggests that inventories are not a liquid asset and would be a drag on company efficiency. From a liquidity viewpoint, if inventory is turned over quickly, the liquid character of inventory can provide funds if needed in the short term.

The inventory-to-sales ratio gives us an opportunity to illustrate the technique employed by Robert J. Hodrick and Edward C. Prescott, professors of economics at Carnegie-Mellon at the time of their research, to filter or decompose the time series of observations of the inventory-to-sales ratio.[13] This appears as Figure 10.5. Any given economic time series can be expressed as the sum of a growth component and a cyclical component. There may also be a seasonal component to the data, but since seasonally

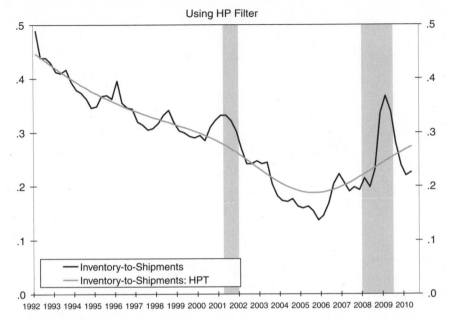

**FIGURE 10.5**   Decomposing Inventory to Shipments Ratio Using the HP Ratio
*Source:* U.S. Census Bureau.

adjusted data is being used, that component has been accounted for in the series tested.

In this framework, the HP filter optimally extracts a growth trend that moves smoothly over time but is uncorrelated to the cyclical component. One key advantage of the HP filter is that once the growth and cyclical components are estimated, it can be seen at any point in time, whether a series is moving below the trend growth (slowdown) or above the trend (boom). This feature of the HP filter helps decision makers identify the stage of the business cycle (expansion or contraction) for any time series with particular reference to application to financial ratios.

## Liquidity

After efficiency, economists ask a number of questions: What is the character of the firm or industry's liquidity? What is the ability of the firm to meet its financial obligations as they become current? Can the company gather enough cash to repay its debts in the short run? The current ratio (Figure 10.6) provides a gauge of the liquidity of the company. The larger

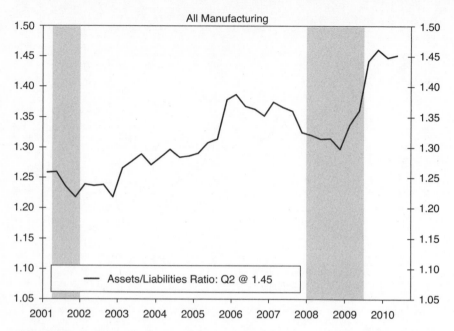

**FIGURE 10.6**   Current Assets/Current Liabilities
*Source:* U.S. Census Bureau.

the current ratio, the larger the safety margin of short-term creditors. The current ratio equals current assets divided by current liabilities. Current assets include cash, short-term securities, receivables, and inventories. Current liabilities are the ongoing interest expense and utility bills that accrue in the short run to any business.

From the earlier discussion on inventories, it can be seen that the current ratio is not invariant to economic factors, particularly the impact of growth on inventory levels and value. A sharp downturn in the economy, such as what occurred in the period from 2007 to 2009, suggests a rapid depreciation of the value of existing inventory, which in many cases would be sold at discount prices. In addition, a rapid slowdown in the economy and thereby top-line sales would lead to less cash on hand in the short run than expected and hence a lower current ratio than expected. This aspect of sensitivity to the economic cycle highlights the need for the analyst or decision maker to monitor changes in the economy that might impact measures of the current ratio and therefore the estimate of the liquidity of the enterprise. For Richard Brealey (professor at the London Business School) and Stewart Myers (professor at MIT), in this case, the quick ratio is the answer.[14] They argue that some assets are closer to cash than others, particularly inventories, since when trouble comes, as it always does, inventories are sold at fire-sale prices. Therefore, a second liquidity measure would consider only such current assets as cash and marketable securities. In addition, Brealey and Myers also caution that a firm could also borrow longer-term and then invest in short-term securities. This would typically happen in a steep yield curve environment. As a result, the current ratio would look much better than the actual liquidity of the firm on a long-term basis.

Likewise on the liabilities side, a rapid change in short-term interest rates may signal a rapid rise in interest expense on short-term debt. In addition, the existence of short-term debt should also be noted in the case that credit availability is limited. In this situation, firms do not have the ability to turn over their short-term debt as easily as they had assumed—another example of lessons learned in the capital markets during the period 2007 to 2009.

Using the current ratio, analysts can introduce the concept of the stability ratio, which helps them identify the stability of any time series such as the financial ratios reviewed here. The stability ratio is simply the standard deviation of a series expressed as a percentage of the mean, where a higher value of the stability ratio is an indication of the higher volatility of a series. The standard deviation alone does not help analysts identify a volatile series unless they compare that standard deviation to the mean. Table 10.3 lists the calculations for the stability ratios for financial ratios as well as

**TABLE 10.3**  Stability Ratio

|  | Mean | Standard Deviation | Stability Ratio |
|---|---|---|---|
| Debt-to-Equity | 62.883 | 18.878 | 30.020 |
| Debt-to-Net Worth | 70.664 | 8.379 | 11.858 |
| Current Assets-to-Liabilities | 1.317 | 0.065 | 4.968 |
| Return on Earnings | 13.266 | 3.361 | 25.332 |
| Return on Assets | 2.067 | 0.806 | 39.012 |
| Earnings Per Share | 44.575 | 21.972 | 49.292 |
| Interest Expense | 19.532 | 4.764 | 24.393 |
| Corporate Profits | 8.038 | 13.524 | 168.237 |

Series Start Dates:
1970: Debt-to-Equity, Debt-to-Net Worth, Interest Expense.
1985: Return on Earnings, Return on Assets.
2001: Current Assets to Liabilities.
*Source:* Federal Reserve Board, U.S. Census Bureau, Compustat, and Factset.

corporate profits. For three series—the debt-to-equity ratio, the current ratio and corporate profits—it appears that the debt-to-equity ratio is the most volatile series when judging based on the standard deviation. Yet, once there is an adjustment for the size of the values of the mean, profits are more volatile. This is in better accord with the prior beliefs on the volatility of profits.

## Leverage

In all three of the last business cycles in the American economy as well as the Asian financial crisis of the late 1990s, the role of leverage was a primary factor driving the expansion on the upside as well as the depth of the recession on the downside. Despite these experiences, we remain uncertain on how to judge when too much leverage is too much and under what assumptions of growth and interest rates can/do we target a set of leverage ratios as break points for prudent financial management.

**Interest Expense and Corporate Cash Flow**  Interest expense as a percent of corporate cash flow provides a practical measure of business leverage owing to the timing of the series and the correlation of interest expense to the five economic factors. Measures of leverage have taken on greater significance in recent years given the recent downdraft in credit availability and questions about the ability to refinance that debt. At the start of the recession in 2007, nonfinancial corporate net interest expense as a percentage of corporate cash flow was around 22 percent and then dropped to 12.8 percent in the second quarter of 2010 (Figure 10.7). In that year, interest expense relative to corporate cash flow was below its long-term average and certainly benefitted from low interest rates. These low rates have also provided the incentive for strong high-grade and high-yield debt issuance during the recovery.

As would be suspected, the interest expense ratio is not invariant to changes in the economic environment. In fact, interest expense is positively correlated to the CPI measure of inflation as well as the 5- and 10-year Treasury rates, as would be expected. In addition, stronger economic growth and profits are correlated with a lower interest expense ratio as both growth and corporate profits are drivers of the denominator corporate cash flow. As evidenced by the spikes in the net interest expense ratio in Figure 10.8, this ratio is very sensitive to weakness in the economy. In this figure we use the Hodrick-Prescott (HP) filter, as in earlier chapters, to provide a simple technique to allow the analyst a first cut at splitting the cyclical and longer-term patterns of any variable under study. The filter is discussed in

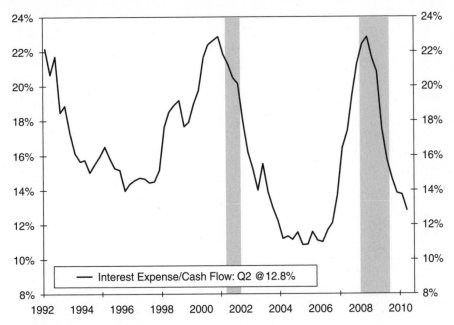

**FIGURE 10.7** Interest Expense/Corporate Cash Flow
*Source:* U.S. Census Bureau.

further detail in the appendix. Slower growth drives slower corporate cash flow and this pattern has been consistently evident since the 1960s. This pattern reinforces the principle expressed earlier that when analysts deal with financial ratios they need to be aware of the independent patterns of the numerator and denominator for any ratio.

## Debt-to-Equity Ratio

Another measure of leverage focuses on the degree to which the financial support to the enterprise is supported by liabilities—short- and long-term debt—relative to an owner's equity. In general, a higher ratio provides less protection for creditors. Since corporate earnings fluctuate over the economic cycle, higher levels of debt are associated with higher interest payments and therefore greater pressure on any given flow of corporate earnings. The debt-to-equity ratio reflects decisions made by corporate leadership on their capital structure and has implications for financial risk. This financial risk is only recognized when the volatility of the earnings stream that accrues to stockholders challenges the life of the corporation. The larger the

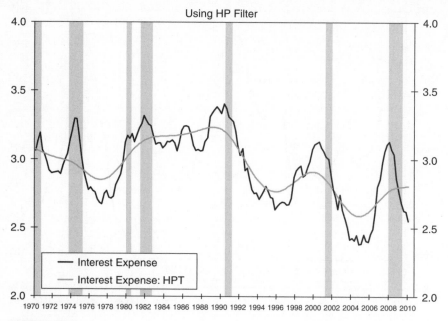

**FIGURE 10.8** Decomposing Interest Expense Using the HP Filter
*Source:* U.S. Census Bureau.

fixed interest expense for a given capital structure, the greater the probability that a given pattern of corporate earnings will fall below that fixed interest expense at some time during the business cycle. Unfortunately, increased leverage is taken on during the good times, but then comes home to roost when the inevitable economic slowdown or recession occurs, as it always does.

Barrie Wigmore, a researcher at Goldman Sachs at the time, cites the pattern in the 1980s when credit quality deteriorated as the credit and business cycle expansion continued. High-yield bonds, bonds issued by below-investment-grade corporations, issued later in the 1980s had poorer balance sheets and debt coverage than bonds issued earlier in the cycle.[15] This is a familiar pattern in financial markets, where the longer the economic cycle, the more likely it is that the quality of some financial instruments will actually deteriorate, perhaps because the last recession is more distant and our memories discount the past more aggressively when there is so much money to be made today.

## TAKING A CLOSER LOOK: INTEGRATED RESOURCES

The experience of Integrated Resources, a financial services company located in New York City, is instructive.[16] Integrated Resources engaged in insurance and money management and its capital structure was tilted toward high-yield debt and preferred stock. Its funding was not being generated by operations; in fact, it was cash flow negative. From 1984 to 1988, revenues and assets climbed for Integrated Resources, but operating income declined while indebtedness rose. Between 1984 and 1988, long-term debt rose from $359 million to $917 million. Bank and commercial paper indebtedness rose from $240 million to $563 million over the same period. By mid-1989, the need for debt financing outreached the willingness of the market to finance that debt. On another note, Integrated's senior debt was rated investment grade as late as June 1989 by Standard & Poor's. In 1990, Integrated filed for bankruptcy.

One lesson from the 1980s is that credit quality deteriorates as the volume of issuance increases in what may be the fashion of the day. We have seen this with high-yield bonds. In the 1990s, it was the dot-com era. Over the last decade, it was subprime lending. There is a clear cycle of credit quality in capital markets and we continue to ignore it, since, well, this time it is different.

The recency bias reigns supreme for decision makers. Recent increases in leverage appear successful, so the envelope is stretched and continues to be stretched. Business leaders only remember recent success and forget the longer history of the credit and economic cycle. People Express was an example of this credit cycle in which the edge of the envelope continues to be stretched until the debt burden breaks the company. Launched in 1981, the airline, a low-cost alternative to the major airlines, began service from Newark, New Jersey, to a number of American cities and by 1983 began service to London. In 1985, People Express purchased Frontier Airlines. In addition, People Express bought Britt Airways and Provincetown-Boston Airlines. Along with these purchases came a load of debt, a danger signal in the airline industry, which is noted for its fierce competition. Over time, other airlines developed better pricing schemes to compete with People Express, while labor problems and the difficulty of integrating Frontier's passengers to a no-frills airline spelled trouble. People Express then attempted to change its business model and added first class service. Eventually, People Express sold Frontier to Texas Air and merged the remaining operations into Continental Airlines. The cyclical pattern of increasing leverage in an industry as competitive as airlines simply did not work. The initial success led to a bias on management's part that the recent success meant success over the entire business cycle. This is unlikely in a world of cycles and straight-line extrapolation.

Increased leverage indicates a higher level of risk for both lenders and stockholders. Leverage in any institution not only threatens the institution's existence, but also the value of the portfolio for lenders as well as the investments of stockholders. The advantage of leverage is that profits accrue to a smaller group of shareholders. The disadvantage of such leverage is that risk rises when profits and cash flows fall, as they inevitably do at some point in the cycle. In those cases where leverage has been limited due to the foresight of management, the slowdown in cash flow puts stress on the company but does not threaten failure. In contrast, aggressive assumption of debt means that the company faces insolvency when interest exceeds cash flow. Yet the typical procyclical behavior of the credit cycle—companies leverage up in expansion—requires a careful balancing act for decision leaders. The choice is how much leverage to take on when the marketplace is willing to accept higher leverage as the business cycle moves on, while knowing that there is a cycle and that trying to deleverage, along with every other firm, in a slowdown or recession is extremely difficult. Differences in leverage over the cycle reveal management's attitude toward risk and alternative strategies to financing the organization.

For many leaders, the game becomes one of guessing cyclical turning points. As illustrated in Figure 10.9, there is clearly a pattern in the debt-to-equity ratio and that pattern has persisted over several cycles. While some analysts might have a tendency to smooth earnings over time—by employing average of earnings over several years—the problem is that, as evidenced by the volatility of corporate profits, there is no tendency for earnings to bounce back after a fall or sink back after a rise. Current earnings act as a better guide to the future than any past average of prior earnings. Mandatory interest payments are a barrier that must be jumped each quarter and yet earnings vary over the cycle. Large debt levels remain a problem in the face of earnings variability, as the economy and credit cycles are a fact of business life.

## Market Value Ratios—A Closer Look at the Price/Earnings Ratio

Market values dominate the daily business headlines and the volatility of these values conveys an impression of a casino. The price/earnings ratio of

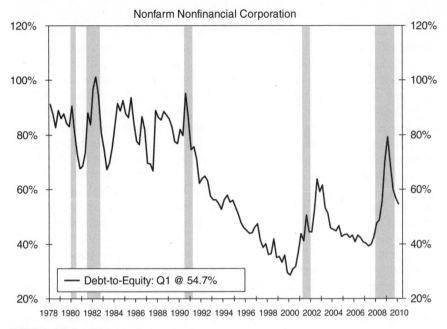

**FIGURE 10.9**  Debt-to-Equity Ratio
*Source:* Federal Reserve Board.

equity, for example, varies over the business cycle. In contrast, many equities are often characterized as low or high P/E ratio stocks as if that were a permanent classification. As a measure of market valuations, the P/E ratio equates to the price assigned by the open financial market compared to the earnings per share of the equity in question. The underlying theory is that the value of an asset is determined by the present value of the expected net earnings stream to be generated by the asset. Immediately, the importance of expectations and the role of economic factors in shaping those expectations are obvious. The earnings stream reflects the expected future path of economic growth. With so many multinational companies in the S&P 500, the role of the dollar exchange rate also has an important impact on earnings. Finally, the present value is impacted by the expected paths of inflation and interest rates over time. When expectations change, market valuations change as well. As discussed earlier, financial markets and the economy move when actual economic values differ from expectations. In turn, these changes in expectations also reflect changes in the economic information that help form these expectations. As a result, what may appear as irrational volatility in asset prices to some observers, is often a response to changes in the economic fundamentals. Market valuations are not set in an environment of certainty; the company and economic fundamentals are developed in an environment of uncertainty. Valuations reflect the expected stream of earnings; when expectations change, so do prices. Since different investors have different expectations, buyers and sellers are willing to trade financial and real assets and traders believe they have got a deal. Different expectations allow the markets to trade. Also note that the P/E ratio can change as the numerator and denominator change at different rates. An "expensive" stock with a high P/E could be more reasonable if earnings (the denominator) rise over time. Alternatively, a fair valued stock with a modest P/E could become more expensive if earnings trail off. In fact, much of equity research is devoted to forecasting earnings changes that will alter the valuation of equity. A high P/E stock reflects the expectation by investors that earnings and dividends will be high relative to the discount factor—interest rates. Therefore, expectations for economic growth and interest rates play a big role in the pricing of equities and the differences between the actual and expectations will drive changes in equity valuations.

Another way to look at valuation and the dynamics of the markets is to reverse the expression of the P/E ratio to earnings as a percentage of the market price, because this allows a simple comparison on valuation compared to bonds. In this case, when interest rates rise, the rising return on bonds will lower the valuation for equities since the P/E ratio will fall below that of the return earned on bonds.

The P/E ratio presents a number of statistical properties that are of interest to decision makers and can be easily captured with simple statistical techniques. First, decision makers want to know whether the P/E ratio tends to return to the same average value over time, that is, is the mean reverting? Second, how volatile is the P/E ratio, and does that volatility hide the basic message of the P/E series? Third, can a long-run trend be identified for the P/E ratio distinct from the economic cycle? For decision makers, characterizing the economic or financial variable that is the focus of interest is a must. Too often, the time-series characteristics of the focus variable are skipped over and immediately the researcher moves to forecasting the variable. Errors in modeling are common when the dependent variable is unexamined.[17]

Does P/E contain a trend? To test for a trend in any economic variable is to run a regression of the variable over time. If the coefficient of the time variable is statistically significant, the series has a linear trend. The coefficient sign will determine whether the variable has an increasing or decreasing trend. In addition, in Figure 10.10 we employ the Hodrick-Prescott filter to identify the pattern of the P/E ratio relative to its trend. This technique was reviewed earlier, but a bit of review would be instructive. The Hodrick-Prescott filter separates the pattern of any time series into two components—its trend and the cycle about the trend. The technique is fairly simple and its advantage to decision makers is that, when applied to any times series, we have the ability to see where the latest observations of that series are relative to trend. We get a sense whether the deviations of the latest observations are getting off track relative to trend—perhaps we should find out why and possibly take some action.

In Figure 10.10 the rise above trend in the P/E ratio during 1987 and again in the late 1990s would have suggested that a thoughtful analyst would have at least investigated the deviation and decided whether any actions were warranted.

There are two major types of trends—linear and nonlinear. A linear trend indicates a constant growth rate and a nonlinear trend is associated with a variable (not constant) growth rate. Leverage has had a rising trend while efficiency variables such as the inventory-to-sales ratios have declined over time.

How does the economic variable vary between economic cycles over time? The character of the American economy is that each expansion and recession is different. There is always a new normal despite all the hype that

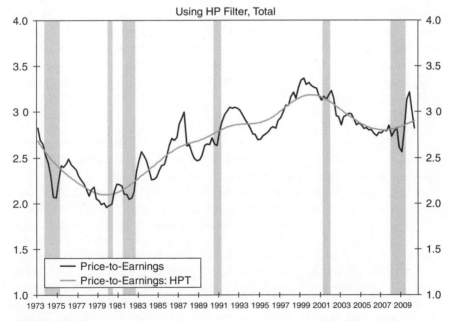

**FIGURE 10.10** Decomposing Price to Earnings Using the HP Filter, Total
*Source:* Compustat and Factset.

**TABLE 10.4**  P/E Ratio—Total

| Period | Mean | S.D. | Stability Ratio | Trend |
|---|---|---|---|---|
| 1961:M2-1970:M11 | 17.690 | 1.980 | **11.190** | Non-linear: U-shaped |
| 1970:M11-1975:M3 | 14.780 | 3.890 | **26.320** | Non-linear: Inverted U-shaped |
| 1975:M3-1980:M7 | 9.190 | 1.640 | **17.850** | Non-linear: U-shaped |
| 1980:M7-1991:M3 | 12.230 | 2.970 | **24.280** | Non-linear: Inverted U-shaped |
| 1991:M3-2001:M11 | 20.870 | 4.090 | **19.600** | Non-linear: U-shaped |
| 2001:M11-2009:M6 | 17.650 | 2.700 | **15.300** | Non-linear: U-shaped |
| 1961:M2-2009:M6 | 15.980 | 4.870 | **30.476** | Non-linear: U-shaped |

some would attach to whatever the new is in economic trends. There are always new trends. One simple approach is to calculate the mean and standard deviation of the financial variable under study for each economic cycle and test whether the mean and standard deviation differ between cycles, which are shown in Table 10.4.[18] Therefore, there are seven business cycles since 1961. By comparing the ratio of the standard deviation to the mean, analysts can identify how any financial factor varies over different cycles. Also, the stability ratio helps to identify for any company what elements of its costs and sales have the greatest volatility and thereby the greatest risk. These calculations are introduced here since they are simple and they provide an easy check on any time series and would provide a clue that perhaps any changes over time should be more closely analyzed for good decision making purposes. Based on the stability ratio reported in Table 10.4, the 1970 to 1975 business cycle was the most volatile cycle for the P/E ratio. On the other hand, the time period from 1961 to 1970 showed the most stable cycle for the P/E ratio. Moreover, there was a nonlinear trend for the P/E ratio.

Each economic cycle differs in the five key economic factors that drive financial markets. Unexpected rising inflation was the driving factor for the 1970s. In the 1980s, there was better-than-expected economic growth, lower taxes, less regulation, lower inflation and interest rates—and stronger than expected performance in equity markets. By the 1990s, globalization began to play a role in setting interest rate and growth expectations. Technology began to influence productivity and inflation estimates as well. The globalization of production began to alter the relative competitiveness of many American corporations.

As a result, changing values for economic drivers would be expected to alter what investors would expect as a fair valuation for equities. Values

**TABLE 10.5**   Pearson Correlation Coefficients

|  | P/E Consumer Staples | P/E Industrial | P/E Total |
|---|---|---|---|
| CPI | −0.62195 | −0.62060 | −0.70717 |
| 10YT | −0.62116 | −0.41003 | −0.66132 |
| Dollar | 0.71837 | 0.55085 | 0.81814 |
| 5YT | −0.58854 | −0.41159 | −0.65479 |
| Growth | 0.22747 | 0.27501 | 0.08012 |
| Profits | −0.05558 | 0.08742 | −0.03973 |

Data dates back until at least 1972.
Bold indicates statistical significance at the .0001 percent level.
*Source:* Compustat, Factset, U.S. Census Bureau, and Bureau of Economic Analysis.

for the P/E ratio, like other financial ratios, are not invariant with respect to the economy. As illustrated in Table 10.5, the P/E ratio has a strong, statistically significant negative correlation to inflation and interest rates, as would be expected. Higher inflation and interest rates would increase the discount rate applied to future earnings and thereby lower the market's P/E ratio. Meanwhile, industrial and staples P/E ratios are positively correlated to economic growth, as would be expected as well.

Spurious regression results are likely to pop up when the dependent variable that analysts are trying to model has a trend in its level form, termed a *unit root*, and is considered nonstationary. Therefore, analysts first must test any dependent variable, such as the P/E ratio, for the unit root/nonstationarity. That is, each series in any analysis should be a stationary series in the sense that its mean and variance are constant over time. If not, if the series is nonstationary, then most likely the variance changes over time and any statistical test of significance will not be reliable. The P/E ratio is a dependent variable in much analysis, so a test for stationarity appears to be a necessity, that is, we need to be sure the series is stationary so our tests of statistical significance will be reliable.

Using a nonstationary dependent variable in a regression may produce very positive reported statistical results when there is no underlying meaningful relationship between the variables. This situation exemplifies the problem of spurious regression. In contrast, a stationary series fluctuates around a constant mean and has a finite variance that does not depend on time—hence it is mean-reverting. This statistical behavior allows the researcher to identify the underlying economic relationship. In Table 10.6, clearly the P/E ratio has a unit root at the level form, except for the most recent business cycle (2001 to 2009). Therefore, level form of the P/E ratio should not be

**TABLE 10.6**   P/E Test for Stationarity

| Period | Unit Root Test |
| --- | --- |
| 1961:M2-1970:M11 | Unit Root |
| 1970:M11-1975:M3 | Unit Root |
| 1975:M3-1980:M7 | Unit Root |
| 1980:M7-1991:M3 | Unit Root |
| 1991:M3-2001:M11 | Unit Root |
| 2001:M11-2009:M6 | **No Unit Root** |
| 1961:M2-2009:M6 | Unit Root |

*Source:* Compustat and Factset.

employed in any regression analysis. The first difference of the P/E ratio is stationary and good for the analysis.

The HP filter allows researchers to separate cyclical and long-run trend growth components, which enables them to identify whether any macroeconomic series is above the long-run trend growth or below the long-run trend growth. HP distinguishes cyclical and trend influences.

Financial ratios serve as indicators of economic and financial success. Unfortunately, these ratios can also be a crutch and barrier to good decision

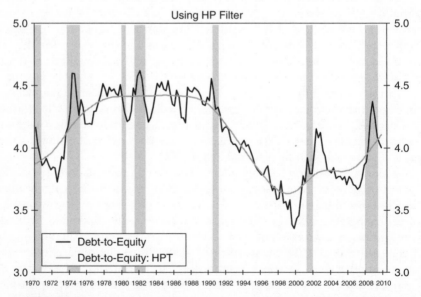

**FIGURE 10.11**   Decomposing Debt-to-Equity Ratio Using the HP Filter
*Source:* Federal Reserve Board.

making. Analysts tend to immediately move to make judgments based on a single financial ratio without reference to the economic context. In addition, financial ratios are not simply indicators, but are also targets for management. The problem for research derives from the behavioral response where both the observation of the behavior (by the analyst) and the public reporting of it can change the behavior observed. The intervention of researchers can change the nature of the relationships being studied.

Any attempt to apply a framework for evaluating a financial ratio needs to account for the difference in the degrees of autonomy for financial ratios. For example, the laws of physics and chemistry are autonomous, not subject to the actions of the analysts. But in the behavioral sciences, the actions that influence the pattern of financial ratios are not independent of the researcher's actions or opinions. Also, financial ratios are part of a larger economic system and therefore are both independent and a dependent variable in any model or framework.

Finally, in the economic framework, the role of expectations comes to the fore. Analysts expect that a company or industry or, in some cases, a country will track a certain financial ratio. Deviations from those expectations lead to sharp movements in asset prices, as evidenced at the national level by the deviations from budget targets of countries such as Greece or Ireland.

Financial ratios are an indicator of financial success for decision makers, but are also part of the broader financial and economic system. Working within that framework gives decision makers the context for making informed decisions about their firm and the economy in general.

## DISCUSSION QUESTIONS

1. How would you react to the following economic changes and their expected feedback impact on critical financial ratios? We are looking for both analysis and your intelligent reaction.
   a. Change—expected weakening economy; your target is the return on assets.
   b. Change—expected sharp rise in key input prices; your target is earnings per share.
   c. Change—expected rise in short-term interest rates as the Fed tightens; your target is working capital turnover.
   d. Change—expect slower consumer spending and anticipated increase in the Fed funds rate; your target is the current ratio.
   e. Change—expected slower productivity and thereby rising unit labor costs suggests that EPS may be under downward pressure; your target is the P/E ratio.

2. Financial ratios represent a difficult problem of identification. Any given financial ratio can be interpreted as a target for its management, an indicator of success by an equity or credit analyst, or an instrument of policy in order to signal the markets about the quality of company operations for future funding.
    a. Discuss the issues involved with the lack of autonomy of a selected financial ratio such as the P/E ratio.
    b. What are the issues with a model where the P/E ratio is the dependent variable in any analysis?
    c. The state of the economy has a very direct influence on financial ratios and particularly the P/E ratio. How might you evaluate the movements in the P/E ratio over the cycle as an indicator of market expectations or as a financial ratio that simply reflects the stage of the business cycle and tells us very little about the individual company?
3. Financial ratios serve as indicators, but not as proof about the financial condition of a company. Consider the following and comment on the pros and cons of each approach.
    a. An analyst focuses on one financial ratio as the indicator of performance for a firm, an industry, and equities in general. You might note here how often investment strategists will judge the equity market on the basis of a single ratio, often the P/E ratio, as evidence of the market being either cheap or expensive.
    b. Financial ratios represent the financial picture of a company. However, nonfinancial data, also critical to a company's performance is not represented. How might this be an issue in the evaluation of a company?
    c. What factors might account for the persistent differences in financial ratios between companies in the same industry?
    d. Seasonality will influence the level of cash and inventories for any given company. What other influences might a factor such as seasonality have on other financial ratios?
    e. Selected financial ratios, particularly those linked to leverage, appear to have changed over time. What might account for this long-term trend?

## NOTES

1. C. A. E. Goodhart, "Monetary Relationships: A View from Threadneedle Street" (papers in *Monetary Economics* (Reserve Bank of Australia) I, 1975).
2. T. Haavelmo, "The probability approach in econometrics," *Econometrica* (1944).

3. William H. Greene, *Econometric Analysis,* 6th ed. (Upper Saddle River, NJ: Pearson Prentice-Hall, 2008), 133–134.

4. In this work we abstract from the use of ratios across industries and firms and simply focus on the broader macroeconomic influences on financial ratios.

5. Roger Lowenstein, *Origins of the Crash: The Great Bubble and Its Undoing* (New York: Penguin Books, 2004).

6. ExCom included Robert McNamara, Secretary of Defense, Robert Kennedy, Attorney General, and Ted Sorenson, the president's counsel, along with several others.

7. Robert F. Kennedy, *Thirteen Days* (New York: W.W. Norton, 1969).

8. The famous line uttered by Captain Renault in the movie *Casablanca,* 1942, Warner Brothers.

9. A business case I have found very useful as a review of financial ratios is the case study from the Harvard Business School by William Bruns, *Introduction to Financial Ratios and Financial Statement Analysis,* Harvard Business School, 9-193-029, September 13, 2004.

10. One note here is that when conducting research at the firm level, net income does not include interest charges and dividends, as this allows interfirm comparisons because differences in capital structure, reflected in different interest charges, will not affect the ratio. See Baruch Lev, *Financial Statement Analysis* (Englewood Cliffs, NJ: Prentice-Hall): 15.

11. At the firm level, comparisons are made difficult since different ages for different assets would have different historical prices.

12. Baruch Lev, *Financial Statement Analysis,* 34.

13. R. J. Hodrick and E. C. Prescott, "Postwar U.S. Business Cycles: An Empirical Investigation," *Journal of Money, Credit and Banking* (1997), 29(1): 1–16. For an application of the economic time series of corporate profits, see John Silvia and Azhar Iqbal, "Three Simple Techniques to Analyze a Complex Economic Phenomenon: The Case of Profits," *Business Economics* 45, no. 2 (2010). Edward C. Prescott won the Nobel Prize in Economics in 2004.

14. Richard A. Brealey and Stewart C. Myers, *Principles of Corporate Finance,* 3rd ed. (New York: McGraw-Hill, 1988): 651–658.

15. Barrie Wigmore, "The Decline in Credit Quality of Junk Bond Issues, 1980–1988," *Financial Analysts Journal* (September/October): 53–62.

16. James Grant, *Minding Mr. Market* (New York: Farrar Straus and Giroux, 1993), 263–266.

17. This review of a few simple statistical techniques expands on the work in John Silvia and Azhar Iqbal, "Three Simple Techniques to Analyze a Complex Economic Phenomenon: The Case of Profits."

18. We define the business cycle as trough-to-trough, which means that we are measuring the business cycle from one trough, or bottom, to the next. This gives us more data to work with now, since we can include the trough-to-trough period of November 2001 (one trough) to June 2009 (most recent trough). If we had used peak-to-peak, our data sample would end at the last peak of the cycle in 2007.

## RECOMMENDED READING FOR SERIOUS PLAYERS

Bruns, William. *Introduction to Financial Ratios and Financial Statement Analysis.* Harvard Business School, 9-193-029, September 13, 2004.

Lowenstein, Roger. *Origins of the Crash: The Great Bubble and Its Undoing.* New York: Penguin Books, 2004.

Kennedy, Robert F. *Thirteen Days.* New York: W.W. Norton, 1969.

Bodie, Zvi, Alex Kane, and Alan J. Marcus. *Investments.* New York: McGraw-Hill/Irwin, 2008.

# CHAPTER 11

# Fiscal Policy as Agent of Change

In late 1990, President George H. W. Bush, a Republican, and the Democratic majority in Congress decided to levy a luxury tax on yachts. The theory was that a 10 percent tax would not discourage anyone willing to spend $100,000 or more on a yacht and that such a tax would raise revenue without impacting the economy. The tax failed on both counts, as it, unfortunately, halted the purchases of yachts, raised unemployment among marina workers, and raised far less revenue than planned. Three effects were immediately obvious. The tax on the rich was not paid by the rich, since they did not buy anywhere near the number of yachts that policy makers estimated. Second, since there were far fewer yacht sales, there was far less revenue raised for the federal government. The 1991 revenue yield was one-half that estimated by the Joint Committee on Taxation in 1990. Finally, since there were far fewer yacht sales, there were fewer yachts produced and therefore far less need for the carpenters, the fiberglass and metal workers, or any of the direct or indirect (transportation, sales, support) staff involved in the business. According to the Joint Economic Committee, the yacht tax destroyed 7,600 jobs in the boating industry. The yacht tax was a disaster paid for by the average blue collar marina workers through the loss of their jobs. Congress, coming to its senses, repealed the tax in 1993.[1]

Fiscal policy—through spending decisions and tax law changes—tops the list of agents of change that alter a framework for decision making. Moreover, a change in one direction today is likely to be reversed in a few years, as the 2010 debates over the so-called Bush tax cuts, health care legislation, and financial reform indicated. In fact, much of the post–World War II period has witnessed a back and forth, give and take on government spending and tax policy. As evidenced by the yacht tax, many fiscal policy moves generated a different outcome from what was expected, exemplifying the law of unintended consequences.

For decision makers, changes in fiscal policy, either in terms of government spending or taxes, affect incentives to produce or invest. Fiscal policy reallocates resources in the economy through spending—through changes in tax laws. Changes in fiscal policy alter the rules of the game. However, these rules and their impact change over time. Spending patterns are sometimes reversed and tax policy often is reversed. But both spending and tax policy and the all-too-frequent changes in those policies that impact the structure of the American macroeconomy and thereby the framework for decision making. Leaders are left with a dual challenge:

- First, they must recognize that fiscal policy will change over time as the political winds blow in different directions.
- Second, the framework leaders employed to evaluate the impacts of any fiscal policy change also evolve over time. In the present era, this framework is being challenged by the larger than normal federal fiscal deficits relative to past levels.

Changes in fiscal policy alter incentives to consume, save, work, and invest. These changes therefore impact the pace and character of economic growth, inflation, interest rates, and corporate profits. Building on earlier work, in this chapter we evaluate how changes in fiscal policy, primarily at the national level, affect the outlook for economic factors. This leads, in turn, to choices that alter the economic framework and the operational choices for our institutions within this new framework.

## FISCAL POLICY OVER TIME: ALTERING INCENTIVES AND REWARDS OF RISK TAKING

The framework for fiscal policy and the economy have evolved from the initial Keynesian multiplier approach of the 1960s. The multiplier approach assesses the incremental change on economic growth from a given change in fiscal or monetary policy. For example, if policy makers choose to increase federal spending by one billion dollars and overall growth would rise by two billion dollars, then the multiplier would be estimated at two. One critical assumption of this approach is that the impact of the policy action would not be offset by changes elsewhere in the economy, for example, through higher inflation or interest rates. Yet, during the 1970s, inflation and inflationary expectations altered market activity, interest rates and inflation reacted to changes in fiscal policy. Expectations also evolved as market participants anticipated future policy actions. In the 1980s and 1990s, the globalization of capital markets altered the model again. In recent years, concerns about future deficits reestablished the influence of David Ricardo. Ricardo argued that people today would discount the implied future tax burden in today's federal spending and would increase their saving and effectively offset at least part of the fiscal stimulus pursued by the federal government.[2] This concern by some economists and policy makers about future tax burdens affected some analysts' expectations about the strength of any fiscal stimulus program taken today in contrast to any stimulus undertaken in the 1960s. The framework for evaluating any change in fiscal policy has changed over time.

## The Simple Sixties

Simplicity was the theme for fiscal policy in the 1960s. The fiscal policy framework at the time was based in the work of the British economist John Maynard Keynes, one of the most influential economists of the twentieth century. His major work, *The General Theory,* was written during the Great Depression and presents the view, counter to the classical economics of the time, that output and employment reflected the movements in the demand for goods and services and that prices and wages did not automatically clear the marketplace. Competitive markets did not, automatically, deliver full employment and growth in the economy. Keynes introduced the concept of a multiplier and argued that an increase in government spending, or a cut in taxes, lifts aggregate demand in the economy and thereby, in the short run, gives rise to a higher level of output in the overall economy.[3] In this simple model, the size of the increase in aggregate demand is enlarged by the multiplier process whereby the initial increase in federal spending leads to subsequent spending in the overall economy and to a larger, multiplied, increase in overall economic growth.

This fiscal stimulus process was explicitly short-term and relied on a number of simplifying assumptions that fit neatly into the practical experience at the time. In the 1950s and up to the period of the so-called Kennedy tax cuts (the Revenue Act of 1964, actually passed after President John F. Kennedy was assassinated, but proposed by him in 1961), the framework of the economy reflected four key elements that allowed the full impact of fiscal policy changes to be felt: excess capacity in labor and product markets, an abundance of low interest savings rates, a mostly closed economy with limited trade, and a monetary policy authority that did not face concerns of rapid inflation. Over the next 20 years, however each of these elements changed its behavior and ultimately has led to a very different framework for fiscal policy success in the present decade. It is also important to note that the Kennedy tax cuts were the largest tax cuts as a percent of national income in the post–World War II period, so estimates of their effectiveness would tend to be positive relative to the later tax cuts. Also, the structure of the economy was very different in the 1960s, as defense spending made up over 40 percent of the federal budget—a much higher number than later in the twentieth century.[4] The large defense spending component allowed for greater and quicker changes in federal spending and a sharper pickup in the economy in response to an increase in federal spending. This contrast is notable in the pickup in the economy, in part, due to the Reagan defense buildup in the 1980s and the lack of pick-up today as many "shovel-ready" programs were not ready at all and such spending must be spread out over many years.

In our decision-making framework, the implications of any change in fiscal policy must be evaluated within the context of the broad markets that characterize the macroeconomy. In the 1960s the assumptions underlying the Keynesian fiscal policy model fit the background of the economy. However, decision makers must understand that the framework of the economy is constantly changing. A fiscal policy change in the present is likely to have a very different impact from one of 50 years ago. The success of tax cuts and the impact of fiscal multipliers reflect the underlying behaviors in the economy that existed in the early 1960s. Unfortunately, success is seldom taken in context. The success of the Kennedy tax cuts led policy makers to an over-confidence bias—a very positive self-assessment of their ability to manage the economy by changes in fiscal policy. The bias arose due to the constant evolution of the economic framework for decision making, yet, unfortunately, the mathematical models retained assumptions that did not pick up the change in the economy. Economic modelers apply constant add-factors in the short run in their spreadsheets to replicate reality until the correct relationship can be developed in the model. Even then, since the world is not perfect, these models retain many add-factors for the simple variety of outcomes possible.

Owing to the experience of the 1960s, many economists and policy makers believed they could rely on precise mathematical models to generate precise real world results. Such overconfidence was severely thwarted in subsequent years as the precise mathematical and multiplier models fell short of predicted precision. This can be seen in the experience of the 2009 fiscal stimulus program. The first shot across the bow started with the tax surcharge experience of 1968.

**First Crack in the Simplistic Model—The Tax Surcharge of 1968**   By late 1967, the economy was growing rapidly and inflation was picking up. Policy makers contemplated three actions to slow aggregate demand—a tighter monetary policy, a curtailing of federal spending, and a temporary tax hike. A tighter monetary policy was dropped because monetary policy had been tightened in 1966 and had led to a credit crunch and a sharp housing correction. Cutting federal spending also lost backing—both the Vietnam War and the War on Poverty were in full swing, so no cutbacks were contemplated. This was the era of both guns and butter, an era of supreme confidence in our economic models and our military superiority. Finally, policy makers settled on a temporary tax hike, a surcharge on incomes that would be applied retroactively to 1968 incomes and then expire mid-1969. The thinking at the time was that the 1968 surcharge would act as the reverse of the 1964 tax cut.

But the tax surcharge did not work. Fiscal policy had been oversold as simple plumbing where aggregate demand could be manipulated by tax law and spending changes to achieve any level of aggregate demand. The surprise response to the tax surcharge was a sharp drop in saving, not consumer spending. Since households knew the tax surcharge was temporary they wouldn't alter their permanent lifetime spending plans.

Owing to this reaction, economists began viewing the spending plans of households and firms as based more on a sense of their lifetime income than on current year's income. This makes sense given that many people take a long-term view of their finances when they buy a car or a home or start a business.[5] One lesson then that should have been learned is that temporary tax changes do not alter individual behavior when those tax changes are viewed as temporary. Over the years many fiscal spending and tax initiatives have failed since they were temporary and did not alter the true underlying behavior of households and businesses. Our latest example was the lack of follow-through on a sustained housing recovery in 2010 after the end of the First-Time Homebuyer Credit.

Policy makers at this time, and at many other times since World War II, have fallen victim to a second bias—the anchoring bias. In this case, policy makers base decisions on the current economic situation as if that situation is the state of affairs for the long run, not a temporary phase of the business cycle. In this way, many temporary policies become permanent policies even though the circumstances that led to those policies have long passed. For example, many state and local governments pass temporary tax increases that remain for years. Temporary federal excise taxes on long-distance phone calls and other activities remain in place long after the initial rationale disappeared. Decision makers allow their anchoring bias to distort their estimates of the longer-run issues and the outlook for the economy. In government spending, the policy of zero-based budgeting is an attempt to remove the anchoring bias. Many so-called federal and state budget cuts are

## TAKING A FURTHER LOOK

Policy makers continue to be surprised when no long-term change in economic activity results. For example, in the spring of 2010, a first-time homebuyer credit led to a brief increase in home sales. But then home sales quickly dropped, even dipping below the weak levels that existed before the credit was put in place. The temporary provisions altered the timing of economic activity, but not the underlying fundamentals. The volatility in the growth of federal spending (Figure 11.1) illustrates that such volatility adds to the perception that changes in spending are often more temporary in orientation than long-term. Federal spending thus increases economic volatility to a higher level than desired as households and business decision makers attempt to make long-run plans.

**FIGURE 11.1**    Federal Government Spending Ex. Interest Payments
*Source:* U.S. Department of Commerce, U.S. Department of the Treasury, and Wells Fargo Securities, LLC.

actually reductions in the pace of growth of spending and do not address whether the current level of government spending is too high or too low. Budget discussions start anchored at the current level of spending and few discussions are held about the proper scale of funding. In sum, the framework of the economy has evolved but existing tax law and spending plans continue to move ahead based on the past.

## Inflation and the Global Integration of the U.S. Economy

The late 1970s witnessed sharp movements in market interest rates. Inflation had shot up in the mid-1970s and increased again in 1979 to 1981. The oil shocks of this period clearly indicated that the economy in the United States was no longer a closed economy. By the early 1980s, the import penetration of Japanese automobiles suggested that increases in domestic aggregate demand would partly go into import purchases. American industrial superiority now faced global competition. Therefore, estimates of the impact of changes in fiscal policy could no longer assume that an exogenous change in fiscal policy would have the full effect associated with earlier multiplier calculations. Now any impact was eroded by offsetting changes in interest rates, an import leakage from trade, and a rise in inflation.

Credit markets and the role of interest rates in the economy had certainly changed by the early 1980s. The abundant supply of low-interest savings and checking deposits in the economy of the 1960s had disappeared. Households increasingly held interest-sensitive money market mutual funds and interest-earning checking accounts. As a result, expansionary fiscal policy that would lead to rising income would also increase demand for a more limited supply of credit and thereby generate an interest rate increase. The concept of crowding out became a greater part of the framework debate. Crowding out referred to the problem that increases in the demand for credit to fund debt-financed federal government spending would raise interest rates and thereby reduce the funding of real private investment in the economy.

Crowding out might be better judged by how close the economy is to full employment. Therefore the impact of fiscal policy on moving the economy forward depends on where the economy is today relative to its potential.[6] Thus, the size of the fiscal policy multiplier is not independent of the conditions of the economy at the time policy is implemented. This also gives rise to another bias in decision making—the bias of the illusory correlation. There is a tendency in public policy discussions to jump to a conclusion about a relationship when no relationship exists. Often, many economic events are occurring at the same time and identifying how much of a change in any economic series is due to the impact of another series is difficult. For fiscal policy, changes in monetary policy often occur at the same time. The individual effect of a policy is very difficult to discern.

Along with the change in interest rates, government purchases and further private purchases of domestic goods and services will tend to drive up prices in the economy and, at least in the short run, drive up measured inflation. Increases in prices and measured inflation reduce the real income of households that do not benefit directly from the increased federal spending. Moreover, any increase in government purchases shifts resources away from the private sector, which is not involved in supplying the federal government's needs. This phenomenon is sometimes called real crowding out.

Finally, the globalization of capital markets introduces another channel of change in the response of the economy to a change in fiscal policy. Increases in federal spending drive up interest rates which attracts foreign financial inflows. Expansionary fiscal policy that leads to a rise in economic growth, higher real interest rates and higher expected returns on real investment does attract foreign capital inflows. This was certainly the experience of the United States in the early 1980s as we shall review later in this chapter. Under the floating exchange rate regime that has existed in the United States since 1971, capital inflows are associated with an appreciation of the dollar exchange rate. Subsequently, the higher dollar will induce additional buying of foreign products and thereby increase imports, while suppressing exports and leading to a deterioration of the trade balance.

Higher interest rates, higher inflation, and an appreciating currency all diminish the multiplier effect of a fiscal policy action. By the late 1970s, rising inflation and rising interest rates dominated the economic picture while a depreciating dollar added to the inflation and dollar woes. At the same time, income tax rates were very high and fiscal deficits were mounting in the context of economic weakness. There was clearly a need for a different path for fiscal policy and a new framework for evaluating its impact.

## Reagan Tax Cuts and the Role of Fiscal Deficits in the Policy Debate

The Reagan tax cuts in the early 1980s brought in a different focus for fiscal policy. The Economic Recovery Tax Act of 1981:

- Included an across-the-board reduction in marginal income tax rates by 23 percent over three years.
- Indexed the individual income tax.
- Created a 10 percent exclusion on income for two-earner married couples.
- Allowed all working taxpayers to establish IRAs.

- Reduced business taxes with the accelerated depreciation on investment spending.
- Reduced windfall profit taxes.
- Expanded provisions for employee stock ownership plans (ESOPs).
- Raised the estate tax exemption from $175,625 over time to $600,000 in 1987.

The cuts placed an emphasis on supply-side incentives to provide for growth, with greater incentives to production by reducing the cost of capital and lowering the marginal tax rates on income. The objective was to provide incentives for greater work effort along with increased saving and investing. The tax cuts were helped at the time by the natural momentum of the underlying economy and the maturation of an educated baby boom cohort that was just entering its most productive years. In addition, the gradual decline in interest rates and inflation added to the fiscal stimulus, thereby lifting growth in the early 1980s.

Two developments during this period complicated the implications of fiscal policy for decision makers and came back to haunt them in recent years. First, the period of expansionary fiscal policy of the early 1980s and a pickup in real economic growth led to a sharp appreciation of the real exchange rate. This, in turn, created a deterioration of the trade balance but did not fully offset the fiscal stimulus. There was also a secondary impact. All sectors of the economy did not grow in line with the overall fiscal stimulus. Export-oriented firms and domestic firms that depended on strategic imported goods suffered as the trade balance deteriorated.

Monetary policy impacts had always been viewed as uneven since it acts through the interest rate and credit channels. It is expected to affect housing and interest rate–sensitive sectors first and most significantly. Yet, fiscal policy was anticipated to have a generally positive impact across the board. With the rising globalization and floating exchange rates of the post-1971 era came the influence on trade via an expansionary fiscal policy. Fiscal expansions that drove up the dollar exchange rate had an offsetting impact on the economy. The trade balance deteriorated and firms that competed against foreign firms for sales in the U.S market felt the impact of rising import competition.

In addition, there came a realization that increasing aggregate demand via fiscal policy would be met increasingly by an increase in aggregate supply that would be composed of a higher share of foreign imports than domestic production. The United States had an economy with rising domestic demand that was increasingly being met by global supply. Therefore, part of any fiscal stimulus would be lost through imports where the income gains would be spent abroad and not spent domestically in the United States.

Second, the rapid rise in federal budget deficits and mounting federal debt led to increasing concerns about the deficit-financing implications of expansionary fiscal policy. In late 1985, Congress passed the Gramm-Rudman-Hollings Act that put in place provisions to limit the growth of federal spending. The focus on deficit financing and its interest rate impacts also has led to the recognition that over the last 40 years the burden of the deficits has fallen on different generations. In the 1950s and 1960s, modest deficits went to financing the infrastructure of the schools and interstate road building. The benefits to such spending accrued primarily to the present generation of voters. By the 1980s, the growth of entitlements as a driving force behind federal spending growth and deficit finance meant that there was an intergenerational inequity between who is paying taxes today and who receives the benefits. In addition, deficits today are financed by bond issues that will have to be paid by future taxpayers, many of whom have not yet been born.

The lessons of the 1980s have been that the impact of any given fiscal change would be different given the changes that were occurring over time in the economy. Decision makers need to recognize that the factors that make up the framework of the economy will influence the effectiveness of any fiscal policy initiative and therefore the potential increase in economic growth that drives top-line revenue growth. When estimating economic impacts, decision makers must remember several lessons that influence the outlook for the impact of any fiscal policy.

First, the state of the economy has a tremendous influence on the multiplier process. That is, the process by which a given jolt of federal spending leads to further spending in the economy depends critically on the level of confidence of consumers, savers, and business firms. Where consumers are highly uncertain of their economic situation, a federal stimulus would not be respent by consumers as much as it would when certainty exists. Instead, consumers likely would increase their savings and pay down debt, as evidenced by the reaction to the 2009 stimulus program. In addition, what Keynes called the "animal spirits" of businessmen will influence their willingness to invest in equipment and hire workers. A cautious business leader is not likely to aggressively pursue opportunities offered via current tax cuts if the outlook for the economy or future taxes and regulation is negative. This same line of argument would apply as well to a tax cut program. Tax cuts, in the face of high levels of uncertainty, would generate more savings, rather than spending in the short run, such that any multiplier process would be subdued. Both spending and tax cuts act within the same economic framework.

These lessons came back with a vengeance in 2009 and 2010 as the fiscal stimulus program underperformed expectations dramatically due to several factors. First, consumer confidence remained very low given the losses of jobs—unemployment remained near 10 percent—and the dramatic decline in asset wealth—particularly in housing. The high unemployment rate and declines in asset wealth led consumers to remain cautious despite the fiscal stimulus applied to the economy. Uncertainty and the loss of animal spirits trumped the expansionary impact of federal spending. Meanwhile, expectations for health care costs due to federal mandates and the threat of higher marginal tax rates raised the uncertainty premium for any firm to hire future workers. Higher health mandates raised the cost of labor. Higher taxes reduced the returns of investing in businesses. Moreover, the uncertain impact of financial reform legislation has raised the cost of lending for financial firms which will, in turn, limit credit supplied to both consumers and businesses. Financial and regulatory uncertainty will prompt financial lenders, particularly banks, to maintain higher levels of precautionary reserves. Private firms, facing tighter credit standards, remain cautious about investing in business expansion and will maintain higher levels of cash than otherwise. This background explains why the estimates of President Barack Obama's administration of an 8 percent unemployment rate were not borne out and why a sustained, rapid, expansion of the economy, that was generally expected, never happened.[7]

Second, fiscal policy for the period of 2009 to 2010 had a radically different impact on credit and debt from 50 years ago. The early 1960s experienced low inflation and interest rates. In this environment, further federal spending did not encroach on the limited credit supply of the American economy. Moreover, a modest increase in federal debt did not significantly increase the risk of debt monetization by the Federal Reserve and thereby did not suggest higher inflation in the future. Today, however, increased credit demands by the federal government represented uncertainties that impact how decision makers defined their view of the economy. Leaders asked: How will foreign investors, particularly the Japanese and Chinese (suppliers of credit), respond to increasing federal deficits (increased demand for credit) in an atmosphere where federal deficits are large and expected to continue going forward? The dependence of the United States Treasury debt issuance on the kindness of foreign investors is illustrated in Table 11.1.[8]

Also, leaders wanted to know: How will investors react to the risk that the Federal Reserve, in an attempt to promote growth and avoid deflation, will increase the money supply by buying Treasury debt and effectively monetizing the federal deficit? As illustrated in Figure 11.2, the economic framework of prior years is far outside the Fed's 2009 balance sheet. This suggested a heightened level of inflation and interest rate risk for investors and decision makers.

**TABLE 11.1** Value of Foreign-Owned U.S. Long-Term Securities and Share of the Total Outstanding

| | Billions of Dollars | | | | | | | |
|---|---|---|---|---|---|---|---|---|
| | June 2002 | June 2003 | June 2004 | June 2005 | June 2006 | June 2007 | June 2008 | June 2009 |
| **Marketable U.S. Treasury** | | | | | | | | |
| Total Outstanding | 2,230 | 2,451 | 2,809 | 3,093 | 3,321 | 3,454 | 3,621 | 4,591 |
| Foreign-Owned | 908 | 1,116 | 1,426 | 1,599 | 1,727 | 1,965 | 2,211 | 2,604 |
| Percent Foreign-Owned | 40.7 | 45.5 | 50.8 | 51.7 | 52.0 | 56.9 | 61.1 | 56.7 |

*Source:* U.S. Department of Treasury.

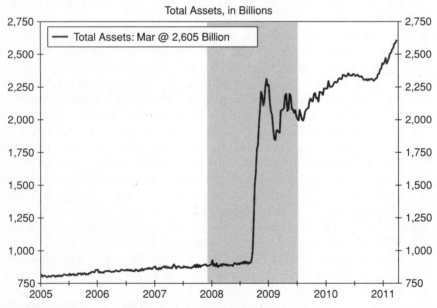

**FIGURE 11.2** Federal Reserve Balance Sheet
*Source:* Federal Reserve Board and Wells Fargo Securities, LLC.

In the past, increases in future deficits in a rapidly growing economy did not dramatically increase risk perceptions of the United States as a net debtor. In the 1960s, the debt was primarily internally held—Americans owed the debt to themselves. The United States had a positive position on its current account (the balance in trade on goods and services, as well as transfer payments) and was in a positive position on net income (Americans received more income on their investments abroad than they paid to foreigners). The country's balance on its current account was positive in the 1960s, but in recent decades has turned increasingly negative.[9] In part, the rising deficits in the current account reflect the continued growth of our imports relative to our exports. In recent decades, with the current account in deficit, see Fig. 11.3, the United States has also experienced a net capital inflow as foreigners on balance have purchased more American financial and real assets here than Americans have purchased abroad. Currently, there is a growing concern that the trend pace of growth in the United States economy has slowed and therefore the United States is less able to support debt repayments in the future consistent with keeping payments current on these assets owned by foreigners and generating the capital required to finance our own growth at a pace that maintains control of our fiscal deficits.

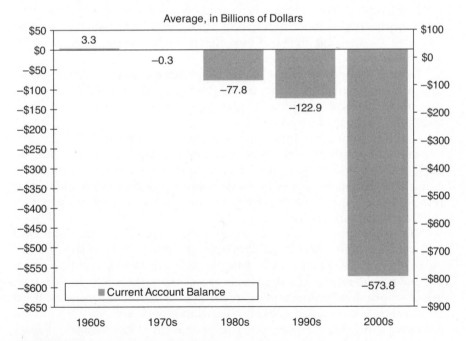

**FIGURE 11.3** Current Account Deficit
*Source:* Federal Reserve Board and Wells Fargo Securities, LLC.

Unfortunately, the downside to the success of the Kennedy tax cut of 1964 was that it introduced an overconfidence bias that persists to the present day. Policy leaders continue to be hampered by an overreliance on large-scale, precise mathematical models to forecast the impact of fiscal policy, without recognizing the sensitivity of the model to change over time and the special conditions of the 1960s. In a series of debates in the late 1960s, Milton Friedman, professor of economics at the University of Chicago, and Walter Heller, professor of economics at the University of Minnesota, began the discussion about the relative strength of monetary and fiscal policy and this debate continues today.[10]

## PUBLIC POLICY AND PRIVATE EXPECTATIONS— THE LUCAS CRITIQUE

Robert Lucas, professor of economics at the University of Chicago, made a simple observation with very important implications: Public policy actions do not simply act on the economy, but also alter the economic model. Policy makers need to take into account the impact of any policy on expectations.[11] In addition, as expectations change so will the impact estimated for any given policy initiative. For example, when car prices are discounted and financing eased, buyers expect another round of pricing and financing incentives. So they wait for the next round to buy. Retail shopping reflects the seasonal patterns of sales and promotions.

In recent years, the Federal Reserve's policies have been aimed specifically at altering inflation expectations. Over time, the Federal Reserve had announced its commitment to its growth and inflation targets in a direct attempt to shape those expectations.

On fiscal policy, the approach under Presidents Kennedy, Reagan, and Obama has been to expand federal spending and cut taxes to signal to the public that the federal government intends to boost economic growth. In part, the intention of such policy is to install confidence in the public that better times are ahead and thereby reduce the level of caution on the part of consumers and businessmen.

However, there are two problems for policy makers regarding both fiscal and monetary policy: (1) The public's belief about the sustainability of such a policy and whether that policy is clearly stated so that everyone knows what it is and (2) can estimate its impacts. In recent years, there have been a number of proposals regarding temporary tax cuts or spending programs. What should private sector agents, such as households or businesses, expect about such programs? Are they temporary or permanent? How much confidence can a household or business have in spending or hiring with a temporary tax credit? Businesses cannot hire a permanent employee with a temporary tax cut. How about energy credits? What is the estimated after-tax return on investments undertaken today when future tax rates on dividends and capital gains are likely to change?

Uncertainty also arises for initiatives in regulatory policy. In the aftermath of the passage of Sarbanes-Oxley (2002) there was a sharp drop in initial public offerings of equity ownership for private companies. This halt to activity is actually typical of the period following any major legislation, as we have seen again in the latest health care reform bill. There is a distinct implementation lag as regulators work through the law to set the details of implementing any law. In recent years, the emergence of discussions on financial reforms first creates uncertainty in the marketplace about what Congress might pass. Then, with the passage of new financial regulations there is the implementation lag until the regulators, such as the Fed or the Securities and Exchange Commission, set in motion clear enough rules so that financial institutions know what the rules are going forward. Over the past two years, this policy process has led to caution on the part of lenders owing to their expectations that the implementation of such regulation will be more restrictive going forward. This is not a case against regulations. Rather, it is a suggestion that both policy makers and those regulated should recognize that working through new rules takes some time and there are no overnight solutions. Policy initiatives do not simply act on the economy, but also on expectations and thereby the structure of the economy itself.

## INTERDEPENDENCE BETWEEN FISCAL AND MONETARY POLICY

While recent fiscal policy initiatives have been oriented toward economic growth, monetary policy has often been geared toward providing long-run price stability while also promoting economic growth. At times such policies can act in the same direction, but at other times they differ. In developing an outlook for growth, inflation, the dollar exchange rates, and interest rates, it is this mix of policies that matters. Fiscal actions alone do not tell decision makers enough for them to make thoughtful decisions.

Moreover, policy makers' actions may also influence the decisions of the other policy makers and alter economic expectations. Under both President Ronald Reagan and President Bill Clinton, debate on fiscal policy was often couched in the context of how the Fed would respond to a change in fiscal policy.

In the early 1980s, during a period of expansionary fiscal policy, the Federal Reserve under Chairman Paul Volcker was committed to stabilizing the money supply as a target to ultimately control inflation. The expansionary fiscal policy (tax cuts and spending increases) was associated with a rise in aggregate demand and income. Increases in income will lead to a rise in the demand for transaction balances and checking accounts, which grow in line with income. For example, as an individual's income grows, the size of the average balance of their checking account grows as well. Similarly, as a nation, as the national income grows, the size of transaction balances kept in checking accounts grow as well. Therefore, given a fixed money supply, a rise in money demand would be associated with a rise in market interest rates. This is consistent with the growing economy in the early years of the 1980s recovery. A period of rising interest rates would also generate additional capital inflows from abroad in response to those higher interest rates and thereby a rise in the dollar exchange rate.

The Mundell-Fleming model of an open economy helps explain how these macroeconomic impacts arise. Robert Mundell[12] and Marcus Fleming[13] worked together at the International Monetary Fund and published their initial groundbreaking work in the early 1960s. Their work followed the initiative of Canada to float its exchange rate. Mundell, a native of Canada, began to investigate the implications of a floating exchange rate regime at a time when the dollar was still linked to gold and many foreign currencies were in turn linked to the dollar.

The model allows a decision maker to understand the general relationships between fiscal policy, monetary policy, and their effects on a large open economy such as the United States. Beginning with the upper left corner of Figure 11.4, a standard macro model shows the relationship between interest rates and the level of output (GDP) or income of the economy. In the short run, the equilibrium value, where the domestic demand equals the money supply, establishes the rate of interest. This rate of interest can be transposed onto the net capital outflow graph that illustrates the relationship between net capital outflows, capital leaving the economy, and interest rates. This relationship is rather intuitive. Investors seeking the highest return on their investments will move capital based on their rate of return, the interest rate. If interest rates increase in the United States compared to another economy, such as Japan, then capital will flow from Japan to the United States. Conversely, if interest rates decline in the United States, investors will seek higher gains on their investment overseas, and the capital leaves the economy. The net capital outflow of the economy can then be related to the level of net exports, which, in turn, establishes the exchange rate for the economy in the short run. The relationship between capital outflows, net exports, and the exchange rate is slightly less intuitive. When capital leaves the economy, capital outflows increase, and the net supply of dollars increases. The result is that the exchange rate declines. In most cases, this basic model of a large

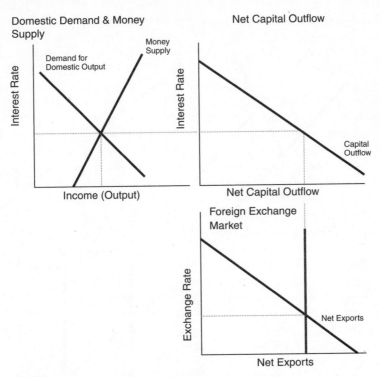

**FIGURE 11.4** Mundell-Fleming Model of an Open Economy
*Source*: Mankiw's *Macroeconomics*, Chapter 12.

open economy allows the decision maker to understand how fiscal policy may impact the economy.

Let's look at the previous explanation of expanded fiscal policy in the context of the Mundell-Fleming model as seen in Figure 11.5. The expansionary fiscal policy increases the demand for domestic goods and thus the GDP increases. As a result, interest rates rise, decreasing capital outflows. This decrease in capital outflows leads to a reduction in the supply of dollars which, in turn, leads to appreciation of the exchange rate. The increase in the exchange rate makes American goods more expensive relative to foreign-produced goods, resulting in a reduction of net exports. This example shows how changes in fiscal policy can be modeled using this framework. However, the Mundell-Fleming model is a model of short-run relationships and the long-run outcome of a policy change may be very different. The long-run effects of fiscal policy are discussed later in this chapter.

By the middle of the 1990s, the Fed had moved away from targeting the money supply and focused on interest rates. In this environment, an

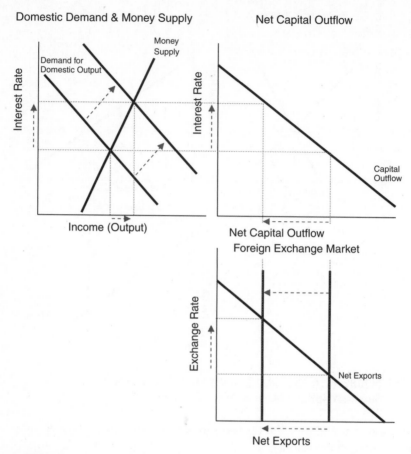

**FIGURE 11.5**   Fiscal Policy in the Mundell-Fleming Model

expansionary fiscal policy would be accompanied by a rise in aggregate demand that would tend to increase interest rates. To offset the upward pressure on interest rates, the Fed increased the money supply and this led to an increase in output. Any crowding out due to increased federal spending was partially offset by central bank easing. Both the dot-com boom of the 1990s and the housing boom in 2005 to 2008 were assisted by an easy monetary policy that kept interest rates too low.

There is an important link between the shocks to the economy and the policies pursued to offset or address these shocks. The sources of many of these shocks, such as changes in technology or labor productivity, lend themselves to obvious fiscal or monetary policy moves. However, in many cases, some economists and business leaders have argued that the economy might work through these shocks better rather than having policy makers attempt to offset these shocks in the short run, which leaves prices or markets in a false short-run equilibrium that cannot be sustained over time. In addition, a shock to the monetary or credit system may call for an offsetting monetary response but, in fact, be met by a fiscal response that only distorts market performance.

Consider the case where there is an exogenous increase in market uncertainty and therefore a widespread increase in the demand for liquidity. This occurred after the collapse of Lehman Brothers in 2008. Here the drive for liquidity triggered a rise in credit demand and a large drop in the supply of credit to the marketplace. In response, the economy weakened and inflation slowed. The Federal Reserve responded by increasing liquidity to the marketplace. But what if fiscal policy were expanded at the same time to offset the income effect? Effectively, there could have been a further increase in interest rates in response to the fiscal policy stimulus, which would be counterproductive to the efforts of the central bank. Once again, it is the mix of policy that influences the patterns of growth, interest rates, inflation, and the value of the dollar. For decision makers, the issue is not just what fiscal policy does, but rather how the mix of fiscal and monetary policy addresses the economic shock or makes it worse.

## POLICY IN THE CONTEXT OF EXPECTATIONS AND INFORMATION

*Congress and the JCT live in an imperfect world, and must act with imperfect information.*

—Alan Auerbach[14]

Institutional constraints on how Congress estimates the impact of tax legislation is an excellent signal to private sector decision makers that forecasts must be made in an imperfect world with imperfect information. However, although Congress and the Joint Committee on Taxation (JCT) face political constraints, private sector analysts must include good-faith estimates of the impact of policy. Typically there is a disconnect between Congressional estimates and private sector estimates of the economic impact of the same legislation. This disconnect is because different institutions have different policy mandates. As emphasized by Alan Auerbach, professor of economics at the University of California, Berkeley, dynamic forecasts may not be reliable given the intense political atmosphere in which forecasts are made.[15]

Sizing up the impact of changes in fiscal policy is made difficult due to the interaction between both what is being passed and how the markets react to what has been passed. Following the Lucas critique, a change in policy means a change in the economy as well as a possible change in the expectations and behavior of consumers and business people. Consumers and business leaders anticipate change. They act based on their vision of their economic interests and their experience with prior economic policy initiatives, which is consistent with the rational expectations model. The model for adaptive expectations, where expectations are built entirely on past experience, does not fit the behavior we see in the marketplace today.

Therefore, in estimating the feedback from policy changes, consumers and business leaders make the best estimate they can, given their framework on how the world works. In recent years, the model of fiscal changes and the estimated impact of those fiscal changes on the economy have evolved due to the greater influence of changes in inflation, interest rates, and global capital markets that have been described in earlier chapters.

Unfortunately, the impact of policy is frequently different from what was anticipated. Often this is a result of the movement of other factors in the economy. Nevertheless, this surprise to expectations still moves the markets and alters the expectations of consumers and business leaders. For example, the stimulus program of 2009 certainly did not deliver on the promises made. However, the context of the fiscal stimulus, just as much as the composition of the stimulus, was a driving force. The overwhelming issues in the credit market put a damper on the impact of the fiscal stimulus that was too much to overcome. Any housing recovery was hampered by the lack of equity for many homeowners, and thereby a limited ability to refinance. Many banks and financial institutions had limited capital and widespread uncertainty about the liquidity and marketability of many financial instruments. In addition, as we shall see shortly, the stimulus was a one-time-shot program, and therefore would not likely deliver a sustained push to the economy. Given the hurdles to success, the surprise would have been that the fiscal stimulus would deliver what policy makers promised. Research by Kenneth Rogoff, professor of economics at Harvard, and Carmen Reinhart, professor of economics, emphasize the challenges to any economic recovery in the face of a financial crisis.[16] In today's economy, the challenge to economic growth centers in the financial sector and the problems associated with a lack of capital and liquidity.

Another challenge to estimates of the effectiveness of a fiscal policy is the constraints put on congressional staffs. Dynamic estimating has been a long-term issue. The core problem is that estimates by the JCT are limited by the committee's ability to incorporate dynamic changes in the economy. That is, changes in tax policy alter individual behavior—increased saving, for example—and the committee needs to estimate the responsiveness of behavior to change. Of course, this approach is open to significant variability, as in any forecast of future revenues based on a change in tax law. For any change in tax law there is the challenge of estimating the response of taxpayers, as well as additional changes (e.g., interest rates) in the economy that also need to be considered.

Similarly, congressional staffs are often asked to evaluate the impact of proposed legislation as it is written. For example, JCT assumes that phase-ins and sunsets for legislative provisions will occur as scheduled and does not make assumptions on future congressional actions—perfectly reasonable, given the institutional constraints of the JCT. That is, the congressional staff assumes that if the tax law is scheduled to end, that law will end even though the political realities of Washington suggest that the tax legislation will be renewed. On the spending side, for example, assumptions that restraints on Medicare payments to doctors will be put in place while each time the deadline approaches for implementation the existing rules are kept and restraints are postponed once again. The alternative minimum tax impact on middle income Americans has, in a similar way also been regularly postponed by Congress.

On the revenue side, estimates are often made for two predicted streams of revenue, one under current law and another under a proposed new law. Yet we know that both current law and the proposed law do not exhaust the range of possible outcomes. As in the case of the alternative minimum tax, current law is not likely to be sustained. As for the proposed law, there is a chance that the proposals will be rejected. What is needed is an estimate of revenues under a scenario that would require judgment on the likely outcome relative to some current baseline revenue estimate. However, this would require a judgment on likely outcomes by the congressional staff that would imply a political judgment on what Congress will actually accomplish. As a result, the congressional staff can estimate at times revenue losses even though actual revenues will rise. We see the possibility in some cases where the proposed law may yield less revenue than current law since the current law may include provisions that Congress is unlikely to retain for political reasons.[17]

Congressional estimators are not asked to judge whether such constraints are reasonable. Moreover, these analysts sometimes find that their estimates are artificially constrained by time period and patently unlikely circumstances such as the termination of tax provisions or spending programs that are highly politically popular. Contrary to some commentators, JCT estimates do reflect taxpayer reactions to the new law, although, like many estimates, the degree of response is highly variable.

Putting aside the revenue implications, where the macroeconomy is concerned, congressional staffs are limited in their analysis by the assumption that the labor supply and labor demand and saving and investment markets are fixed. There is not a feedback loop—changes in the tax law would affect the overall economy and that would impact future tax revenues but this loop is assumed away in the analysis. For Congress, this assumption, no macro response due to changes in incentives, is another institutional constraint given the number of tax estimates asked for by the congressional staff and the need to compare revenue impacts across proposals. Over the very short run, these assumptions of a lack of response to incentives may appear workable. However, in some ways the task of the estimators is similar to asking the skipper of the Titanic to plot a course that assumes no icebergs. The assumptions are simply not tenable over time and distort rather than clarify the implications of policy alternatives.

For private sector estimators, these assumptions are not workable. Private firms need to deal with the world as it would be if a tax proposal is put into effect. Estimates of the macro impact of tax policy do introduce an element of arbitrariness into the process, but also contain a sense of realism. The test of the private sector outlook is how well it works given all the vagaries of the economy. Therefore, private and public sector estimates of the impact of any fiscal program can differ not because there is a conspiracy, as some critics might contend, but rather because the goals of the public and private sector estimators are different.

## LONG-RUN EQUILIBRIUM VERSUS SHORT-RUN EQUILIBRIUM

It is important to recognize both the short-run and long-run implications of fiscal policy changes despite what Washington policy makers want to portray as the impacts of their policy initiatives. This is particularly true in cases where the budget cost and economic implications of policy changes are considered.

In addition, fiscal policy estimates may not alter inflation, interest rates, and exchange rates in the short run. However, if fiscal policy is effective over time, economic growth will improve and that will alter the future path of the key drivers such as inflation and interest rates. As the economy changes, expectations of consumers and business leaders will also change and that will, in turn, change the framework of the economy.

In the short run, prices and interest rates may be unchanged in response to a fiscal policy initiative. But if the economy improves, the demand for credit will lift interest rates and increased demand for goods will drive up prices. In the long run, the real growth of the economy will be driven by the fundamentals of technology, labor, and capital productivity. So while fiscal policy can temporarily improve the economy, sustained growth is not the product of additional fiscal stimulus unless such stimulus can release the potential of the economic fundamentals that drive long-term growth. The transition from short-run to long-run fundamentals helps to explain the internal dynamics of the economy, the chapter's next topic.

## Understanding the Impact of Change: The Dynamic Nature of Economic Adjustment

When estimating the feedback from any fiscal policy initiative, regardless of the initial framework employed to characterize the workings of the economy, the dynamic pattern of the economy must be recognized. The short-run response to a fiscal stimulus will be different from the long-run response. And the character of the response in terms of the economic factors that matter—growth, inflation, interest rates, and the dollar—also changes over time. Expectations play a key role in the process as well.

Initially, a fiscal stimulus program should lead to an increase in demand for goods and services. In the short run, the aggregate supply in the economy should not change; an increase in output should be accompanied by a rise in inflation and interest rates. In fact, in the later half of 2009 both inflation and interest rates did rise relative to where they were prior to the stimulus program. The rise in growth, inflation, and interest rates set up its own internal dynamic. The rise in prices tends to reduce real incomes and lower consumer demand. The rise in interest rates tends to dampen investment spending at the margin.

Here the dynamic of expectations comes into play. With inflation greater than expected, the willingness of producers, labor, and capital to supply goods and services at the prior, lower inflation and price level diminishes. As a result, the aggregate supply in the economy diminishes, leading to slightly higher inflation and slightly reduced output. The bargain-basement, recession-driven price discounts starts to disappear and normal pricing starts to reassert itself. Over time this dynamic process plays out until an economy finds itself in balance, where expected inflation and actual inflation match up.

This process matches the actual experience of the United States economy in 2009 to 2010. Initially the stimulus added to growth; inflation and interest rates rose. Then, over time, the impetus of the stimulus faded and both inflation and interest rates declined. In the end, the pace of growth, inflation, and interest rates slowed back to a pace in line with the pre-stimulus economy.

The experience of the fiscal stimulus of 2009 brings out four key points for those responsible for monitoring developments in the overall economy, which are enumerated in Table 11.2. First, the stimulus did add to economic growth in the short run. Second, over the intermediate term, changes in economic drivers such as inflation and interest rates relative to expectations

**TABLE 11.2**   Real GDP, CPI, and 10-Year Treasury Note

|                            | Q3-2009 | Q4-2009 | Q1-2010 | Q2-2010 |
|----------------------------|---------|---------|---------|---------|
| Real Gross Domestic Product | 1.6    | 5.0     | 3.7     | 1.6     |
| Consumer Price Index        | −1.6   | 1.5     | 2.4     | 1.8     |
| 10-Year Note                | 3.31   | 3.85    | 3.84    | 2.97    |

*Source:* U.S. Department of Commerce, U.S. Department of Labor, and Federal Reserve Board.

led to changes in the pace of economic growth. Third, over a longer period, the economic growth rate returned to a pace similar to the pre-stimulus pace since the underlying long-term growth drivers of labor, capital, and technology didn't change. Finally, the internal dynamics of the economy suggest an up-then-down pattern to growth and other economic factors that would not be characteristic of a typical straight-line spreadsheet forecast for company planning. It could be argued that the stimulus did not have a long-run effect since it did not alter the public capital stock (infrastructure) that the United States experienced during Franklin D. Roosevelt's administration. Over the next few years we shall see the evidence on this stimulus package.

## WHEN THE LONG-RUN OUTLOOK IMPACTS TODAY'S BEHAVIOR

Increasingly, the public has become concerned about the long-run burden of the entitlements shown in Table 11.3. Historically, fiscal stimulus has been proposed as a countercyclical tool that stimulates economic growth by adding to aggregate demand. In recent years, this view has changed and there may be a change in the structure of expectations that will impact how fiscal policy is seen.

To what extent do taxpayers today discount the future tax burdens implied in current spending? This question is increasingly important for two reasons. First, the impending retirement of the baby boomer generation and the duration of quality care they will require suggest a larger drain on the Social Security and Medicare systems than prior generations incurred. Yet, the generation of taxpayers after the baby boom is smaller and will likely face an increase in their tax burden to support the boomers. Second, the extent of the current fiscal deficits (Figure 11.6) is outside of the long-term experience of taxpayers. These deficits represent a possible significant change in traditional economic frameworks, with implications for growth, inflation, and interest rates that would be part of any forward-looking business plan.

**TABLE 11.3** Components of the Federal Budget

|  | Percentage of GDP | | |
|---|---|---|---|
|  | 1970 | 2007 | 2020 March Baseline |
| Revenues | 19.0 | 18.5 | 20.3 |
| Outlays | 19.3 | 19.6 | 23.3 |
| Social Security, Medicare, and Medicaid | 3.8 | 8.2 | 11.1 |
| Defense | 8.1 | 3.9 | 3.6 |
| Other Mandatory Spending and Non-Defense Discretionary Spending | 6.0 | 5.8 | 5.3 |
| Net Interest | 1.4 | 1.7 | 3.2 |
| Deficit | 0.3 | 1.2 | 3.0 |

*Note:* Figures are shown net of offsetting receipts where relevant. CBO Director's Blog, March 9, 2010.

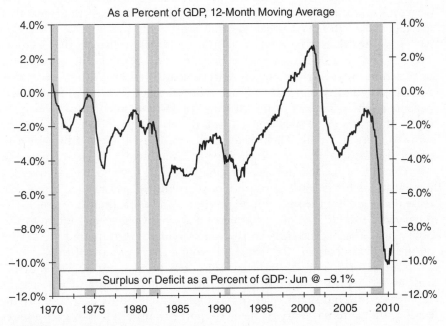

**FIGURE 11.6** Federal Budget Surplus or Deficit
*Source:* U.S. Department of the Treasury and Wells Fargo Securities, LLC.

Large, continued fiscal deficits would promote continual Treasury borrowing, which could upset the demand/supply balance of domestic and global capital markets and further alter the economic framework of the economy.

## POLITICAL BUSINESS CYCLE: POLITICAL REALITIES FOR PRIVATE DECISION MAKERS

Government policy, at all levels, is influenced by voters and special interests. Political interest reflects the sources of income, wealth, employment, regional, demographic, or personal characteristics.

Trade tariffs in America throughout the nineteenth century reflected the influence of different regions and different industry groups to use the federal government to seek economic advantage. In England, the source of income from trade or land influenced the development of the Corn Laws and the evolution of trading and shipping over time. The Corn Laws in the first half of the nineteenth century limited the importation of grain into England to help support higher prices to the benefit of the landed classes. Those who derive most of their income from labor seek special privileges to protect that income; those who derive their income from profits, rent, retiree benefits, welfare or health care benefits, or capital gains seek to protect that income. The tax code is a litany of special interests. For example, it is important to remember that any attempt by government to control health care costs on one side means that incomes are reduced to those who provide those benefits to the recipients of health care. This is true in each case when we speak of proposals to cut defense spending, ethanol, and farm subsidies or infrastructure spending. Each of these categories is supported by powerful political interests that reflect the income received by each of these categories.

The size of income also has become a special interest. Many program qualifications for federal, state, and local programs have income limits. Yet these limits are not the same for all programs and these limits are simply the outgrowth of the bargaining that takes place between special interests and politicians. The middle class has become an interest group, and the debate on the Bush tax cuts in 2010 revolved around the definition of rich.

Sources of income by industry or profession also appear to be a special interest as tax laws and special subsidies persist, often for years, to support certain industries relative to others. By region or degree of urbanization, the patterns of government support can differ as each group seeks special interest legislation to support urban mass transit or soil conservation, more highways through rural areas, or energy and environmental subsidies for special projects that benefit only a specific region. Age, religion, and gender differences give rise to special interests that seek greater federal aid. The long list of special interests explains the continual increase in government spending as a way to rob Peter to pay Paul in a way that would not be possible without government help.

Rent seeking refers to the exploitation of political means to achieve an increase in rent or income beyond that would be achieved in the private marketplace. Much of what is called special interest legislation is simple rent seeking and is the driving force behind the growth of government spending over the last 50 years. Given the natural inclination for special interests to seek rent and for politicians to attempt to satisfy them, growing governmental spending bills are likely to remain an issue for some time.

Those seeking the rent or special provision that generates that rent are usually well versed in applying political pressure, while the public at large is not. The information available to the public at large is limited, but is very well known to the special interest group seeking to collect the rent. Therefore, in every major piece of legislation there are special, "mid-night" provisions that benefit special interests in some way. To quote a leading textbook on public finance: "Politicians, rent-seeking special-interest groups, and bureaucrats vote themselves programs of ever-increasing size."[18] For decision makers, this is a reality behind the expansion of the government and the implied future burden of taxes on income.

Alternatively, we can also see cases where legislation recognizes needs that can't be addressed by the marketplace, and some legislation is designed to address the needs and problems created by an increasingly unequal distribution of income and wealth in the country; such legislation would impact the opportunities for all in society. There are also cases in which powerful business groups manipulate legislation to protect/support their industries, sometimes in ways that don't benefit society. This was very true in the nineteenth century when many firms and industries employed tariffs as barriers to competition. Such concerns about the restraint of trade and the conspiracy of industrialists were very prominent in the writings of capitalism's original philosopher, Adam Smith.

> *People of the same trade seldom meet together, even for merriment and diversion, but the conversation ends in a conspiracy against the public, or in some contrivance to raise prices.*[19]

Finally, on the spending side, there is the sunk cost bias in much of public policy. Public spending projects, special tax provisions, and many temporary agencies appear to have a life of their own, especially when such programs appear to be failing. Since politically inspired programs have such large political cost for failure, there is a bias to escalate the commitment to a program in which there has already been a substantial prior investment of time or money.

## FISCAL POLICY IN AN OPEN ECONOMY: THE UNITED STATES IN THE TWENTY-FIRST CENTURY

Increasingly over the past 30 years, the influence of fiscal policy on an economy must be seen in the context of the framework of an open economy, especially with the ascension of China to the World Trade Organization and the globalization of capital markets.

For the United States, an expansion of fiscal policy leads to an increase in aggregate demand and thereby an increase in both output and interest rates. The higher interest rate is critical in attracting foreign financial capital into the country to help finance the deficit, although the higher rates also have a negative impact on domestic investment. In addition, as the capital inflow to the United States rises, the dollar exchange rate appreciates. The higher exchange rate alters the trade balance as exports diminish in competitiveness and imports tend to rise. The trade balance tends to deteriorate.

Over time, the growth of the global capital markets and the incentives of both public and private investors in those markets have given American policy makers both opportunities and risks that continue to evolve. The outlook is for continued federal spending and large deficits. Federal spending, interest rates, and the dollar exchange rate will depend on the willingness of foreign investors to buy American financial instruments. With the outlook for continued large fiscal deficits, the risk going forward is that foreign investors will be less willing to buy Treasury securities, and even more so private securities, at currently low interest rates or the dollar exchange rate. This is the issue in the next chapter.

## DISCUSSION QUESTIONS

1. As a member of your investment management team you are asked to present your observations on the outlook for growth, inflation, and interest rates, given your evaluation of the following changes to the macroeconomy for 2011.
   a. A $400 billion fiscal stimulus program is announced for 2011.
   b. A temporary corporate tax cut is put in place just for 2011.
   c. The Bush tax cuts are dropped by Congress in an attempt to reduce the federal budget deficit.

    d. Monetary policy shifts from a focus on controlling the money supply (Volcker style) to pursuing a constant interest rate policy (Bernanke style).

    e. Cap and trade is passed with implied increases in taxes on carbon production.

2. Treasury Secretary Geithner, as quoted in the *Wall Street Journal*, August 2, 2009. "...while there were signs that the recession was easing, a key element to getting the U.S. economy back on track was to bring down the country's surging deficits. We will not get this economy back on track.... unless we can convince the American people that we're going to have the will to bring these deficits down...." You are asked to present to your employee pension management team an assessment on the following.

    a. Discuss your thoughts on the inside/outside lag that the secretary faces on altering fiscal policy.

    b. Discuss your thoughts on what is the impact of the current large fiscal stimulus package on growth, inflation, interest rates, and the dollar.

    c. Differentiate the impacts of sustained current policy on your four benchmark variables compared to Geithner's suggestion that future policy will bring deficits down. How might global (e.g., Chinese) investors react?

    d. If the Fed altered its current easy policy with an effective exit strategy to withdraw liquidity, how might this reinforce/frustrate Geithner's policy with respect to the expected outcomes on your four benchmark variables?

    e. How would you suggest the committee view Geithner's comments with respect to your understanding of adaptive/rational expectations and the role of the Lucas Critique?

3. Over the last 50 years the impact of fiscal policy changes has been altered by the evolution of the economic framework. In recent years the impact of fiscal stimulus appears to be far less effective than many thought.

    a. How might the state of the financial markets have influenced the response of the economy to the fiscal stimulus?

    b. How might the growing globalization of capital markets have impacted the effectiveness of fiscal policy over the last 30 years?

    c. How might the impact of fiscal stimulus been impacted by the expectations that the federal budget deficits associated with current stimulus efforts may be more permanent than some expected?

    d. How might have the sovereign risk problems in Europe impacted perceptions of the path of U.S. deficits?

    e. How might the Ricardian equivalence theme have impacted taxpayer assessments of future tax burdens and therefore saving and consumption behavior?

## NOTES

1. Kwame Holman, "Rising Tide," *PBS Newshour*, January 1, 1996.
2. Douglas Bernheim, "Ricardian Equivalence: An Evaluation of Theory and Evidence," *NBER Macroeconomics Annual* (1987), 263–303.
3. This Keynesian approach is outlined in many undergraduate macroeconomic textbooks and follows the tradition of the writing of John R. Hicks, "Mr. Keynes and the Classics: A Suggested Interpretation," *Econometrica* 5 (1937): 147–159.
4. William Ahern, *Comparing the Kennedy, Reagan and Bush Tax Cuts* (Washington, DC, Tax Foundation, August 2004).
5. Milton Friedman, *A Theory of the Consumption Function* (Princeton, NJ: Princeton University Press, 1957). Milton Friedman later won the Nobel Prize for his work in this area.
6. Roger W. Spencer and William P. Yohe, "The Crowding Out of Private Expenditures by Fiscal Policy Actions," *Federal Reserve Bank of St. Louis Review* (October 1970, 12–24).
7. Christina Romer and Jared Bernstein, "The Job Impact of the American Recovery and Reinvestment Plan," January 9, 2009.
8. Bureau of the Public Debt, Table 1, *"Summary of Public Debt Summary of Treasury Securities Outstanding, Total marketable held by the public less bills,"* Various issues.
9. Economic Report of the President, 2010, 448, Table B-103.
10. Milton Friedman and Walter W. Heller, *Monetary vs. Fiscal Policy* (New York: W.W. Norton, 1969).
11. Robert E. Lucas, Jr., "Econometric Policy Evaluation: A Critique," Carnegie Rochester Conference on Public Policy 1 (Amsterdam: North-Holland, 1976), 19–46.
12. Robert A. Mundell, "Capital mobility and stabilization policy under fixed and flexible exchange rates," *Canadian Journal of Economic and Political Science* 29, no. 4 (1963): 475–485. Reprinted in Robert A. Mundell, *International Economics* (New York: Macmillan, 1968).
13. J. Marcus Fleming, and J. Marcus, "Domestic financial policies under fixed and floating exchange rates," *IMF Staff Papers* 9: 369–379. Reprinted in Richard N. Cooper, ed., *International Finance* (New York: Penguin Books, 1969).
14. Edward D. Kleinbard, Joint Committee on Taxation, "Inside the JCT Revenue Estimating Process," January 2008.
15. Alan Auerbach, "Dynamic Revenue Estimation," *Journal of Economic Perspectives*, Vol. 10 (1996): 141–157.

16. Carmen M. Reinhart and Kenneth S. Rogoff, *This Time Is Different: Eight Centuries of Financial Folly*, (Princeton, NJ: Princeton University Press, 2009).
17. Edward D. Kleinbard, op. cit., 4.
18. Harvey Rosen, *Public Finance*, 7th ed. (New York: McGraw-Hill Irwin, 2005), 136.
19. Adam Smith, *Wealth of Nations*, 1776.

## RECOMMENDED READING FOR SERIOUS PLAYERS

Ahern, William. *Comparing the Kennedy, Reagan and Bush Tax Cuts*. Washington, DC: Tax Foundation, August 2004.
*Economic Report of the President*, one issue in February each year.
Rosen, Harvey. *Public Finance*, 7th ed. New York: McGraw-Hill Irwin, 2005.

# CHAPTER 12

# Global Capital Flows: Financing Growth, Creating Risk and Opportunity

*The whole world has become a city.*

—Fritz Stern[1]

**B**y 1872 the fraud of the century could no longer be kept secret, in part because there is no honor among thieves. Stock of the Credit Mobilier (the American construction company set up by the Union Pacific Railroad to build the first transcontinental railroad) was placed in the hands of those who would do the most good for the corporation. Stock went to congressmen, senators, the speaker of the House of Representatives (James G. Blaine), the vice president of the United States (Schuyler Colfax), and a future president (James Garfield). But so rich was the fraud and so prevalent is greed among men that, when frustrated that they weren't getting their fair share, some of the thieves blew the whistle. Sometimes too much is not enough. By summer 1872 the *New York Sun* had the story. By September, credit became tight and the railroads turned from issuing bonds to borrowing short-term. A global credit crisis and the longest officially recorded depression in United States history was about to unfold. Congressmen Oakes Ames and James Brooks were both censured for their role in the scandal. As Charles P. Kindleberger (former professor of economics at MIT) argued, booms and busts are transmitted in many ways—surprise moves in commodity and security prices, interest rates, short-term capital movements, gluts and shortages of essential products, and, of course, psychological panic and greed.[2] German investors had been major supporters of American railroads and western land development. But when the indemnity for the Franco-Prussian War had to be paid in gold, investments came to an abrupt halt. The year 1873 stands out as the first *significant* (Kindleberger's emphasis) international crisis. It certainly would not be the last. In recent times, in less than 20 years there has been a series of financial/currency shocks.[3] In 1992, Britain withdrew from the exchange rate mechanism (ERM) when they could no longer maintain the currency peg. In 1994, Mexico devalued the peso despite having a fixed exchange rate regime. In 1997, Thailand decided to float its currency, the baht, after continued efforts to support the fixed exchange rate to the dollar were just too costly. In other countries, such as Indonesia and South Korea, capital inflows had driven up real estate prices to levels that were not sustainable, given the decline in economic activity that began to spread. Russia defaulted on its debts in August 1998, as a result of a decline in commodity prices in 1997 which prompted slower economic growth in the face of large Russian federal budget deficits. Housing finance, 2007 to 2010 in the United States, and the government debt crisis in Greece (2010) are just two more in a long line of distinguished debt crises. The surprise to decision makers would be if the future had no shocks. That is very unlikely—so we prepare.

As in our prior efforts, we start with a simple framework for decision making, which here is focused on the role of global capital flows. These flows have become increasingly important as the growth of trade in goods and services has also grown over the years. Within this framework, we highlight the importance of the impossible trinity that limits options for public decision makers, but also represents significant opportunity/risk trade-offs for private decision makers. Next, we explore the evolution of global imbalances, particularly as they reflect the decisions made in the American economy and the implications for opportunity and risk for any strategic vision for any institution—public or private. Finally, we review the basic tenet of both economic and public policy decision making in a global setting—that is, all countries are not alike. This tenet is frequently forgotten in both private and public policy discussions.

## BUILDING A FRAMEWORK FOR UNDERSTANDING

How should decision makers respond to a financial crisis? Should decision makers respond? What are the risks associated with any given response? What are the assumptions? The framework leaders use must put into context the ways in which the global capital markets have influenced the path of the key economic factors of growth, inflation, interest rates, the dollar, and corporate profits. The challenge for decision makers is that there are clearly global imbalances today in trade and capital flows, countries with large current account deficits and those with current account surpluses, countries with large fiscal deficits and those countries helping to finance those deficits.

How should leaders respond to such imbalances? What are the risks to growth, inflation, interest rates, and the dollar? What explicit and implicit assumptions underlie the global economic model, and if these assumptions are wrong what would happen to this economic framework?

In the twenty-first century, the global nature of trade and capital flows has influenced the success of both private and public institutions—often in surprising ways. As evidenced by both the 2008 to 2010 Great Recession and the euro-area sovereign debt problems, the challenge for decision makers is to recognize when the latest data suggest a deviation from their basic framework and then act on it. Over the short run, interest rate volatility has shown a tendency to surprise the most astute bond manager, as seen in Figure 12.1.

The deterioration of the United States current account deficit suggests a fundamental imbalance over the long term, with uncertain consequences for global capital markets and for the financial survival of many businesses. Yet, the rhetoric of policy makers contains an undertone of the anchoring bias, in which the past serves as America's reference point to the future and distorts an evaluation of where the country is today. Is the United States still the one dominant economic power that can dictate to other countries that they are

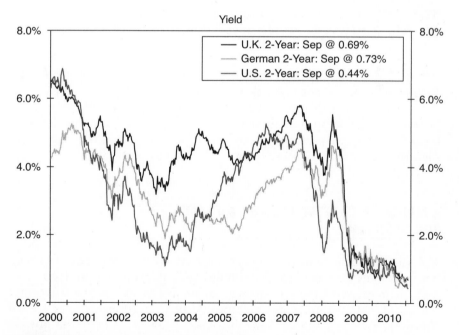

**FIGURE 12.1**  Two-Year Government Bonds
*Source:* Bloomberg, LP and Wells Fargo Securities, LLC.

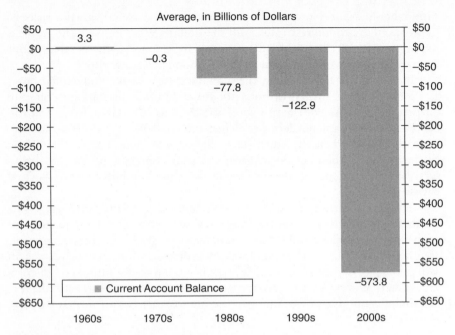

**FIGURE 12.2** Current Account Deficit
*Source:* U.S. Department of Commerce and Wells Fargo, LLC.

following the wrong path in trade and exchange rate policy? Is China still an emerging nation that requires import protections? Is Europe a coherent region with similar cultural, work and leisure, and saving and investment preferences so that all nations can agree on a similar framework for both fiscal and monetary policy? The evidence of the past 10 years (Figure 12.2) suggests that all three of these frameworks need to be updated.

## A MODEL OF CAPITAL FLOWS TO FRAME OUR DECISIONS

The Mundell-Fleming model applied in a previous chapter is that of a small, open economy with perfect capital mobility. This economy can borrow or lend all it wants in the world financial markets and this does not alter the world interest rate. This model would be characteristic of the United Kingdom, France, Canada, Australia, and Singapore.[4] The world interest rate for these countries is exogenously fixed. In a small economy with perfect capital mobility, an increase in the domestic interest rate would generate a large flurry of incoming capital and thereby drive back down the interest rate. The international flow of capital is fast enough and large enough to keep the domestic interest rate equal to the world interest rate.

In the goods market, consumer spending is a function of income, prices, and household wealth. Investment is a function of the interest rate and expected final sales. The international sector reflects the relationship between the exchange rate and net exports. Here net exports (exports less imports) are inversely related to the exchange rate. A stronger domestic currency weakens net exports as exports become relatively more expensive and foreign imports relatively cheaper. A decline in net exports is associated with a decline in national income.

In the case of floating exchange rates, like those of the United Kingdom, the exchange rate is set in the marketplace and therefore fluctuates, given the changes in economic activity, such as an expansionary fiscal policy. In this case, the expansion of fiscal policy would increase aggregate demand and increase the exchange rate, but, given the constraint of the money market, the level of income does not change over time. When income rises, interest rates would rise as well. But in an open economy, any rise in interest rates would bring in capital from abroad and drive the interest rate back down to the global equilibrium rate. Capital inflows drive up the value of the British pound. The appreciation of the pound makes British goods more expensive relative to foreign goods, reducing net exports. The fall in net exports offsets the expansionary impact of fiscal policy on economic growth. In a closed economy, interest rates would rise; in a small, open economy no such increase happens since the domestic interest rate remains equal to the global interest rate.

In contrast, the alternative expansionary policy to an increase in the money supply in a small open economy would be a depreciation of the exchange rate. While an increase in the money supply cannot alter interest rates as in a closed economy, an easier monetary policy can lead to a depreciation of the currency and an increase in national income in a small open economy. An easier monetary policy in an open economy initially lowers interest rates, but it would then generate a capital outflow as investors would seek higher returns elsewhere. As investors move their money they convert domestic currency into foreign currency, thereby lowering the value of the domestic currency relative to the foreign currency. So in a small, open economy, an easier monetary policy would increase national income by lowering the exchange rate rather than the interest rate.

Hong Kong, as a small open economy, has pursued a fixed exchange rate tied to the dollar. Other countries that do the same include many Caribbean countries, Jordan, Panama, the United Arab Emirates, and Venezuela. The fixed exchange rate system was initiated in 1944 at Bretton Woods, New Hampshire, as a means to provide financial stability in the post–World War II period. Each of the 44 countries that attended the conference pledged to follow a monetary policy regime to maintain a fixed exchange rate to gold. At the time the United States possessed the leading role in the global economy and many currencies were pegged to the dollar. China today could also be characterized as a fixed exchange rate system, at least over short periods of time. Using fiscal policy, an economy such as Hong Kong could increase government spending. Aggregate demand would then increase, as would the relative value of the domestic exchange rate. However, under a fixed exchange rate system, a central bank would buy foreign currency and sell the domestic currency in order to stabilize the value of the domestic currency. In the process, the central bank would increase the domestic money supply, and unlike the flexible exchange rate regime, the increase in the money supply would be consistent with an increase in economic growth in the short run.

Using monetary policy directly, however, would present a central bank with a problem. An increase in the domestic money supply would lower the exchange rate in the very short run. But because the central bank is committed to maintaining a fixed exchange rate, it must enter the market and buy the domestic currency to restore its original value; when it does so, the central bank reduces the money supply to its original value. Monetary policy using the money supply as a tool is not effective for a small country under a fixed exchange rate regime. By fixing the exchange rate, a central bank gives up control of the money supply.

A country with a fixed exchange rate regime can change the exchange rate and thereby devalue its currency. Alternatively, a country can revalue its currency upward. Devaluation can expand net exports and raise national income. A revaluation would reduce net exports and lower national income.

## The Impossible Trinity

The trade-off between exchange rate flexibility and an independent monetary policy and capital mobility is expressed in the concept termed the "impossible trinity," or in Mundell's terms, the "trilemma."[5] It is impossible for a country to have free capital flows, a fixed exchange rate, and an independent monetary policy. Countries such as Canada, Australia, and the United Kingdom have opted for free capital movements and thereby also an independent central bank monetary policy, but they accept exchange rate volatility. The independence of the central bank is important, as these countries seek their own sovereign monetary policy and want to avoid the straitjacket of a fixed exchange rate system in which monetary policy would be driven by the base peg country's currency—most likely the U.S. dollar for

Canada or the euro for the United Kingdom. Recall that the United Kingdom had already tried the ERM system with disastrous results in 1992.

China, in contrast, has fixed its exchange rate while maintaining capital controls and an independent central bank. On the other hand, Hong Kong has fixed its exchange rate while adopting free capital mobility, but has no independent monetary policy. Its domestic money supply must adjust to maintain the targeted exchange rate of the monetary policy of another country—the United States.

If Hong Kong engaged in a monetary expansion, a decline in domestic interest rates would occur but global rates would remain unchanged. An arbitrage then becomes possible. Investors could borrow in Hong Kong dollars and then lend at a higher interest rate globally. With no capital controls, investors would continue to do this arbitrage. Selling Hong Kong dollars would lower their value in the marketplace. Hong Kong would then defend the peg to the U.S. dollar by selling reserves to buy back its own currency in order to raise its value in the marketplace. Unfortunately, the central bank would exhaust its reserves defending the currency, and so the initial monetary policy easing would have to be reversed. If not reversed, Hong Kong would continue to lose foreign exchange reserves until it devalued its currency.

### Evolution in the Post–World War II Environment for Economic Drivers

Over the past 40 years, beginning with the United States break from gold in 1971, the behavior of each of the five economic factors has been increasingly impacted by global economic developments.[6] For example, the pace of American economic growth has seen a rise in the share of economic activity driven by exports and imports. The globalization of production for the needs of foreign emerging and industrialized markets has meant that American production facilities are increasingly located abroad. The passage of the North American Free Trade Agreement and the accession of China to the World Trade Organization have reduced trade barriers. This has generated downward pressure on the prices of foreign imported goods and thereby helped slow the pace of inflation in the American economy. The rise in capital outflows from Japan and China has lowered interest rates in the United States relative to what they would have been otherwise. Domestic corporate profits have benefitted from access to foreign markets. Many of the nation's largest firms are true multinationals, with the foreign share of their sales and profits above 50 percent. Finally, the dollar initially gained in stature as a reliable trading vehicle as global trade opened up. Many emerging markets and commodity markets have denominated their trading accounts in dollars. Recently, however, questions have been raised about the value of the dollar given the imbalances of America's trade, capital, and federal budget accounts. The combination of large current budget deficits and estimated large future deficits due to entitlements and our global military commitments suggest future pressures on debt finance and the dollar in the years ahead.

Unfortunately, business and political models of how the world works are often cast in concrete. Leaders give lip service to the idea that change is constant, but then build models that are rigid and inflexible.

**Mexico, Emerging Asia, and the Confirmation Bias of Analysts**    Prior to the election of 1994, the administration of President Carlos Salinas of Mexico accelerated the pace of federal spending and thereby increased the federal deficit. To finance the deficit, the Mexican government issued tesobonos, which were Mexican sovereign debt denominated in pesos but indexed to the U.S. dollar. These tesobonos were issued to finance Mexican domestic spending and were linked to the dollar as a form of insurance on the currency value for foreign investors. At the time, Mexico had a fixed exchange rate system and free capital flows, and therefore the tesobonos relied for their credit rating based on the fixed exchange rate to the dollar. However, when Mexican fiscal deficits rose, the risk premium on Mexican assets rose, and foreign investors wanted to sell pesos and buy dollars. Unfortunately, the Mexican central bank lacked the foreign reserves to maintain the fixed exchange rate system. The bank then bought Mexican Treasury securities to maintain its balance sheet reserves—but this kept interest rates from rising, which led to further capital outflows as investors shed the peso. Inevitably, the peso was devalued despite the Mexican government's verbal commitment not to allow this to happen. The Mexican government could not roll over its debt and defaulted. With a fixed exchange rate system and free capital flows, the Mexican central bank could not conduct an independent monetary policy and attempt to maintain a monetary base or set of interest rates independently. The impossible trinity claimed another victim.

At the time, investment research supported the theme that Mexico was an emerging economic power and therefore capital investment in Mexico was a good idea. This is often the case in countries, or investment concepts, that offer outsized opportunities with little perceived risk. This was especially true for the Mexico. Given its close location bordering the United States and the euphoria surrounding the recent signing of NAFTA, Mexico could make a strong case that it had a bright future. Investors and portfolio managers often rely on information that confirms their existing views and avoid or downplay information that would disprove their hypotheses or beliefs. This is what happened in Mexico. Yet, a careful examination of the fundamentals of what was happening in Mexico, not a wish about what might happen in the future, may have saved a lot of investment pain.

The negative signs were there. First, as in many countries, fiscal stimulus was employed prior to the election to boost the economy and win votes. Second, credit standards had been loosened in the years prior to the crisis while hyperinflation had persisted from 1985 to 1993. Finally, declining oil prices brought into question the fiscal deficit issues for the entire economy.

During the mid-1990s, the Asian economic miracle of rapid growth was hailed by economists and the business media.[7] Thailand, Indonesia, and South Korea grew rapidly during this period. Thailand, for example, grew over 9 percent between 1985 and 1996. But a thoughtful decision maker could already make out the outline of another visit from the impossible trinity. Free capital flowed strongly into the developing Asian economies as the independent central banks maintained high interest rates to attract foreign investors. Asset prices rose rapidly. However, that old nemesis—the overconfidence bias—asserted itself and overcame any caution. Thailand, Indonesia, and South Korea had large private current account deficits, but these countries maintained fixed exchange rates against the dollar—a model that could not work over time. Free capital flows and a fixed exchange rate preclude an independent monetary policy to set interest rates. By 1994, the Federal Reserve under Chairman Alan Greenspan, who was concerned about inflation reoccurring in America, began to raise interest rates. Hot-money flows shifted from Asia to the United States, raising the value of the dollar. Since countries such as Thailand had their currency pegged to the dollar, the higher U.S. dollar value made Thai exports more expensive and therefore less competitive in the global marketplace. The Thai current account position deteriorated further.

Given the fixed exchange rate regimes in place, the markets bet against the Thai baht. When Thailand failed to effectively defend the baht in June 1997, the crisis was on. The baht devalued rapidly and the Thai stock market fell over 70 percent.

When Thailand floated the baht, questions were raised about Indonesia. The Indonesian central bank widened the rupiah trading band, that is, the band or range that the Indonesian central bank would allow its currency, the rupiah, to trade within before any aggressive exchange market intervention would be taken. However, the global trading community quickly sensed the contradiction in policy. Indonesia replaced the managed floating currency regime with a free-floating exchange rate arrangement. However, both the rupiah and the Jakarta stock exchange dropped in value, as seen in Figure 12.3. Meanwhile, many Indonesian businesses had borrowed in dollars. When they had to repay, they bought dollars and sold rupiah, thereby putting further downward pressure on the currency. Indonesia's long-term debt was downgraded to junk status by Moody's. Over the next year, real growth in the Asian economies fell for Thailand, Indonesia (Figure 12.4),

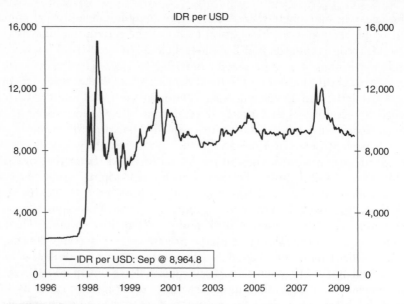

**FIGURE 12.3** Indonesia Exchange Rate
*Source:* Bloomberg, LP and Wells Fargo Securities, LLC.

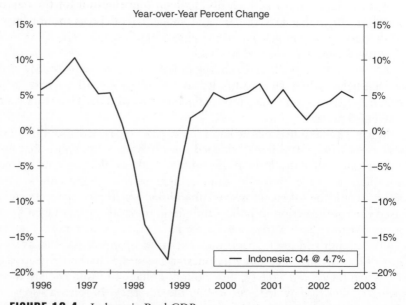

**FIGURE 12.4** Indonesia Real GDP
*Source:* Badan Pusat Statistik, IHS Global Insight, and Wells Fargo
Securities.

Malaysia, South Korea, and the Philippines. Japanese GDP fell sharply and business bankruptcies rose as well.

The Asian crisis led to a sharp fall in the price of oil, as expectations of recession led to a drop in demand for industrial commodities such as oil. Lower oil prices put subsequent pressures on Russia due to reduced oil revenues and therefore large federal deficits there. This, in turn, contributed to the 1998 Russian financial crisis and the notorious collapse of the famed hedge fund Long-Term Capital Management.

For the modern global capital markets, a framework for decision makers is one that reflects the Mundell-Fleming model. This approach allows decision making to characterize countries by: their choices of currency systems— fixed or floating; by their system of capital controls—open or closed; and by their type of central bank—independent or dependent. Using this framework, we can analyze policy decisions to stimulate the economy in Mexico or manage interest rates in Thailand and Indonesia that would set up pressures on interest rates, exchange rates, and inflation that must be addressed by market adjustments or policy choices as the framework for the global capital market system evolves over time. In some cases, market responses will inevitably alter the system and the country's economy in very abrupt and harmful ways, as witnessed in the cases outlined here. Alternatively, this basic framework will allow change, as with the Chinese revaluation of the fixed rate peg in 2005 while there was no devaluation for the renminbi from 1997 to 1998 due to the lack of convertibility and capital flows at that time.

For decision makers, signals of imbalances in the global capital markets are the clues to making choices about what a new model will look like and what business decisions on international direct investment and currency hedging are needed. Over the past 40 years, since the delinking of the dollar to gold under the Nixon administration, the framework of the United States economy in the global capital markets has been changing, which is the subject of the next section.

## THE AMERICAN FRAMEWORK IN GLOBAL CAPITAL MARKETS: THE EVOLUTION OF IMBALANCES

Over the past 40 years, a growing United States current account deficit and deteriorating net international investment position (Figure 12.5) have raised the risk profile for the current mix of interest rates, inflation, growth, and the dollar exchange rate.[8] This is not an issue of all or nothing; rather it is the pattern of deterioration that leads a good decision maker to consider whether

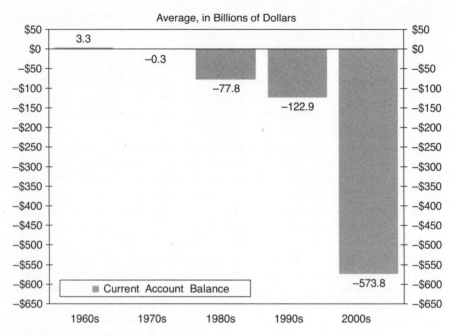

**FIGURE 12.5**  Current Account Deficit
*Source:* U.S. Department of Commerce and Wells Fargo Securities, LLC.

the current system is sustainable in the face of continued pressures. The capital markets in the United States benefit from several major advantages. For example, perceptions of crony capitalism are less prevalent in the United States than in Mexico or the emerging nations of Asia.[9] Capital markets in the United States are very liquid, in the sense that transactions take place smoothly and at a price very close to quoted prices within the bid (buy) and offer (sell) quotes, and the Treasury market, in particular, is very deep in the sense of having many issues over a broad maturity range. Also, in the United States, property rights and the rule of law are highly regarded. However, economic fundamentals are changing and the risks of a significant change in one or more of the country's economic drivers should be considered. The federal fiscal deficit is the economic driver that most bears watching today. During the past two years the federal fiscal deficit has been 8 to 10 percent of the GDP and this percentage has been the largest since World War II. Unfortunately, these deficits are expected to remain large for the foreseeable future and therefore questions arise about what market adjustments will take place for interest rates, inflation, and exchange rates in the future such

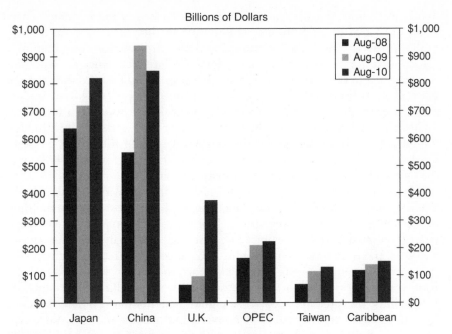

**FIGURE 12.6**   Top Holders of U.S. Treasuries
*Source:* U.S. Department of the Treasury and Wells Fargo Securities, LLC.

that these deficits will find a home in the portfolios of foreign and domestic bond investors.

Meanwhile, the major buyers for Treasury securities are the foreign governments of Japan and China (Figure 12.6) and, most recently, the Federal Reserve under its large scale asset purchase program. The goal of the Federal Reserve in the short run is to increase its balance sheet, which will increase available bank reserves and thereby, hopefully, increase bank lending in the economy. For the Fed, the goal of such easing is a revival of the economy after the Great Recession. Meanwhile, what are the limits of foreign interest in buying Treasury debt given our view of the large current account deficits the United States economy continues to run? In the short run, the Chinese and Japanese appear to buy Treasury debt as part of an attempt to manage their exchange rates against the dollar and support their export markets.

Over time, however, there is likely to be an underlying shift in the framework of the demand and supply of United States Treasury debt in the capital markets. On one side, the rise in external indebtedness, reflecting the increasing supply of federal debt, makes financial markets in the United

States, as well as globally, more vulnerable to a loss of market confidence. This could lead to an ominous combination of diminished capital inflows at the current interest rate, inflation, and dollar depreciation combination if foreign investors were to fear greater future inflation/currency devaluation, for example. In the extreme case, a sudden stop in capital inflows is not the most likely or most relevant case for decision makers. Too often, leaders think of economic outcomes as either/or outcomes: a boom or a recession; inflation or deflation; capital inflows continue or they stop suddenly. In fact, the most likely outcome here is the gradual decline of the dollar, a rise in interest rates, higher inflation, and slower growth—all of which will impact the best-laid plans for any senior strategy meeting.

It was not always like this. In the early years following World War II, the Marshall Plan, the Truman Doctrine, and the subsequent rebuilding of Europe led to a perceived dollar shortage. The demand for American exports created a trade surplus and a strong dollar. By the late 1950s, however, the issue of current account imbalances appeared. Investments by American firms and citizens abroad exceeded the current account surpluses from trade. As long as foreign central banks were willing to accumulate U.S. dollars, the imbalances could be maintained. But under a gold standard system, foreign liabilities could be converted into a demand for gold which could lead to a run on these reserves. By the mid-1960s, official liabilities exceeded the gold stock.

Economic fundamentals in the United States were also changing. Although the framework of international currency and gold exchange markets had not altered, supports for that system were eroding. During the 1960s, inflation rose and the real value of the dollar declined. The real exchange rate—the terms of trade—reflected the relative price of goods between American and other countries. Foreign goods became relatively cheaper to domestic goods, so imports rose while exports declined. Moreover, the trade balance worsened.

With the fixed exchange rate system of the post–World War II period, the central banks of Europe bought dollars to defend their pegs to the dollar. However, buying dollars meant an increase in their domestic money supply and therefore a higher pace of inflation. By 1971, the dollar-gold link was broken as President Richard Nixon suspended the convertibility of the dollar to gold—large U.S. current account deficits were leading to gold outflows at a pace that would have emptied the gold coffers and made the fixed exchange rate link to gold untenable. The fixed exchange rate system was abandoned in 1973, and a floating rate system adopted.

During the 1980s, President Ronald Reagan's expansionary fiscal policy, along with Fed Chairman Paul Volcker's continued cautious monetary policy, led to an appreciation of the dollar. Foreign investors reacted to a renewal of economic growth, as well as high real interest rates, by investing in the American economy. Dollar strength and the economic recovery increased imports.

The importance of "import leakage" first came to the attention of decision makers in the 1980s. Prior to that time, the consumer preference for imported goods was not a significant factor in the multiplier process or in the country's trade competitiveness. However, beginning with the oil shocks of the 1970s, the rising price of gas initially drove many consumers to purchase Japanese automobiles. By the 1980s, consumer electronics were also becoming the province of Asian producers. As a result, a rising share of any increase in domestic demand was spent on foreign imported goods. This impact was reinforced by NAFTA in 1994 and China's ascension to the World Trade Organization.

Dollar appreciation in the early 1980s led to a worsening of the United States trade balance and a rising current account deficit. At that same time, the federal fiscal deficit rose as the Reagan defense spending programs and tax cuts began to impact the economy by altering market expectations for growth and interest rates going forward. By the end of the 1980s, the United States had become a net debtor as the net income flows became negative as a result of continued large current account deficits.

As for the economic framework, the United States was a large, open economy with flexible exchange rates, free capital flows, and an independent central bank. As a large economy, changes in interest rates in the United States by the Federal Reserve altered global interest and exchange rates and the competitive positions of firms importing or exporting around the globe. In recent years, there has been a growing concern among economists that increases in the federal fiscal deficit will lead to a rise in credit demand relative to the supply of credit such that interest rates may rise sharply in the United States.

Another issue that confronts decision makers is that capital is not perfectly mobile across the globe. Many investors exhibit a home bias, tending to overweight their native land in their investment allocations.[10] Differences in yields will persist across countries and a single global interest rate is unlikely to emerge. Also, countries with huge current account surpluses, such as China, do not allow the free outward flow of capital. Therefore, although there may be a global savings glut in theory, there is much less of one in practice. Ben Bernanke, then a governor at the Federal Reserve, raised the issue of the global savings glut in a speech in 2005 with the view that economies outside the United States (Japan, Western Europe) had slow-growing or declining workforces and therefore their domestic savings outpaced their investment opportunities.[11] Since citizens of those populations needed to provide for their retirement, they would invest in the United States due to its superior offering of investment opportunities. The expectation was that private investors would increase their allocation of financial assets, especially equities, toward the United States. Meanwhile, foreign central banks increased their holdings of United States sovereign debt until they had purchased a significant majority of these obligations in recent years.

The higher the expected, after-tax, risk-adjusted rate of return on American investments relative to those abroad suggested that foreign investors would continue to invest in the United States and that United States investors would more likely keep their investment capital working in their own economy. As a result, the net flow of financial capital is negatively related to the rate of return that is, as a first approximation, a function of the interest rate. This net flow can be a positive or negative depending on whether a country is a net lender or borrower in the capital markets.

In contrast, in a closed economy, there is no international flow of capital so that domestic saving equals domestic investment. Since World War II, many countries have liberalized their capital accounts and allowed capital inflows into the country, sometimes with very disastrous results. The sudden rush of foreign capital seeking investment opportunities can sometimes overwhelm small financial markets. Such capital inflows drive up asset prices and thereby leads to overly optimistic assessments of the opportunities, while downplaying the risks of investing abroad.

Of course, this investment scenario is nothing new, as the South Sea bubble shows. After the Treaty of Utrecht in 1713, which divided up Spanish territory and dealt with succession, the Caribbean and Central America were open to British economic development. The South Sea Company, a monopoly, was set up by the British to trade with the Caribbean. A government monopoly should have been a clear signal of problems to come. In 1719, the company proposed to the government that it would offer its stock to the public for additional subsidies and concessions. In 1720, the public sale was conducted and the price of company stock soared. Other companies were created and proposed, including "a company for carrying on an undertaking of great advantage, but nobody to know what it is."[12] By the winter of 1720 the scheme had collapsed. Like Credit Mobilier, the company had distributed much of the stock to the political leadership to assure a proper hearing of petitions from the company. The romance of extraordinary returns in exotic countries appeals even today.

A large, open economy such as the United States is in a unique position to be able to influence global capital markets. The more the United States lent abroad following World War II, the greater the availability of capital to Europe and Japan and the lower the interest rate borrowers in those countries faced. In contrast, in recent years, the more the United States borrows, the higher the global rates.

In this case, one issue is that as a net borrower, the United States is taking financial capital from poorer countries. At first glance, this may appear unfair. Yet, in the marketplace the American economy offers higher risk-adjusted rates of return compared to those poorer countries whose legal and property rights systems are of lower quality.

In addition, global capital mobility is also influenced by a home bias. Investors prefer, at the margin, to hold their wealth in domestic rather than foreign assets, all else being the same. Such a preference may reflect imperfect information. Domestic investors find it difficult to evaluate foreign opportunities in countries with incomplete accounting standards and an uncertain rule of law. After all, it is the risk-adjusted rate of return that matters. Therefore, global interest rates, while they do move together, do not equalize, as evidenced below in Figures 12.7 and 12.8, even for advanced industrial economies.

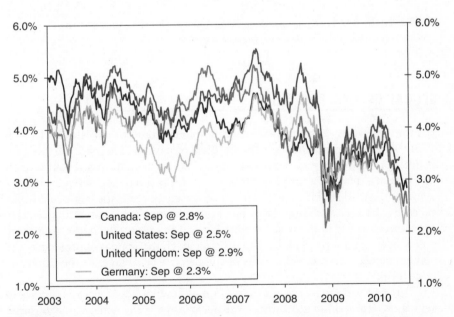

**FIGURE 12.7**   10-Year Government Bond Yields: The U.S., Canada, and Western Europe
*Source:* Bloomberg, LP and Wells Fargo Securities, LLC.

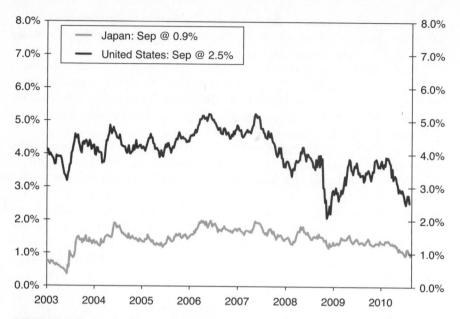

**FIGURE 12.8**   10-Year Government Bond Yields: The U.S.–Japan Spread
*Source:* Bloomberg, LP and Wells Fargo Securities, LLC.

## GLOBAL INTEREST RATES

For the American economy, savings can finance domestic investment as well
as investment abroad through the outflow of capital. The pace of these investments reflects the ex ante expected rate of return on domestic and foreign
investments. The net capital outflow also reflects a balance between the net
exports, the trade balance, and capital flows where the trade balance is influenced by the real exchange rate. The real exchange rate reflects the relative
price levels in the comparison countries and thereby reflects the monetary
policy in each country. Finally, the nominal exchange rate is expressed as the
real exchange rate times the ratio of the foreign price level to the domestic
price level.

During the Reagan era, the expansion of fiscal policy led to an increase in
aggregate demand but a decline in the net savings of the American economy.
There followed a reduction of the supply of credit and then an increase in
the equilibrium interest rate. The rise in the equilibrium interest rate reduced
domestic investment and the net capital outflow from the United States. A
decline in capital outflow reduced the supply of dollars going abroad and

then led to an increase in the exchange rate and a concomitant decline in net exports. In a large open economy, both investment and net exports decline; whereas in a closed economy the drop in savings is entirely met by a drop in real investment.

One response to the Asian crisis in the late 1990s taken by many Asian central banks was to accumulate foreign exchange reserves, particularly dollars. By their accumulation of dollar reserves, these countries were able to stabilize the dollar exchange rate when they funded the current account deficit of the United States in the early years of the twenty-first century. And in doing so, they helped maintain the competitiveness of their countries' export sectors. The strategy supported high export growth to the American economy and also low interest rates in the United States. But eventually there would be significant consequences down the road.

The model of capital flows changed over time. That has generated interesting feedback effects and choices for business decision makers. The traditional approach is to view capital flows as a means to equalize ex ante expected rates of return for investors across the globe. The model focuses on private sector decision makers. However, after the Asian crisis, central banks entered the marketplace with a different objective function—currency stability. Their purpose was to allow their exporters to increase market share and thereby grow the economy through exports. In the short run, manufacturers in Asia gained at the expense of the competitiveness of American manufacturing firms. In addition, lower-than-market interest rates fed the consumer boom in durables, automobiles, and housing. The overleveraging of the consumer was on, especially in America. Meanwhile, low interest rates and the securitization of credit lead to the overbuilding of commercial real estate as well. The implications of the current account deficit and the change in the capital flows' incentive model were not well understood then, but the principle remains the same. Over time, the economic framework underlying an activity, such as trade and housing, can change simply due to a change on the financial background of that activity. Changes to the framework call for an evaluation of the feedback effects and how choices are made. Unfortunately, the distortions in pricing of consumer and real estate credit were overlooked while the party was going on.

Global imbalances had been a theme for a number of analysts, including Steven Roach, chairman of Asia for Morgan Stanley, who has long written on this imbalance issue. For the markets, the question should be: How would such imbalances be resolved? Imbalances in the current account reflected the inequity between saving and investment in the United States, as well as the distortion in growth models between the export-led growth model of emerging Asia and the consumer-led demand model for the United States. Beyond the timing of the eventual correction, there is the issue of speed and severity. Will the adjustment be smooth, or, as is typical of financial markets, faster and broader than anyone could anticipate?

One issue referred to before that has been a growing issue over the last 40 years is the responsiveness of United States imports to increasing aggregate demand and incomes in the United States. Over this period, rising aggregate demand and consumer income has been associated with rising appetites for foreign goods and thereby generated interest in the American market for foreign suppliers. Faster growth at home increased American imports more than foreign GDP growth increased exports from the United States.[13] Our propensity to import for a given gain in income is higher than other countries' propensity to import from us. This suggests that any improvement in the current account deficit for the United States would not be as rapid as many policy makers would like to believe. Once again, the framework for the capital flows model was changing. The outstanding current account deficit of the United States was likely to remain larger and stay around longer than earlier expected. Moreover, the usual routes to a correction, dollar depreciation and growth abroad, do not appear to be providing the traditional solution to resolving these global imbalances.

In fact, the imbalance between Asian savings and domestic consumption in the United States could actually continue for longer than many expect since the current system serves the goals of everyone involved. In this sense there is an uneasy balance between the parties at opposing ends of the fulcrum. Can either rider step off the seesaw? In this view, Asian savings help to finance domestic consumption in the United States in order that that consumption can be met by Asian production. So far that approach appears to be moving forward, but, knowing the history of rapid changes in the global economy, anything is possible. The issue is that disrupting this uneasy balance is an all or none move, and sometimes getting off the seesaw can be awkward and very painful if not done carefully.

In addition, the imbalance associated with the growing net international investment position raises an associated risk on the financial side of the global picture. The position of the net international investment as a share of GDP in the United States remains large relative to America's share of exports as a share of the economy. Income payments associated with meeting the obligations of the nation's foreign debts put a burden on the economy, as any debt payments do for any flow of income for any debtor.

There is another delicate balance here—a portion of income meets America's debt obligations, and, unfortunately, those debt obligations appear to be continually rising over time. The growth of interest payments will continue with the rise in current account deficits. The history of current account deficits for the United States suggests that the imbalances will continue and therefore these are signals to decision makers that some adjustment will have to occur. Such an adjustment could potentially result in a large, sharp

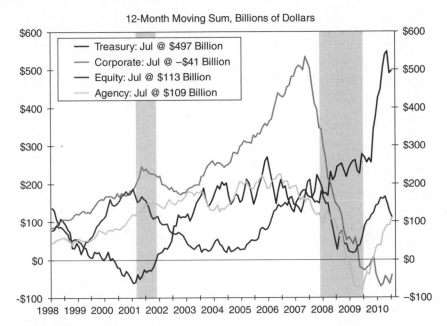

**FIGURE 12.9**    Foreign Private Purchases of U.S. Securities
*Source:* U.S. Department of the Treasury and Wells Fargo Securities, LLC.

movement in interest rates, inflation, growth, or the exchange rate, or all four. The problem of meeting growing interest payments is further complicated by the allocation of capital to sectors that do not generate the export earnings needed to pay those interest bills.[14] As illustrated in Figure 12.9, there has been a decided shift in foreign financing of American debt issuance away from corporate and equity financing and toward Treasury finance. This reallocation of financial capital may have negative consequences for the financing of private and public sector financing over the long term.

## RISKS AND OPPORTUNITIES: NOT ALL COUNTRIES FIT ONE MOLD

One of the premier challenges that decision makers face across the globe is that countries differ by their choice of the free or fixed or dirty floating exchange rate systems, their willingness to allow the central bank independence, and their willingness to allow free capital flow in and out of the country. Here we refer to the dirty floating exchange rate system as a system where the currency exchange rate is free to float but with significant central government intervention to insure stability over time and limit the influence

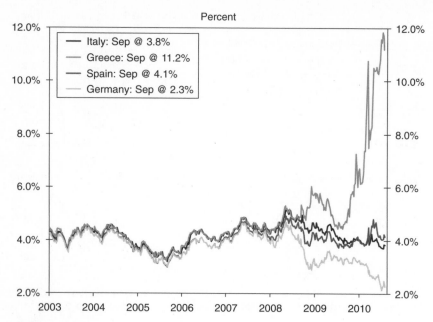

**FIGURE 12.10**    10-Year Government Bond Yields
*Source:* Bloomberg, LP and Wells Fargo Securities, LLC.

of market forces. This will be familiar to readers as a characterization of the
Chinese approach today. In addition, some countries peg their currencies
to other countries outside their trading region, which can create significant
short-run imbalances in trade.

In the period from 2009 to 2010, the conventional wisdom of a stable
euro area was overturned, which was reflected in sovereign debt interest
rates as seen in Figure 12.10.

With the election in October 2009 of a new Greek government, there was
little hint of what was to come. Yet, much like the experience of Mexico, a
change of governments often allows the new leadership to take a fresh look at
fiscal finances. The picture was not pretty. On November 5, 2009, an update
of the government's budget indicated an estimated deficit of 12.7 percent of
the GDP for 2009, more than four times the initial December 2008 estimate.
On December 8, the rating agency Fitch cut Greece's rating to BBB+ from
A–, with a negative outlook. The race to higher yields was on. With yields
around 5 percent in early December, 10-year Greek bond yields peaked at
over 12 percent by early May of 2010.

Greece did not actually make the first cut in 1999 for the euro, since
Greece did not meet the criteria for membership; for example, its debt-to-
GDP ratio was more than twice the limit for entry to the euro. When Greece

was accepted and the currency fixed in June 2000, there were concerns about its high inflation rate and large government debt and deficits as a percentage of the GDP. Since the restoration of democracy in 1974, Greece had a long history of large fiscal deficits, and these deficits were a means to finance public sector jobs, pensions, and social benefits. With the economic slowdown in 2008, state revenues tumbled and the deficit for 2009 was revised from 6.0 to 12.7 percent by the Papandreou government.[15] On April 27, 2010, Standard & Poor's downgraded Greek debt to junk amid fears of default by the Greek government.[16] In May, nationwide strikes and demonstrations were held to protest the government's proposed austerity measures of spending cuts (cuts in pay and allowances for public sector workers) and tax increases (extraordinary tax on corporate profits, increased taxes on alcohol and cigarettes). Many investors sold part of their positions in European equity and bond markets as a way to minimize currency and growth risks. The European sovereign debt crisis began.

As illustrated in Figure 12.11, government debt as a percent of the GDP is a significant problem for Greece, Ireland, Portugal, and Spain. On September 30, 2010, the financial ratings firm Moody's downgraded Spanish sovereign debt from AAA to AA+. Since 2007, Ireland, Portugal, and Greece

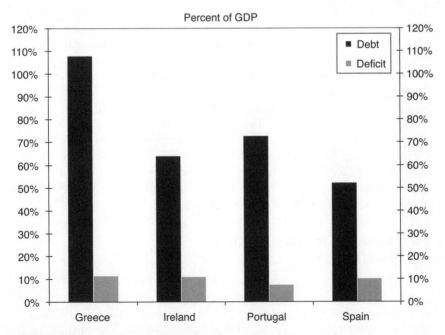

**FIGURE 12.11** Government Debt and Deficits
*Source:* Eurostat and Wells Fargo Securities, LLC.

have all been downgraded by Moody's. Has the sunk cost bias impacted the decision by the European leaders to retain all current members of the euro community even though many of the original qualification criteria are being ignored and fiscal constraints are being thrown to the wind? Moreover, the relief package for Greece was not an easy decision, as Germany, for one, was very reluctant to agree to the package.[17]

> *It is a grave mistake to assume that the sovereign debt crisis that is unfolding will remain confined to the weaker euro zone economies.... It is a fiscal crisis of the western world. Its ramifications are far more profound than most investors currently appreciate.*
>
> —Niall Ferguson[18]

For Niall Ferguson, professor of history at Harvard University, there is no such thing as a Keynesian free lunch. Ferguson asserted in February 2010 that "Deficits did not save us and the impact of the multiplier has been much less than the proponents of the stimulus hoped." He is correct. Analysts have projected continued large fiscal deficits for the foreseeable future. This brings into question the safe haven value of United States Treasury debt over the long run. As concerns about debt repayments increase, the market will move those key economic factors that drive the economic success of the institutions. Fears of default will lead to a drop in the supply of credit to the United States from foreign lenders; this will drive up real interest rates and thereby weaken domestic investment in the United States and the outlook for long-run growth in the United States. In addition, the Federal Reserve's recent moves to quantitative easing will promote growth in the economy in the short run, but would also provide an upward bias to inflation and nominal interest rates over time. Discussion of quantitative easing has also been associated with a drop in the value of the dollar relative to the euro, although the actual easing has not occurred. This demonstrates the role of expectations in moving investors and decision makers to anticipate policy changes and to move ahead of those changes.

## Going Forward: Imbalances, Risks, and Opportunities

In 2010, the pace of economic growth was slower than many had anticipated and Federal Reserve easing is aimed at promoting that growth. However, in a global context, Fed easing also will lower the value of the dollar. Over time, a weaker dollar puts upward pressure on inflation and pushes nominal long-term interest rates higher, especially given the continued large financing burden of federal debts. Over the longer run, as monetary stimulus wears away, the economy will slow to its natural trend growth rate. That rate is often slower than the rate associated with stimulus; in addition, there is a downshift in the growth of corporate profits.

The problem is that the sunk cost bias may be showing up for both fiscal and monetary policy. Fiscal policy is focused on another stimulus to get the economy going, although the budget and deficit implications are increasingly out of line with historical perceptions of prudent practice. Similarly, monetary policy is treading in new territory with quantitative easing, although the inflation risks of such a policy appear to be rising while the exchange value of the dollar declines. The benefit-cost balance of further policy actions raises the question: Is it worth it?

For domestic investors, current low yields on United States Treasury debt provide very little protection against the risk of accelerating inflation. For foreign investors, there is little protection for exchange rate losses. Present trade and current account deficits for the United States suggest that the financing burden of these deficits will force a change in the key economic factors that drive success. The big downdraft in foreign purchases of securities issued in the United States during the Great Recession was actually by private investors, not official foreign investors (Figure 12.12). This strikes

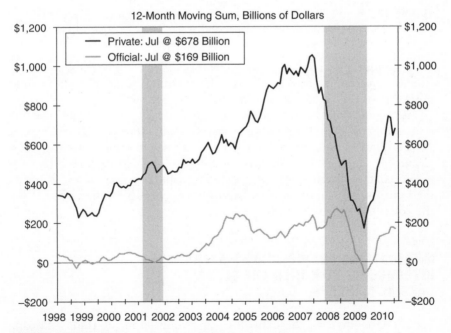

**FIGURE 12.12** Foreign Purchases of U.S. Securities
*Source:* U.S. Department of the Treasury and Wells Fargo Securities, LLC.

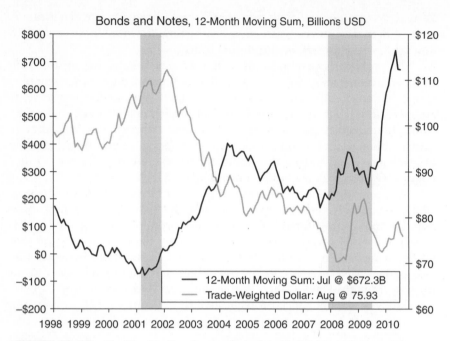

**FIGURE 12.13** Net Foreign Purchases of Marketable US Treasury Securities
*Source:* U.S. Department of the Treasury and Wells Fargo Securities, LLC.

at the argument that the dollar and Treasury market will be stable, since the Chinese government, an official buyer, has a strong incentive to maintain its purchases of United States securities to stabilize the dollar.

Along the same lines, the link between Treasury purchases and the dollar is also more complex than some might suppose (Figure 12.13). Over the 2002 to 2005 period, the dollar actually weakened in value as Treasury purchases fell. During the Great Recession the dollar-Treasury link did appear to fall into the pattern that Treasury buying helps the dollar theory. Yet, with the recovery, Treasury purchases by foreign investors have strengthened, but the dollar has gone sideways.

## IMPLICATIONS FOR DECISION MAKERS: INTRODUCING RISK INTO THE GLOBAL CAPITAL MARKETS

For the last 40 years, there has been an evolution in the trade and capital markets as well as the political balance of power associated with the international community. The economic framework has continually evolved over this period and so must the thinking by decision makers. Currently, a large United States current account deficit is associated with large and rising fiscal deficits. The Fed is engaged in discussions about quantitative easing, with which the nation has had very limited experience. The outlook for growth is a more moderate path relative to United States history since World War II, since the country is no longer a closed economy and the country's economic model has been adopted, in part, by many new players, who are now our toughest competition. The inflation outlook is highly uncertain, not just risky. The Federal Reserve may have the ability to provide just enough monetary stimulus to avoid deflation, promote moderate inflation, and yet avoid accelerating inflation, which would engender rising inflation expectations. However, increasing inflation expectations would drive up short- and long-term interest rates. Once again, the challenge is: Can those rates rise just short of discouraging economic growth? Moderate inflation is a worthy goal, but given the global context of uneven growth and trade flows, the soft landing for inflation remains very uncertain.

Meanwhile, the moderate inflation outlook is a core input to the expectations for the dollar going forward. Disappointing economic growth and accelerating inflation would be a difficult scenario for the global capital markets and create negative expectations on the outlook for the dollar. Expectations concerning corporate profits remain highly volatile given the uncertainty surrounding growth, inflation, and interest rates. A significant percentage of corporate profits for American companies are earned abroad. Therefore, a volatile dollar would have a negative influence on corporate profits and the reliability of those profits to support growth in the economy.

## Framework

What does that leave for a framework? The United States has a floating rate currency with fairly free capital flows and an independent central bank. At the same time, President Barack Obama's administration is engaged in an expansionary fiscal policy that is unlikely to become very restrictive in the near term. Fiscal deficits are being financed, in part, by both private and official foreign investors who are sensitive to the exchange rate risks of dollar depreciation. For some time, the Fed will maintain an easy monetary policy that is likely to sustain its easing bias through a quantitative easing program directed at raising the inflation rate. But this strategy also has some chance of weakening the currency over time. This type of quantitative easing program has not been conducted before in the post–World War II period. There are significant risks that such a program could generate unanticipated results for expectations of inflation, interest rates, and the dollar.

## Change

What type of changes should decision makers look for over time? Given the fiscal and monetary policy commitments, job growth should improve and with that, consumer incomes and spending. However, the Federal Reserve remains concerned about the low pace of inflation and therefore it will continue to employ large-scale asset purchases (also termed quantitative easing) to increase inflation. An easier monetary policy suggests weakness for the dollar, but better economic growth and higher interest rates should lift the dollar over time. Finally, positive economic growth will likely improve corporate profits over time and offset the negative impact of a stronger dollar.

## FEEDBACK, ALTERED EXPECTATIONS, AND BUILDING THE NEW FRAMEWORK

With an altered economic model, what can decision makers expect going forward in the context of a globalized world? Both fiscal and monetary policies are geared to providing greater growth than at present. Yet, the pace of growth may be less than what the public expects, or enough to produce the economic environment that would qualify as normal given our post–World War II history.

Inflation expectations are in flux; therefore, the assumptions underlying the new framework are not clear. In terms of our strategy, we are dealing with significant uncertainty. What is the pace of inflation that will satisfy the Federal Reserve's goals for growth and unemployment? How much inflation is enough? How much is too much? What distance away from deflation is adequate to assure the Fed that the risk of deflation is de minimis? Moreover, what is the economy's actual transmission mechanism from the start of the Federal Reserve's buying of Treasury debt today to the possible increasing in the rate of inflation tomorrow? What about the timing of any possible inflation increase in the future? How does quantitative easing work in an economy that is operating below capacity? These questions point up the principle that our strategy is not a simple step forward, but a step into an area about which there is more uncertainty than risk and our strategy must therefore reflect the broad possibilities of outcomes.

Interest rates are an example of the dynamic character of economic events and the difference in economic impacts between the short run and the long run. Over the short term, further Federal Reserve easing will lower long-term interest rates through an easing of credit pressures and the traditional liquidity channel, whereby the Fed lowers interest rates by providing greater liquidity through bank reserves. However, over time a successful monetary policy will generate greater economic growth and rising inflation pressures and thereby higher long-term interest rates. This pattern is further complicated by the uncertainty surrounding the impact of long-term fiscal deficits on the expected increased demand for credit and how the public will discount future tax burdens. The risk for decision makers at this point is that the turn in interest rates is as swift as the rise in interest rates during 1994 to 1995 when the Fed raised interest rates to head off a potential rise of inflation.

Dollar issues are no less complex. Over the last 40 years there has been a rising integration of global capital markets. And, in particular, there has been a close integration of America's fiscal deficit finance and the willingness of Japanese and Chinese investors to intervene to support the dollar's value to sustain their export markets. Over time, Japan and China will likely develop greater trading relationships with Asia and Latin America. This will reduce their incentive to support the dollar at current values. In addition, the Fed's goal of increasing inflation over the period ahead may also put downward pressure on the dollar. As in the inflation model, as the Lucas critique would suggest, current policy changes alter the economic model when actors such as foreign and domestic investors change their expectations of the fundamental forces moving economic activity.

Corporate profit growth will reflect the impact of policy on growth, inflation, and interest rates. However, the growth of the global trading environment suggests that the importance of the dollar will grow in estimating the path of corporate profits. As trading relationships increase and more United States–based firms engage in direct investment or partnerships abroad, the impact of exchange rate fluctuations on earnings will grow over time. Once again, the economic framework for estimating a key economic factor such as corporate profits is evolving.

## Choices

For the global policy leadership, the challenge of rebalancing the savings and investment, consumer and export-led economies will be a political as well as an economic problem. Interest groups benefit from the current arrangement and will be very hesitant to change, as was the British landed gentry in an earlier era when facing growing industrialization and the globalization of the British economy.[19] Yet, the reality is that failing to make the hard choices and updating the framework of the global economy will not alter the continuous evolution of the economy. Failing to choose is a choice and often a decision for failure in an evolving global credit market. For example, in recent years we have seen the euro community not come to grips with the outsized fiscal deficits of several countries until the change was forced on them and the adjustment costs were much greater than they would have been otherwise. In addition, the United States has not come to grips with its outsized promises on entitlements and the credit-financed lifestyle of consumers that has recently come to grief. Meanwhile, China—dependent on the export sector—is also in a difficult position, needing to adjust to a sharp deterioration in the dollar that will impact both export sales and the value of the central bank portfolio.

## A NEW FRAMEWORK AND THE OVERCONFIDENCE BIAS

Political rhetoric has suggested that the overconfidence bias is alive and well in public policy on the global level. Commentary from the euro community, the United States, and China suggests that their way is the real way forward and that others should adjust to satisfy the internal political and economic goals of that society. Each region has a very positive self-assessment of its framework. Yet, from another perspective, there appears to be an overreliance on the precise balance of trade and capital flows to sustain what appears to be an increasing greater imbalance between export dependent and consumer-generated economic growth engines for different regions of the globe. For example, economic growth in the United States has become increasingly consumer dependent while relying on capital inflow to finance both public and private sector spending. Meanwhile, many emerging economies are export dependent for growth, while also exporting out capital as loans to industrialized countries. The present experience of the global economy suggests that intellectual rigidity in the face of macroeconomic volatility is a sure prescription for further crises along these same fault lines. Perhaps a bit of innovation is needed and to that we now turn.

## DISCUSSION QUESTIONS

1. You are the international sales manager for a high-tech equipment manufacturer based in the United States. Explain how the alternatives of a benign resolution or a hard landing to the United States current account deficit would impact your expectations for growth, inflation, interest rates, and exchange rates.
   a. How will this alter your expected foreign sales in the year ahead?
   b. What role would you expect the Chinese Central Bank to play in avoiding the hard landing?

    c. What are the implications for growth, inflation, interest rates, and exchange rates in the short run from Chinese intervention?

    d. In the long run?

2. Debates on free trade versus protectionism often circle around the interests of producers versus consumers.

    a. Using the example of the Corn Laws in Britain, discuss the positions of farmers, consumers, and manufacturers in this debate.

    b. How might the Corn Laws case provide a framework for the evaluation of the impacts of NAFTA?

    c. Assume you are a producer of low cost textile goods and trade barriers protecting the textile industry are going to be reduced. What might your advice be to management?

    d. How might the adage "what you see depends on where you sit" apply to trade policy?

3. The impossible trinity theme creates an interesting challenge for those leaders in a multinational firm who are responsible for exchange rate management.

    a. Explain the impossible trinity concept.

    b. How might this impossible trinity present a problem of exchange rate and inflation volatility between currencies and economies for countries that adopt different corners of the trinity?

    c. Contrast the positions of the United States and China on the trinity. How might their respective positions explain the influence of domestic politics and international aims?

## NOTES

1. Fritz Stern, *Gold and Iron: Bismarck, Bleichroder and the Building of the German Empire* (London: Allen & Unwin, 1977), 189.
2. Charles P. Kindleberger, *Manias, Panics and Crashes* (New York: Basic Books, 1978), 118.
3. The era from 1880 to 1913 is considered the golden era of global capital markets, given the fairly free flow of capital at that time. For a recent review of that era and its lessons for today, see Lee E. Ohanian and Mark L. J. Wright, "Capital Flows and Macroeconomic Performance: Lessons from the Golden Era of International Finance," *American Economic Review* (May 2010), 68–72.
4. Robert A. Mundell, *International Economics* (New York: Macmillan, 1968) and J. Marcus Fleming, "Domestic Financial Policies under Fixed and Floating Exchange Rates," *IMF Staff Papers* 9 (November 1962), 369–379.
5. Robert A. Mundell, "Capital Mobility and Stabilization Policy under Fixed and Flexible Exchange Rates," *Canadian Journal of Economic and Political Science* 29(4)(1963): 475–485.

6. The United States break from gold in 1971 reflected the Nixon administration's wish to stop the gold outflow, as persistent trade deficits were draining our gold stock.
7. For a review of the Asian miracle and the aftermath, see "Ten Years After: Revisiting the Asian Financial Crisis," edited by Bhumika Muchhala, Woodrow Wilson International Center for Scholars (October 2007).
8. A useful business case in providing background for the American experience that I have used here is by Laura Alfaro and Rafael di Tella, *The U.S. Current Account Deficit in 2005*, Harvard Business School, 9-706-002, revised December 7, 2005.
9. Crony capitalism simply refers to a nominally capitalist economy in which political links have an overwhelming influence on the success of any business and open, competitive markets are very limited. Friendships and family ties drive the economic success of an institution more than its competitive prowess.
10. For more on the home bias, see Cheol S. Eun and Bruce G. Resnick, *International Financial Management*, 3rd ed. (New York: McGraw-Hill Irwin, 2004), 370–374.
11. Ben Bernanke, "The Global Savings Glut and the U.S. Current Account Deficit," remarks at the Sandridge Lecture, Virginia Association of Economics, Richmond, Virginia, March 10, 2005.
12. John Train, *The South Seas Bubble, Famous Financial Fiascos* (Burlington, VT: Fraser Publishing, 1985).
13. Peter Hooper, Karen Johnson, and Jaime Marquez, in "Trade Elasticities for G-7 Countries," Federal Reserve Board of Governors, International Finance Discussion Papers 609 (1998).
14. Maurice Obstfeld and Alan M. Taylor, *Global Capital Markets: Integration, Crisis, and Growth* (Cambridge: Cambridge University Press, 2004).
15. "Greece's Sovereign-Debt Crunch: A Very European Crisis," *The Economist* (May 2, 2010).
16. Jack Ewing, "Cuts to Debt Rating Stir Anxiety in Europe," *New York Times*, April 27, 2010.
17. "Merkel Economy Adviser Says Greek Bailout Should Bring Penalty," *BusinessWeek*, February 15, 2010.
18. Niall Ferguson, "A Greek Crisis Is Coming to America," *Financial Times*, February 10, 2010.
19. For more on rebalancing the global economy, read Stephen S. Roach, *The Next Asia* (Hoboken, NJ: John Wiley & Sons, 2009).

## RECOMMENDED READING FOR SERIOUS PLAYERS

Kindleberger, Charles. *Manias, Panics and Crashes*. New York: Basic Books, 1978.
Obstfeld, Maurice, and Alan Taylor, *Global Capital Markets: Integration, Crisis, and Growth*. Cambridge: Cambridge University Press, 2004.
Roach, Stephen S. *The Next Asia*. Hoboken, NJ: John Wiley & Sons, 2009.

# CHAPTER 13

# Innovation and Its Role in Economics and Decision Making

**A**fter the misadventures of Adam and Eve, the need for cloth and the transformation of cloth into clothing became a necessity. Yet, for centuries, the transformation was done by hand and thus was very expensive. Most people went through every day with the same clothes on their backs. This is where innovation comes in, and the results are quite contrary to the impression often conveyed by critics of technology. In 1856, Isaac Singer brought together the earlier advances of others into the sewing machine—Elias Howe had obtained a patent on an earlier machine in 1846. Singer's two major advancements were the now familiar straight needle with a back-and-forth shuttle motion and the action of feeding the cloth through the machine in a continuous fashion. Three advancements came about: speed, flexibility to work with seams of any length, and, very important for the overweight nineteenth-century person, the ability to sew on a curve.

Contrary to conventional wisdom, the sewing machine increased the importance of the individual worker by making each person individually more productive and as a group it increased the supply of clothing to the markets so that the lower prices brought in more buyers, thereby leading to the boom in apparel demand for all households. More women entered the workforce and more families enjoyed a greater variety of clothes than ever before. By the twenty-first century, Adam and Eve could shop at the mall on Saturday and pick out that perfect outfit for their Sunday walk in the garden.

Innovation meets a need. In this chapter, the focus is on economic needs and the application of a vision to alter a current economic framework for the production, distribution, or marketing of goods and services. In some cases, the need has been driven by a prior change or shock to the economic framework. In other cases, the innovation itself changes the framework as the innovation meets an unexpressed need in the marketplace. Innovation meets an induced change or induces change by itself. The innovator sees an opportunity or creates that opportunity. In some cases, a new good is introduced, such as the iPod. In other cases, a new means of production is introduced or expanded—Nucor steel and the advancements in mini-mill manufacturing, electric arc furnaces, and continuous thin slab castings are examples. In some cases, a firm will open new markets—for example, Kroger and the growth of the suburban grocery store. Finally, an entire industry can be reorganized to fit a new generation—with the growth of laptops an old order was broken down.

Innovation provides the secret element in success for any organization and yet that same innovation is hard to measure and illustrate using our tools. However, we know it when we see it. In this chapter, we begin with an examination of the character of both evolutionary and revolutionary change in the economic framework. Second, we highlight how changes in economic forces such as inflation, interest rates, and exchange rates have played their role as forces for innovation in the economy. Next, we turn to the interrelationship between innovation and our decision-making process, where we see how innovation can alter our actions at each stage of that decision-making process. Innovation and risk taking are two sides of the same decision-making coin and in the next section we take a look at risk-taking and prospect theory and their impact on the willingness to innovate. Finally, we highlight the innovations in economic thought that have addressed the most significant decision-making challenges of their day.

## INNOVATION AND THE ECONOMY

Successful leadership always has a vision for the future. Leaders who have this vision can see opportunity in changes in the economy or they can create change by recognizing the unmet needs of a society. This section reviews the elements that shape successful innovation in an economic setting.

### Growth

Innovations alter the productivity of capital (better machines) and that of labor, and thereby change the potential output of the economy. Clothing became more abundant and cheaper. Altering economic growth is the explicit intention of the entrepreneur, and thereby he changes the decision-making framework for the economy.

In the short run, David Ricardo, a Jewish-Portuguese immigrant to England, lost his battle on the Corn Laws, which were the laws that limited agricultural imports, particularly corn from the United States, and thereby favored the landed, agricultural interests at the expense of consumers. In the long run, however, Ricardo provided one of the most enduring insights into economics and the advantages of free trade. Trade offers the possibility of raising the potential output of any country and increasing its rate of growth. Ricardo's innovation was recognizing that even though one country could be more productive in producing two different goods, by specializing in the production of one good and allowing another country to produce the other, each country could take advantage of its comparative advantage. For Ricardo, the comparison was between cloth, produced in his new country, England, and wine, produced in his old country, Portugal. Trade, especially with the Dutch and Portuguese at the time, was the means for increasing national wealth far beyond what each of these small countries could achieve on its own. Ricardo recognized the changing nature of the global economy at the time and wanted to alter the existing economic framework.

Unfortunately, Ricardo lost out to the landed interests in England who wanted high tariffs to protect their high prices, a carryover from the Napoleonic war period. But Ricardo's innovation in thinking about trade survived the Corn Laws and still serves as the intellectual basis for trade expansion today and the counterargument against trade protectionism.

In the United States in the post–World War II era, the attitude was one of growth and suburbanization. After the Great Depression and the rationing during World War II, the consumer wanted more of everything and a greater variety of it. For the grocery business, this meant a shift in vision from meeting basic needs of the Great Depression and war consumption to seeing a future with more choices in a suburban atmosphere. Jim Collins, management consultant and former professor at Stanford University, lays out the contrast between A&P and Kroger as two different visions of the growth potential of the consumer and the changing character of the American economy.[1] A&P stores tended to be urban, small, and not automobile-friendly, with very limited parking in very dense urban locations with little street visibility. In the 1930s A&P was the number one grocery chain in America, operating more than 16,000 stores. Kroger, which believed the future lay in greater consumer choice, built brighter, cleaner stores, with more variety, in a suburban environment. A&P failed to recognize that the framework had changed. By 2009, Kroger was America's largest supermarket chain and A&P, while still in existence, had slipped far behind.

Technology can enhance labor productivity. Despite the technology skeptics, the Luddites, technology has underlaid economic advancement in the United States since its beginnings and led to higher real wages for workers and more employment.[2] In 1824, Senator Daniel Webster, acting as a private attorney, argued before the United States Supreme Court that federal law on interstate commerce overrode New York's grant of a steamship monopoly on the Hudson.[3] Breaking up the steamboat monopolies on the Hudson and Mississippi allowed technology and innovation to move forward, bringing down the cost of shipping and lowering transportation costs for all goods being shipped. Years later, Abraham Lincoln would win other cases in favor of the railroads and lowering costs, once again allowing innovation to proceed and serve new markets.[4] Sometimes technology and innovation need the assistance of the law.

## TAKING A CLOSER LOOK

Eli Whitney and the cotton gin, a device that separated cotton fibers from the seeds much more quickly and efficiently than could be done by hand, lowered the cost of cotton cloth, which led to an increased supply of cotton for apparel manufacturers. Lower prices created greater demand among the public during the antebellum period, and, unfortunately, also increased the demand for more labor—slave labor—that was required to produce enough cotton to keep up with the demand. Moreover, the land that grew the cotton became more valuable and so did the importance of cotton exports to Europe. By 1860, the American South was providing the majority of the world's supply of cotton. Alternatively, the transcontinental railroad and all the innovations that attended it, such as the truss bridge, altered the economics of transportation costs. The railroad also opened up vast tracts of land—to the detriment of the Plains Indians—and led to an increase in the amount of agricultural goods that could be produced, resulting in lower prices on these products sold in the Eastern United States and Europe. Meanwhile, the telegraph altered the cost of communication across space, and ended the romantic era of the Pony Express. In the twentieth century, the radio and the automobile again changed the costs of communication and transportation and thereby raised the potential growth of the economy by reducing the transaction costs of everyday production, marketing, and shipping.

Technology transformations often produce "lumpy" changes in growth—growth spurts—in a way not captured by the smooth, linear projections of spreadsheets or the smoothing process of economic forecasts. Instead, such changes are abrupt. The economy adopts a new framework for decision making that leaves the old order with an abundance of capital and creates a new order of entrepreneurs who can now take advantage of new opportunities. In the mid-1990s, the rapid adoption of Internet communication once again lowered the costs of consumer and business communication, creating new winners—Yahoo! and Google spring to mind—as well as a host of losers like newspapers and the post office. These sudden changes require a very quick adoption of the new framework and require leaders to forgo decision-making biases such as sunk costs. Lumpy changes, driven by technology, are part of the business cycle approach to the economy. These growth spurts build on the commentary of Harvard economist Joseph Schumpeter, who envisioned that significant economic innovation was intermittent, not continuous, and reflected an ebb and flow of innovations and subsequent reactions and secondary waves of innovation. Innovators act like a wave that creates movements in economic life.[5]

Innovation creates change in the framework for how the economy can grow and at what pace. The builders of the transcontinental railroad saw the opportunity that could be gained from lowering transportation costs, changing the way Americans travel, and creating a national marketplace. In other cases, such as the cotton gin, the thrust was to solve a problem in production and thereby lower the production costs and create new markets. In the twentieth century, the Internet altered the framework for communication and marketing and thus forced many firms to alter their methods for reaching the customer.[6]

Innovation can be either evolutionary, as in the new and improved version of the latest dishwashing detergent, or revolutionary, in terms such as Schumpeter's creative destruction. Evolutionary change is incremental and does not alter the competitive position of the players in the industry or in the global economy. In the economic framework these changes do not bring into question the future of the organization. They are the subject of the monthly departmental meeting, the quarterly meeting of the board of directors, or the company's offsite meetings.

In contrast, revolutionary change brings into question the range of future structures of the organization. Rapidly rising gas prices in the 1970s brought into question the structure of the automobile companies and the industry itself. Globalization in the post–World Trade Organization era and the rise of the Chinese and Indian economies brought into question the pricing power and ultimately the competitiveness of firms on the global scale. Revolutionary change creates a new industry while old industries lose prominence. During World War I, European and Russian grain production had declined; many men were at war in Europe and the Bolshevik Revolution had begun in Russia, and the physical destruction of men and horses limited gearing up production after the war. The war took a terrible toll on horses due to their use in cavalry and in supply trains that were easy targets for enemies. Horses were employed for reconnaissance and logistical support during the war. They were better than mechanized vehicles at traveling through deep mud and over rough terrain. Yet, horses were no match for machine guns, and gradually tanks replaced them over the term of the war.[7] Therefore, when companies like John Deere introduced farm tractors during the 1920s, they got a double-barreled boost from high grain prices and limited capital (work horses) available to produce the crops. The plow and horses were soon displaced. With higher prices for their crops, the farmers could afford the tractors and Deere, and others, enjoyed a bumper crop of success, so to speak. While evolutionary change is fairly common and is consistent with the steady growth of the firm, revolutionary change is relatively rare and results in a large-scale transition to the way economic growth and the needs of the economy are met. At the outset, the iPod and the iPhone were disruptive innovations that rendered competitors and their products out of touch with consumer needs. After the iPod and iPhone introductions, competitors brought forth evolutionary improvements with better products, but all within the realm of improving on the new idea.

A revolutionary innovation can give a competitor a sustained advantage over other competitors over a long period of time and this often alters the structure of the industry, while evolutionary change grants only a temporary competitive advantage. The revolutionary innovation generates alternative future options that we reviewed in an earlier chapter. In contrast, evolutionary change represents movement along the existing strategy model. For example, Southwest Airlines has a revolutionary approach to airline travel and has sustained a comparative advantage for some time as compared to other airlines. Meanwhile, many of its competitors will focus on the incremental improvements in their airplane seating and domestic airline routes. In the first case, for Southwest Airlines the changes they have implemented were revolutionary, while in the second case, many of the changes other airlines have introduced have more of the evolutionary pattern.

### Inflation: A Force for Financial Innovation and Consumer Choice

During the late 1960s and especially in the late 1970s, inflation became a revolutionary force that altered the framework for households, businesses, and financial institutions. Rising inflation drove market interest rates above government interest rate ceilings on bank deposits and thereby led to the innovation of financial instruments that would appeal to savers and investors willing to stray from insured deposits. This was a step away from the Depression-era attitude of safe deposits backed up by the Federal

Deposit Insurance Corporation. Money market funds came into being in 1971 as a means of offering savers a return on their money that would exceed the returns on bank deposits, which were subject to the restrictions of Regulation Q. These Regulation Q limits operated like a price control scheme, with nominal interest rates fixed in the face of rising inflation that effectively lowered the real return to savers. Price controls distort the economic incentives to save and, in this case, hurt both savers and banks by limiting price competition for savings. Such distortions in the market generally lead to innovation around the distortion, and money market funds were the answer. The Merrill Lynch Ready Assets Fund was started in 1975 and shot up to $40 billion of assets in just one year. This innovation was followed in 1977 with the introduction of the Merrill Lynch Cash Management Account, which allowed customers to write checks against their balances. By 1980, money market fund assets rose to $80 billion and in mid-2010 these funds stood at $1.1 trillion.

This revolutionary change altered the asset allocation model for savers and the business model for banks. Small savers could earn a market rate of return when their returns on bank deposits were capped. Meanwhile, banks suffered from disintermediation—the withdrawal of deposits from depository institutions because the returns were limited by Regulation Q. Over the next 10 years, evolutionary change followed as regulators gradually dismantled Regulation Q requirements and competition for consumer deposits rose, as did inflation and interest rates.

### Interest Rates—Volatility and Risk

By the early 1970s, the rise in interest rates created a need for businesses to hedge interest rate risk and its associated volatility. The era of low, steady interest rates was over. The new era of higher, more volatile, interest rates that were set in the market was about to begin.

In 1975, the Chicago Board of Trade (CBOT) began trading futures contracts on Government National Mortgage Association certificates (GNMAs). In the following year, the Chicago Mercantile Exchange (CME) began trading Treasury bill futures contracts. In her commentary on interest rate futures written in 1980, Judy Menich, economist at the Federal Reserve Bank of Cleveland at the time, concluded that "Interest-rate futures have the potential to modify substantially the way in which business is conducted in the capital markets."[8] Indeed, they have. In a study released in 1984, the Commodity Futures Trading Commission (CFTC) argued that financial futures were not destabilizing, as claimed by some, and that they actually added to market liquidity.[9] Initially, then, the interest rate futures market was considered an innovation that offered far greater benefits than costs and was a net positive to the economy. In later years, futures, like almost all products and services, pushed the limits of the envelope and created more problems than benefits; but that too leads to new innovations.

Volatility in interest rates was not a new development by the 1990s. In fact, interest rates have spiked up and down frequently over the last forty years. Yet commitments to contracts that are based on fixed interest rates have in them the risk of interest rate volatility and thereby also contain in them the seeds of a future sunk cost bias on the part of both sides of a contract. For borrowers, the risk of refinancing at a higher interest rate in the future is always present. Many borrowers, therefore, lock their interest rate today for financing tomorrow by using futures. During the interest rate rise that occurred between 1994 and 1995, however, Gibson's Greetings, a greeting card company headquartered in Cincinnati, Ohio, and Orange County, CA, both lost big when their interest rate bets went against them. Both institutions and their advisers failed to see the volatility in market interest rates as anything more than passing. Their positions became a sunk cost as interest rates rose. Both institutions did not limit their losses and did not accept the loss as a sunk cost, but instead stayed with their interest rate bet while rates continued to rise. In 1994, Orange County declared bankruptcy while Gibson's Greetings took a loss and later settled a suit with Bankers Trust on the interest rate trades.

## Dollar and Hedging Exchange Rate Risk

With the end of the gold-dollar fixed exchange rate in 1971, the new world of exchange flexibility brought the need for exchange rate hedging, and its risks, to the forefront of multinational businesses. Well, at least some firms grasped the risks. Franklin National's speculation on foreign exchange markets came to an abrupt end in the spring of 1974. The stock was suspended from trading in the open market by May. Up to that time, that was the largest bank failure in American history.

In 2010, the volatility in the euro-dollar exchange rates, illustrated in Figure 13.1, reflected the changing perceptions of risk and opportunity when two currencies and the respective outlooks for the economy change. With the revelations of the sovereign debt problem in Greece, examined earlier in our review, and then subsequently also in Ireland and Portugal, subjects for a future essay, the euro declined sharply against the dollar. Talk of further quantitative easing by the Federal Reserve put downward pressure on the dollar.

Over the longer term, the greatest exchange rate challenge for the dollar and decision makers will most likely be the dollar-yuan exchange rate, which

**FIGURE 13.1**   Euro-Zone Exchange Rate
*Source:* Bloomberg LP.

is illustrated in Figure 13.2. Here, the makings of a more fundamental change in exchange rate parities and the risk of revolutionary change in the relative merits of the two currencies over a very short period of time can be seen. This revolutionary change will require rapid choices by decision makers in a very different global economic framework from what they have experienced in the past.

## Innovations and the Decision Making Framework

Contrary to popular impressions, decision making is critically intertwined with innovation and its impacts at any point within an organization. Innovation is not just a responsibility for the engineering department. In fact, it is often the failure to deal with innovation that leads to the downfall of many organizations.

The initial framework for any decision takes the existing economy at face value, but with the expectation that change will alter that framework in the future. Continuous change, the dynamic movement of the economic system, has been an underlying theme running throughout this chapter.

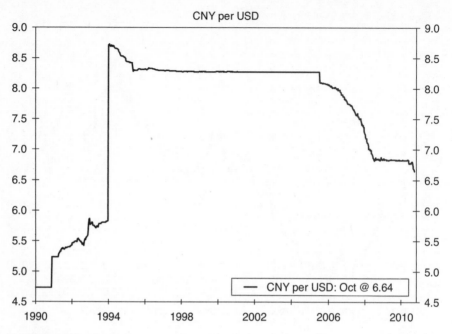

**FIGURE 13.2** Chinese Exchange Rate
*Source:* Bloomberg LP.

Innovation is a process of altering the framework of the enterprise model. In terms that might be comparable to Thomas Kuhn's[10] (professor at University of California at Berkeley at the time of the publication of the *Structure of Scientific Revolutions*), the existing economic framework can be likened to normal science. For example, within the existing framework physical stores are thought to be the only way to sell books or music CDs. This model is the way the world is and nothing else can be imagined. Then along comes change, or, in Kuhn's words, the anomaly. The anomaly is a result that does not fit the normal science paradigm and must be dealt with by decision makers. The crisis comes when widespread acceptance of the anomaly becomes apparent and this violates the rules of normal science. Selling books and music CDs through the Internet increasingly became the norm. The old economic framework is antiquated and inefficient to meet the needs of the public. Now the search for the new paradigm begins—the search for a new framework that allows for the anomaly and still explains the prior accepted experience. The anomaly is resolved within the new paradigm (framework) which provides a much richer view of the economy.

## The Initial Framework: Normal Science

In the current framework for the economy, decision makers must anticipate change either by their own initiative or through a change in their surroundings. Economists are constantly searching for a better way of doing something or searching for that better thing, that unmet need, to help them see the world differently, much as Copernicus or Newton saw the physical world differently. For John Maynard Keynes, the classical economic framework of his day asserted that there was an automatic link between saving, investment, and interest rates. The price of credit would adjust to make it so. But Keynes saw that the model of wages and prices operated differently from the classical framework. Keynes asserted that wages and prices *do not* automatically adjust to create a new equilibrium. On the contrary, especially in the short run, nominal wages and prices are "sticky," and therefore the existence of an excess supply of labor or goods could manifest itself, at least in the short run. As a result, the market will not automatically reestablish full-employment equilibrium in the economy. This was the point that prompted Keynes to advocate for government action to increase spending in order to raise aggregate demand and thereby increase output and employment toward full employment.

Milton Friedman also saw the received model as lacking. His view was that the short-run models failed to give enough emphasis to the role of money and its behavior over time. The demand for money depended on long-term factors and the rate at which people turned over money—velocity—was stable over time. Therefore, while there may be periods of imbalances in the economy over the short run, it is the long-run framework that matters. Short-run changes in policy do not alter the long-run path of the economy.

In recent years, this debate about policy effectiveness in the short and long run has continued, particularly regarding the effectiveness of the fiscal stimulus of 2009. As reviewed earlier, as long as inflationary expectations remain subdued, the increase in aggregate demand should lift economic growth. However, as expectations for interest rates, inflation, and the dollar change over time, both the aggregate demand and supply in the economy change and thereby so does the equilibrium output and pace of inflation. Unless the underlying capital, labor, or technology changes in the economy, the equilibrium long-run output (or it's growth rate) remains the same.

Friedman won his Nobel Prize in economics based on his observation on the difference between the behavior of consumers over the short and long run. According to the received framework for the economy, consumer spending will reflect changes in household income. Upon observation, however, consumer spending appeared to fluctuate much less than the received model would have suggested. How can we explain the anomaly? Friedman postulated that consumer spending is based on expected lifetime income and not short-run income. For example, young couples will invest in their education and also purchase a home with the expectation that they will pay off their debts and earn a return on their education over their working lifetime.

In part, this observation on lifetime income helps to explain why temporary tax changes do not alter consumer spending patterns over time. In 1968, the temporary tax surcharge did not slow consumer spending. The first-time homebuyer credit of 2009 altered the short-run timing of home purchases, but did not have any sustained impact on consumer spending. Temporary tax policy alters the timing of spending, but not the underlying growth of spending in the long run.

### Change as the Anomaly

Initially, business leaders can cast their framework as a given, but know that change is indeed a constant and they must adapt their framework to the changes they see. Innovations can be evolutionary or revolutionary and leaders know that they must execute and adapt any strategy in an economic context that is likely to change. In the late 1970s, changes in the level of gasoline prices as well as how those prices were set (by cartel rather than by free markets) suggested that the prior model for production, distribution, and sales in a cheap energy world was no longer relevant.

Innovation was forced on the trucking and automobile industry. Customers expected more fuel-efficient vehicles in light of the rising gas prices and concerns about the environment.

In the financial markets, as discussed earlier, the change in consumer interest in money market funds was a response to higher than expected inflation. Alternatively, business leaders can initiate change and this is often the most exciting part of the innovation that has characterized financial markets since the 1970s. The emergence of money market funds as a competitor to bank deposits is one example. Lehman Brothers introduced high-yield bonds in 1977 for the bond underwritings of LTV (Ling-Temco-Vought) and Pan Am Airlines, yet true innovation began in this area in the early 1980s with the repricing of risk in the marketplace. Bonds are one of several sources of capital for a business. Below-investment grade (junk) bonds paid an interest rate out of line with the actual historical default risk experience of those bonds. Moreover, these bonds were higher in the capital structure than equity and therefore were to be paid off before equity owners received anything. Investors reasoned that the default risk was mispriced. Simply stated, the history of pricing for high-yield bonds revealed that the implied default risk premium that was paid on these bonds in the marketplace exceeded the realized default experience of these bonds, as Michael Milken, a trader at Drexel Burnham, had claimed. Institutional investors, such as insurance companies, pension funds, and mutual funds as well as savings and loan institutions saw the opportunity to buy yield in excess of the risk of default. In addition, Drexel developed a second innovation, a secondary market for these bonds, which gave the market liquidity. The CNN network and the MGM Mirage were products of the early years of high-yield bond finance.

Milken's innovation was based on his exploitation of information that presented an anomaly between market pricing and actual experience. The adjustments in the marketplace since then brought about a huge increase in below-investment grade bond issuance and a broadening of the capital base for many companies, thereby adding to economic stability in the overall economy. Unfortunately, a federal grand jury indicted Milken in 1989 and in 1990 he pleaded guilty to six counts of securities and tax violations. In 1982, Milken and his brother founded a family foundation to support medical research and education. In a November 2004 cover story, *Fortune* magazine called him "The Man Who Changed Medicine." Innovation continues even if the context changes, as we know from the history of Carnegie and Rockefeller in the past and Gates today.

Securitization was another innovation that improved the functioning of the credit markets. It added liquidity to the markets and helped to offer originators of a loan product the means to package and sell off the portfolio if desired. Securitization converts nonmarketable instruments, such as the home mortgage, into publicly traded securities such as mortgage-backed securities. Automobile loans, credit card receivables—any asset or revenue stream—could be pooled and shares of the revenues sold to investors. Innovation created a secondary market for these instruments and thereby increased the total size of the lending market.

Asset-backed debt for the mortgage market began back in the early 1980s and by 1984 the mortgage-backed market grew to $1.6 trillion. The key legislation change in favor of the markets was the Secondary Mortgage Market Enhancement Act of 1984, which exempted mortgage-backed securities from margin requirements. In addition, the law preempted state laws that restricted depository institutions from purchasing mortgage-backed securities.

## Feedback and Choices

With feedback and choices come many decision-making biases. When analysts model the implications of any actual or proposed change, there is a tendency to bias their judgment. Innovation is a test of the underlying assumptions and orthodoxies associated with the old framework. To downplay the old ways in order to create a new way of doing business requires breaking down biases while leaders brainstorm for new solutions.

The anchoring bias problem is very obvious when the question is asked about why Montgomery Ward failed to innovate.[11] In the post–World War II years, Sewell Avery, president of the company, saw another Great Depression ahead, as depressions historically tended to follow wars. Avery failed to innovate, kept a high level of cash, and did not expand. Sears Roebuck did expand and became the nation's leading retailer. What Avery failed to see was that Americans had increased their savings during the war and were ready to spend. Germany and Japan were destroyed and the United States was the main manufacturing power in the world; that would generate strong personal income growth in the years ahead. In five years, Sears doubled its sales while Montgomery Ward's sales barely moved. In 2001, Montgomery Ward was closed down.

For Digital Equipment, innovation created its success but also its demise. The sunk cost effect of a historical investment in equipment and talent in the originally successful line of computers became a hindrance to innovation in the future. Digital was a leader in the minicomputer market in the 1960s and 1970s. The supermini computers were competitors to the larger mainframe computers. Yet innovation in the computer industry is relentless. In the late 1980s, the business microcomputer rose and the 32-bit systems of the 1990s meant the end of the competitive advantage of the minis. Ken Olsen, co-founder of Digital Equipment Corporation in 1957, dismissed the first microcomputers with the comment that "There is no reason for any individual to have a computer in his home." Digital did not investigate the microprocessor technology until after IBM launched its PC. Digital's architecture and software were not competitive in the new marketplace. The firm's sunk cost commitments to its technology and a workforce dedicated to supporting that technology could no longer compete in an environment that required a quantum leap to a new technology, not incremental changes over time. In 1998, the remnants of Digital were sold to Compaq.

Innovations by an upstart are frequently met by an overconfidence bias by established players.[12] Nucor steel was not one of the established big steel companies of the Northeast. Yet its bets on technology and culture and the personality of its leader, Ken Iverson, gave it the momentum to grow steadily over time. Nucor became *the* low-cost steel company in the United States. Nucor's innovations were in its technology, but also its labor relations. All 7,000 employees' names appeared in the annual report. Everyone except safety supervisors and visitors wore the same color hard hats. All employees received support for post-high school education for their children, and employees shared in the profits in a good year. In contrast, Bethlehem Steel, once the second-largest steel producer in America, failed to innovate both in its technology and its culture. Labor strikes, corporate aircraft, an executive country club, and executive rank determined shower priority at the club.[13] By 2001 Bethlehem Steel had declared bankruptcy.

Innovators frame problems as opportunities rather than as possible failures. Thomas Edison said he had found 1,000 ways not to make a light bulb, but one way to make it work. That one way made all the difference. Innovators frame problems in a way that does not constrict debate or the range of solutions that will be considered. Innovators put multiple frames on the same issue. In an innovating culture there is a willingness to fail and allowance for people to make useful and intelligent mistakes.[14]

## INNOVATION AND THE PATTERNS OF PROGRESS

Movements over economic cycles and structural economic changes over time reinforce the role of innovation in raising a society's standard of living while improving the prosperity for the innovator. The search for spices and trade improved the wealth of small countries such as the Netherlands and Portugal far beyond what they could have achieved domestically. Innovations such as the Erie Canal, the cotton gin, the steamboat, and the transcontinental railroad all significantly altered the production and transportation elements of the American economy and raised the nation's prosperity in the nineteenth century.

In the early years after World War I, John Deere and the farm tractor business illustrates the revolutionary character of innovation. Structural changes in both the demand for farm tractors and the supply-side production of those tractors led to a revolution in farm productivity and output. By 1924, John Deere had introduced its Model D and International Harvester had its Farmall. Both were significant innovations in farm tractor technology and by 1926 farm surpluses became an increasing issue.

Innovation in the twentieth century is best represented by the rapid turnover on the Who's Who list in business—the Dow Jones Industrial Index. A listing of companies from the World War I to the post–World War II period shows a story of constant change and innovation. Three firms that have dropped out of the Dow Jones, Bethlehem Steel, General Motors, and Woolworth, were not brought down by a single event.[15] Instead, there was a process of evolutionary change. These companies exemplified the principle of path dependence—each company stayed too long with the familiar way of doing things, their sunk costs, and that led to their demise as industry leaders over time. Meanwhile, innovative companies like Nucor, Toyota, and Kroger gathered momentum over time.

For the twenty-first century, the character of the business cycle in the United States and certainly the pattern of the nation's long-term growth will reflect the globalization of trade and finance that is altering the decision-making framework. Agreements such as NAFTA and WTO compel individuals and firms to step up to the challenge of innovation. Moreover, that challenge will be constant. Decision makers will have to overcome the sunk cost bias time and time again. For the Portuguese, their initial opportunity was to search for a way to the East after the Ottoman Turks took Constantinople in 1453. Portugal's great age of innovation and exploration began with the voyages of discovery around Africa. Yet, when a great opportunity opened up for them with Columbus's offer, they stumbled over their sunk cost bias and failed to explore what was to be the Western Hemisphere.

For the United States today, there is the anchoring bias that frames much public debate in the country—a belief that America is still in the hegemonic position of the early post–World War II period, not part of the globalization and trade and capital flows of the twenty-first century. Globalization and the emergence of Asia as an economic power commands decision makers to focus on the evolution of the global economy and seek out opportunities in a world whose cyclical and secular trends will be very different from the way they were in the latter half of the twentieth century.

Information has become the competitive edge for innovation today. Michael Lewis's book *Moneyball* highlights the effective application of information by Billy Beane, general manager of the Oakland Athletics, in building a winning team, despite having far less money to spend on talent than teams such as the New York Yankees and the Boston Red Sox.[16] Throughout the book Lewis cites the decision-making biases inherent in the baseball establishment. For example, the biggest bias is the belief and the operational principle that money determines outcomes. Moreover, traditional measures of success, such as the slugging percentage or hitting percentage, do not deliver the success that is promised, as very often good hitters are poor fielders or weak base runners. Mike Lewis makes the point that the way we traditionally process information is flawed in baseball and, in my view, often flawed in the private sector. The challenges to Oakland's management in overcoming those information biases are similar to the challenges facing private and public sector decision makers. On a final note, to support the thesis that money doesn't buy success in baseball, we would note that neither of the 2010 World Series teams—San Francisco and Texas—is at the top of the baseball salary spectrum. It is not how much you spend, but how you spend it.

Reach and richness represent two facets of information that prescribes success. Many Internet franchises—Google, YouTube, and Facebook—are built on the ability to deliver reach for advertisers. Mobile phone service quality is described in terms of its reach to millions of households. Cable or satellite television service is defined by its richness in terms of the number of channels provided and, in recent years, the number of channels available in HD. News is 24/7 and even the popular business news channels, such as CNBC and Bloomberg, have correspondents around the globe.

Having lots of information is a significant advantage, but how is it processed and distributed? For Gordon Moore and then Andy Grove, as CEOs at Intel, processing information meant starting with a clean slate, similar to the concept of zero-based budgeting in public finance, and then imagining what you would decide if there were no sunk costs. After this exercise, they asked: Would we be in this business today if we were just starting out? Grove and Moore decided to exit the memory chip business.[17] Facing numerous low-cost providers and a drop in demand in 1984, Moore and Grove met in mid-1985 in Grove's office and made the decision to get out of the memory chip business and into the microprocessor field. For Grove, that period of time became a period of their strategic inflection point and by 1992, Intel had become the largest semiconductor company in the world.[18] In contrast, Polaroid, a leader in instant photography, passed on developing digital photography. The impact of sunk costs, both in technology and manpower, limited their innovation to doing better at what they already did— evolutionary change, rather than a revolutionary change.

Walter Annenberg's challenge was how to distribute information. In the early 1950s, there were both national and local television channels, but no way to know what the programming was about so as to make informed choices. Annenberg began publishing *TV Guide* in 1952, contrary to the advice of his financial advisers. Prior to that, Annenberg took over his fathers' publishing business, including the publication of the *Philadelphia Inquirer* and *The Daily Racing Form.*

In the future, Internet social networks like Facebook that gather, process, and distribute information from millions of individuals acting on their own will be a source of innovation. The information is sometimes rumor; in other cases, it is incorrect. The motives of some of the creators of the information are suspect. Yet, for many decision makers, these social networks are a vehicle that will help people make better decisions.

Biases in information gathering, processing, and distribution are significant barriers to the innovator and entrepreneur. The innovator seeks change. Those who oppose change are easily caught by the confirmation bias. It easy to gather the conventional wisdom to demonstrate that it is wiser to stay with what is than to venture off into the unknown, which always has lots of risks and uncertainties.

The current situation benefits also from the anchoring bias. Decision makers are very comfortable with what they know and are uncertain about venturing into new areas.

Finally, an innovator needs to exercise caution about the illusory correlation between bits of information that may not tell the whole story. Man's first attempts to fly followed the correlation that since birds have wings and can fly, therefore the same would be true for man who had wings—unfortunately, it was not that easy. The correlation between flying and having wings was just too simple. Manned flight had to wait for the Wright brothers.

For Nicholas Dreystadt at General Motors, the correlation of successful black people and Cadillac ownership did convey practical information that led to his innovation in marketing to an overlooked part of society and revived the Cadillac brand. For the innovator, the opportunity lies in recognizing a correlation and asking why.

## RISK, INNOVATION, AND PROSPECT THEORY

Framing decisions as risk versus reward is the essence of financial market decision making. From the very first class in finance, the trade-off between risk and reward becomes the cornerstone of financial analysis.

Today, people take for granted that most mortgages are amortized, that is, paid off during the lifetime of the mortgage. Yet, before the Great Depression, home mortgages were short-term, non-amortizing loans with a balloon payment due when the loan matured. The risk in this case was refinancing risk, that is, the borrower could not refinance due to credit issues or unemployment. Alternatively, the price of the home declined during the Great Depression and an appraisal to meet the loan requirements could not be obtained. Finally, many banks went out of business and the borrower could not find a lender. In the post–World War II period the amortization approach to paying off the loan came into play to minimize the refinancing risk. Until the housing crisis brought about by the securitization of mortgages, this amortization approach worked.

However, changes in credit qualifications and financing options effectively reintroduced the refinancing risk for many homebuyers in recent years. For many homebuyers, the original mortgage was very short-term, two years in some cases, and thereby there was a risk that refinancing could not be obtained at that time. In addition, there were small or no down payments for many home purchases. There was very "little skin in the game" for many homebuyers and very little incentive to make the payments when times got hard. The Great Recession brought hard times and a wave of foreclosures when the refinancing problem again appeared.

Risk can reappear in an instrument, such as the home mortgage, when the conditions underlying that instrument change. The amortization of the home mortgage and the initial down payment ensured that the homebuyer had skin in the game. Forgetting that lesson, buyers and lenders were lulled into thinking that home buying and financing had little risk; they failed to recognize that the conditions minimizing that risk were also the conditions that were being eroded by the overconfidence bias of the buyers and lenders in the system.

The practical drift in mortgage lending had its political roots as well. The political incentive was to extend home ownership through lending and financing through the government-sponsored enterprises, GSEs, such as Fannie Mae and Freddie Mac, even though the credit quality of the lending was being downgraded over time. Unfortunately, the political payoff for such lending added to the inability to back away from what appeared to be a free lunch for policy makers, lenders, investors, and homeowners.

Interest rate and exchange rate risk prompted the innovation in financial markets for futures and options contracts on the exchanges to hedge those risks. This followed on the original agricultural futures contracts to hedge the risks associated with price volatility. In a familiar pattern in financial markets, innovation is constant. Since the 1960s, the innovations of commercial paper, Eurodollars, high-yield bond, and securitization have all had their boom periods, corrections, and resurrections as innovations with staying power that provide a service to the general public.

## Innovation, or Its Prevention, in Public Policy

Contrary to popular perception, innovation does take place in public policy, although often preventing innovation or protecting others from innovation is often a public policy goal. In the face of high inflation, Paul Volcker, as chairman of the Federal Reserve, headed monetary policy off in a new direction in favor of money supply targets, inflation control, and the willingness to accept the costs of interest rate volatility and a recession as the price of ensuring long-run price stability. The Great Recession brought many innovations in monetary policy recently as the Fed sought to deal with the collapse of the housing market and its associated financial marketplace downdraft. These innovations included, among others, lending dollars to foreign central banks, creating a range of emergency liquidity facilities to meet the funding needs of key nonbank participants, and the purchase of large amounts of longer-term securities.[19]

In fiscal policy, innovation took the form of the Kennedy and Reagan tax cut programs, as well as the attempt to slow down federal spending through the Gramm-Rudman-Hollings Balanced Budget Act of 1985. This was followed in 1990 by the Budget Enforcement Act, which was an agreement negotiated between President G. H. W. Bush and Congress. This act created two new budget control procedures. First, annually appropriated spending now faced a budget cap. Second, a pay-as-you-go, or PAYGO, provision was put in place for entitlements and taxes.

There are, however, a number of biases that limit innovation in fiscal policy. For example, most federal spending reflects the problem of path dependence—decisions made in the past limit the options today. Treasury debt issued in the past requires interest expenditures today. But the biggest issue is entitlements. Promises made in the past have molded the expectations for recipients or near recipients today. Yet the political office holders who made these promises did not fund them at that time, nor are they responsible for delivering on those promises now. It is easy to promise benefits to existing voters and ignore their costs for voters who may not even be born yet, but will have to pay sometime in the future.

Trade policy is another area where change and innovation are challenged by the sunk costs of existing competitors. New free trade agreements with Colombia, South Korea, and Panama would bring down artificial barriers, taxes, and transaction costs, but at the price of the sunk costs of politically-interested groups in those countries who vote. For a political decision maker, the influence of prospect theory is paramount. Taking down trade barriers can lower costs to consumers, firms, and institutions that import goods for production and final use. Yet, there are also risks where goods and services produced by established players in the market may not be competitive with the imported goods and services. This could mean plant closures and lay-offs. Often, the risk of these plant closures exceeds the future benefits of lower consumer prices in the political calculus. This occurs since the costs are visible and very concentrated, while the benefits are very diffuse and therefore obscured.

## INNOVATION, ECONOMIC THOUGHT, AND THE BIG CHALLENGES OF THE DAY

Over time, the big challenges facing a society and its economic welfare of-ten require innovation in thinking that questions the conventional modes of thought. For Thomas Malthus, the question was one of poverty, but the lesson for decision makers is the challenge and sometimes failure of long-term forecasting. Malthus was a reverend and a British scholar who studied political economy and demography and the problems of popula-tion growth and the demand for food. Malthus saw a world of geometric population growth that would limit a society's advancement in economic and moral terms; he contrasted the geometric population growth against the linear gain in agricultural production and projected a cycle of grind-ing poverty and a stagnant standard of living. What Malthus missed was innovation, in terms of population and agricultural spheres, as well as a sampling error.

First, Malthus made his observations on society in the early industrial age when better health lowered death rates and population did rise rapidly. However, he missed the advances in medicine that soon followed. This increased the quality of life for many people and led to changes in people's lifestyle choices. Better medicine improved the survival rate of children, and therefore reduced the incentive for large families. Second, the agricultural and industrial revolution altered living patterns and led to greater urbanization and thereby smaller families than he had projected. Third, education improved, and with that came a postponement of marriage and families that again reduced the rate of population growth. These evolutionary changes in the nineteenth century have given way to revolutionary changes since World War II, with birth control and better education and employment options for both spouses leading to a desire to have fewer children. The change has been so great that the question today has been turned on its head. Will there be enough people around to support economic growth given the low birth rates in Western Europe? And, if immigration is the answer to population growth, will that change the character of Western Europe?

For David Ricardo, the problem was that of trade. During the Napoleonic wars, agricultural interests in England, especially the landowners, had benefitted from high grain prices during wartime. Naturally they wanted to keep prices high after the wars given that the farm land, buildings, and tools were all sunk costs and were unlikely to earn a market return anywhere near what could be earned in farming.

In contrast, the new entrepreneurial class of the emerging industrial revolution wanted lower prices for their workers so that they could pay lower wages while also seeking more foreign markets for the goods they could now produce on a greater scale. Ricardo argued in favor of free trade among countries based on his work on comparative advantage and the specialization of labor. In the short run, the voters of what was—the landowners and agricultural interests—won, while the voters of what could be—the industrialists—lost. In 1815, Parliament passed the Corn Laws, prohibiting imports of grain below a certain price. Ricardo argued for free trade and against trade protectionism to no avail—in the short run. Over time, the balance of political interests changed as consumers and industrialists gradually gained the political power to abolish the Corn Laws in 1846. As an aside, the widely read magazine, *The Economist*, was founded in September 1843 by James Wilson with the help of the Anti-Corn Law League and his son-in-law Walter Bagehot later became the editor of that magazine.[20] Benjamin Disraeli, later to become prime minister, was opposed to the repeal of the Corn Laws but did not attempt to reinstate them as prime minister. The tide in favor of free trade had turned.

Since David Ricardo's time, the theory of comparative advantage and the benefits of specialization have stood up in the halls of academia, but have struggled, failed, and succeeded in many various forms in the halls of a country's legislature.

With the onset of the Great Depression on a global scale in the 1930s, the classical economic framework appeared out of touch. Wages and prices did not adjust over time to restore full employment or active markets in the buying and selling of goods and services. Instead, there appeared to be permanent excess of employment and a lack of output overall for the needs of the population. The solution that John Maynard Keynes advocated was central government spending in the short run to stimulate the economy, along with the acceptance that this would mean fiscal deficits for a time as well. Inadequate private sector demand called for pro-government action to deal with that problem—infrastructure spending and public works—to get the jobs and income machine going again. The budget would be balanced over the business cycle. The classical orthodoxy, however, persisted as policy in the United States through both the Hoover and Roosevelt administrations (Roosevelt's tax increases of 1937 were aimed at balancing the budget, but, instead, set the economy back again). Not until the Kennedy tax cuts in 1964 was Keynes' fiscal prescription put into place.

Today, the Keynesian fiscal stimulus argument has been widely accepted in public policy circles, but balancing the budget over the business cycle has been ignored. As a result, concerns about the implications of large sustained deficits on interest rates, the dollar exchange rate, and incentives for growth and employment have now taken center stage. To reduce these deficits, some policy makers have called for higher marginal tax rates, but these calls have raised concerns about incentives for innovation. Meanwhile, the expansion of entitlements over the last 40 years has lessened the incentives to work, save, and innovate, while also boosting future deficit estimates in a way Keynes would not have anticipated.

For Milton Friedman the question was the stability of consumption in the face of volatility of income. Keynes' approach to consumption was that household spending depended on household income. Yet, for Friedman, the volatility of income was not accompanied by a similar volatility of household spending. The answer lay in the concept of lifetime expected income. Households spend over their lifetime based on their expected lifetime earnings. Early in this life cycle approach to consumer spending, the household takes on debt to finance the house, the car, and the appliances, expecting to pay off the debt in the future. In addition, over the working years, households save for retirement. In this way, households smooth out their spending compared to their income and so consumer spending is not as volatile as income.

Consumer spending therefore reflects a longer view of income. For policy, this helps explain why actions such as temporary tax increases or decreases or the recent First-Time Homebuyer Credit program only alter the timing of consumer spending to take advantage of a bargain, but do not alter the permanent spending pattern of consumption and therefore did not jump-start the housing market as some analysts expected.

For Adam Smith, the division of labor as well as the innovation and self-interest of the owners of economic resources (land, labor, and capital) provided the basis for economic prosperity. Self-interested competition, therefore, promotes the good of the society. Smith also discussed taxes, saying that citizens should support the state in proportion to their abilities. Today the debate is about that proportion and to what extent the activities of the state are too big and should be reduced, as well as whether the state is engaging in the wrong activities and should alter its spending. What exactly is the balance between the state and the private economy, and how does that balance evolve over time? The framework of this question is always changing, as people's expectations about what the state should do has, in recent years, appeared to hit the limits of what can be afforded in a global economy with limited resources and unlimited desires.

For all those who innovate:

> *Jack Sparrow*: Now . . . bring me that horizon.
>
> —*Pirates of the Caribbean: The Curse of the Black Pearl*,
> 2003, Disney Pictures.

## DISCUSSION QUESTIONS

1. Innovation appears as an intermittent phenomenon. A burst of innovation was associated with the railroads in the post–Civil War era, radios and cars dominated the 1920s, and dot-com innovations characterized the mid- to late 1990s. Change does not appear to come at a constant rate. In contrast, in some cases where small changes are constant, innovation appears to be evolutionary.
   a. What factors might account for the two different characteristics of innovation?
   b. Innovation conveys a temporary monopoly on the innovator. What factors might influence the durability of that monopoly?
   c. What role does/should the federal government play in supporting innovation?
   d. What does Kuhn's model of normal science and a paradigm shift suggest innovation and the acceptance of change?

2. Is change and innovation an anomaly or the normal state of affairs in any science or society? Why?

3. Innovation faces a number of decision-making challenges. The challenge to Galileo is famous. What is the impact of the following biases on decision making and how is innovation either accepted or rejected?

   a. Impacts on the estimate of feedback.

   b. Anchoring bias.

   c. Sunk cost effect.

   d. Choice as impacted by prospect theory.

4. Public policy is often portrayed as protecting what is and ignoring what is possible. How might this view be reflected in the tendency of society to advocate tariffs and protectionism?

## NOTES

1. Jim Collins, *Good to Great* (New York: HarperCollins, 2001).

2. The Luddites were an early nineteenth-century group of textile workers who protested against the introduction of better quality looms that incorporated the newest technology and threatened to put workers out of a job. In some cases, the Luddites destroyed some of the machines.

3. *Gibbons v. Ogden,* 22 U.S. 1 (1824), discussed in John Steele Gordon, *The Business of America* (New York: Walker and Co., 2001), 75–79.

4. *The Illinois Central Railroad Company v. Brock Hays, et al.,* 19 Ill. 166 (1857) and *The Illinois Central Railroad Company v. Morrison,* 19 Ill. 136 (1857).

5. Joseph Schumpeter, *Theory of Economic Development* (Cambridge, MA: Harvard University Press, 1934), 214–231.

6. One business case that offers a structure for innovation is by Scott D. Anthony, Matt Eyring, and Lib Gibson, "Mapping Your Innovation Strategy," *Harvard Business Review* (May 2006).

7. Hedley P. Willmott, *World War I* (New York: Dorling Kindersley, 2003).

8. Judy Z. Menich, *Interest-rate Futures*, Economic Commentary, Federal Reserve Bank of Cleveland, June 16, 1980.

9. Commodity Futures Trading Commission, "A Study of the Effects on the Economy of Trading in Futures and Options," December 1984.

10. Thomas Kuhn, *The Structure of Scientific Revolutions*, 1st ed. (Chicago: University of Chicago Press, 1962).

11. John Steele Gordon, *The Perils of Success*, in *The Business of America*, Walker and Co., 2001.

12. Jim Collins, *Good to Great*, p. 167 for example.

13. John Stromeyer, *Crisis in Bethlehem* (Pittsburgh: University of Pittsburgh Press, 1986).

14. Daniel Kahnemann and Amos Tversky, *Choices, Values, and Frames* (Cambridge: Cambridge University Press, 2000).
15. Bethlehem and Woolworth, along with others, were dropped from the Dow-Jones index in 1997 and replaced by a number of firms including Hewlett-Packard and Johnson & Johnson. General Motors and Citigroup were dropped in 2009 and replaced by Cisco Systems, Inc. and the Travelers Companies.
16. Michael Lewis, *Moneyball* (New York: W.W. Norton, 2003).
17. Andy Grove, *Only the Paranoid Survive* (New York: Currency/Doubleday, 1999).
18. Ibid., 85–97.
19. See Donald L. Kohn, *The Federal Reserve's Policy Actions during the Financial Crisis and Lessons for the Future*, Remarks at Carleton University, Ottawa, Canada, May 13, 2010.
20. Bagehot is frequently quoted in times of financial crisis because of the view he presented in his book, *Lombard Street,* that a central bank must lend only against good collateral and at penalty rates.

## RECOMMENDED READING FOR SERIOUS PLAYERS

Buchholz, Todd G. *New Ideas from Dead Economists*. New York: Penguin Group, 1999.
Kahnemann, Daniel, and Amos Tversky. *Choices, Values, and Frames*. Cambridge: Cambridge University Press, 2000.
Kuhn, Thomas. *The Structure of Scientific Revolutions*, 1st ed. Chicago: University of Chicago Press, 1962.
Lewis, Michael. *Moneyball*. New York: W.W. Norton, 2003.

# The Hodrick-Prescott Filter

The Hodrick and Prescott (HP) (1997) filter has two justifications: one theoretical and one statistical. The theoretical part of the HP filter is connected with real business cycle (RBC) literature, for instance, in the RBC world the trend of a time series is not intrinsic to the data but it is a representation of the preferences of the researcher and depends on the economic question being investigated. The popularity of the HP filter among applied macroeconomists results from its flexibility, which can accommodate these needs since the implied trend line resembles what an analyst would draw by hand through the plot of the data. The selection mechanism that economic theory imposes on the data via the HP filter can be justified using the statistical literature on curve fitting.

The conceptual framework presented by Hodrick-Prescott can be summarized as follows:

$$y_t = g_t + c_t \tag{A.1}$$

for

$$t = 1, 2, 3 \dots T$$

Where $T$ is the sample size. A given series $y_t$ is the sum of a growth component $g_t$ and a cyclical component $c_t$. Actually, there is also a seasonal component but, as the data is seasonally adjusted, this component has already been removed by those preparing the data series.

In this framework the HP filter optimally extracts a trend ($g_t$) that is stochastic but moves smoothly over time and is uncorrelated with the cyclical component ($c_t$). The assumption that the trend is smooth is imposed by assuming that the sum of squares of the second differences of $g_t$ is small.

An estimate of the growth component ($g_t$) is obtained by minimizing;

$$\underset{[g_t]_{t=-1}^{T}}{Min} \left\{ \sum_{t=1}^{T} C_t^2 + \lambda \sum_{t=1}^{T} [(g_t - g_{t-1}) - (g_{t-1} - g_{t-2})]^2 \right\} \qquad \text{(A.2)}$$

$c_t = y_t - g_t$, cyclical component ($c_t$) is deviation from the long run path (expected to be near zero, on average, over long time period) and smoothness of the growth component is measured by the sum of squares of its second difference.

$$\Delta^2 g_t = {}_{(1-L)^2} g_t = [(g_t - g_{t-1}) - (g_{t-1} - g_{t-2})] \qquad \text{(A.3)}$$

Where $L$ denotes the lag operator, for example, $Lx_t = x_{t-1}$. The parameter $\lambda$ is a positive number that penalizes the variability in the growth component ($g_t$). The larger the value of $\lambda$, the smoother is the solution series. For a sufficiently large $\lambda$, at the optimum all the $g_{t+1} - g_t$ must be arbitrarily near some constant $\beta$ and therefore the $g_t$ arbitrarily near $g_0 + \beta t$.

This implies that the limit of solutions to equation (A.2) as $\lambda$ approaches infinity is the least squares fit of a linear time trend model. In this context, the "optimal" value of $\lambda$ is

$$\lambda = \delta_g^2 / \delta_c^2$$

where $\delta_g$ and $\delta_c$ are the standard deviation of the innovation, in the growth component ($g_t$) and in the cyclical component ($c_t$), respectively.

Another interesting observation would be the squared second difference of the trend component ($g_t$), which is multiplied by a factor ($\lambda$) and it is a very small term. Even very large changes in $\lambda$, therefore, influence the cyclical component $c_t$ modestly (Zarnowitz and Ozyildirim, 2006). Users of the HP filter select a value for $\lambda$ to isolate those cyclical fluctuations that belong to the specific frequency band the researcher wants to investigate. For example, Hodrick-Prescott favored $\lambda = 1600$ for quarterly data and for annual observations, $\lambda$ values of 400 or 100 have been used. For monthly data, the value of $\lambda$ has been set equal to 14, 400 by Zarnowitz-Ozyildirim.

Now we discuss some potential issues related with cyclical component ($c_t$). By definition $c_t = y_t - g_t$ and $y_t$ is the natural logarithm of a given time series, one advantage of using log form instead of level form, the change in the growth component ($g_t$), $g_t - g_{t-1}$, corresponds to a growth rate. First, it is a general consensus among macroeconomists that many macroeconomics series contain a unit root when expressed at level values, so $y_t$ may be one of those series (non-stationary at level). Second, intuitively, the growth component ($g_t$) should be non-stationary, as growth reflects a trend in a series over time (often a long run trend growth) component of a given series, and this trend will tend to be very smooth over time.

As cyclical component ($c_t$) is deviation from growth component, and it is expected to be stationary, the economy's output should exhibit reversion to the trend growth; and the effect of shocks, though they may persist over time, should decline and eventually die out. In other words, the stationarity of $c_t$ implies that no matter what kind of fluctuations in the series, deviations from its long-run growth component ($g_t$) are temporary and series will move, on average, smoothly over time.

One key advantage (along with many others) of the HP filter, is that once we estimate the $g_t$ and $c_t$, we can see, at any point of time, whether a series is running below the trend growth (slowdown) or above the trend (boom). This feature of the HP filter contains a useful policy implication that may help policy makers in their future decision-making process. For instance, $y_t$ is the U.S. real GDP (log form) and $g_t$ its long-run growth path; let the U.S. economy continuously grow (positive growth rate) but at a rate less than the $g_t$ for a period of say, two years. So the U.S. economy doesn't experience a recession, usually defined by negative growth rate (more specifically, two consecutive quarters of negative growth rate, although it is not true for the 2001 U.S. recession), and yet the economy has at times suffered sustained periods of below-trend growth and thereby higher unemployment. It is certainly possible to conceive of a severe and long slowdown causing more hardship than a mild and short recession. In fact, long slowdowns in employment and demand growth have occurred repeatedly in recent times even while output and supply growth held up well, which is supported by the process of technology and productivity (Zarnowitz-Ozyildirim). So with the help of the HP filter we can see where we stand now—are we in slowdown or not? Rather than waiting for a recession, slowdowns also demand serious consideration of alternative actions by decision makers. For example, a slowdown in employment and demand growth can lead to disappointing sales and rising inventories which call for action on the part of a decision maker.

Figure A.1 shows real GDP and its long-run trend based on an HP filter. During the last two U.S. recessions (2001 and 2007 to 2009), the HP- based trend peaked much earlier than the NBER's determined peak (beginning of the recession). Moreover, a continuous decline in the long run trend growth should caution policy makers as it is consistent with a slowdown or a recession in the near future, as depicted by Figure A.1.

The U.S. corporate profits growth and long-run trend based on an HP filter are plotted in Figure A.2. The long run trend growth is a leading indicator as it has peaked before the beginning of a recession during last two U.S. downturns/cycles.

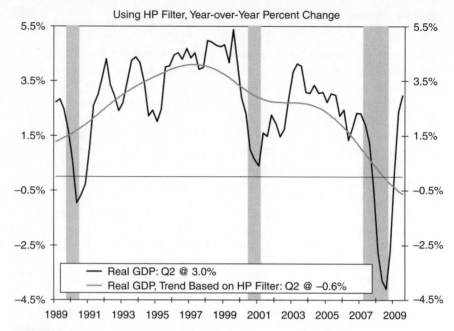

**FIGURE A.1**  Decomposing Real GDP
*Source:* Federal Reserve Board and Wells Fargo Securities, LLC.

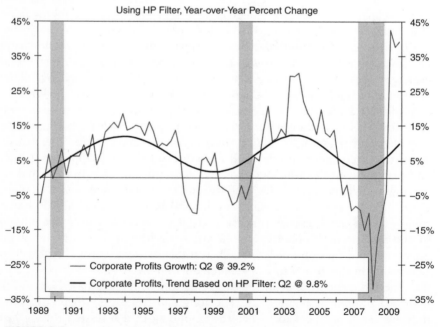

**FIGURE A.2**  Decomposing Corporate Profits Growth
*Source:* Federal Reserve Board and Wells Fargo Securities, LLC.

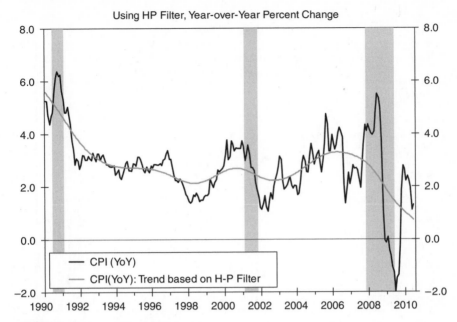

**FIGURE A.3** Decomposing CPI
*Source:* Federal Reserve Board and Wells Fargo Securities, LLC.

In Figure A.3, we plotted U.S. CPI growth and its long-run trend based on an HP filter. The long-run trend is a good benchmark to evaluate whether prices exert an inflationary pressure (above the trend growth) or deflationary pressure (below the trend growth) and may signal the need for action by a central bank.

The 10-Year Treasury rate and its long-run trend based on an HP filter are shown in Figure A.4. The 10-Year Treasury is also a leading indicator since during the last two recessions, the log of the 10-Year Treasury was much higher than the long-run trend before the beginning of recessions.

## AUTOREGRESSIVE CONDITIONAL HETEROSCEDASTICITY (ARCH)

The basic version of the ordinary least squares (OLS) model assumes that the expected value of all error terms, when squared, is the same at any given point. This assumption is called homoskedasticity, and it is this assumption that is the focus of the Autoregressive Conditional Heteroscedasticity (ARCH) models.[1] Data in which the variances of the error terms are not

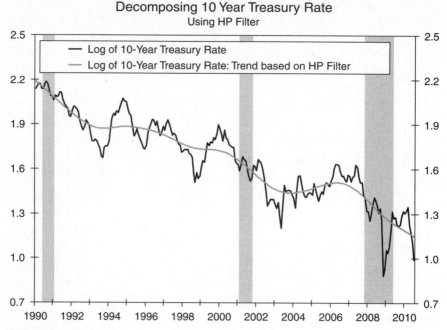

**FIGURE A.4**   Decomposing 10-Year Treasury Rate
*Source:* Federal Reserve Board and Wells Fargo Securities, LLC.

equal, in which the error terms may reasonably be expected to be larger
for some points or ranges of the data than for others, are said to suffer
from heteroscedasticity. The standard warning is that in the presence of
heteroscedasticity, the regression coefficients for an ordinary least squares
regression are still unbiased, but the standard errors and confidence inter-
vals estimated by conventional procedures will be too narrow, giving a false
sense of precision. Instead of considering this as a problem to be corrected,

**TABLE A.1**   The Comparison between the ARCH and OLS Models

| | Mean Square Error (MSE) | |
| --- | --- | --- |
| Variable | ARCH | OLS |
| CPI | 0.370 | 0.541 |
| 10-Year Treasury | 0.274 | 0.304 |
| Real GDP | 0.731 | 1.090 |
| Profits | 46.380 | 65.410 |

ARCH models treat heteroscedasticity as a variance to be modeled. As a result, not only are the deficiencies of least squares corrected, but a prediction is computed for the variance of each error term. As Table A.1 shows, the mean square error (MSE) based on the ARCH model is smaller than the OLS model. Therefore, the results based on the ARCH approach are more accurate.

## NOTE

1. Engle, Robert F. 1982. "Autoregressive Conditional Heteroskedasticity with Estimates of the Variance of United Kingdom Inflation." *Econometrica* 50(4): 987–1007.

J ohn E. Silvia is a managing director and the chief economist for Wells Fargo. Based in Charlotte, North Carolina, he has held this position since he joined Wachovia in 2002 as the company's chief economist. For the past four years John has taught in the MBA program at Wake Forest and those lectures serve as the basis for the material of much of this book.

Prior to his current position, John worked on Capitol Hill as senior economist for the U.S. Senate Joint Economic Committee and chief economist for the U.S. Senate Banking, Housing and Urban Affairs Committee. Before that, he was chief economist of Kemper Funds and managing director of Scudder Kemper Investments, Inc. In 2009, John was named one of the Top 10 forecasters for the last four years by *Bloomberg News* and the No. 2 forecaster by *USA Today* for 2008.

John holds BA and PhD degrees in economics from Northeastern University in Boston and has a master's degree in economics from Brown University. Currently John teaches part-time in the MBA program at Wake Forest University.

John serves as a member of the Blue Chip Panel of Economic Forecasters and also serves on an informal advisory group for the Federal Reserve Bank of Philadelphia. He serves as chair for the Economic Advisory Committee of both the Securities Industry and Financial Markets Association (SIFMA) Economic Advisory Roundtable and the American Bankers Association.

John was a director of the National Association of Business Economics (NABE) and was former president of the Charlotte Economics Club. He has also served on economic advisory committees to the Federal Reserve Bank of Cleveland, the Federal Reserve Bank of Chicago, and the Public Securities Association.

A strong supporter of education and civic affairs, John serves as a member of the Business Advisory Council at the Walker College of Business at Appalachian State University in Boone, North Carolina, and on the President's Council for Charlotte's Central Piedmont Community College. He has previously served as a board member of the British American Business Council of North Carolina and served on the Economic Development Board for the State of North Carolina, a special appointment by the Governor. He also served on the Business Advisory Committee for the City of Charlotte.

# What's on the Companion Web Site

*We are what we repeatedly do.*

—Aristotle

**T**his book provides a framework for decision making, which can be applied to the various situations we all face in business. To reinforce these new behaviors and solidify this framework in the mind of the reader, we've added a companion website.

For additional case studies, graphics, links to additional information, and checklists for every chapter in the book, please go to www.wiley.com/go/economicdecisionmaking (password: silvia123). This will help you apply the framework to a range of examples, and help you test yourself by making real decisions in a practical setting.

A&P/Kroger, 337
Absolute Income Hypothesis, 23
Alternative paths, 182–184, 190–191
American Recovery and Reinvestment Act, 138
Anchoring, 15–16
Anchoring bias, 71–73, 97, 112, 134–135, 184, 191, 276, 350, 351
Annenberg, Walter, 351
AOL and Time Warner, 189
Apollo 13, 195–196
Argentina, 46–47
Asia:
   crisis in, 310–313, 321
   emerging nations of, 14, 314
   globalization and, 350
   trading relationships, 331
Assumptions, 2–3
Asymmetric information, 109, 192, 193, 194
Auerbach, Alan, 289
Auto industry:
   Cadillac and GM, 111
   information and, 117
   innovation and, 346
Availability bias, 108–109, 244–245
Average expected return, 217–221
Avery, Sewell, 348

Baby boom, 145, 151
Balance in economy, determining, 85–86
Bank lending, 63, 102, 150
Barings Bank, 199–200
Barriers to entry, 192
Benchmarking growth, applications for, 24–26
Berlin Wall, 74, 75
Bernanke, Ben, 317–318
Bethlehem Steel, 348–349

Biases:
   anchoring bias, 71–73, 97, 112, 134–135, 184, 191, 276, 350, 351
   availability bias, 108–109, 244–245
   confirmation bias, 2, 50, 111–112, 135, 190–191, 246, 310–313
   decision making and, 242–244
   decision-making biases to watch, 244–248
   evaluated alternatives and, 184
   framing, 111, 113, 190
   group think, 51
   home bias, 317, 319
   illusory correlation, 70–71, 111, 113, 114, 135, 246, 352
   innovation and, 351, 354
   mental, 15
   normalization of deviance, 66–68
   overconfidence, 15, 210–211, 332
   recency bias, 2, 208–210, 259–260
   recognizing change as a process, 68–70
   subpar results and, 190–191
   sunk cost bias, 9, 248, 326, 327
BlackRock, Inc., 133
Blind pool investments, 141
Bonds:
   high-yield, 225–226, 258
   two-year government, 305
Boskin Commission, 37
Brealey, Richard, 73, 254
Budget Enforcement Act, 353
Bureau of Economic Analysis (BEA), 26, 28, 84
Bush, George, 271, 353
Bush tax cuts, 271
Business model, information and, 117–119

Cadillac, 111, 352
California Big Four, 179
Canada, 286, 306, 308

Capital flows, model of. *See also* Global
    capital flows
  generally, 306–308
  impossible trinity, 308–309
  Mexico/Asia/confirmation bias, 310–313
  post–World War II period/economic
    drivers, 309–310
Capital flows, poor countries and, 92
Capital markets:
  in the 1980s, 208–210
  and allocation of capital, 230–232
  average expected return/variability of
    returns, 217–221
  credit crunches, 224–226
  economic change as driver, 202–204
  economics/expectations/information,
    205–208
  engine of analysis, 200–201
  feedback process/credit cycle, 221–224
  generally, 199–200, 232–235
  Great Recession and, 212–213
  internal cyclical changes/overconfidence
    bias, 210–211
  irony and paradox, 211–212
  and life cycle of institution, 226–230
  perspective of change over time, 201–202
  risk/reward calculation, 213–215
  traded/non-traded goods, 215–216
  wake-up call, 216–217
Capital stock:
  forces impacting growth, 85
  output growth and, 86–87
Carter, Jimmy, 160
CBOT. *See* Chicago Board of Trade (CBOT)
CDS. *See* Credit default swaps (CDS)
Central Intelligence Agency (CIA), 109
CFTC. *See* Commodity Futures Trading
    Commission (CFTC)
Change. *See also* Shocks
  as the anomaly, 346–347
  barriers to, 4–6
  character of, 145–146
  economic, as driver, 202–204
  economic adjustment and, 293–294
  evolutionary, 339, 340
  feedback from, 246–248
  framework and, 166–170
  generally, 3–4
  identification of (*see* Identification of
    change)

introducing, 9–10
  modeling, 146
  over time, perspective of, 201–202
  as process, recognition of, 68–70
  in savings rates, 88
  short/long responses to, 76–78
  sources of, 6–7
Chicago Board of Trade (CBOT), 341
China:
  capital outflows, 309
  as emerging nation, 14
  exchange rates and, 45–47, 308
  growth rates in, 134
  import protections, 306
  trading relationships, 331
  U.S. Treasury securities and, 315
  in WTO, 298, 309, 317
Choices:
  failing to choose, 331–332
  feedback and, 347–349
  and information choke points, 119
  innovation vs. old model, 10–11
  method of making, 17–18
  taking advantage of change, 12–17
CIA. *See* Central Intelligence Agency (CIA)
Civil War, 179, 180
Clinton, Bill, 285
Closed economy, 318
Coincident indicators, 61–62
Cold War, 140
Collins, Jim, 337
Commercial paper, 229
Commodity Exchange, 205
Commodity Futures Trading Commission
    (CFTC), 341
Community banking, 102
Compensation of employees, 33
Competitive advantage, information and,
    103–104
Conference Board, 60
Confirmation bias, 2, 50, 111–112, 135,
    190–191, 246, 310–313
Consumer:
  activity, 60–61
  choice, 340–341
  spending, 28, 357
Consumer price index (CPI), 37–38, 63, 167
Convertibility Law, 46
"Corn-hog" cycles, 76
Corn Laws, 82, 296, 355

Corporate bond spreads, 143
Corporate cash flow, 256–257
Corporate profit growth, 331
Corporate profits tax, 91
Creative destruction, 104–105
Credit:
  aspects of, 170
  constraints, 222
  crowding out, 277
  quality of, 150, 151, 218
Credit crunches:
  high-yield bonds and, 225–226
  Regulation Q and, 224–225
Credit default swaps (CDS), 208
Credit risks, ranking of, 222, 223
Credit spreads, 142, 143–144, 171, 216,
  217
Creditworthiness, 227
Crowding out, 277
Cuban missile crisis, 246
Culture, 13
Currencies. *See* Exchange rates
Cyclical and structural change:
  bias in decision making, 66–73
  coincident indicators, 61–62
  cyclical patterns, linear projections,
    57–59
  evolution of a framework and, 73–78
  forces of economic success, 55–57
  generally, 78–80
  lagging indicators, 62–64
  leading indicators, 59–61
  moving average (MA), 65–66
  trends and cycles, identifying, 64–66
Cyclical change, benchmark for, 25–26
Cyclical patterns, linear projections:
  identifying change, 59
  recessions and, 57–59

Debt-to-equity ratio, 257–260, 261
Debt to GDP ratio, 243
Decision making:
  biases and, 242–244
  framework, innovations and, 343–344
Decision-making biases to watch:
  choices, 248
  evaluating change, 245–246
  feedback, 246–248
  framework set up/availability bias,
    244–248

Deficit to GDP ratio, 243
Department of Commerce, 26, 32, 84
Digital Equipment Corporation, 348
Disruptive innovations, 104–105
Diversification, 190
Dollar:
  appreciation, 317
  and hedging exchange rate risk, 342–343
  weakening of, 326, 328, 329
Dot-com boom, 288
Drexel Burnham, 347

Econometric models, 138–141
Economic adjustment, dynamic nature of,
  293–294
Economic benchmarks:
  applications for, 24–25
  for cyclical change/secular growth, 25–26
  GDP, components of, 27–36
  generally, 23–24
  inflation, 36–41
Economic cycle, 172–173
Economic dynamism:
  exchange rate and, 95–96
  flow of capital, 92
  framework for growth, 83–88
  generally, 81–83, 97–99
  growth/opportunity/preservation, 96–97
  institutions, savings/investments, 90–92
  overcoming geography, 92–95
  population growth/westward expansion,
    88–90
Economic growth factors, 50
Economic Recovery Tax Act of 1981,
  278–279
Economic risk(s):
  biases/building framework, 134–135
  interdependencies among, 135–138
  useful risk model, 132–134
Economic shocks. *See* Shocks
Economies of scale and scope, 187–189
*Economist*, 355
Edison, Thomas, 349
Efficiency ratios. *See* Profitability ratios
Emerging market countries, 96, 134
Energy prices, 76–77. *See also* Oil prices
English Corn Laws, 82, 296, 355
Equity market decline, 75
ERM. *See* Exchange rate mechanism (ERM)
EU. *See* European Union (EU)

European sovereign debt crisis, 325
European Union (EU), 239
Evolution of frameworks, 18–19
Ex-ante interest rate, 42–43, 164
Exchange rate mechanism (ERM), 304
Exchange rates:
  altering of, 95–96
  economic dynamism and, 95–96
  fixed system, 307–308, 316
  flexible, 317
  floating, 307
  nominal exchange rate, 94
  real exchange rate, 94–95
  relative price/many relatives, 45–48
  risk, innovation and, 353
Expansionary fiscal policy, 95
Exports. *See* Net exports
Ex-post interest rates, 42, 209

Fannie Mae and Freddie Mac, 164, 176,
  223, 353
Federal budget surplus/deficit, 295
Federal Deposit Insurance system, 340–341
Federal fiscal deficit, 314
Federal funds rate, 43
Federal Housing Administration, 213
Federal Reserve:
  asset purchase plan, 315
  balance sheet, 170, 171, 282
  banking system and, 168
  debt monetization, 281
  as de facto central bank, 45
  establishment of, 162, 218
  Federal Funds rate set by, 43
  inflation and, 160, 208, 209, 284
  lagging indicators and, 63–64
  LTCM and, 211
  monetary policy and, 40
  "quantitative easing," 176, 326, 327, 329,
  330, 342
  Regulation Q, 224–225
  Treasury bond portfolio of, 50
Feedback:
  choices and, 347–349
  effects, 74, 75
  process, credit cycle, 221–224
Ferguson, Niall, 326
Financial innovation, 340–341
Financial Institutions Reform, Recovery and
  Enforcement Act, 225

Financial ratios:
  biases to watch, 244–248
  correlations among ratios, 244
  decision making/biases, 242–244
  framework development and, 240–248
  generally, 237, 267–270
  information and (*see* Financial ratios as
    information)
  targets, indicators, or instruments,
    237–240
  theory, 242
Financial ratios as information:
  debt-to-equity ratio, 257–260
  generally, 248
  leverage, 256–257
  liquidity, 253–256
  market value ratios, 260–267
  P/E (price/earnings) ratio, 260–267
  probability/efficiency ratios, 248–253
Firefighting tragedy, 191
First Time Homebuyer Credit, 275
Fiscal deficits, 278–284
Fiscal policy:
  equilibrium, long-run vs. short-run,
    292–294
  expansionary, 278, 316–317, 329
  generally, 271–272, 298–300
  innovation and, 353
  long-run outlook/today's behavior,
    294–296
  monetary policy and, 279, 285–289
  in open economy, 298
  political business cycle, 296–298
  risk taking (*see* Risk-taking, fiscal policy
    and)
Fiscal stimulus. *See* Stimulus program
Fleming, Marcus, 286
Floating exchange rates, 307
Fordney-McCumber Tariff of 1922, 82–83,
  84
Framework:
  for economy, 345–346
  principles for new, 153–155
Framework development:
  assumptions, 2–3
  biases and, 2, 332
  creating a framework, 7–9
  decision making, 17–18
  education and, 3
  evolution of frameworks, 18–19

feedback and, 11–12, 146–149, 330–332
financial ratios (*see* Framework
  development, financial ratios and)
generally, 1–2, 19–22
information and, 116–117
innovation vs. old model, 10–11
introducing change, 9–10
policies for growth and, 90
problems/solutions, 3–7
taking advantage of change, 12–17
Framework development, financial ratios
  and:
  decision making, biases and, 242–244
  decision-making biases to watch,
    244–248
  generally, 240–241
  Pearson correlation coefficients, 241
  theory, 242
Framing, 111, 113, 190
Free capital flows, 45
Free-trade agreements, 97. *See also* North
  American Free Trade Association
  (NAFTA)
Friedman, Milton, 284, 345–346, 356

GDP. *See* Gross domestic product (GDP)
GDP deflator, 39–41
General Motors (GM), 111, 349, 352
Geography. *See* Economic dynamism
Germany, 13, 72, 231, 326, 348
Global capital flows. *See also* Capital flows,
  model of
  American framework/imbalances,
    313–320
  building a framework, 304–306
  decision makers and, 328–330
  feedback, expectations and, 330–332
  generally, 303–304, 332–334
  global interest rates, 320–323
  model of capital flows (*see* Capital flows,
    model of)
  overconfidence bias, 332
  risks/opportunities, 323–328
Global interest rates, 320–323
Globalization:
  Asia and, 350
  capital markets and, 202, 231, 278
  of housing demand, 215
  interest rates and, 264
  open global economy and, 18

in post-WTO era, 339
of trade, 161
GNMAs. *See* Government National
  Mortgage Association certificates
  (GNMAs)
GNP. *See* Gross national product (GNP)
Going public, 229
Gold:
  discoveries, 170
  prices, 70
Golub, Bennett W., 133, 135–136
Goodhart, Charles A. E., 238
Goodhart's Law, 238
Goods market, 307
Government National Mortgage Association
  certificates (GNMAs), 341
Government purchases, 32
Government-sponsored enterprises (GSEs),
  353
Gramm-Rudman-Hollings Act, 280, 353
Great Depression:
  bank failures and, 224
  Cadillac sales during, 111
  debt payoff and, 131
  exchange of financial capital, 202
  fears of another, 23, 203
  Federal Reserve and, 218
  global scale of, 356
  home mortgages and, 352
  money supply and, 170
  as period of thrift, 55
  tariffs and, 83
"Great Moderation," macroeconomic
  volatility and, 211
Great Recession. *See also* Recessions
  assumptions and, 242
  capital markets and, 209, 212–213
  changes of, 146
  credit and, 170
  decline in real final sales, 35
  home prices and, 138
  household lending and, 131
  intensification of, 108
  low savings rate and, 86
  monetary policy and, 175, 354
  professions not viable in, 77
  refinancing/foreclosures, 352
  risk, reward and, 131, 327, 328
  subprime lending and, 212–213
  U.S. Treasury securities and, 315

Greece, 128–129, 133–134, 239, 267,
  324–326, 342
Greenspan, Alan, 311
Gross domestic product (GDP):
  benchmarking growth and, 24
  debt/deficit to GDP ratio, 243
  government purchases, 32
  gross private domestic investment,
    28–32
  net exports, 32–34
  personal consumption, 27–28
  real final sales, 34–36
  real GDP, 26, 89, 112, 126, 127
  volatility in, 126, 128
Gross national product (GNP), 32
Gross private domestic investment:
  equipment and software spending, 29
  generally, 28
  inventories and, 29, 30
  residential investment, 29, 30
  slowing demand and, 30–32
Group think, 51
Growth:
  framework for, 83–86
  higher output and, 86–87
  innovation, economy and, 336–340
  opportunity, preservation and, 96–97
  policies for, 90
Growth business, information in, 104–106
GSEs. *See* Government-sponsored enterprises
    (GSEs)

Haavelmo, Trygve, 238
Hedging exchange rate risk, 342–343
Heller, Walter, 284
High-yield bonds, 225–226, 258
Hodrick, Robert J., 64, 252–253
Hodrick-Prescott (H-P) filter, 64–65, 66,
    257, 262–263, 266
Home bias, 317, 319
Hong Kong, 45–46, 307–308, 309
Hoover, Herbert, 356
Housing:
  boom in, 77, 288
  correction, 75, 130
  marketing for, 118
  mortgage payments, 131
  prices, deflation, 129–132
  public policy and, 213–214
  recovery in, 275

slowed demand, feedback from, 219–221
speculation, 218
H-P filter. *See* Hodrick-Prescott (H-P) filter
HP ratio, 252–253

Identification of change:
  approaches to, 59
  character of change, 145–146
  feedback and, 146–149
  generally, 141–145
  modeling change, 146
  normalization of deviance, 149–153
Illusory correlation, 70–71, 111, 113, 114,
    135, 246, 352
"Import leakage," 317
Indonesia, 311, 312, 313
Inflation:
  CPI and, 37–38
  double-digit, 160, 161
  expected vs. actual, 129
  Federal Reserve and, 160
  financial innovation/consumer choice,
    340–341
  GDP deflator, 39–41
  generally, 36–38
  and global integration of U.S. economy,
    277–278
  interest rates and, 173–175
  outlook, 329, 330
  pace of, 330
  Phillips Curve and, 125–126
  producer prices and, 38–39
  trends/expectations, 164–166
  unemployment and, 159, 205
  weaker dollar and, 326
Inflation-unemployment tradeoff model, 160
Information. *See also* Financial ratios as
    information
  asymmetric, 102, 109, 192, 193, 194
  "calling it quits"/viewpoints, 108
  choices/choke points and, 119
  as competitive advantage input, 103–104
  decision process and, 106–107, 116–117
  disruptive innovations, 104–105
  economic, 116–117, 205–208
  electronic, 115–116
  in an existing business, 102–103
  generally, 119–122
  innovation and, 350
  interpretation, Cadillac, 111

limited, 184, 193
mathematical models and, 108
in new growth business, 104–106
as part of business model, 117–119
policy, expectations and, 289–292
processing, steps (*see* Information
    processing steps)
quality of, 183, 186
reach and richness of, 103–104, 106
in *Trading Places* (film), 101
Information processing steps:
    1- gathering economic/business
        information, 107–109
    2- interpreting information, 109–114
    3- distributing information, 114–116
Innovation:
    and decision making framework, 343–344
    disruptive, 104–105, 340
    dollar/hedging exchange rate risk,
        342–343
    economic thought, challenges and,
        354–357
    and the economy, 336–349
    generally, 335–336, 357–359
    growth and, 336–340
    inflation and, 340–341
    interest rates and, 341–343
    vs. old model, 10–11
    and patterns of progress, 349–352
    public policy and, 353–354
    risk, prospect theory and, 352–354
Institutions, markets before, 162
Institutions, savings/investment and:
    corporate profits tax, 91
    generally, 90–91
    technological progress, 91–92
Integrated Resources, 259
Intel, 351
Interest expense, 256–257
Interest Rate Control Act of 1966, 225
Interest rates:
    debt burden and, 128
    ex-ante, 42–43, 164
    ex-post, 42, 209
    global, 320–323
    inflation and, 173–175
    negative real, 160
    nominal, 42, 160, 174, 208
    real, 166, 174, 209
    real nominal, 41–45

risk, innovation and, 353
short vs. long run, 330–331
volatility, risk and, 341–342
International Monetary Fund, 160
Internet:
    emergence of, 105–106
    information distribution, 115–116
    social networks, 117–118, 351
    web sites, 118
Inventory valuation adjustment (IVA), 49
Ireland, 239, 267, 325
Irony and paradox, 211–212
IVA. *See* Inventory valuation adjustment
    (IVA)
Iverson, Ken, 348

Japan, 13, 72, 231, 309, 315, 319, 348
JCT. *See* Joint Committee on Taxation (JCT)
Jobless claims, 60, 61
John Deere, 349
Joint Committee on Taxation (JCT), 271,
    289, 290–291

Kahneman, Daniel, 152
Kennedy, John F., 109, 246, 284
Kennedy tax cuts, 273, 274, 284, 353, 356
Key economic growth factors, 50
Keynes, John Maynard, 23, 24, 144, 273,
    280, 326, 345, 356
Keynesian multiplier, 272
Kroger/A&P, 337
Kuhn, Thomas, 344
Kuznets, Simon, 23, 24

Labor market:
    Berlin Wall and, 74, 75
    unemployment rate and, 63
Labor Statistics, Bureau of, 126
Lagging indicators, 62–64
Latin American countries:
    political stability and, 87
    trading relationships, 331
Laubach, Thomas, 128
Leading indicators, 59–61
Lehman Brothers, 134, 195, 197, 346
Lev, Baruch, 251
Leverage, 256–257
Lewis, Michael, 350
Limit pricing, 193–194
Lincoln, Abraham, 179, 187, 338

Liquidity, 253–256
Liquidity effect, 170
Long-run adjustment, 170–172
Long Term Capital Management (LTCM), 41–42, 210–211, 274, 313
Louisiana Purchase, 199, 200
LTCM. *See* Long Term Capital Management (LTCM)
Lucas, Robert E., 92, 284–285

Maastricht Treaty, 239
Malthus, Thomas, 354–355
Mankiw, Greg, 91
Marginal product of capital (MPK), 84
Market manipulation claims, 205
Markets:
  before institutions, 162
  unexpected events and, 162–166
Market value ratios, 260–267
Marshall Plan, 316
Medicare, 291, 294
Menich, Judy, 341
Mergers and acquisitions, 113–114
Merrill Lynch, 341
Mexico, 48, 310, 313, 314, 324
Milken, Michael, 346–347
Miracle on the Hudson, 195
MLS. *See* Multiple listing service (MLS)
Monetary policy, 279, 285–289. *See also* Exchange rates
Money:
  change, framework and, 166–170
  economic cycle/quality spreads, 172–173
  generally, 160–162, 176–178
  inflation, interest rates and, 173–176
  lessons learned, 175–176
  markets before institutions, 162
  risk, accounting for, 172–173
  short-run/long-run adjustment, 170–172
  unexpected events, markets and, 162–166
*Moneyball* (Lewis), 350
Montgomery Ward, 348
Morgan Stanley, 321
Mortgage-backed market, 347
Moving average (MA), 65–66
MPK. *See* Marginal product of capital (MPK)
Multicolinearity, 134
Multiple listing service (MLS), 118

Multiplier process, 280
Mundell, Robert, 286, 308
Mundell-Fleming model, 286–288, 306, 313
Myers, Stewart, 73

NAFTA. *See* North American Free Trade Association (NAFTA)
Napoleonic wars, 355
National Bank of Commerce, 172
National Income and Product Accounts (NIPA), 48–50, 84
Navigation Acts, 81–82
Net exports, 32–34
New-growth enterprise, information in, 104–106
Newspaper business, 104–105
New thinking, 195–197
1980s, the, 208–210
NIPA. *See* National Income and Product Accounts (NIPA)
Nixon, Richard M., 42, 316
Nixon administration, 204, 313
Nominal interest rate, 42, 160, 208
Non-durable goods, 28
Non-traded goods, 215–216
Normalization of deviance, 66–68, 149–153
North American Free Trade Association (NAFTA), 74, 82, 93, 210, 309, 310, 317, 350
Not seasonally adjusted (NSA) sales, 110
NSA. *See* Not seasonally adjusted (NSA) sales
Nucor steel, 348, 349

Obama, Barack, 111, 128, 281, 284
Obama administration, 329
Oil prices. *See also* Energy prices
  oil shocks and, 77, 129, 160, 204, 208–209
  pattern of, 112–113
Olsen, Ken, 348
Ottoman Empire, 81, 350
Output, level of, 86–87, 88
Overconfidence bias, 15, 210–211, 332

Panic of 1907, 172, 218
Paradox and irony, 211–212
PCE. *See* Personal consumption expenditure (PCE) deflator

P/E (price/earnings) ratio, 237, 238, 240, 260, 261–267
Pearl Harbor, 153
Pearson correlation coefficients, 241, 249
Penn Central Railroad, 203–204
Penn Square, 71
People Express, 259–260
Personal consumption, 27–28, 76
Personal consumption expenditure (PCE) deflator, 39–41
Phillips, A. W., 159
Phillips Curve, 125–126, 159
Political stability, savings rates and, 87
Ponzi scheme, 153
Poor countries, 92
Porter, Michael, 230
Post–World War II period:
  anchoring bias and, 72
  baby boom and, 145
  British nationalization and, 89
  capital flows/economic drivers, 309–310
  capital markets and, 203, 204
  capital stock and, 85
  economic drivers and, 309–310
  emerging markets and, 227
  fixed exchange rate system, 316
  government spending/tax policy, 271
  growth and, 135, 337
  home prices and, 129
  illusory correlation and, 70
  inflation in, 125
  leverage/risk taking and, 132
  manufacturing economy of, 201
  subsidization of industries and, 56
  U.S. power and, 96
Predatory pricing, 194
Prescott, Edward C., 64, 252–253
Probability, risk and, 183–184
Probability/efficiency ratios, 248–253
Process:
  choices and, 12–17
  decision making, 17–18
  evolution of frameworks, 18–19
  feedback, 11–12
  framework for, 7–9
  innovation vs. old model, 10–11
  introducing change, 9–10
Producer prices, 38–39
Production possibilities curve, 92–95

Profitability ratios:
  inventory to sales ratios, 251–253
  return on assets, 249–251
  return on equity, 248–249
Profit(s), 48–50
Profits expectations, 207
Progress, innovation and, 349–352
Prospect theory, 97
Protectionism, 74
Public policy:
  growth and, 83–84
  housing market and, 213–214, 222
  innovation and, 353–354
  investments and, 74
  leadership in, 224
  Lucas critique and, 284–285
  makers of, 93
  real/financial economy and, 211
  risk and, 131–132

Quality spreads, 172–173
"Quantitative easing," 176, 326, 327, 329, 330, 342

Ratios. *See* Financial ratios
Reagan, Ronald, 284, 285, 316–317, 320
Reagan tax cuts, 278–284, 317, 353
Real capital, market for, 200–201
Real final sales, 34–36
Real wages, 89
Recency bias, 2, 208–210, 259–260
Recency effect, 108–109
Recessions. *See also* Great Recession
  double dip, 128
  narrow focus on, 57–59
  recoveries following, 201
  risk taking and, 132
Regulation Q, 224–225, 341
Reinhart, Carmen, 290
Resource allocation, 207–208
Retail sales, SA and NSA, 110
Return on equity, 248–249
Returns, average expected/variability of, 217–221
Ricardo, David, 272–273, 336–337, 355–356
Risk:
  accounting for, 172–173
  alternative paths and, 182, 184

Risk (*Continued*)
  assessments, 192, 227–228
  dollar/hedging exchange rate, 342–343
  generally, 197–198
  interest rates and, 341–342
  opportunity and, 323–328
  probability and, 183–184
  in refinancing, 229–230
  strategic thinking and, 183
  uncertainty and, 180–181, 182, 184, 186
Risk aversion, 142, 143–144, 170
Risk modeling/assessment:
  biases/building framework, 134–135
  change, identifying, 141–153
  econometric models and, 138–141
  economics and, 124–129
  generally, 123–124, 155–158
  housing prices and, 129–132
  initial framework/model, 132–134
  interdependencies among risks, 135–138
  mean/standard deviation and, 133
  new model, 153–155
Risk premiums, 129
Risk/reward calculation, 213–215
Risk-taking, fiscal policy and:
  generally, 272–273
  inflation, U.S. economy, 277–278
  Reagan tax cuts/fiscal deficit, 278–284
  simple sixties, 273–274
  tax surcharge of 1968, 274–277
Roach, Steven, 321
Rogoff, Kenneth, 290
Roosevelt, Franklin D., 133, 294, 356
Rothschild, Nathan, 107

SA. *See* Seasonally adjusted (SA) sales
Sarbanes-Oxley, 285
Savings/investment decision, institutions and:
  corporate profits tax, 91
  generally, 90–91
  technological progress, 91–92
Savings rates:
  Great Recession and, 86
  level of output and, 87
  political stability and, 87
  rise/decline in, 88
  signals for prosperity, 87–88
Scale economies, 187–189
Schumpeter, Joseph, 104

Seasonally adjusted (SA) sales, 110
Secondary Mortgage Market Enhancement Act of 1984, 347
Secular growth, benchmark for, 25–26
Securities and Exchange Commission, 285
Securitization, 108, 347
Sense making, 191
September 11, 2001 terrorist attacks, 181, 182, 195
Sewell, Avery, 135
Shocks:
  from demand side, 75
  ex-ante rate of return and, 168–169
  financial, 134
  framework development and, 8, 10
  housing market and, 129–132, 218
  oil shocks, 77, 129, 160, 204, 208–209
  policy makers and, 288–289
  response to, 5, 181
  sources of, 9
  from supply side, 78
Short-run adjustment, 170–172
Smith, Adam, 357
Smoot-Hawley Tariff Act of 1929, 82–83, 84
Social networks, 117–118, 351
Social Security, 294
South Seas Company, 77, 318
Spreadsheets, 108–109
Stagflation, 205
Stewart Myers, 255
Stimulus program, 111, 128, 138, 280–281, 293–294
Strategic barriers, 192–195
Strategic thinking, levels of:
  altering the vision, 184–195
  applying new thinking, 195–197
  considering alternative paths, 182–184
  generally, 180–181, 197–198
  short-run planning, 181–182
Structural barriers, 192
Subprime lending:
  credit quality and, 150, 151
  delinquencies and, 220–221
  just another market, 212–213
  riskiness of, 222
Subsidies, 74
Sunk cost(s):
  attachment to, 73
  bias, 9, 15, 248, 326, 327

effect, historical investment and, 348
influence of, 152
strategic barriers and, 193

Tariff barriers, early, 82
Tax Reform Act of 1986, 91,169
Tax surcharge of 1968, 274–275
Taylor, John B., 175
Taylor rule, 175
Technological progress, 91–92
10-year Treasury rate, 43, 44, 240
Tilman, Leo M., 133, 135–136
Time series, 137
Time Warner, 189
*Tobin's Q*, 206–207
Traded goods, 215–216
Trade policies, 48, 354
Trade routes, early, 81
*Trading Places* (film), 101
Transcontinental Railroad, 179–180, 181
Treasury:
    borrowing, 296
    debt, 128, 326, 327
    dollar theory and, 328
    market, 314
    rate, 43
    securities, 298, 315
Treaty of Utrecht, 318
Tresky, Amos, 152
Truman Doctrine, 316

Uncertainty:
    alternative paths and, 182
    generally, 197–198
    multiple dimensions of, 196
    risk and, 180–181, 183, 184, 186, 195
Unemployment:
    inflation and, 205
    stimulus program and, 280–281
Unemployment rate, 62–63, 159
United Kingdom, 307, 308
United States:
    debt payoff and, 283, 322
    economy, real growth in, 111–112
    fiscal policy, 21st century, 298
    global capital markets and, 313–320

in post–World War II period, 96
    westward expansion of, 88–90
U.S. Treasury. *See* Treasury

Variability of returns, 217–221
Vaughn, Diane, 149, 150
Venture capital:
    capital markets and, 227–228
    decision making, 114
Vertical integration, 190
Vietnam War, 275
Vision, altering:
    barriers to entry, 192
    biases, subpar results and, 190–191
    diseconomies of scale, 188–189
    economies of scale/scope, 187–188
    entry/exit for firms, 186–187
    generally, 184–186
    strategic barriers, 192–195
    vertical integration/diversification, 190
Volcker, Paul, 160, 170, 208, 285–286,
    316–317, 353

Wage inflation, 159
Wake-up call, 216–217
Wal-Mart, 102
Ward, Montgomery, 23, 24
War on Poverty, 275
Wealth effect, 76
Web sites:
    business model for, 119
    generally, 118
Webster, Daniel, 337
Whitney, Eli, 338
"Winner's curse," 190
World Trade Organization (WTO), 74, 82,
    93, 298, 309, 317, 339, 350
World War I, 145, 202, 339, 349
World War II, 23, 24, 30, 55, 129, 131, 224,
    314, 316, 318. *See also* Post–World
    War II period
WTO. *See* World Trade Organization
    (WTO)

Yacht tax, 271
Yield curve, 43, 44, 171–172